AGAINST THE APOCALYPSE

Against the Apocalypse

Responses to Catastrophe in Modern Jewish Culture

David G. Roskies

Harvard University Press
Cambridge, Massachusetts, and London, England
1984

Printed in the United States of America
10 9 8 7 6 5 4 3 2 1

Publication of this book has been aided by a grant from the Andrew W. Mellon Foundation.

This book is printed on acid-free paper, and its binding materials have been chosen for strength and durability.

Library of Congress Cataloging in Publication Data

Roskies, David G., 1948–
Against the apocalypse.

Bibliography: p.
Includes index.
1. Yiddish literature—History and criticism.
2. Hebrew literature, Modern—History and criticism.
3. Jews—Europe, Eastern—Persecutions. 4. Jews in literature. 5. Holocaust, Jewish (1939–1945), in literature. I. Title.
PJ5120.R67 1984 839′.09′09358 83-18663
ISBN 0-674-00915-0

דער מאַמען —

וואָס דורך איר האָט דער עבֿר

אויפֿגעבליט אין אונדז

Acknowledgments

IN stark contrast to many of the works discussed herein, this book was written under optimal conditions. There was ample time to refine my thinking (eight years from start to finish); there was money to subsidize my writing (assistance from the Memorial Foundation for Jewish Culture and a very generous grant from the Abbell Research Fund of the Jewish Theological Seminary of America, not to mention a sabbatical leave); and, most important, there was the help of friends and editors.

Thirteen of my colleagues from the Jewish Theological Seminary, along with Roger Shinn from Union Theological Seminary and the late Isaiah Trunk from the YIVO Institute, collaborated with me in an interdisciplinary course that I was privileged to teach in 1977 and 1979 on the subject of this book. Three of the papers prepared for the course, by Shaye Cohen, Ivan Marcus, and Mortimer Ostow, were subsequently published. And so I owe special thanks to Neil Gillman, whose brainchild it was. As the writing progressed, individual chapters were read by John Felstiner, Avraham Holtz, James Kugel, Ivan Marcus, and Abraham Nowersztern, who gave freely of their expertise. Yechiel Szeintuch and Abraham Nowersztern of the Hebrew University were kind enough to share their unpublished research, without which Chapters 8 and 9 could not have been written. But the one person who kept me honest and kept me bold; who scrutinized each detail, generalization, and mixed metaphor; who revised all my translations of poetry or redid them from scratch; who sometimes read as many as four versions of the same chapter—is Hillel Schwartz. I hope the result is worthy of his efforts.

Guiding me through the final stages were the two most gracious and conscientious editors I have ever encountered, Maud Wilcox and Maria Ascher. Penny Goldenberg, working after hours, did all the typing and retyping without a complaint.

I am, in addition, indebted to the many individuals and publishers who granted me permission to use verse quotations in the text. Sources of these quotations are acknowledged in the notes.

Other acknowledgments are harder to formulate because they span many years of listening and learning. The most thoroughly secular and hard-nosed training in the nature of Jewish expression was gleaned at the dinner table, from my sister Ruth Wisse. Particularly fruitful were the winter evenings we spent in 1973, in an unheated Jerusalem apartment, exploring the ghetto poems of Abraham Sutzkever. Dan Miron, my teacher in more formal settings as well, revealed that Yiddish literature could be read as an indictment of modern Jewish culture, something my Yiddish School teachers would never have allowed. The motivation to connect all this to rabbinic and medieval sources came from my exposure to the Seminary, where nothing is real if it does not partake of the classical heritage. And the knowledge that there was life after the book was knowledge born of my past three years with Shana, my wife.

D.G.R.

New York City
7 September 1983
ערב ראש השנה תשמ"ד

Contents

Illustrations

AGAINST THE APOCALYPSE

CHAPTER ONE

Ruined Cities of the Mind

And the city stood in its brightness when years later I returned,
My face covered with a coat though now no one was left
Of those who could have remembered my debts never paid,
My shames not forever, base deeds to be forgiven.
And the city stood in its brightness when years later I returned.

Czeslaw Milosz

THERE are said to be Moroccan Jews who have kept the keys to their ancestral homes in fifteenth-century Spain and Portugal. When, in the 1950s, the exiles dispersed yet again—to France, Quebec, and Israel—these metal relics from Seville and Granada, Lisbon and Barcelona, became perhaps their most tangible link to their great Sephardic past. Such keys may not in fact exist; but even so, they intrigue as metaphors. Something like a key, for instance, must have been passed on from parents to children as part of the Jewish emigration during and after World War II. How else can I understand why the immediate but severed past exerted such an enormous claim on my loyalties? The Lithuanian city of Vilna in particular, with its unique blend of tradition and secularism, became something of a lost temple to me, a symbol of what eastern European Jewry had achieved in its eight hundred years of settlement. Though my parents had left Vilna in 1930, almost two decades before I was born, its people and places were more real to me than those of Montreal. In our family, distances were measured according to a prewar map: a shopping expedition to St. Catherine Street in Montreal, for example, was described in terms of the distance from my mother's former house on Zavalne, corner of Troke, to the Vilna train station. When I actually had occasion to walk the latter route in 1971, I knew my way instinctively, despite the new street signs—Komsomol Street, Red Army Avenue, Lenin Boulevard.

As I grew familiar with the avenues and alleyways of the lost city, heard and repeated stories and songs about the workers, marketwomen, merchants, children, and intellectuals who had lived in each courtyard (my mother's memory!), I felt an almost paralyzing sense of personal loss. I had been born too late. When, at the age of fourteen, I came upon the chronicles of Vilna's destruction in my parents' library and recognized so many names, the terrible knowledge of how these people had met their deaths made of their memory a personal mandate. The chronicles became my sacred texts, the irreplaceable keys entrusted to my possession, and the extraordinary repertoire of ghetto songs learned at commemorative gatherings formed my liturgy.

Vilna took on different meanings for me at different times. There was the adolescent's morbid fascination with the details of death and torture; the teenager's thrill with the exploits of the partisans, whose presence loomed even larger when I met some of them in my own living room; the anxious probing of the college student into spiritual resistance, especially into the paradoxical philosophy of the scholar Zelig Kalmanovitsh; the religious fervor of the twenty-two-year-old intent on finding a ritual framework for commemoration; and finally the adult's search for that which could be rescued from Vilna for future generations.

The landscape of ruined cities is best retrieved through the poets—from Homer and Jeremiah to Cavafi and Milosz. They know how to make Troy and Jerusalem, Alexandria and Warsaw, the center of a transcendent vision. In my case, a surrogate city in French Canada, with its Catholic churches, its river and mountain, its babble of tongues, somehow intimated the loss of the birthplace I never knew. There was even an Old City, though it lacked a wall. As in Vilna, the Jewish community in Montreal was trilingual: Hebrew and Yiddish continued to serve, in concert and competition, as lingua francas, while English was adopted for negotiating with the outside world in much the same way as Russian and Polish had been in the past. Language, then, was one of the essential keys. In the Jewish treasure house of my youth, only Yiddish held out a promise of breaking the barriers of class and time; it was the main code of entry into the life of the Jewish collective. From my earliest vantage point, beneath the piano at my parents' literary evenings, I came to realize that immersion in a particular foreign culture had nothing to do with hermetic insularity, that writers who chose Yiddish as their medium were not immediately consigning themselves to mediocrity. From my contact as a teenager with working-class Jews who spoke Yiddish and could rattle off more folk sayings than I would ever know, I came to realize that no one group could speak for all of eastern European

Jewish civilization and that books alone could not provide the answer to my quest.

For the most part, I ventured no further than the classroom; but this was far enough, since a network of excellent day schools was one of the central achievements of the Lithuanian Jewish community in Canada. My teachers stressed the coherence of the eastern European Jewish heritage, the inseparability of Hebrew and Yiddish, the interface of religion and culture. As Zionists, they were careful to temper the tales of past glory with a celebration of national rebirth. Our teacher, Shimshen Dunsky, once assured us that the very classroom we were sitting in was living proof of Jewish continuity. As secularists, Dunsky and his colleagues sought new forms of ritual that would retain the idioms of tradition. As citizens of a modern democracy, they imparted a sense of Jewish pride without ever dwelling on anti-Semitism or rallying us to action "for the sake of the six million."

Montreal was a city of survivors. Everyone knew who these were, not because of their tattooed numbers (which marked very few) but because they were so active in communal affairs and because they gathered each year in public mourning. There was the city-wide commemoration in the spring and the smaller gatherings of the Bundists (members of the Jewish Labor Bund) and the *landslayt* (people from the same town or region) on the dates on which their ghettos had been "liquidated." My parents, who escaped the Holocaust by a hairsbreadth, lit memorial candles on August 16 for Bialystok and on September 23 for Vilna, to honor all their family whose actual death dates would never be known. And we, the youngsters, were called upon to recite poetry, sing ghetto songs, and light the six candles. There was no conspiracy of silence, no stigma. We could see adults crying in the synagogue or school auditorium, and sometimes we cried too. What made the survivors special in my eyes was that they were at least a decade younger than my parents and most of my teachers. Through them I could more easily imagine my growing up in eastern Europe when Yiddish culture was still flourishing. I especially envied the survivors of the Vilna ghetto the cultural life they had created. The diary of Herman Kruk, the chronicler of the Vilna ghetto, recorded more events in one month in the ghetto than Montreal could offer in a year. Judging by the vitality of those who had survived, by their ghetto slang and unforgettable songs, there seemed nothing more real than a people defying its own destruction.

And so, those growing-up years spent in a communal network of home-school-street with close ties to Lithuania—ties that were further strengthened by an influx of proud and vocal survivors—led me to a more general understanding of Jewish responses to catastrophe. Like Nathan Wachtel, who visited the descendants of the Incas to unearth the "deep structure" of their national trauma as expressed in folk rituals of commemoration, I absorbed the rhythm of yearly remembrance. Going beyond my observer status, I started thinking of ways to perpetuate the cycle. And this is what I learned.

When the unit of destruction is not the individual but the collective, when an entire Jewish population of a town or a city is gone, and when the disappearance of each community is known by date and there are dates enough to fill the calendar, then the task of remembrance threatens to eclipse all else. Yet the remnants of that same collective, those who feel the loss most keenly, manage to incorporate even so vast a destruction. In the showpiece synagogue of Vilnius, formerly the *khorshul* (choral synagogue) of Vilna, there is now a memorial plaque to the right of the Ark such as one sees in almost any Ashkenazi (that is, of the Franco-German Jews and their descendants) synagogue in the world, except that the Vilna plaque lists only the names and death dates of the surrounding towns, not the anniversary of each murdered Jew. Their given names wouldn't fit anyway—not on that wall or any other. Because the unit of destruction was so great, shortcuts are inevitably taken. Each year, as the ranks of the commemorators thin and those left look to their own immortality, the story of the town's destruction—be it that of Vilna, Warsaw, Lodz, Bialystok, or any other—becomes increasingly simple, and heroes emerge to give the story coherence. When Jews now mourn in public, therefore, they preserve the collective memory of the collective disaster, but in so doing fall back on symbolic constructs and ritual acts that necessarily blur the specificity and the implacable contradictions of the event.

I once had the privilege of addressing the Vilna *landsmanshaft*, the association of Jews who hailed from there, at one of their gatherings. I used songs of the Vilna ghetto and ghetto theater as sermonic texts. After the program, a former partisan came up to me. In the ghetto, in 1942, he had posted placards denouncing the establishment of a theater, but now he admitted to second thoughts. He realized that the hymns, laments, lullabies, love songs, and theatrical numbers I had sung had apparently served to mediate the two polarities of ghetto life: the movement for radical action, predicated on the knowledge of genocide, and the inward response of those who made Yiddish and Hebrew culture the expression of shared fate and hoped-for regeneration. Perhaps, he concluded, theater had been a legitimate form of resistance after all.

The issue of resistance also came up at a small Holocaust seminar conducted by Abba Kovner in New York City on May 14, 1979. When asked about Zelig Kalmanovitsh's unequivocal opposition to the ghetto fighters, Kovner visibly blanched and then told of his two secret meetings with "the prophet of the ghetto." That must have been an extraordinary sight: a young radical Zionist, a leader of Hashomer Hatsair, the left-wing Zionist youth movement, seeking the endorsement of a middle-aged Jewish scholar before embarking on a venture with life-and-death consequences for the entire collective. "Kegn aza rishes ken men nit geyn mit keyakh," Kalmanovitsh argued: "Against evil of such magnitude one cannot go with force. Our strength is our powerlessness. We are fated to be like all of Abraham's children." More astonishing still was Kovner's admission that had he been ten years older at the time, Kalmanovitsh's case for Jewish tradition would have won him over and the call to arms would not have gone out. This encounter, in other words, exemplified two competing systems of memory which intersected at the notion of martyrdom but which diverged in their sense of the text. For Zelig Kalmanovitsh, the text was the historical as well as the active force. The notion of "Abraham's children," so central to the covenantal idea of the Torah, made all action impossibly allusive and therefore elusive. For Abba Kovner, the text was the source which could be acted upon but was not yet (at his age) the center of history.

The hidden purpose of memorial gatherings may very well be to reconcile these inherent contradictions that lie beneath the surface. Only the trained anthropologist, however, or the privileged visitor can ever glimpse this internal drama. For me, the training ground of home and school proved too limited a terrain in which to glean all the necessary insights. Fortunately, there were other points on the map where the Jewish collective had regrouped and where private wounds were being nursed in fuller view of the public.

When, as a nineteen-year-old student, I came to Israel, with George Steiner in my head and Jewish cosmopolitanism in my heart, the Six-Day War had just released a new messianic wave. Among its heralds was a Yiddish writer, Leyb Rochman, one of a handful of survivors from Minsk-Mazovieck. The slaughter he had witnessed seemed to have sharpened his youthfulness, his hasidic fervor, and his passionate love for Jerusalem. Through Rochman's uncompromising Zionism, I first came to recognize Israel as the legitimate heir to the traditions I had been seeking to link the past to the diminished present. The touchstone of his reality was the People—not some disembodied Event, but Jews of flesh and blood who had perished and other Jews whose fate it was to live on. With prophetic logic, he reserved his harshest judgment for his own people and their wholesale glorification of the eastern European past, for the deceptive panaceas of the American present, and for the threatened promise of the Israeli future.

I made many trips to Tel Aviv to hear Yiddish spoken in cafés and to meet some of the legendary figures of Vilna: Alexander Libo, Mark Dworzecki, and Abraham Sutzkever. Of Sutzkever I can only say, in the cadence of the Passover Haggadah: were he only a leading Yiddish modernist—*dayyenu,* it would have been enough. Or only the proud son of Vilna Jewry; or only the poet of the ghetto and forests; or only the bard of national rebirth; or only the standard bearer of Jewish excellence—each in its own right would have been enough. If my own understanding of "survivorship" differs from the commonplace, it is due in large measure to Leyb Rochman and Abraham Sutzkever. As writers, they are worlds apart: without the Holocaust, Sutzkever would have continued to build the Temple of Yiddish in Vilna, whereas Rochman sooner or later would have made his way to Palestine. As survivors, they made their personal odysseys the emblem of the nation's miraculous rebirth.

Later, in more sober moments in North America, I discovered that this quest of mine to link the postwar present to the prewar past, to repossess the Hebrew frontier as the living home for Yiddish, to take in the New City as well as the Old, was nothing more than a romantic exercise. It was surely no accident that of all the urban landscapes I had visited on my travels, those which pretended to be the most authentic were the least so. I had found Vilna-Vilnius inhabited by Lithuanians from the provinces. The Jewish quarter had been reconstructed to match a late-Gothic dream-plan, like nothing any living person could remember. As for the new Jerusalem, nothing could have been further from its redesigned appearance than the image of eastern European "ghettos": no cramped alleys would ever again block access to the Wailing Wall. In North America, meanwhile, Hungarian hasidim and reformed hippies reclaimed Borough Park and Crown Heights as terra sancta, to live there in precarious isolation. My students ask me if this is what the shtetl was like.

Just as the eastern Europe I sought was nowhere on the map, the survivors of eastern Europe could not tell me what I needed to know. The people I turned to for guidance were themselves parentless and homeless. Fragmented, self-serving memories were all they could offer. Deep down, they did not believe that I or anyone else could be their heir. Too much had been lost and too much would be censored. Outwardly, they behaved as survivors of earlier catastrophes had behaved in the past: they were quick to (re)marry and bear children, to join together in groups and commemorate, to commit their experiences to writing. Beneath the social masks a new order had been established in which people were ranked according to what they had suffered: those whom the Soviets had dragged off to the Far East were considered luckier than those who had endured Nazi occupation; those in the ghettos and forests had been luckier than those in the camps; those in a work camp had been luckier than those in a death camp, and those who had survived had been luckier than those who had perished. This closed system would produce no heirs. Only those who had shared in the unknowable experience were accorded status. It made of history a mysterium tremendum.

So one day the survivors awoke to hear themselves acclaimed secular saints, the purveyors of a new gospel. As people who had "actually lived through Hell," they were endowed with almost mystical powers. Their lives were said to be doubly cursed, because to go on living after Auschwitz was to recall the horror and to wrestle anew with the moral collapse of the world. People who had never experienced starvation or mass graves or crematoria now looked upon the survivors as a higher order of human being, as God's messengers from the planet of destruction.

Before all the historical evidence was in, myth had already displaced history and the survivors had involuntarily displaced the murdered millions. In effect, not the survivors but their civilization had died a double death. There was a twisted road *to* Auschwitz, but another twisted road led away from it—a posthumous victory for the murderers if there ever was one. Why else did the Nazis burn books, letters, photos, and religious objects in huge pits, if not to ensure that the iconography of death would be accessible to all but attributable to no single group of victims? With rigorous planning and methodical execution, they left the world with only an enormous freak show of atrocity pictures—motion pictures, even—by which to remember a civilization more than a millennium old.

Three are the orders of reality: that of the present, that of the murdered Jewish people, and that of the world they left behind. The more I try to confront and connect them, the more I am forced to look at the dirty pictures, to visit the peep show that opens into the chamber of horrors with lampshades made of tattooed human skin. To avoid the defilement seems impossible. Yet in living with the shame of it, how can one avoid falling prey to the easy mediation of myth, a path that so many have followed?

An analogy has often been drawn with the Jews in Roman times. When the Temple of Jerusalem was destroyed in 70 C.E. by the emperor Titus, Jews lost all access to the sacrificial cult as performed by the High Priest—just when their need for purification could not have been greater. Under rabbinic leadership, surrogate structures were created, centered on the synagogue and house of study. Chief among them was the vicarious reenactment of the Temple service. Even today, the gory details of the sacrificial blood, the counting-out ceremony of the High Priest sprinkling the blood of the bullock in the Holy of Holies, and the act of prostrating oneself on the ground have lost none of their cultic power. If anything, they have gained in awesome splendor—because of the Holocaust.

There is a desperate need, I believe, for more rites and ceremonies by which to retrieve the grandeur of European Jewry and by which to expiate Jewish degradation—rites such as the yearly memorial performance of Verdi's Requiem in the fortress town of Terezin; Jerzy Grotowski's staging of the modern Polish classic *Acropolis* in concentration camp uniforms; José Limón's choreography to Zoltán Kodály's *Missa Brevis in Tempore Beli.* Ultraorthodox Jews send wedding invitations to their murdered relatives, addressing the cards to the death camps where they perished; but for most of us the Holocaust is not an intimate family affair, and death is not the mythic flip-side of life.

How, then, does one mourn effectively when there is no way back and the ruins will never be rebuilt? Perhaps the answer lies in the question itself: by taking that which is most sacred, most fraught with meaning, and demolishing it with the force of the Holocaust, the mourner-survivor approximates the actions of the enemy and thus arrives at a permanent break which leaves a few sacred shards while shattering the vessel for all time. When I reach back over the abyss, I see most clearly the perversion of the biblical promise, the cynical revocation of the covenant. Long ago, in the middle of the Israelite camp, where each of the tribes had its allotted place, there was a Tent of Meeting which housed the Tabernacle of the Lord, where the right person could enter, see God, and live, but where unauthorized entrance was punished with immediate death. Of the many subsequent calamities that signaled a breach of convenantal promise, foremost was the burning of the Temple in Jerusalem, followed by a very long exile and, eventually, the extravagant destruction of the Jewish people in Europe. Gathered from their dispersions, "From Warsaw, Paris, Prague, and Salonika" (in the words of Yitzhak Katzenelson), by the most modern of technological means, European Jews were once again brought together in a single camp. Those who were chosen were herded into chambers where a cloud of gas descended upon them and no one ever came out alive.

Such irreconcilables cannot coexist in anxious juxtaposition without the Profane of the Profanes canceling out the Holy of Holies; the biblical text cannot sustain the onslaught. Believing this was so, I wrote a Holocaust liturgy to prove it. I had just left Montreal, "the Jerusalem of Canada," and had entered a world which was indifferent to the past, which denied that anything of value had been lost. Jewish-sponsored universities and a Jewish state, the argument went, showed that things were better than ever before (I refer here to the late 1960s), and such self-congratulation filled me with apocalyptic rage. After several false starts, I vented that rage against God as the surest way to drive my message home—and discovered, to my amazement, that by invoking His Name, even in vain, I was reaching out for meaning, that by subjecting the ancient text to violence I was merely doing what my ancestors had done since the beginning. The memory of sacrilege and murder was always channeled back into the sources of greatest holiness, making Jewish culture the crucible into which even the Great Destruction could be melted down. What's more, in this late adolescent rebellion of mine, I was playing out a question that came to polarize and even politicize the community: Is the Holocaust an event or an Event? Does it admit of analogy or is it sui generis, an indescribable manifestation of evil that stands at the cataclysmic end of history?

It now seems to me that to approach the abyss as closely as possible and to reach back over it in search of meaning, language, and song is a much more promising endeavor than to profess blind faith or apocalyptic despair. The alternative, to focus solely on the Event itself, succeeds only in robbing the dead of the fullness of their lives and in inviting the abstraction of the survivor into Everyman, the Holocaust into Everything.

With emancipation and the loss of Yiddish and Hebrew everywhere but in Israel, Jews have let slip the cultural strand that always tied each catastrophe to the one before. The Jewish people are at the point of turning the tables on themselves, of allowing the Holocaust to become the crucible of their culture. I have set out to challenge this apocalyptic tendency by arguing for the vitality of traditions of Jewish response to catastrophe, never as great as in the last hundred years. And responses to the Holocaust do not mark the end of the process. Elsewhere in the Jewish world, where the war still goes on, traditions of remembrance have been revived, and that too is part of my story.

A book that on the surface deals with finality, endings, disruption, and desecration is really a study in continuities and internal transformations. Jewish catastrophe is a subject whose paradoxical nature—life in death—challenges some of our basic assumptions. For a number of years I identified with George Steiner's essay "A Kind of Survivor," a cosmopolitan manifesto. In it he writes: "The Israeli Jew cannot look back too often; his must be the dreams not of night but of day, the forward dreams."[1] But even looking forward, Israeli Jews make use of traditional motifs. On a recent visit to Tel Aviv's busiest district, I came upon a building marked "Library to Perpetuate the Memory of the Fallen Soldier." The library houses some two thousand volumes that have appeared since 1945—diaries, memoirs, letters, and the artistic legacy of individual soldiers who fell in Israel's wars. After 1967, the motif of the Akedah—the binding of Isaac on Mount Moriah—reasserts itself in these volumes: the parents of the Palmach generation, that elite corps of Palestinian freedom fighters, now have to send their own sons—young men my age—into war. This isn't, I grant, the kind of continuity I had hoped for, and much in these memorial volumes is new and unconventional; but it leaves no doubt in my mind that of all Jewish traditions, the response to catastrophe remains the most viable, coherent, and covenantal.

READING oneself back into history has obvious pitfalls. Yet my own upbringing in a collective Jewish environment could not have been totally anomalous. I am neither the first nor the last to see ruined cities in my mind's eye, and I have reason to believe that the views of catastrophe I shall be describing here were inculcated from childhood into other eastern European Jews and were everywhere reinforced. Not long ago, for instance, I visited one of my mother's Israeli friends, Regina, and brought a fountain pen as a gift. Regina, who studied with Eisenstein in Moscow and is the first professor of film history at an Israeli university, tested the pen just as her father had taught her to do in Bialystok before World War I: she wrote the word "Amalek," and then crossed it out. Here was a lapsed daughter of her people heeding the ancient call of Deuteronomy: "Remember what Amalek did to you on your journey, after you left Egypt . . . You shall blot out the memory of Amalek from under heaven. Do not forget!" (25:17, 19). A quarter century of Yiddish secular life in Vilna followed by another quarter century of professional success in communist Poland had done nothing to dim what Regina had learned about memory from an ultraorthodox father in Bialystok. Memory is an aggressive act.

Of course, this still does not prove that previous generations had nothing but destruction on their minds. It is today's Jews, not they, who live with an awareness of perennial crisis, which is precisely what impels the younger generation to go out in search of traditions. The very ideal of historical continuity, wrote Hannah Arendt, is a modern constuct, a substitute for traditional faith.[2] Everything in modern critical theory teaches one to beware of seamless progressions.

On the other hand, the research of Nathan Wachtel and Paul Fussell shows that the response of individuals and collectives to crisis situations is governed by preexisting patterns. In Wachtel's formulation: "Every event occurs in a context already *there*, made up of institutions, customs and practices, meanings and patterns which both resist and sustain human activity."[3] Fussell's dictum, that "one notices and remembers what one has been 'coded'—usually by literature or its popular equivalent—to notice and remember" is equally relevant to the subject at hand.[4] Working backward according to these guidelines, I shall try to define the traditions of Jewish response to catastrophe in terms both of popular and high culture, ritual practice and individual perspectives. I shall focus on Jewish liturgy as a central repository of group memory in the premodern period (till the end of the eighteenth century) and as that body of custom most readily accessible to the average Jew.

The antitraditionalist revolt of the intellectuals, which is to be the major concern of this book, began in the nineteenth century and reached its peak in the aftermath of World War I and the Bolshevik Revolution. For convenience' sake, I have grouped the writers of this movement into six generations, roughly twenty years apart, with the inevitable arbitrariness that this entails, though I hope to show how the social and historical forces that shaped each generation were quite distinct.

As the modern revolt gathers momentum and each successive generation rejects, expands, severs, and combines the systems and strategies for coping with catastrophe that have evolved over two millennia, the full nature of the enterprise and the extent of this qualitative break with the past become fully apparent only when the culture of Jewish eastern Europe is examined in its bilingual (and, to a lesser degree in this book, trilingual) expression. In and of itself, this represents no methodological breakthrough, and the interested reader will note my profound debt to those literary critics, some of whom I have studied with, who stood above the Great Rift between Hebrew and Yiddish out of ideological or scholarly commitment. (Those of the first type include Ba'al Makhshoves, A. R. Malachi, and Dov Sadan; those of the second include Shalom Luria, Dan Miron, Gershon Shaked, and Khone Shmeruk.) Joining Hebrew and Yiddish sources is also important to illustrate their numerous points of contact (many of which have gone unnoticed), as well as their significant differences. There is much common ground, for instance, in the rejection of messianism for political radicalism and in the emphasis on the individual's sensations in the encounter with disaster. But when the Hebrew writers essentially abandoned European Jewry to its fate in 1930 and transferred the entire Hebrew publishing industry to Mandatory Palestine,[5] Yiddish writers assumed greater prominence by design and default. Thus, the dramatic resurgence of Yiddish writing in the Nazi ghettos has as much to do with the prior defection of Hebrew intellectuals as with the sudden creation of a Yiddish-speaking audience solely dependent on internal resources.

From a bilingual perspective, the modern movement is seen to run a cyclical rather than linear course. Antitraditionalism peaked around 1930 and then circled back upon itself in the face of ever-growing persecution. My discussion in Chapter 7 marks this turn in the modern period by detecting the hidden continuities, the affirmation of faith and communality, in the works of Sholem Aleichem and others—a symmetrical arrangement that I did not anticipate. Similarly, my original intent to end on a resounding note of regeneration was frustrated by the unmistakable signs of discontinuity. Jews who appear on the cross as symbols of collective martyrdom point to a universal constituency that would not respond to Jewish archetypes. And as surely as this is a book written in English, the language of the most recent Jewish dispersion, it is just as certain that the culture described here is gone.

Even as defined, the subject is too large for any one person. I could not, for instance, have undertaken a survey of authentic ghetto writings were it not for the meticulous research of Yechiel Szeintuch, or have chosen to focus on a specific eastern European school of Jewish literary response had Sidra Ezrahi not been there before me to evaluate the full range of postwar writing on the Holocaust. In a book parallel to my own, Alan Mintz brings to life the exemplary texts of Hebrew literature—ancient, medieval, and modern—through interpretive readings of the highest order.

All of this critical theory, however, casts doubt not only upon one's own motives but also upon the very materials one studies. Arranged on one of my bookshelves are all of the classical sources on Jewish catastrophe, edited and annotated. Together they form a coherent literature of destruction where only discrete texts and regional customs existed before. A Tradition, in other words, was reinvented by the moderns out of earlier scattered traditions that were made manifest, reshaped into canonical form, and given a secular sanction quite apart from their original place within the culture as a whole. The earliest anthologies on my shelf go back only to the 1880s. Though the Cossack uprising under Bogdan Khmelnitsky in 1648–49 inspired a wide range of testimonies and memorial prayers, all but one chronicle, *The Deep Mire* (1653), remained scattered in private libraries and local synagogues. When Jonas Gurland, the government-appointed rabbi of Odessa, began their publication in 1887, he was prompted by a mixture of piety and patriotism.[6] The persecutions of old were proof of the Jewish claim to Mother Russia, a claim that recent pogrom-mongers had sought to challenge.

Gathering the sources was a modern way of closing ranks, of reaffirming the essential unity of Jewish experience as one vale of tears through space and time. The harder the times, the more desperately intellectuals clung to a notion of historical continuity. The 1920s were a period of bitter disillusionment for many eastern European Jews. In an emotional essay, Simon Bernfeld explained the pathos of his present hour.[7] Writing as a veteran of past struggles for emancipation, he declared that past struggles had failed to curb the hatred of the Jews. No sooner did they enter the life of nations than bloodshed began. Through all the centuries of persecution Jews had stifled their anger in the constant hope of peaceful coexistence, whether civil rights had been offered them or not. Now this self-imposed censorship had to be lifted, he argued, if they were to withstand the newest onslaught of history, the aftermath of World War I and the Russian Revolution. And so Bernfeld assembled *The Book of Tears,* a vast chronological survey of Jewish responses to suffering that was calculated to revive the flagging spirits of a people who had broken faith with God and with grand political solutions.

Bernfeld's was by no means a majority view in the 1920s and 1930s. Zionists, for instance, read the failure of emancipation as a mandate for political sovereignty. Lord Balfour had offered the first real endorsement. When the Arab riots of 1936 seemed to threaten the very basis of this dream, the young Zionist historian Israel Halpern began work on a counteranthology, *The Book of Valor,* to chronicle not the suffering but the resistance to persecution.[8] The first volume, *From Masada to the Beginnings of Emancipation,* appeared at the lowest ebb of Jewish history, in 1941. By the time volumes two and three were off the press, the battle for independence had been fought and won, vindicating Halpern's agenda. The collection was then forgotten, until another period of despair set in. In the wake of the Yom Kippur War, a group of Israeli academicians prevailed upon the publisher to put out a new edition. Now I, too, can own a set.

The pieces do fit together to form a continuum of Jewish response to catastrophe. The books on my shelf aren't distorting the truth. The only caveat is this: whereas Jews have always seen that history has patterns, the codes were transhistorical, governed by God. The moderns elevated the patterns to the status of a tradition so that they might claim either that Thou shalt reconsecrate it (Bernfeld) or that Thou shalt recreate it (Halpern). The various anthologies, popular histories, translations, and studies were themselves the responses of Jewish intellectuals to the upheavals of their day, an attempt to make Torah out of history.

Although the response of Jewish intellectuals to historical traumas, be it scholarly or imaginative, is eminently worthy of study, to stop there would be to miss the dramatic interplay of history and culture, of memory and behavior, of the elite and the masses. During the past 150 years, as we shall see, history has conspired with literature to repeat the patterns of persecution—or so, at least, it appeared to the Jews of eastern Europe schooled in the exercises of collective memory. This sense of déjà vu has cut across all strata and all age groups, so that everyone—a Jewish mother protesting her son's abduction in the synagogue of Minsk in the 1840s, a Russified officer fighting in World War I, a fourteen-year-old member of the Young Pioneers in the Vilna ghetto—could recognize the unprecedented horrors as something already experienced. The greater the catastrophe, the more the Jews have recalled the ancient archetypes.

The Holocaust was the most demonic of conspiracies between literature and life. Designed as such by the Nazis (one of Hitler's professors had studied at the Hebrew University in Jerusalem), it was perceived by the Jews as a return to the hoary past. This, of course, raises a host of painful questions as to the role that the memory of past destruction played and continues to play in the politics of Jewish survival. Would the Nazis have succeeded in deluding Jews into repeating past responses had it not been for a tradition that constantly rehearsed the destruction? Or shall we say that without a patterned, collective response to catastophe, all Jews might ultimately have perished? And is it possible to generate new responses in the postwar world when the enemy still chooses the holiest day of the calendar to launch its attack?

In reply, let me cite two openly programmatic anthologies of Jewish response to catastrophe, one put out by the Warsaw branch of the Zionist youth movement Dror in July–August 1940 and the other by a survivor some four decades later. The first Jewish book in Nazi-occupied Warsaw was a 101-page mimeographed anthology in Yiddish called *Suffering and Heroism in the Jewish Past in Light of the Present.*[9] Four hundred copies were distributed to the youth leaders of Dror by the underground press, under the joint editorship of Yitzhak Zuckerman and Eliyohu Gutkovsky, a translator of Maimonides into Polish and of Marx into Hebrew.[10] Like Halpern in his *Book of Valor,* slated to appear a year later, the Warsaw editors emphasized the theme of self-defense and the Zionist revolution, but there were enough materials from the Crusades and the Khmelnitsky massacres to suggest that the Jewish people had been sorely tested before. Without this profound historical awareness, there could not have been a last stand in the ghetto.

From Abba Kovner, who issued the first and most passionate call for Jewish armed resistance and who later was party to the fierce battle for the Negev, has come a rallying cry for collective survival in the name of past martyrdoms. At the entrance to the Nahum Goldman Museum of the Jewish Diaspora, in Tel Aviv, Kovner has prefaced his ultramodern exhibit with a richly illustrated book entitled *Scrolls of Fire.*[11] Despite the abstract artwork, everything in that book suggests a liturgical orientation: the title, taken from a work by Chaim Nachman Bialik; the division into fifty-two chapters, one for each week of the year; the careful selection of sources that cuts across the centuries and spans Jewries east and west. One begins with the Destruction of the Temple and ends with a prayer to commemorate all the freedom fighters down to the present day, only to begin the scroll all over again. And so, Jews come full circle: via Ponar and Auschwitz, back to the Bible and prayerbook; through the whirlwind, back to the word.

CHAPTER TWO

The Liturgy of Destruction

Our rabbis have taught: When the First Temple was about to be destroyed, bands upon bands of young priests with the keys of the Temple in their hands assembled and mounted the roof of the Temple and exclaimed, "Master of the Universe, as we did not have the merit to be faithful treasurers these keys are handed back into Thy keeping." Then they threw the keys up towards heaven. And there emerged the figure of a hand and received the keys from them. Whereupon they jumped and fell into the fire.

B. Ta'anith 29a

FOR Gershon Levin, a medic serving in the tsarist army in 1916, the shock of recognition was immediate when his regiment marched through the ruins of Husiatyn, a town that straddled the border between Galicia and Russia: "Only then did I grasp the Destruction of Jerusalem, for whenever I had read the Book of Lamentations in *heder*, or heard *kinot* recited on the ninth of Av, the description always appeared to be grossly exaggerated. But on seeing what the Russians did to Husiatyn in the twentieth century, I could easily imagine what the Romans must have done to Jerusalem some two thousand years ago."[1] The total and willful destruction of a once-prosperous Jewish community, a center of hasidic piety, awakened Levin's childhood memories which in turn validated the oldest record of Jewish disaster. In a single instant of personal and cultural recall, the event fell into place along the scale of earlier catastrophes.

Yet on closer inspection, nothing in his comparison really holds. As a soldier, Levin surely didn't mean to equate the first "world" war in history, raging across Europe in 25,000 miles of trenches, with the Roman subjugation of a tiny rebellious province, the destruction of its capital, and the dispersion of its people. And as an emancipated Jew, he surely didn't accept the traditional theological grounds for destruction. In Levin's mind, Husiatyn validated the historicity of the ancient texts, not their teleology. He did not protest the innocence of the victims directly to God or think in terms of retribution. If Levin's analogy fits, it is because he was reacting to the Jewish dimensions of the tragedy in line with a Jewish pattern of response. The Russians had destroyed Husiatyn house by house, leaving only the Catholic church intact, and they had expelled the entire Jewish population, down to the last cripple.[2] Levin's shock on entering the town triggered a leap across historical time: such things had not happened since the days of the Temple; but however terrible the present devastation, memory confirmed that it was not impossible. As real as was the ruin of the Great Destruction, it was perhaps just as certain that the Jews should endure. The other recourse was to science fiction: Levin was also reminded of H. G. Wells's dead town on the moon.

On seeing Husiatyn razed, Levin invoked the supreme paradigm of Jewish collective disaster. The strength of his religious training came through in a moment of intense pain, when the tragedy of his people intensified the challenge to his personal identity. The tradition resurfaced in secularized form as a flashback to the historical Jerusalem.

This sense of recapitulation is a constant in Jewish history—first, because Jews remember in a highly selective way and, second, because the enemy remembers too, knowing where Jews hurt most, what it is they live by, and what they are ready to die for. Galicia was not simply overrun by the Russian army; it was rendered almost devoid of Jews. An object of particular violence were the symbols of Jewish grandeur, the lavish courts of the hasidic dynasties. In 1917 the synagogue of the rabbi of Sadeger was destroyed. This is how it appeared to one eyewitness:

> When my eye caught sight of the eastern wall, I was totally shaken by what I saw. The elaborate ornamentation on the ark, including the ten commandments up above, remained intact. But in the middle of the empty ark itself a huge [Eastern Orthodox] icon [of Jesus] had been placed.
>
> *Tselem baheykhal,* "an idol in the sanctuary," flashed through my mind. And this shocked me more than all the pogroms I had witnessed. An ancient response began to awaken within me, an echo of the destruction of the Temple . . . I felt that a terrible sacrilege had been perpetrated here, a desecration of *both* religions. The brutal hand of a soldier run wild had exacted the same reprisal from God as from man.[3]

It takes a very modern sensibility to perceive a double desecration. Indeed, this detailed and gripping tableau is the work of S. Ansky, a man equally at home in both Russian and Jewish culture, whose chronicle of the Great War has inspired much of the discussion in the chapters to come. Ansky, for all his erudition, would not have remembered the idol in the sanctuary were it not for the rabbinic practice of combining events into a single date, and, in the case of catastrophe, of clustering acts of desecration: "Five calamities befell our ancestors on the seventeenth of Tammuz and five on the ninth of Av. On the seventeenth of Tammuz the tablets of the law were broken, the daily burnt offering ceased, the walls of Jerusalem were breached, wicked Apostomos burned the law and set up an idol in the Temple" (Mishnah Ta'anith 4:6). That Ansky should join the idol in the sanctuary with the destruction of the Temple, though historically the two events were quite distinct, is just what the rabbis had intended. By supplying the pivotal date, they did not mean to recall a precise coincidence of historical anniversaries—traditions varied as to which of the two Temples, Solomon's or Herod's, was meant where, and no one quite remembered who this wicked Apostomos was—but to set the time of the first event, that primal act of a broken covenant that anticipated all the shattered stone down through the ages. The Law had been defiled once and yet again, always on the same day. Now that the date had been fixed in the mythic past, the punctual became transtemporal, reaching across the millennia from Sinai to Sadeger.

The paradigms of destruction and desecration served Levin and Ansky differently. Levin articulated what I would define as the Jewish dialectical response to catastrophe: the greater the immediate destruction, the more it was made to recall the ancient archetype. Ansky's invocation of the past was more complex. What he recognized in the soldier's deed was not a mere repetition of the anti-Semitic act, but a double desecration, a parody of Apostomos in the sanctuary of the Lord, a breach in the covenant of humanity at large. Ansky saw the act of defilement as an assault on the system of sanctity as a whole. Levin and Ansky were not up to anything new. Both uses of the archetypes—one as literal recall, the other as sacred parody—have been around at least since the fall of the First Temple, and it is to the scholars, preachers, and poets of the rabbinic period (70–500 C.E.) that we must look to trace the development of a normative aboveground tradition of response to catastrophe—a tradition that was taken up by medieval Ashkenazic Jews and that finally became the property of eastern European Jews in modern times.

WHEN the survivors of the First Destruction (the fall of Jerusalem in 587 B.C.E.) cast around them for comparisons, what they found seemed anything but consoling:

> The chastisement of my poor people
> Was greater than the punishment of Sodom,

> Which was overthrown in a moment,
> Without a hand striking it.
>
> (Lam. 4:6)

Once, when a city had broken faith with God, its punishment had been divine and instantaneous—a merciful death compared to the brutal and prolonged siege of Jerusalem. Before 587 B.C.E., what might have seemed rhetorical excess in the dire predictions of Amos (4:11) and Isaiah (1:9) had been surpassed in historical actuality: Jerusalem fared worse than Sodom and Gomorrah. In the very act of searching the sacred texts for figurations, however, and in recalling the exact formulations of their prophets, the exiles from Jerusalem were acknowledging the hand of God, the truth of the true prophets, and, by implication, the deservedness of their punishment. In this way the analogy to Sodom both mitigated and intensified the immediate destruction by reaffirming, however obliquely, the ongoing contract.

The affective weight of catastrophe was increased by its tie to a holy covenant. Whatever happened had direct bearing on the divine prognosis for the chosen people. What's more, Jews flaunted the contract so that anyone intent on wreaking havoc could directly attack the centers of sanctity.

When the Israelites were in the wilderness and the terms of the covenant were still being dictated, the Lord served notice that no Ammonite or Moabite was to enter His sanctuary, even piously and peaceably (Deut. 23:4). What could be bleaker than to stand at the other end of the journey, with the Temple desecrated and the nation dispersed? At such a moment the sacred contract seemed irremediably breached.

> The enemy stretched out his hand after all her [Zion's] precious things.
> She saw that the heathen entered her sanctuary,
> Concerning whom you had commanded:
> "They shall not enter your assembly."
>
> (Lam. 1:10)

This was an open act of imperial dominion, one that any conqueror could be expected to perpetrate against the central symbols of an enemy's strength: palace, temple, vestal virgins, and oracles. Later, when Israel lost the symbols of its temporal power, its new convenantal trappings—the portable Torah, the surrogate temples, the Halacha (rabbinic Law), and Jewish practice—came under attack instead. In a way, this made Jews less vulnerable, since no conqueror until modern times could possibly destroy all the sanctums.

So the enemy had known where to attack, and the survivors would rehearse their sense of defilement again and again, because recalling the covenant in the context of destruction was a step toward spiritual renewal. The perceived desecration had a unifying effect when the covenantal promise was invoked in group dialogue with God, just as the attempt to put cataclysm on a continuum implied a shared, communal memory. What of the individual, however? If the polity itself needed assurances of continuity in its moment of crisis, then the individual's need to make peace with a polity that had just been sundered must have been all the more intense.

The voice of the individual sufferer—not as personification but as paradigmatic loner—does indeed emerge out of the communal ruin of Jerusalem. "Ani hagever," the survivor cries, announcing the sudden shift in perspective in the Book of Lamentations. These two words will reecho for the next two and a half thousand years, each time an individual stands up to bear witness to atrocity:

> I am the man whom the Lord has shepherded
> With the rod of His wrath;
> Me he drove on and on
> In unrelieved darkness.
> (Lam. 3:1–2; emended reading)

Haunted by another voice from the past, the Psalmist's shepherding Lord, the individual's anguish gives the exultant hymn of old a new and bitter twist. Here the function of the earlier text is not to subdue or mitigate or mollify or soothe or reconcile. By echoing the psalm in the context of bitter exile, the survivor is voicing a protest against God. For a brief instant the suffering individual registers despair by making the most hallowed and hopeful of texts the target of desecration. Far from being a mere device, this resort to literature is an attempt at a very human counterassertion: if God can do this, for whatever reason, then Jews can do something equally grotesque at the human level. If God mutilates, so can Jews—not of course on the same scale, but in microcosm.

Lest these seem exaggerated claims based on a single emended reading of a verse from Lamentations, it should be pointed out that the Jewish device of twisting Scripture, of subjecting the earlier canon to radical reinterpretation by means of subtle reformulations, is now recognized as central to the Bible as a whole. It is but one instance of innerbiblical midrash—of scribal, legal, aggadic (legendary), and prophetic exegesis that eventually formed the basis of rabbinic teaching.[4] After the exile, the need for such interpretive procedures was especially great.

Viewed in this larger context, the survivor's tactic of inverting Scripture can be seen as a means of keeping faith. This is so despite the terror and aloneness of the individual, who is cut off not only from God but also from the collective, with its easy recourse to the fund of past experience. At that moment of crisis, individuals have the ability and the freedom to reinterpret and radicalize the tradition. They can take the supreme act of profanity and convert it to sacred use, creating their own personal "sacred parody"—to borrow out of context from the English devotional poet George Herbert.[5] It is parody in a double sense. Most directly, the sacred text is put to irreverent use, but what triggers this response on the part of individual sufferers is their desire to imitate the sacrilege, to disrupt the received order of the text in the same way as the enemy, acting at the behest of God, disrupted the order of the world.

Some parody, of course, *is* destructive, which raises the question of how to tell faithful mimes from their cynical counterparts. What makes individual sufferers people of faith is their willingness to accept the covenantal framework of guilt, punishment, and restitution; or, to put it differently, it is in the self-imposed limitations of their parody. Theirs is an anger deflected through the hallowed texts, a highly mediated and ritualized form of anger. By making the text seem for a while crazy and corrupt, the individual sufferer expands its meaning, allowing subsequent sufferers to enter the breach. And once the shepherd's psalm is put through the fire of catastrophe, the lyric ode can be used as a song of defiant affirmation.

This technique of imitating the breach of God's promise in the parody of Scripture has been variously called "symbolic inversion"[6] and "countercommentary"[7] by those who recognize its use only in the modern age. In fact, it is one of two basic forms of Jewish response to catastrophe. The first response—to locate the catastrophe on a continuum—is an act of collective faith. But to mimic the sacrilege allows the individual to keep faith even as the promise is subverted.

What conceptual choices did survivors of the Great Destruction have back in 587 B.C.E.? On the one hand they had access to the mythic, cyclical view of "eternal return."[8] Up until that year, the royal Davidic tradition of temple, priest, and king had flourished in Judah as the official state religion. It was an overwhelmingly mythic world view, having borrowed its kingship terminology lock, stock, and barrel from Egypt and Mesopotamia. Competing with it was the biblical, Sinaitic religion which had been revived some thirty-four years before (in 621 B.C.E.) by Josiah and which was championed by the prophets and their followers. It was the historicist view of unique events that had changed things forever, the product of God's all-powerful will.

Logically one might have thought that with destruction, the cyclical world view would have prevailed, for the linear perspective carried with it a great deal of insecurity. It was easier to live with the constant of natural instability, to placate the gods on a cyclical basis, than to face an all-powerful God who made one's claim to the land and the favorable outcome of the story contingent upon the performance of His commandments. Nothing in the biblical narrative drove this terror home more forcefully than the list of Mosaic curses (the *Tokheḥa*) in Leviticus 26 and Deuteronomy 28. Even the untrained ear can recognize in this catalogue of horrors an ancient stratum of the biblical tradition—one, indeed, that Israel shared with other Near Eastern peoples. A terrifying list of curses generally accompanied the terms of a treaty, to warn of the punishment the gods would exact for breach of promise.[9] The biblical terms were drawn from the spheres of nature and technology and from the realm of universal human endeavor. The heavens and the earth would repudiate Israel for breach of contract:

> The skies above your head shall be copper and the earth under you iron.
> The Lord will make the rain of your land dust, and sand shall drop on you from the sky, until you are wiped out.
>
> (Deut. 28:23–24)

Every human initiative would be frustrated—planting, harvesting, building, mating—"until you are driven mad by what your eyes behold" (Deut. 28:34).

Here they were, as Deuteronomy described them, recently liberated from Egypt, on the eve of their nationhood, and hanging over their heads was not only the specter of famine, pestilence, and drought but a threat more terrifying still because it was rooted in their historical experience. Though they had not yet conquered the land, Moses was laying out in detail the ultimate threat of siege, defeat, and exile. This last set of threats resonated deeply because it forced the Jews to look back and become *fixed* on the past: "He will bring back upon you all the sicknesses of Egypt which you dreaded so, and they shall cling to you" (verse 60). Noah was granted a new covenant after the flood. Abraham was promised that his people would be as numerous as the stars in the skies. But now all would revert to chaos. "And as the Lord once delighted in making you prosperous and many, so will the Lord now delight in causing you to perish and in wiping you out; you shall be torn from the land which you are about to invade and occupy" (verse 63). Even the means of exile were laid out: "The Lord will send you back to Egypt in galleys, by a route which I told you you should not see again" (verse 68). The ultimate curse, then, was the nightmare of mythic repetition. Nothing was worse than history's turning back on itself.

Fortunately, the way out of the circular trap was charted in the curses themselves. Angry as God might be, He never withdrew from the covenant. Destruction or exile spelled not abandonment by God but punishment, and if the people returned to the ways of the Lord, He would return them not to Egypt but back to the Promised Land: "Then the Lord your God will turn your captivity and take you back in love. He will bring you together again from all the peoples where the Lord your

God has scattered you" (Deut. 30:3). Restoration, not blind repetition, was the proper direction for history to take, a linear route that ended in Zion and that depended entirely on man's contractual agreement with God. If this grandiose theme seems rather at odds with its modest desert setting, it was because the curses owed their final redaction to a period after the catastrophic fall of Judah, when the exiles desperately needed to hear that just as the biblical threats had been fulfilled, so too would the promised restoration.[10]

There was an extraordinary tension at work here between the linear, God-centered approach and the mythic cycles of the gods; but with the destruction and exile, as the examples of Lamentations and the Tokheḥa have shown, the Sinaitic, historicist world view came to its full power. Just as the author(s) of Lamentations (or Jeremiah alone, according to tradition) saw the First Destruction as the fulfillment of the Mosaic curses—Zion's enemies had indeed become her masters (Lam. 1:15), the Jerusalemite women during the siege had indeed devoured their children (4:10), and the "sword of the wilderness" (5:9) now ruled over all the survivors—so too did history intrude on an inherited list of treaty stipulations for the sake of this grand design of threat, fulfillment, exile, and return. And as for sacred parody—the stylistic equivalent of being driven mad by what your eyes behold—it was the first step toward the human writing of history. Lamentations introduced the individual and particular sufferer who did *not* claim to be metonymic—who was an accident, an aberration, a shepherd whom the Lord had somehow abandoned. This, in turn, raised the terrifying question: To what degree was the devastation, too, a mere historical accident and not the culmination of a grand mythic design? Hence, the pathetic attempts in Lamentations to awaken God's mercy, to insist that even suffering must be good (3:26–30), that both "weal and woe" proceed from the word of God (3:38), and, for lack of any new theology to advance, the concluding, desperate hope to "renew our days *as of old*" (4:21).

Within the two basic forms of Jewish response to catastrophe were embedded both the mythic and linear-historical sense of human eventualities. The great catastrophe seemed to demand a double consideration and a double trial: to make sense of the "accident" by linking it to a string of similar past "accidents" in some not incredible way, and to give the violence a mythic power while accepting the covenantal implications.

SO long as the priests and prophets were around to placate God's wrath, the burden of His infallible memory was easier to bear. When all at once the mediators were eliminated, leaving the Temple of

Solomon despoiled and the best of the people dispersed, the terror could not have been greater. Whence was the word of God to come if the destruction had been caused, according to Lamentations (2:14), by the charlatans who prophesied "oracles of delusion and deception"? To buttress their authority, the true prophets relied increasingly on their powers of interpretation and on the utterances of earlier prophets. The discontinuity of exile, however, left prophecy more suspect than ever. The rabbis looking back after the fall of Herod's Temple would conclude that since the First Temple's ruin, prophecy had been taken from the prophets and given to the sages—*ḥakhamim* (B. Baba Bathra 12a). This left the text itself as the sole arbiter of sacred history, and scribes and scholars as its truest guides.

After the exile, the book that had been regarded as the inviolable source of the law and as the chronicle of the people's beginnings took on a radically new dimension, becoming the blueprint for its future as well. This placed the burden of historical recapitulation and interpretation squarely on the shoulders of man. Of course only God could ever be expected to know and remember everything in its finest detail, but since the God of History was not imprisoned in history, it was sometimes left to man to remind Him, as it were, of His promise that each exile would be followed by a new exodus to freedom. The resort to history had to be the resort to human parallel. The "reminding of God" was the reassertion of human continuity: *we* remember; we've stored away the promises all the way back to Abraham and Adam.

No analogies, therefore, were ever to be drawn at random. Ideally, the choice of archetypes would fulfill a triple purpose: to give the immediate event a biblical sanction, thereby to alert God to the grand design of history and to assure the survivors of their own place on the continuum.

In contrast to Lamentations, which was relentless in its causality and almost documentary in style, the prophetic consolation delivered in response to the fall of Solomon's temple was extravagant in its use of archetypes. Ezekiel and Second Isaiah were the two main prophets of the exile, and each created a unique blend of history and myth to instill hope among the exiled community. Ezekiel's visionary scenario was spectacular. He prophesied the war of Gog and Magog, the embodiments of pure evil, whose sole function was to attack Israel, suffer defeat at its hands, and be devoured in a great sacrificial bloodbath. In magnificent detail he laid out a blueprint for spatial renewal in a Temple flowing with restorative waters—a new Eden.[11] Finally, he gave Jews their most palpable myth of redemption, the Valley of the Dry Bones. The force of this splendid vision of destruction, renewal, and resurrection derived from its wealth of detail, the product of a speculative mind[12] that could plot a military campaign without any regard for historical necessity, or reconstruct the physical landscape of Israel down to the exact architectural requirements of the new Temple, or breathe life into dead bones, limb by limb.

Second Isaiah drew his consolation from the record of events past and prophesied. The trauma of history is behind you, he announced, for Israel "has received at the hand of the Lord / Double for all her sins" (40:2). To prove the beneficence of the future, he offered a revisionist reading of the past, beginning with Creation itself. Whereas the rebuilding of the Temple is what most excited the imagination of Ezekiel, who was himself a priest, Second Isaiah restructured the course of history as a new exodus. Whatever fears of blind reversal had been instilled by the Mosaic curses were now forever allayed by the series of miracles the Lord was about to enact *in history,* miracles that would surpass anything that had come before. This time, God would not only destroy the historical enemies and return the exiles to the land, but also irrigate the desert in the process (Isa. 40–51).

The remythification of history became the very essence of the apocalyptic thinking that flourished in Palestine from about 200 B.C.E. to 100 C.E. Whereas the nation and its institutions were very much alive in the minds of the prophets of the exile, who therefore could still affirm the restoration of God's kingdom in the historical realm, the apocalyptists increasingly despaired of the political and religious structure of the nation and therefore shifted their restorative program onto the visionary realm. The visionary impulse, according to Paul D. Hanson, was greatest when the sense of *real* power was in decline.[13] And as the Jews of Palestine smarted under the rule of the Greeks and later of the Romans, there was every reason to despair of temporal power. Thus, although the vision of restoration was common to both prophets and apocalyptists, the latter laid claim to revelationary powers beyond anything that had ever been accepted before. The apocalyptists purported to disclose, at least to a select group of believers, things that Scripture did not explicitly say or declared to be beyond the reach of the human intellect—things such as the secrets of nature, history, and divine retribution. Apocalypticism, in Ithamar Gruenwald's enthusiastic appraisal, "could digest almost anything."[14]

The rabbis could not have disagreed more. In the struggle for hegemony in the real world, there was no room for initiates who claimed that only a few would be saved, regardless of the deeds of the many—those few who had prepared for the Coming of the Messiah. Except for the Book of Daniel and certain "proto-apocalyptic" segments in Isaiah and Zechariah, the vast body of apocalyptic speculation was suppressed. The triumph in late Second Temple times of Pharisaism over the rival camps of Sadducees, Zealots, the Qumran sect, and the Essenes, to name the chief contenders, left the Sinaitic tradition as the exclusive route to sanctity. Scripture, as interpreted by the Sages of Yavneh and Usha (the Tanaim), was the touchstone of reality. Paradoxically, it was by setting the biblical canon apart that the rabbis of Yavneh guaranteed its future hold on the Jewish imagination. The rabbis of the tanaitic period (100–200 C.E.) believed that after the exile, God had distanced Himself from history.[15] They admitted that they no longer knew what He was doing in the here and now. The only assurance of truth, the only reliable record they had of God's speaking to humankind, was in Scripture. But what more did they need? If the Bible revealed the pattern of the whole of history, then all subsequent events could be made to fit the biblical paradigms. The rabbis' concern was for the larger configurations of history as prefigured in Scripture, not for its concrete, contemporary particulars.[16]

Historical events were reinterpreted in light of the earlier dialogue between God and man. Once the synagogue replaced the Temple, once prayer replaced the sacrificial cult, once rabbis and preachers succeeded the priests and prophets, then all visions of past, present, and future were restructured to fit a new liturgical mold. Henceforth, the contexts of memory were all to emanate from Scripture, study house, and synagogue. Multiple copies of the Temple key were reentrusted to the synagogue wardens for safekeeping.

Working on the biblical premise that man must appease God to win back His favor, the tanaitic rabbis codified an elaborate schedule of public fasts, to be implemented especially in times of drought. The rite of special prayers, later incorporated into the penitential service of the High Holiday liturgy, concluded with a set of supplementary blessings to be recited by the leader of prayer. These six blessings together provide an encyclopedic overview of the biblical heroes for whose sake the Lord reversed the course of nature: Moses at the Red Sea, Joshua in Gilgal (Josh. 6, 7, 10), Samuel in Mizpah (1 Sam. 7:5–9), Elijah on Mount Carmel (1 Kings 18:36–39), Jonah in the belly of the fish, and kings David and Solomon in Jerusalem (2 Sam. 21; 1 Kings 8–9). Each followed a similar formula: "May He who answered Moses and our fathers at the Red Sea also answer you and listen to the sound of your outcry on this day. Blessed art thou, O Lord, who rememberest forgotten things" (Mishnah Ta'anith 2:4).

This was a celebration not of the natural but of the historical—more precisely, of the historical intervention of God in nature. The pathos of this prayer consists in the Jews' daring to imagine that God would act and the course of the world be reversed *for them* as it was for Moses, Joshua, Samuel, et al. The rabbis of the Mishnah were concerned with the past to the extent that it could be used to galvanize the present—and vice versa. They had little patience, as we shall see, for fast days that merely commemorated historical disasters, preferring instead to regulate petitionary fasts and to record the preemptive fasts observed during Temple times. One remembered in order to bring the God of History back into nature.

To make the Torah a book of the eternal present, the rabbis linked it to the calendar, rearranging Scripture toward a metahistorical purpose. Neither the strict chronology of events nor the original historical setting of any given oracle—questions that so preoccupy the modern reader—was allowed to stand in the way. Brevard Childs has amply illustrated the various scribal stratagems for subtly updating, redirecting, and reinterpreting the prophets.[17] The most relevant example for my purposes is Second Isaiah (chapters 40–55), who lived during the Babylonian exile. The scribes put him back in the eighth century to be joined with First Isaiah, of Jerusalem. Robbed of his historical particularity, Isaiah of the Exile could bring a timeless message of hope to all future generations and complete the cycle of destruction to consolation.

Instead of assuming that the modern sense of chronology and history was simply absent from the earlier ("more primitive") world, it may be more correct to assume that the rabbis of the second century C.E. simply rejected as too stupid or too flat the notion of chronology and context as overriding precepts. Though they may have known that Isaiah of Jerusalem lived before Jeremiah and Ezekiel, the rabbis justified having the prophetic books copied in reverse order: "Because the Book of Kings ends with a record of destruction and Jeremiah speaks throughout of destruction and Ezekiel begins with destruction and ends with consolation and Isaiah is full of consolation; therefore we put destruction next to destruction and consolation next to consolation" (B. Baba Bathra 14b). In the scrolls they had before them, Isaiah appeared last, not first as he does in the canonical order that has come down to us, and such a violation of chronology seemed perfectly justified in order to end the major prophets on a resounding message of hope.

A far more obvious way of turning sacred history to liturgical use was by the public reading of Scripture. This practice goes back at least to the time of Ezra (ca. 458 B.C.E.), when the relevant passages from the Torah were read aloud and interpreted in the Temple during the pilgrimage festivals.[18] By the middle of the third century B.C.E. the practice was instituted of reading the entire Pentateuch from start to finish on consecutive Sabbaths, and some time before the Common Era *haftaroth,* or supplementary readings from the prophets, were introduced.[19] The importance of the ritualized reading of Scripture can hardly be overstated. First, though the events of biblical history remained unique and irreversible, they were now experienced "cyclically, repetitively, and to that extent at least, atemporally."[20] In the Babylonian system, the cycle was completed each year. Thus, in the course of a person's lifetime the various segments of Scripture became associated with the changing seasons: Joseph with mud and sleet, Balak with the heat of the summer. Second, the reading of the scroll provided the weekly ritual with narrative continuity. Recognizing this, the rabbis in the geonic period (ca. 1000 C.E.) set aside a day at the climax of the Sukkoth festival to mark the Torah's completion and resumption.[21] Third, as the public reading itself became a central ritual act, the interpretation of Scripture in the rabbinic sermon became a major creative outlet. The ongoing embellishment of the Torah became the province not of the select few but of the entire people. Finally, the introduction of haftaroth encouraged the panchronistic reading of Scripture: there is no "before" and "after" in the Torah (B. Pesahim 6b and elsewhere); all parts of it interpenetrate. Thus, the prophets were lifted out of their original context to form a thematic link either with the Torah reading for that Sabbath or with a particular event in the calendar cycle. The prophetic readings were ideally suited to highlight larger themes, such as the pattern of destruction and redemption, which were programmed into the calendar year.

The flowing time of the calendar which subsumed the events of Scripture into a cyclical pattern of triennial or yearly repetitions did not leave much room for the moments of crisis and catastrophe. The rabbis of Yavneh and Usha inherited an extensive if laconic list of commemorative dates for the prohibition of fasting on each Hasmonean military victory and religious reform (dating mostly from the years 167–152 B.C.E.). By the time the rabbis were through with the list, known as Megillath Ta'anith,[22] only Hanukkah and Purim survived intact; the first was spiritualized into the victory of God, not of the Maccabees, and the second was acclaimed as the prototype of redemption-in-a-day affecting men and women alike (B. Rosh Hashanah 18b).

All this activity of canonizing, of codifying, rearranging, and ritualizing historical memory, happened in a period (the first and second centuries C.E.) when the rabbis of Palestine were themselves intensely involved in historical events. Perhaps nothing so reveals how the rabbinic response to catastrophe diverged from that of the biblical prophets, the apocalyptists, and the early Christians as the rabbinic legacy, in law and lore, of the Hadrianic persecutions.

Under Hadrian's rule (132–138 C.E.), as under that of Antiochus Epiphanes three hundred years before, Jews were forced to wage a dual war, one for their political sovereignty, the other for their faith; but with the failure of the military option, the rabbis chose to recall this period as the time of "the wicked government that forbade the Jews to study and practice the Torah" (B. Berakhot 61b). Rabbinic sources provide a long list of Roman edicts, beginning with a ban on circumcision, to bans on observing the Sabbath, eating matzoh on Passover, reading the Scroll of Esther on Purim, reciting the Shema, engaging in public prayer and study, and ordaining rabbis.[23] A different punishment was meted out for violating each prohibition. The enemy had apparently done their homework. The resistance to these Roman edicts was led by Rabbi Akiva and Bar Kokhba.

Unlike Ignatius, who left a passionate testimony on the eve of his martyrdom sometime during Trajan's reign,[24] and unlike Polycarp, whose death in the arena in 155 was retold in complete and vivid detail,[25] the traditions concerning Akiva's death are fragmentary, contradictory, and lacking in any historical focus. In their simplest rendering, "Rabbi Akiva was tried before the impious Tineius Rufus. The time for reciting the Shema arrived. He began to recite it and became very joyful. 'Old man, old man,' said Rufus, 'are you a magician or do you defy torture?' "[26] Akiva later died in prison. More dramatically, it was in the hour of death that Akiva fulfilled his religious obligation, and the meaning of his last heroic act, the proclamation of God's oneness, has been explained by Saul Lieberman as a direct challenge to the emperor's claim to divine authority.[27] But the story *as written* makes no reference to the Romans at all, has no polemical intent, and is addressed solely to an issue of theodicy:

> When R. Akiva was taken out for execution it was the hour for the recital of the Shema, and while they combed his flesh with iron combs, he was accepting upon himself the kingship of heaven [that is, reciting the Shema]. His disciples said to him: Our teacher, even to this point? He said to them: All my days I have been troubled by this verse, WITH ALL MY SOUL, [which I interpret,] "even if He takes your soul." I said: When shall I have the opportunity of fulfilling this? Now that I have the opportunity, shall I not fulfill it? He prolonged the word *eḥad* (one) until he expired while saying it. (B. Berakhot 61b)

The grounds for human suffering had changed if someone as blameless as Rabbi Akiva could be subjected to death by torture. Akiva's martyrdom was taken to mean that the death of the righteous was brought about by nothing else than their resolve to serve the Lord to their fullest.[28]

The model of rabbinic martyr was a compromise among three of many possibilities: the warrior-messiah, such as Bar Kokhba, who fought Rome in the same way that Judah the Maccabee had fought the Syrians; the martyr, the essence of whose life is the manner of his death; and the rabbi, who places the preservation of the Torah above all else—

as did Rabbi Yohanan ben Zakkai, who stole out of beleaguered Jerusalem in order to establish the academy of Yavneh with Roman support. The traditions surrounding Rabbi Akiva drew upon these three, giving as the reason for his arrest either his support for Bar Kokhba's rebellion or his defiance of Roman orders by calling assemblies to study the Torah.

Eventually, all memory of the rebellion was suppressed and Akiva's death was remembered only in the context of an all-out war against Judaism. This left him and the other martyred rabbis as the sole defenders of the faith, whereas Bar Kokhba (which resonates with *kokhav*, star), was demoted in later rabbinic sources to carry the insult of Bar Koziba, the disappointer, a pun on Bar Kosba, his actual name.[29] In a further semantic twist, the martyrs were dubbed *Harugei Malkhut*. The term meant persons put to death for treason against a *Jewish* king and was now adapted to mean Jews who, by virtue or their prominence and nobility, elected martyrdom under the murderous rule of others.[30]

More profoundly, the meaning of Kiddush Hashem, the sanctification of God's Name, was utterly transformed. By the same process that shifted the burden of memory from God to man, Kiddush Hashem became the prerogative of man, rather than of God acting to sanctify His own Name, as we find it in biblical sources.[31] Akiva was not rescued from the fire like Hananiah, Mishael, and Azariah in the Book of Daniel, to bear witness to God's glory through a miracle; he did not claim to be dying for his sins, as did old Eleazar, or the mother and her seven sons in 2 Maccabees. Akiva accepted suffering-with-love as the highest piety, and after him Hanina be Tardion (or Teradion) militantly ventured all for the preservation of the Torah, for which the Romans sentenced him to be wrapped in a Torah scroll and burned (The Tractate "Mourning" 8:12).

These exemplary deeds were then translated into required practice. The Roman attempt to separate public submission from private observance and to drive a wedge between positive and negative commandments was countered by the rabbis of the same or the next generation who formulated new martyrological guidelines (B. Sanhedrin 74a–b): a person should die rather than commit idolatry, adultery, or bloodshed. In times of religious persecution (*bish'at hashemad*), a person should die rather than transgress any commandment, no matter how minor, but only if he or she is forced to do so in public (in the presence of at least ten people). When assimilation, betrayal, and persecution threatened to destroy the whole community, martyrdom, redefined as Kiddush Hashem, was a call to close ranks.

If the rabbis of Hadrian's time inaugurated a new response to catastrophe and if the heroic deaths of some rabbis were duly recorded, then did they not warrant individual saints' days? From the so-called Latter Scroll of Fasts,[32] it would appear that the death dates of five tanaitic rabbis (including Akiva and Hanina) were indeed observed in Palestine, along with the anniversaries of Moses, Aaron, Miriam, Eli the Priest, Samuel, and other biblical greats; but by the early Middle Ages, no vestige remained of any of these fasts except the one for Moses. What I think underlies this disappearance is that Jewish martyrdom could never be a literal *imitatio Dei.* In the Jewish scheme, God is *kadosh,* holy, and therefore the Jew must be holy. God is God by being a negation of the pagan world; a Jew is a Jew by negating pagan society and customs, first and foremost through the observance of the Torah.[33] After the Hadrianic persecutions, the Jew was obliged to be *kadosh* by observing the Torah—or to die.

"During religious persecutions," the tanaitic rabbis ruled, "man is to give his life rather than violate even the least important of the commandments, as it is said, 'And you shall not desecrate My Holy Name' (Lev. 22:32)."[34] What better way was there to promote this new concept of Kiddush Hashem, the Jew's obligation to preserve God's holiness in times of persecution, than to attribute acts of blasphemy to the archcriminal of an earlier time: "Vespasian sent Titus who said, WHERE IS THEIR GOD, THE ROCK IN WHOM THEY TRUSTED (Deut. 32:37)? This was the wicked Titus who blasphemed and insulted Heaven. What did he do? He took a harlot by the hand and entered the Holy of Holies and spread out a scroll of the Law and committed a sin upon it" (B. Gittin 56b). The sexual defilement of Zion and her holy places was central to Lamentations and to the martyrology in 2 Maccabees. The emperor's challenge to God added a new dimension of blasphemy to the desecrated landscape of old. But if God could countenance this most heinous of crimes (the blasphemy, as underscored by the sex) which Jews were now called upon to resist, then here was a sacrilege of double proportions. How could they go on singing His praises as if nothing had happened? The Psalmist's words rang hollow to Aba Hanan, a Tanna of the second century C.E., who threw them back at God.

> WHO IS A MIGHTY ONE LIKE YOU, O LORD (Ps. 89:9)? [Rather one should proclaim:] "Who is like You, mighty in self-restraint? You heard the blasphemy and the insults of that wicked man, but You kept silent! In the school of Rabbi Ishmael it was taught: WHO IS LIKE YOU, O LORD, AMONG THE MIGHTY (*elim*) (Exod. 15:11)? [Read rather] "Who is like You among the mute" (*illemim*)—since He sees the suffering of His children and remains silent! (B. Gittin 56b and Mekhilta 42b)

If you will, it is only a word game, this adding of a single Hebrew consonant, a technique used constantly throughout midrash. Then again, it is about as close as the rabbis themselves ever came to blaspheming; with a tone of defiance, of parody, imitating the emperor's grotesque behavior with the perversion of the sacred text; a counter-statement that would be picked up again by the twelfth-century poet Isaac bar Shalom, and again by angry liturgists in the twentieth century. It makes no difference that Titus was innocent and that if anyone challenged the kingship of God, it was Hadrian, by whose day the Temple was already destroyed. What the rabbis preserved instead was the internal response of a generation suffering under the weight of an unequal covenant.

The rabbis were concerned to answer the emotional and spiritual needs of their time through a revisionist reading of Scripture and, like the apocalyptists, drew heavily on folklore and popular belief. But the rabbis' mandate was a public one, designed to secure a strong popular base, with a message that was universally accessible and universally binding. To this end, rabbinic activity was divided between perfecting a system of legal interpretation, the Halacha, and developing a mythology of the mundane, the Aggadah. Neither corpus was particularly fixated on catastrophe.

The halachic mind, or any legal mind for that matter, harmonizes texts with realities in order to yield a normative decision, and ultimately in the geonic period, a code of behavior. In the process of linking up with Scripture to serve God's will in the concrete everyday, categorical precedents and major decisions are of far greater import than singular occurrences. In this context, the historical anecdote enjoys no independent status whatsoever. A search through tanaitic sources, those closest in time to the events described, will yield, at most, a handy repository of martyrological tales, the eighth chapter of the tractate "Mourning," whose central concern is just that—the rules attending death and bereavement.[35] The deeds of the first- and second-century rabbis are held up as examples of how to die and how properly to honor the dead. It is here that we read of Hanina ben Tardion's torture and death:

> At the time of his execution, they wrapped him in a Torah scroll and set fire to him and to the Torah scroll, while his daughter, throwing herself at his feet, screamed: "Is this the Torah, and this its reward?"
>
> "My daughter," he said to her, . . . "if it is for the Torah scroll that you are weeping, lo, the Torah is fire, and fire cannot consume fire. Behold, the letters are flying into the air, and only the parchment itself is burning." (8:12)

In a later account (B. Abodah Zarah 18a), the details of his torture are laid out in starker detail—tufts of wet wool are placed over his heart to prolong the burning, and the executioner throws himself into the fire as well—but the essentials of the story, its paradigmatic qualities, remain unchanged. The religious leader who fulfills his duties even unto death, who transcends the barbarity of his executioners, transforms the torture into triumphant martyrdom. Hanina's wife is sentenced to die by the sword and his daughter is sent to a brothel, but he, having made the preservation of the Torah the guiding principle in his life, can now endure the torture with equanimity. A greater triumph is achieved on the symbolic level, for by means of this individuated execution, the Romans endowed Hanina's death with universal significance. The letters of the Torah have a life of their own and take leave of the burning scroll in the same way as the soul departs from the human body. The scroll is mere flesh, but its spirit is indestructible.

This story anticipates two directions taken by rabbinic Aggadah in response to catastrophe. In the amoraic period (200–400 C.E.), storytelling traditions such as these about the early rabbis were expanded into small-scale rabbinic biographies, just as rabbinic behavior was read back into biblical times. Abraham, Isaac, and Jacob were refashioned as proto-rabbis. Even the most skillfully dramatized biographical segments, however, were still embedded in a wider body of legal and exegetical concerns, and it was not the course but the meaning of the life that mattered.[36]

In a second direction, the rabbis began to probe beyond human interest stories to such larger issues as God's own response to the tragedy and the relevance of the Torah to history. In the ritual cycle, the summer months of Tammuz and Av were the time when the destruction of the Temple was rehearsed in the synagogue. Thus, for the preacher, it was the ideal occasion to expound on the meaning of Jewish suffering and persecution. The proems, or introductory sections, of the amoraic midrash preserve some of their sermons more or less intact,[37] and in one, the twenty-fourth proem in the midrash on Lamentations,[38] the full flight of the rabbinic imagination is revealed.

It was an ancient Near Eastern motif, of a god who abandoned the city and allowed its destruction,[39] which Ezekiel had alluded to in his vision of restoration (Ezek. 10:18; see also Ps. 78:59–61). But in this case the preacher (Rabbi Yohanan?) was constrained by the particular prophetic reading for that day to begin with a passage from Isaiah instead. MY LORD GOD OF HOSTS SUMMONED ON THAT DAY TO WEEPING AND LAMENTING, TO TONSURING AND GIRDING WITH SACKCLOTH (Isa. 22:12) would be taken to mean that God summoned *Himself* to grieve for the destruction that He had allowed through His absence.

Once the deed is done, the Lord is seized with remorse and returns to inspect the full extent of the damage, guided by Jeremiah. An inconsolable God orders Jeremiah to fetch Moses and the patriarchs, "for they know how to mourn." Poor Jeremiah cannot bring himself to break the news, and he prevaricates as he rouses them from the grave:

Jeremiah: Son of Amram, son of Amram, arise, the time has come when your presence is required before the Holy One, blessed be He.
Moses: How is this day different from other days that my presence is required before the Holy One, blessed be He?
Jeremiah: I don't know.

Since Jeremiah hasn't the heart to do it, the ministering angels "whom he recognized from the time of the giving of the Torah," are left to reveal to Moses what has happened, releasing a veritable orgy of grief:

When the Holy One, blessed by He, saw them, immediately THE LORD GOD OF HOSTS SUMMONED ON THAT DAY TO WEEPING AND LAMENTING, TO TONSURING AND GIRDING WITH SACKCLOTH. Were it not explicitly stated in Scripture, it would be impossible to say such a thing, but they went weeping from one gate to another like a man whose dead is lying before him, and the Holy One, blessed be He, lamented saying, "Woe to the King who succeeded in His youth but failed in His old age!"

The rabbis occasionally hedged their bets with "were it not for the biblical verse black on white, it would be impossible to say," when they portrayed God as suffering with man.[40] These bold anthropomorphisms do more than give graphic expression to abstract theosophical ideas. For to conjure up the moment when God, the angels, the patriarchs, and the prophets see the destruction for the first time, to imagine how each tries to spare the other until they all join in one great and terrible lament, is true catharsis for an audience that has lived with the news for generations and is still no closer to seeing the Temple rebuilt.

Rabbi Samuel ben Nahman's sermon, recorded next in the same proem, takes the dramatic interplay of heavenly and human personalities one step further by animating the Torah and the letters of the Hebrew alphabet. Abraham, the greatest of biblical intercessors, pleads Israel's case before the Lord: "How could You destroy the Temple where I offered my own son Isaac as a burnt offering before you?" God replies: "Your children sinned and transgressed the whole of the Torah and the twenty-two letters in which it is composed." Abraham, never one to dally, calls the Torah and the letters to testify. The Torah's testimony is promptly dismissed when Abraham reminds it of the time (according to a famous Aggadah) when all the nations but Israel refused to accept the Ten Commandments. Then comes the turn for the letters to appear:

The aleph came to testify that Israel had transgressed the Torah. Abraham said to it, "You, aleph, are the first of all the letters, and you come to testify against Israel in the day of their trouble! Remember the day when the Holy One, blessed be He, revealed Himself upon Mount Sinai and opened with you, '*anokhi*, I am the Lord your God' (Exod. 22:2), and no nation accepted you but my children, and you come to testify against my children!" The aleph immediately stood aside and gave no testimony against them.

The beth (rebutted with "*bereishit*, in the beginning God created") and the gimmel (with "*gedilim*, you shall make tassels" [Deut. 21:12]) did likewise. "When the remainder of the letters saw that Abraham silenced these, they felt ashamed and stood apart and did not testify against Israel."

Having silenced the Torah and the alphabet, Abraham returns to his first line of argument, pleading for mercy in the name of his own selfless deeds. Each of the patriarchs follows suit. Jeremiah and Moses are drawn into the act, and the latter denounces the sun for shining on the day of destruction. Playing, finally, to the mothers in the audience, the preacher dwells at great length on Rachel's instances of self-denial. This is what finally sways the judge: "At once the mercy of the Holy One, blessed be He, was aroused, and He said: 'For your sake, Rachel, will I return Israel to their place!' "

Rachel was the homilist's obvious choice because it was she, according to Jeremiah, who wept most bitterly for her exiled children and whom God would be the first to comfort on their return (Jer. 31:15–17). Through this brilliant sermon, the congregants were reminded of their inexorable bond to the Torah, each letter of which carried the full weight of tradition. They were put back into a more benign universe where the past reverberated, the written word literally came alive, and the harsh sentence of history promised to come to an end.

THE conscious rabbinic effort to implode the events of history was a self-imposed limitation of design, not of scope. The scope of the rabbis could hardly have been more immense, reaching back as it did to the wilderness and to before Creation. Their distinct and lasting achievement lay in their complex manner of coding, recording, and commemorating. True to a central strand of the Sinaitic tradition, the rabbis of the first to fifth centuries found complex means of restructuring the past to make it a usable guide for the future.

The coding began with a search for the archetype. Catastrophes that clustered around a single date highlighted the primal event in the wilderness; the breaking of the tablets on the seventeenth of Tammuz culminated in the desecration of the sanctuary by Apostomos. In times of drought, a list of biblical heroes for whose sake the Lord had reversed the course of nature was retrieved from the collective memory; and in times of national crisis, ancient and more recent heroes were recast in a new light. The anonymous mother who sacrificed all her sons during the Maccabean revolt was revived after the Hadrianic persecution in the guise of Miriam. She now challenged her persecutors with the same rhetoric of martyrdom as that used by Christian martyrs, adding a challenge of her own, to Abraham: "Yours was a trial; mine was an accomplished fact!"[41] Exemplary deeds singled out from the maze of conflicting traditions—Akiva dying with the Shema on his lips, Hanina being burned along with the Torah—were dignified with code words from the past, Kiddush Hashem and Harugei Malkhut.

Since the rabbis were also in charge of the "means of production"—deciding on the biblical canon, enforcing the lunar calendar, interpreting the Torah—the recording of historical events was left almost entirely to them. Whole periods of history could evaporate into legend if the rabbis chose to relegate the chronicles to apocryphal status. No wonder historians are still arguing over the basics of the Hadrianic persecution and the Bar Kokhba revolt. There are those who believe the sparse rabbinic accounts[42] and those who do not,[43] while the rabbis, for their part, left tantalizing contradictions. They conflated Hadrian with Titus and even Nebuchadnezzar, and did everything possible to downplay the significance of Bar Kokhba. The events of the time were divorced from world history to fit Jewish history—if one can call a loose string of martyrological tales and anachronistic legends history. What was remembered and recorded was not the factual data but the meaning of the desecration.

Inner and outer dimensions of sacrilege are very hard to separate. The public record usually lists the battles and defeats, the casualties and property damage, while the victims are left to nurse the wounds that no one else can see. However, it is often the subjective reality, not the verifiable acts of destruction, that sets the norm and gives rise to new responses.[44] In Hellenistic times, Jews themselves kept a double set of records, each with its own ideological slant, in response to that famous revolt against Antiochus Epiphanes. The first book of Maccabees, written in Palestine in the second century B.C.E., told of military victories and of one heroic family in particular that liberated the land and restored the Temple. That was the book the rabbis expunged. But the martyrological sections of book two (chapters 6–7), the unverifiable part of the story, survived in midrash and folklore to become the guide for future action and perception.

To test the effectiveness of the rabbinic system, one ought to look at the coding and recording as a prelude to the commemoration—to the transformation of collective disasters into individual rites of mourning and of individual deeds into a model of collective sacrifice. By restructuring the liturgical calendar, the rabbis and their immediate heirs were able to program past events, such as the destruction of the Temple, and past heroes, such as Rabbi Akiva, into the fabric of religious life; and these rituals, as augmented over time, became the living text of Jewish memory.

IN the three weeks between the seventeenth of Tammuz and the ninth of Av, the final stages of defeat and destruction of both Temples were reenacted in the synagogue. To set the stage, not so much historically as morally, the opening chapters of Jeremiah and Isaiah were read during this three-week period. The prophetic warnings spelled out the indictment against Israel with painful clarity:

> For my people have done a twofold wrong:
> They have forsaken Me, the Fount of living waters,
> And hewed them out cisterns, broken cisterns,
> Which cannot even hold water.
>
> (Jer. 2:13)

> Hear, O heavens, and give ear, O earth,
> For the Lord has spoken:
> "I reared children and brought them up—
> And they have rebelled against Me!
> An ox knows its owner,
> An ass its master's crib:
> Israel does not know,
> My people takes no thought."
>
> (Isa. 1:2–3)

The effect of these haftaroth was to confine the congregants within "the narrow places," as this three-week period is called (after Lamentations 1:3), to prepare them for the punishment that was sure to come. And when it came, consolation was quick at its heels, as in the scribal order of the books themselves. Second Isaiah's breathtaking visions of restoration made up the bulk of the haftaroth for the seven weeks after the ninth of Av, the so-called Weeks of Consolation.

The underlying theme of this ten-week period was not destruction per se but exile; and to drive the point home, the rabbis clustered several calamities around the central day: "On the ninth of Av it was decreed against our fathers that they should not enter the land of Israel [Num. 14:29]; the Temple was destroyed both the first and second times; Betar was captured, and Jerusalem was ploughed up" (Mishnah Ta'anith 4:6). As a way of restructuring history to fit the ritual drama, the rabbis once again located the root experience back in the wilderness, the source of all beginnings. When the Israelites accepted the defeatist position of the spies who had just returned from Canaan, they despaired of the Promised Land and wanted to go back to Egypt. The date of this treason was fixed for all time as a day of eternal exile (B.

Sanhedrin 104b). The destruction of the two Temples, sandwiched into a list of five calamities, was but the punishment for the crime committed back in mythic times. Just as the seventeenth of Tammuz was forever the day of broken tablets, so the ninth of Av was the day of eternal exile, when the proudest cities of Israel were laid waste once, and yet again. Members of future generations learned from this systematic congregation of calamities to append their own tribulations to the mythic time scheme; among them was a modern rabbi, who added to the list of disasters that fell on the ninth of Av the expulsion order from England in 1290, the expulsion from Spain in 1492, and the outbreak of World War I.[45] By clustering catastrophes, moreover, the rabbis of the Mishnah insured against the proliferation of commemorative fast days: one day could preserve multiple meanings.

Telescoped and mythologized, history did not readily translate into dramatic ritual. To convey a keen and personal sense of loss, the rabbis enlisted the standard rites of mourning that were later intensified in medieval Germany and France. Thus, for example, it became customary to prohibit weddings and other joyous celebrations as of the seventeenth of Tammuz, while the Mishnah's rules of abstinence went into effect only thirteen days later, on the first of Av. But before going into the ritual detail, it would be useful to consider the comparison that Rabbi J. B. Soloveitchik recently drew between individual and collective rites of mourning in Judaism.[46]

Soloveitchik taught that the three-week period of increased mourning from the seventeenth of Tammuz to the ninth of Av is designed to bring the individual *into* the collective memory of the people of Israel's historical tragedy, whereas the *decreasing* intensity of personal mourning—the rites of *shiva* (seven days) and *sheloshim* (thirty days), and the recitation of the kaddish for eleven months in the synagogue—are designed, in contrast, to bring the individual who is cut off from normal life back into the everyday routine of the Jewish people. This, then, is the way individual Jews prepared themselves during the exact period between the breaching of the walls and the day of destruction; and then, in assembly with other Jews, experienced the desecration of their own sacred space—their *mikdash me'at,* or Temple in miniature.

On the first of Av, mourning customs go into effect: no cutting of the hair or washing of clothes (in France and Germany, no meat or wine, except on the Sabbath). On the eve of the fast day of the ninth, a mourner's meal is eaten, made up of such symbolic foods as eggs and lentils. Bathing, sex, and wearing leather shoes are forbidden, as on Yom Kippur. Unique to the fast day are the symbols of inversion inside the synagogue: the benches are turned over and the curtain over the Ark is gone. Anyone who has seen such a curtain can easily imagine how stark and naked the Ark appears when robbed of its rich embroidery.

The denuding of the most sacred objects in the synagogue, the Torah scrolls, is the closest symbolic equivalent of the Temple's desecration. Like mourners, congregants sit either on the floor or on overturned benches and pray in subdued voices. There is no Torah study, just the reading aloud of appropriate texts of despair. At morning services the men pray unadorned by ritual trappings—without tallith (prayer shawl) or tefillin (phylacteries).

The defamiliarized setting serves as a prelude to the liturgy itself. All of Lamentations is chanted to an appropriate haunting melody, followed by the recitation of kinot. These dirges came into being, perhaps as early as the amoraic period (200–400 C.E.), because the standard liturgy and Scriptural texts were deemed inadequate for expressing one's personal anguish over the collective disaster. A simple and early form of elaboration was to make the last chapter of Lamentations into a workable litany by adding "Woe, what has happened to us!" after each verse. As the rite expanded over time, with widely divergent traditions for the Italian, Ashkenazi (Franco-German), and Sephardi (Spanish) communities, the separate Book of Kinot became the closest thing to an anthology of liturgical responses to catastrophe. In the Ashkenazi rite,[47] almost half of the forty-six kinot in the standard, printed editions were the work of a single fifth- or sixth-century poet, Eleazar ben Kallir, who established the model for later additions.

These kinot, which in the course of some 800 years came to outweigh the primary biblical texts, moved from the theme of destruction to redemption. Sometime after the twelfth century, Judah Halevi's exquisite "Ode to Zion" (written, as it happens, as a nonliturgical poem) was introduced into the kinot and, like Kallir's dirges, soon inspired a string of imitations.[48] Thus, at the far end of the denuded landscape was the vision of Jerusalem rebuilt; the poetic embellishments worked in both directions, adding laments for the more recent destructions even as they emphasized the longed-for restoration of Zion.

There is an obvious connection between mourning and messianism. Take, for example, the ninth-century Mourners of Zion, Jewish fundamentalists living in exile who sold their belongings and returned in sackcloth and ashes to Jerusalem. Despite their initial enthusiasm for this fringe movement within Judaism, the rabbis eventually rejected as heresy the Mourners' single-minded obsession with Jerusalem and its destruction, just as they rejected any literalist approach to Scripture, such as that of the Karaites of the same period.[49] Perhaps, as practical men, the rabbis did not want to push the Messiah's hand. However, they very much wanted to keep the hope of restoration alive. And so they continued to believe that the Messiah would be born on the ninth of Av (based on P. Berakhot 2:4), thus linking the anniversary of the Great Destruction to the new beginning. Centuries later the Jews of eastern Europe heightened the dialectical tension by adding new practices. They turned the rabbinic custom of exempting schoolchildren from classes on the ninth of Av, originally intended as a form of spiritual denial (B. Ta'anith 30a), into a regular free-for-all: heder (school) children ran around all day throwing burrs at the adults. And adult Jews in the Galician city of Brod, in the hope of imminent redemption, tore up their printed kinot at the end of the service—each year.[50] Next year in Jerusalem there would be no more cause for lamentation.

The rabbinic design seems to have been to set limits to mourning lest it spill over into extreme asceticism or a cult of death; at the same time, they left ample room for selective expansion. And so, just as the liturgy for the ninth of Av could move from Jerusalem in ruins to Jerusalem rebuilt, the pendulum continued to swing—sometimes with amazing rapidity—from grief to relief in other ritual spheres as well. In the Middle Ages, a memorial service was added to Shemini Atsereth, the eighth day of Sukkoth when the prayer for rain is recited. This serves as prelude to the festivities of Simhath Torah. The Fast of Esther precedes Purim, the most raucous day of the year, as the Fast of the Firstborn precedes Passover. Along the same lines, Yom Hazikaron, the memorial day for Israel's war dead, ends just as Israeli Independence Day celebrations begin. Taken alone, each catastrophe or rite of commemoration might tip the balance, which is presumably what happened to the Mourners of Zion. What the rabbis did and what their heirs followed through with instead was to incorporate the high and low points, the fasts and festivities, into a permanent tension within the liturgical calendar, which in turn becomes its own self-regulating mechanism.

With all the room for accretion and innovation, one rule was rarely violated: the Liturgy of Destruction did not treat the *individual* victim as worthy of memorialization. There was no place for heroes in the entire three-week period leading into the ninth of Av, despite the cost to ritual intensity. It would have been far easier for a group of the faithful to identify with the fate of an individual than for each individual to reexperience a collective disaster. The Catholic stations of the cross provide a far more dramatic and sequential focus than the prolonged siege of a city repeated at five-hundred-year intervals, but rabbinic hegemony was maintained. Saints' days to commemorate the deaths of individual martyrs were not to be a permanent part of Judaism.

The early Christians pursued the path avoided by the rabbis. The Church appropriated the Book of Maccabees as a canonical text, transforming the grave of the martyred mother and her seven sons into a Christian holy site, with August 1 as the date of commemoration.[51] Contrast what happened to Rabbi Akiva—as good a candidate for sainthood as any of the early Church Fathers.

The Jewish religious imagination combined Akiva's death with that of nine other rabbis who came to be known as the Ten Harugei Malkhut, assembled from different places and different times. Christians revered "the blessed Polycarp, who, martyred at Smyrna along with twelve others from Philadelphia, is alone remembered,"[52] whereas Akiva, who apparently died alone in Caesarea, was remembered in this context as one of ten. Despite the conflicting traditions about Akiva and Judah ben Bava, to name but two of the Harugei Malkhut, in legend they died together. Ten of them were needed to give the story symmetry and to provide a startling analogy to Joseph and his brothers.

This happened in a further transformation when unknown authors, perhaps "Merkavah" mystics at the end of the Byzantine period,[53] combined their separate stories into a mythic drama with biblical antecedents. In Midrash Eileh Ezkerah,[54] Rabbi Ishmael the High Priest, Rabban Simeon ben Gamliel the Prince, Rabbis Akiva, Hanina, Judah ben Bava, Judah ben Dama, Huztapit the Translator, Hanina ben Hakhinai, Yeshivav the Scribe, and Eliezer ben Shamua were called before the emperor to justify the behavior of Joseph's brothers; when the scholars unwittingly (and rather uncharacteristically) fell into the emperor's trap, he ordered them punished for this unexpiated crime. At this point Rabbi Ishmael, the hero of the story, asked for a three-day reprieve and promptly ascended to heaven to question God's design. Gabriel the angel, astonished at Rabbi Ishmael's boldness, ascertained that the verdict had to be carried out because "from the day Joseph was sold by his brothers, the Lord, blessed be He, never found in a single generation [ten] saints who were equal in righteousness to the tribes; therefore the Lord exacts the punishment from you" (page 65). Before descending, Ishmael was also shown a heavenly altar next to the divine throne. "What do you sacrifice on it every day?" he asked. "Are there bullocks and burnt offerings in heaven?" Said Gabriel to him: "Each day we sacrifice the souls of the righteous upon it" (page 66). The story concludes with a detailed description of the death by torture of the ten exalted rabbis.

The two central motifs in this story were profoundly suggestive to twelfth-century Jews who faced similar accusations and attacks in Christian Europe. The selling of Joseph, as H. J. Zimmels proposed so ingeniously, was now seen as a parallel to the selling of Christ.[55] If the former remained the only unexpiated sin from antiquity, then perhaps, the Jews believed, the martyrdom of German Jewry would expiate that other, unmentionable crime as well. Moreover, the motif of the heavenly altar expressed a radical version of vicarious atonement: the ashes of the martyrs were needed in heaven to atone for the sins of their generation. They died for the purification of Israel.[56] And so, in the wake of the Crusades, when an adequate response was needed to the mass martyrdom of thousands of Jews, the legend of Rabbi Akiva, as recast into the myth of the Ten Harugei Malkhut, was transposed into poetic form and eventually incorporated into the Yom Kippur liturgy as a commemoration of *all* mass martyrdoms.

WE come now to the European Middle Ages, wherein lies the real test of rabbinic hegemony. The Golden Age of Ashkenazic creativity, as Gerson Cohen has labeled the years 1000–1300,[57] produced major innovations in talmudic scholasticism, mysticism, and pietism; but what is of concern here, in the study of Jewish responses to catastrophe, is not the elitist forms of cultural self-understanding, but the canonization of memory in the public and communally sanctioned domain. The concern of this book is with liturgy. Here it will be seen how the rabbinic legacy was pushed as far as it could go.

Along with the justified pride in their cultural achievements, the Jews of France and Germany suffered new forms of persecution: the Crusader riots of 1096 and 1146, the first ritual murder accusations in continental Europe, the double disaster of plague and pogrom. A new self-consciousness arose in the sorely tested communities, a local sense of identity and with it—of history. For a brief period, as we shall see, there was even a rush to chronicle the disasters, but what survived was something rather more modest: a system for coding events, additional commemorative dates on the calendar, some new prayers, a new look at the old archetypes. And that was more than enough.

Before the Crusades, historical dates were of little importance. Since, as Yerushalmi reminds us, there were three major systems of chronology in simultaneous use among medieval Jews, it's doubtful whether any date could have universal currency.[58] One of the three systems began with the fall of the Second Temple, but the code words *ḥurban habayit* (the destruction of the Temple) meant both Temples at once. After the eleventh century, persecutions that were perceived as unprecedented either in scope or kind were recalled by their dates: *TaTNU* (1096) and *TaTKU* (1146) for the First and Second Crusades; *TaTKLA* (1171) for the martyrdom of the Jews of Blois and *TaḤ veTaT* (1648–49) for the Khmelnitsky massacres. When calamities stretched over a period of time, the shorthand selected only the most relevant items. The years 1648–49, the period of pogroms, excluded the sixteen subsequent years of foreign invasion that left Poland in a state of permanent ruin. In the twentieth century there have been the Arab Riots of 1929 (*me'ora'ot TaRPaT*) and the Holocaust, known alternately as (*der driter*) *khurbm*—(the Third) Destruction—in Yiddish, and *shoah* in Hebrew.

This shorthand worked according to the old rabbinic stratagem of divorcing catastrophe from secular history so as to fit Jewish history. In the parallel course of secular and sacred time, the date of a catastrophe could itself become a source of sacrilege. The mass martyrdom of the Jews of Mainz was the more memorable for its having occurred on the third day of Sivan, "a day of sanctification and abstinence for Israel in preparation for receiving the Torah, the very day on which our Master Moses, may he rest in peace, said: 'Be ready against the third day.' "[59] In Mainz, the chronicler Solomon bar Simson tells us, Torah scrolls were desecrated on the anniversary of Sinai; the community, comparable only to Jerusalem in saintliness, committed ritual slaughter upon itself in an Akedah without divine intercession.

A date in Jewish history is no neutral set of figures but a meaningful code with potentially redemptive or sacrilegious qualities. "In the year 4856 [1096]," Solomon bar Simson begins his chronicle, "in the eleventh year of the cycle *Ranu* (sing), the year in which we anticipated salvation and solace, in accordance with the prophecy of Jeremiah (31:7): 'Sing with gladness for Jacob, and shout at the head of the nations'—this year turned instead to sorrow and groaning, weeping and outcry." Since the letters of the Hebrew alphabet also have numerical value, dates may yield words of significance, especially if taken to be abbreviations. Jewish, Muslim, and Christian theoreticians in the Middle Ages all used these *gematriot* to refer to crucial dates and to compute the exact coming of the Messiah.[60] By a few important calculations, 1648 was to be the year of glad tidings. How much greater, then, was the despair when it ushered in a reign of terror instead.[61] In the twentieth century, the hope for redemption was especially keen during the summer of 1942, *taf-shin-bet* (5702) on the Jewish calendar; for had not the Lord proclaimed, *veshavtah ha'arets shabbat ladonay*—the land shall observe a Sabbath (*shin-bet-taf*) of the Lord (Lev. 25:2)?[62]

The rabbis of the Mishnah and Talmud had devalued the present. God, in their view, had acted on the biblical past and would act again in the redemptive future, but for the time being, law and lore would be the only bridge back to the beginning and only the Messiah would hasten the end.[63] It was not until the twelfth and thirteenth centuries, among Ashkenazi Jews, that this premise was challenged. The unprecedented spectacle of spontaneous mass martyrdom, of Jews defending against their Christian oppressors and openly defying Christian dogma in the moment of defeat, as well as the failure of political intercession and the physical ruin of such proud communities—all this gave new urgency to the plotting of disasters on a continuum and the search for adequate archetypes.[64] An oft-quoted refrain from the beginning of the twelfth century expresses this recurring sense of the unsurpassed. In the breathing space between the First and Second Crusades, Rabbi Eliezer bar

Nathan tried to come to terms with the mass martyrdom of Jewish Mainz. For theological reasons which Shalom Spiegel explained so memorably in *The Last Trial*,[65] the chronicler chose from among the repertoire of classical analogues the one that most directly addressed the sacrificial response to the tragedy: "Ask now and see, was there ever such a holocaust as this since the days of Adam? When were there ever a thousand sacrifices in one day, [each of them like the Akedah of Isaac, son of Abraham]? Once at the Akedah of one on Mount Moriah, the Lord shook the world to its base!"[66] The archetype, of course, had been radically altered, since nowhere in Scripture did it say that Isaac was actually slaughtered. In its new application as a paradigm of death and resurrection, the Akedah was found wanting when compared to the sacrificial death of so many; yet the events on Mount Moriah continued to structure perceptions and influence behavior. The choice of analogy imparted both a biblical sanction and a sense of election to the martyrs of Mainz.

The response of Franco-German Jewry to the Crusades and blood libels was to retrieve and reinterpret the ancient archetypes of destruction. Martyrdom was the self-sacrifice of the sacred person, hence an Akedah. Mass martyrdom was the destruction of the sacred place, hence a *ḥurban*. On the scales of destruction, the Temple was on one side, all other catastrophes on the other. But since the Temple was *the* archetype, all other catastrophes taken together would not weigh more than the Temple. It was the power and paradox of the Temple as template to make the sufferers realize that no matter how bad things were, they hadn't suffered the loss of a House of God.

With Jerusalem as the model of the perfect community, the concept of Kehillah Kedoshah, or Holy Community, was endowed with new meaning. Intensely pietistic and self-assured in their allegiance to the Law, Ashkenazi Jews elevated their own communities to the status of Kehillot Kodesh, Holy Congregations, bearing witness to God's presence in exile. The term itself, already used in pre-Islamic times, now came to imply a collective martyrdom as the true sign of election. The most famous were the three sister cities in the Rhine Valley—Speyer, Worms, and Mainz—known in abbreviated form as SHUM.[67] For purposes of recall, however, one city was usually chosen to stand for the many. Mainz was to the Crusades as Nemirov would be to the Khmelnitsky massacres, as Kishinev would be to the tsarist pogroms, and as the Warsaw ghetto would be to the Holocaust. Without the metonymic act of the one-for-the-many, commemoration on anything but a local scale would have been impossible. Medieval communities were notorious for their local brand of patriotism. Ashkenazi Jews countered the centrifugal force of persecutions and expulsions by perfecting the act of coding and recording until each commemorative act incorporated the individual, the local community, and the regional community. Not until the twentieth century would the people as a whole be entered into a single word.

And so, with the Crusades, the experience of atrocity was recorded in prose, with names and dates and details; and for the first time, paradigms of individual behavior were preserved in group memory. Yet even these named individuals were ultimately recast into a collective portrait: Akiva's grand improvisation, dying with the Shema on his lips, became the requisite noble death for the people as a whole; the sacrifice of Isaac, the death by fire of Aaron's sons Nadav and Avihu, the suicide of Saul, the trial of Hananiah, Mishael, and Azariah, and—most astonishing—the Temple sacrifice itself[68] were all fused in the crucible of destruction to yield a new model of collective action, a new Jerusalem—the Kehillah Kedoshah.

For all this activity of recording and reinterpreting the recent disasters, what was ultimately consigned to group memory was not the names, places, and events but the perceived desecration. Nothing had really changed on this score since the tanaitic rabbis had laid down the procedures. But the pride of being an elect, of being second only to Jerusalem, gave Ashkenazi Jews the right to challenge God in a way He had scarcely been challenged before—with a collective call for vengeance. Remembering, during the Crusades, increasingly became an act of vicarious aggression.

Sometime in the twelfth century the Sabbath before Shavuoth, the anniversary of the start of the First Crusade, became an occasion to read out the names of the martyrs in the synagogue. With group memory then at its keenest, the remembrance of the dead provoked a pointed call for divine action:

> *Av haraḥamim,* may the merciful Father who dwells on high, in his infinite mercy, remember those saintly, upright and blameless souls, the holy communities who offered their lives for the sanctification of the divine name. They were lovely and amiable in their life, and were not parted in their death. They were swifter than eagles and stronger than lions to do the will of their Master and the desire of their Stronghold. May our God remember them favorably among the other righteous of the world; may he avenge the blood of his servants which had been shed.[69]

The key phrase, "they were swifter than eagles and stronger than lions," had been carefully chosen from David's great dirge on the death of Saul and Jonathan (2 Sam. 1:19–27) so as to appropriate the heroic suicide of King Saul for use as a martyrological paradigm. The appeal for vengeance was then drawn from each section of the Torah, concluding with the Psalmist's battle cry: "He will execute judgment upon the nations and fill the world with corpses; he will shatter the enemy's head over all the wide earth" (Ps. 110:6–7). Since the Sabbath before Shavuoth was the anniversary of the Great Destruction in Ashkenazic communities, it was also deemed fitting to recite the *Av haraḥamim* on the Sabbath before the ninth of Av. Much later, the Jews of eastern Europe took the next logical step and incorporated the prayer into the *weekly* Sabbath rite. And thus it has remained to this very day.

So great was the yearning for God to settle the accounts of history that the call for revenge intruded at the great mythic moments in the liturgical calendar. On Passover, at the dramatic highpoint of the seder, when the door was opened for Elijah the prophet to come in, he was greeted by an outburst of rage: "Pour out Your wrath upon the nations that do not know You and upon the kingdoms which do not call upon Your name. For they have devoured Jacob and laid waste his dwelling place (Ps. 79:6–7). Pour out Your fury upon them, let Your fierce anger overtake them (Ps. 69:25). Oh, pursue them in wrath and destroy them from under the heavens of the Lord! (Lam. 3:66)." Technically there was little innovation here either, since all the passages were biblical citations. But the cumulative effect of so much rage was certainly new, and it is safe to assume that the ritual outburst in its entirety did not predate the Crusades.[70]

In mishnaic times, when drought was of major concern, the names of biblical heroes were invoked to petition the Lord for immediate succor. In medieval times, the locus of anxiety shifted from the ecological to the historical arena, and the call went out not only for relief but also for revenge. How this shift in emphasis gathered momentum from the twelfth century onward can perhaps best be seen in one of the oldest penitential prayers in the siddur (prayer book). It was originally a prayer to be recited in times of drought and was ascribed to Rabbi Akiva in the Talmud (B. Ta'anith 25b). "*Avinu malkenu,*" it began: "Our Father, our King, we have sinned before you." By the early Middle Ages, new formulas were added to the original petition, which were then recited on the Ten Days of Penitence between Rosh Hashanah and Yom Kippur.[71] Centuries passed, and the Jews of Poland suffered their own disaster. What better way, then, of activating God's intercessory powers than to invoke the memory of the recent martyrs?

Our Father, our King, act for the sake of those who were slain for your holy name.
Our Father, our King, act for the sake of those who were slaughtered for proclaiming your Oneness.
Our Father, our King, act for the sake of those who went through fire and water for the sanctification of your name.
Our Father, our King, avenge the spilt blood of your servants.[72]

The most effective means of provoking God, however, were still the most indirect: through sacred parody, by imitating on the human, literary level the sacrilege that God had allowed to be perpetrated in history. The sense of sacrilege felt by Rabbi Meir of Rothenburg as he learned of the public burning of the Talmud in Paris on June 17, 1242 was translated into the opening line of his lament: "*Sha'li serufah ve'esh,* O [Torah], that has been consumed by fire, seek the welfare of those who mourn you"—a take-off on Judah Halevi's famous "Ode to Zion," complete with the same rhyme scheme.[73] There is none of Halevi's wistful longing in this poem of outrage. Was not the Torah given with lightning and fire at Sinai? Now it was consigned to the flames in Paris. And if the Rabbis were found to have blasphemed in the wake of Hadrian's persecution, how much more did their angry words apply in the wake of the Crusades: "There is none like You among the dumb, / Keeping silence and being still in the face of those who aggrieve us."[74] The poetics of sacrilege continued to work both ways, however, consoling even as it bordered on blasphemy. The sacred text became an ever more pliant medium of expression each time new possibilities of violence were forced upon it.

The Black Death was another occasion to cast around for biblical anchor. Current throughout western Europe, it was a disease that honored no national boundaries. Within the second year of the plague, in 1348, the flagellants blamed the Jews for poisoning the wells; Ashkenazic communities were singled out for a double disaster—for plague and pogrom. To express, in poetic shorthand, the vastness of the tragedy, the fourteenth-century poet Barukh ben Yehiel followed a double alphabetical acrostic rivaling the central chapter of Lamentations with its triple acrostic, and to convey the specifically Jewish dimension of this denunciation by water, he ended each stanza with another biblical allusion to water and wells:[75]

> Women slaughtered their children
> As they clutched at the breast
> Suckling at [the moment of] their death—
> THEIR WINE WAS MIXED WITH WATER
> (Isa. 1:22)
>
> Get away, you filth! the [heathens] cried.
> Look now, and see:
> The Jews have polluted and poisoned
> THE WELL AND PIT IN WHICH WATER IS COLLECTED.
> (Lev. 11:36)

One prooftext reinforced the biblical prophecy, while the other reversed its original intent: the waters of Leviticus were to be considered clean, even if a carcass fell into them. More frightening still was the overall echo effect of fifty-six stanzas ending with the word *mayim* (water), in open parody of the solemn prayer for the life-giving powers of rain which had been recited, ever since Eleazar ben Kallir, at the close of the Sukkoth festival.[76]

Though the anger and parody are perhaps those aspects of the commemorative liturgy that have the strongest resonance today, their prevalence in the premodern period ought not to be overstated. The liturgical outlets of group memory allowed for a wide range of emotions, from intense feelings of penitence, as on Yom Kippur (the holiest and most mythic day of all, into which the Eileh Ezkerah prayer[77] on the Ten Harugei Malkhut was introduced some time after the Crusades), to the somber mysticism of Tikkun Ḥatsot—a practice, introduced by sixteenth-century Kabbalists of awakening at midnight, pouring ashes on one's head, and mourning the Destruction and the exile of the Shekhinah,[78] to the revelry of local Purims,[79] which celebrated disasters that had been miraculously foiled. It also happened that persecutions (real or imagined) were enlisted simply to validate liturgical innovation, as if to say: the deeds of the martyrs give special intercessionary powers to this prayer. It was an argument that thirteenth-century Ashkenazi Jews found most compelling. Thus, they explained that the long *Vehu raḥum* ("He, being merciful") prayer recited in the morning service of Mondays and Thursdays was the work of three exiles whom Vespasian or Titus had cast abroad to foreign parts after the fall of Jerusalem; or, alternatively, that the prayer was originally a memorial service for actual martyrs.[80] A more famous legend, still retold in the standard orthodox prayer books,[81] attributed the ancient and awesome *Unetaneh tokef* ("Now let us proclaim") prayer to one Rabbi Amnon of Mainz who, having been mutilated by the archbishop for refusing to convert, spoke the prayer as he died in the synagogue on New Year's Day. (The "real" Rabbi Amnon was probably a Christian saint.)[82]

Ashkenazi Jews surely made history more particular, richer in its timeliness. There is even evidence of the celebration of saints' days in certain communities, though nothing more is known than the fact of their observance.[83] Yet what kept these Jews going in periods of distress were those earlier texts that were least factual, most archetypal, conventional, allusive, anonymous, and timeless—Moses admonishing his people in the desert; Rabbi Ishmael ascending to heaven, where he was shown the altar reserved for the sacrifice of the saints; or Rabbi Amnon, his arms and legs chopped off, composing some of the best lines in the liturgy. The Crusade chronicles, much as they answer to Jews' current need for facts, figures, and individual heroes, were not central to the folk because no place could be found for historical accounts within the synagogue proper,[84] even though their initial purpose, as Gerson Cohen has suggested,[85] may have been to legitimate new commemorative rites, in the same way that martyrological legends were used. The recycled, popular texts, in contrast, all had a defined place in the liturgy.

When the place of the Tokheḥa is reached in the annual cycle of Torah readings, the curses are intoned in a stage whisper. The congregation is drawn together as it awaits the reprieve of Leviticus 26:42 or of Deuteronomy 28:69, when the reader restores the normal modulation. A popular form of scapegoating in eastern Europe was to call up the lowliest artisan for this particular Torah reading and to "pour the curses out" on him.[86] This accounts, at least in part, for why the curses reecho as often as they do—from the midrash, to the medieval chronicles and historical songs, to the works of modern Hebrew and Yiddish writers, to the memoirs of Jewish army officers in World War I, to the diaries of the Warsaw ghetto. Memorial texts do not enjoy an independent literary existence within Judaism; they come alive only within their liturgical context.

EARLY medieval Ashkenaz was a watershed in the Jewish response to catastrophe, insofar as the rabbinic guidelines were stretched to new limits. The temporal, factual, geographic, and emotional range of historical commemoration was greatly expanded, while the "deep structure"—of plotting disasters on a continuum, of rendering the singular event transtemporal, and of acting on the subjective realities rather than the verifiable facts of destruction—was retained. It remains to be seen how the legacy of Ashkenaz held up in the migration eastward, to Poland and the Ukraine, within a very different Christian environment and after long periods of relative calm. Poland, after all, was a haven for Jews who began their eastward emigration after the Black Death.[87] By the middle of the sixteenth century, Poland was entering its own Golden Age.

That the Ashkenazi traditions of remembrance became a source of renewal should come as no surprise. Looking at two contemporary chronicles of Polish Jewry's great catastrophe, the Cossack revolt of 1648–49, we can see precisely how old and new strategies were combined and how the response to catastrophe was one of the ways a community defined its own place on the continuum.

Nathan Nata Hannover's *The Deep Mire* (or *The Abyss of Despair*) began and ended on a liturgical note.[88] In his preface, Hannover adduced a string of *gematriot* to prove that all had been foretold in Scripture, including the date of disaster and names of the villains. Embedded in the title itself were a clever biblical pun and a numerological brainteaser. *Tav'ati biyeven metsulah,* I am sunk in deep mire, said the

Psalmist (63:3), or rather, into a mire of Yevanim = Ionians = Greek Orthodox = Cossacks! As further proof that the Psalmist meant to anticipate the seventeenth-century Cossacks, the numerological value of the passage added up to 730, the same as the words "Khmel[nitsky] and the Tartars joined together with the 'Greeks.' " Also in the preface, Hannover explained that he was about to detail the incidents of collective martyrdom so that the survivors might know when to recite kaddish. The chronicle ended with an eloquent tribute to Polish Jewry as a whole for having embodied each of the six pillars enumerated in the Ethics of the Fathers: Torah, prayer, charity, truth, judgment, and peace. See how vast the scope of collective commemoration had become since the first group of exiles wept by the waters of Babylon!

Hannover began the historical account with a straightforward analysis of the causes for the Cossack revolt, the telltale signs of modern history writing; but his main interest lay with the victims, as the preface had already intimated: their death was the death of martyrs, even if they were killed in flight. In two of the most memorable incidents, Hannover told of the unnamed maidens of Nemirov who devised their own death to protect their chastity—one by tricking the Cossack into shooting her, the other by throwing herself into the river during the wedding procession (page 53). Both were probably folktales that Hannover accepted at face value; the second tale in particular drew on a familiar motif from the Midrash on Lamentations (1:45). There was no longer any need to invoke the Akedah or to recreate the last words of defiance. By Hannover's time, Kiddush Hashem had come to be viewed as the Jewish way of death in times of crisis[89]—a further swing toward the standardization of martyrdom.

The question arose, as it did after the Crusades, whether a disaster of such magnitude could be contained within a system of commemoration that telescoped events back to the beginning. The Temple of Polish Jewry had been destroyed a dozen times over: in Nemirov, Tultshin, Polannoe, Konstantynow, Bar, Lwow, Narol, Zamość, Ostrog, and so on, each described in harrowing detail. By the end, the reader joined Hannover in saying that "all the other diseases and plagues that are not mentioned in this book of Teaching" (Deut. 28:61) had been brought upon the Jews of Poland, exactly as the curses had foretold (page 109). To be sure, *The Deep Mire* was later read in many Polish communities in preparation for the ninth of Av, but there were those who felt that something more was needed. This is what prompted Shabbetai Hacohen Katz to publish his *Scroll of Darkness* in 1651, a manifesto and introduction to penitential prayers on the Khmelnitsky massacres; his stated goal was to justify the establishment of a new commemorative fast day for himself and as many Polish Jews as would follow his example.[90] The force of his argument was the opposite of historical. To lay claim to uniqueness would automatically consign the event to oblivion, for who but the relatives would mourn their dead? The meaning of *TaḤ veTaT* (1648–49) could be apprehended only archetypally, by locating *each* and *every* occurrence on the scale of mythic archetypes and, if possible, by clustering earlier catastrophes together on the same day so as to rival the other loaded dates on the calendar.

This is how Shabbetai Hacohen described the destruction of Nemirov, queen of Polish-Jewish cities:

And in the synagogue, before the Holy Ark, with slaughtering knives they slew the choirboys, the cantors and the attendants. There the sons of our people brought up burnt offerings and sacrifices; they performed an Akedah on themselves as on rams and sheep and goats, and with fragrant smell they rose to the dwelling place of angels. Then the enemy destroyed the synagogue, our surrogate Temple; they rampaged, they removed all the Torah scrolls, both old and new, and tore them to shreds, and cast them aside to be trampled upon by the feet of man and beast, horses and their riders, and they also made sandals and boots called *posteles* out of them and garments of several kinds, and they cast Scripture to the ground and trampled on the parchment with their feet. (pages 252–253)

Hannover treated the same subject without recourse to the Akedah. His was a martyrological account with strictly human dimensions. In Shabbetai Hacohen's retelling, there was hardly an action without its biblical echo. Allusions to the Temple sacrifice were no doubt borrowed from the literary legacy of the Crusades. Specific details were mustered only to document the desecration of the sacred place—for example, that the sacred scrolls were made into boots called *posteles,* and anyone who ever saw a peasant in his primitive boots of bast would cringe at the thought of God's Torah thus degraded.

Now the punctual event was given cosmological significance and was placed within a chain of Jewish martyrdom:

And this took place on Wednesday, the 20th of Sivan, in the month of triple creation, on the very day when the lights of the world were created. Do not read *me'orot,* lights, but *me'eirah,* a day of wrath and malediction for the helpless children, for *gzerat TaTKLA,* the massacre at Blois in 1171, also happened on that day, the 20th of that month, in which we were shamed and humiliated. And the holy congregation of Nemirov was the first to suffer from the worthless rabble.

The midrash tells us that in Sivan, the third month of the original Jewish calendar, the Torah was given, whose every letter, *ALeF, BET,*

GiMeL, is spelled out with three letters; which itself is divided into three main sections; whose body of interpretation is likewise composed of three parts; whose intended recipient, the people of Israel, has three main branches, and so on.[91] Therefore, the atrocity carried out on the Torah scrolls in Nemirov could only be understood as a reversal of *Matan Torah*, a repudiation of God's Law and an event of mythic proportions which eclipsed the light of Creation. So far, this is on the cosmic scale. But why did Shabbetai Hacohen connect it to Blois? If gruesome precedents were what he wanted, twelfth-century Europe provided far bloodier episodes. It was the date he needed. According to the eastern European rite, Blois happened to be immortalized on Yom Kippur. The penitential prayers for the Supplementary (Musaf) Service included the following lines from a poem by Hillel ben Jacob of Bonn:[92]

> On the twentieth of Sivan, the month which matures the fruit and makes them blossom
> In the year 1171 when they were given over into the hands of wicked Thibaut [the ruler of Blois]
> With the Shema on their lips they offered themselves as fragrant offerings
> ALL MY BASKETS [the good and the bad will in time to come] GIVE FORTH FRAGRANCE. (Songs of Songs 7:14, based on Rashi)

The clash of historical calamity and natural time—of God calling up the spring and the slaughter together, as Bialik was later to put it—was absorbed into the fearful progression from the month to the year to the oneness of the One. *Be'eḥad* (with "One") is how the third line begins in the Hebrew. A collective act of martyrdom, the day of Blois, compressed the months of natural time and the dates of historical time into a single, transtemporal juncture.

Every day bore witness to the presence of God, but the day of catastrophe when Jews upheld their faith in the face of divine wrath and malediction was a day pregnant with special meaning. On such a day His Name was revered despite His absence, and His covenant affirmed despite its mortal consequences. The historical details did not matter. What mattered was the perceived continuities. Having suffered the destruction of one's own cultural base, it was essential to reach back through the centuries for the manifestations of faith, defiance, and martyrdom, for the covenantal link of catastrophe peculiar to one's own culture. And so the Sabbaths before Shavuoth and the ninth of Av were set aside for each Ashkenazi community to mourn the victims of the Crusades and to pray to God for vengeance; and so a fast day was declared for Polish Jews on the twentieth of Sivan to recall the end of another Golden Age.

A century after the Khmelnitsky massacres, Kabbalah entered into popular culture when Hasidism swept across eastern Europe, from east to west, countering the forces of modernity moving in the opposite direction. On the very threshold of the new, therefore, when eastern European Jewry might have waked to the promise of reform and enlightenment, the spiritualization of history and the search for hidden structures were revived instead. Hasidism, in addition, provided its followers with something the Jews had lacked for centuries: a dynasty of heroes who mediated between the forces of evil below—heretics, angry Polish dukes, and drunken Ukrainian peasants—and the heavens above. History was the hieroglyphic domain of the holy which only the tzaddik, the holy man, could properly negotiate.

When the revolt of the moderns inevitably came, in the latter half of the nineteenth century, the force of history ultimately proved stronger than that of the intellectuals. In the Warsaw ghetto, the penultimate reference point of Jewish catastrophe, the secular poet Yitzhak Katzenelson made his angry appearance while a few doors down from him the hasidic rabbi Kalonymus Kalmish Shapiro was composing a tract to justify the ways of God. Bialik was quoted as often as Job. The liturgical impulse of Ashkenazi Jews was absorbed by those who railed against it. So compelling was this literature born of destruction and rebellion that it was honored as prophecy in its day and has been offered up as Law in our own period. The rabbis of Yavneh have yet to reply.

CHAPTER THREE

Broken Tablets and Flying Letters

Lomir veynen, lomir shrayen
Tsu dem tsar Nikolayen.

Let us weep, let us cry
To Tsar Nikolai.
Yiddish folksong

THE rebbe of Kopyczynec was safe in Hamburg vacationing at the spas when the Great War began.[1] As the Russians drew near his opulent home in Galicia, the rebbe sent for Lippe Shvager, a hasidic dealer in rare books, and entrusted him with a mission to rescue his most cherished possession—a letter written in 1753 by the Baal Shem Tov, the founder of Hasidism. All his other property, valued at several million crowns, could go to waste as far as the rebbe was concerned, so long as the Baal Shem Tov's letter was salvaged.

Shvager set out on his mission and arrived in Kopyczynec a few hours before the Russian army. He had just enough time to hide the letter in a tin box and bury it under a cellar wall with some of the rebbe's gold and silver. With the Russians suspecting him of espionage, Shvager would not return to the cellar for several months. When he did, he found the wall dismantled and the treasure gone. Shvager was beside himself. He tried again a few days later and to his great joy, discovered the tin box with the letter; but when he opened the box, the letter was blank.

Lippe Shvager related his story in 1917 to S. Ansky, who was supervising a relief effort on behalf of Galician Jewry. Ansky's prior career as an ethnographer made him skeptical of a story too well told and all the more curious to see the evidence. The letter, when produced, was indeed blank. "I've heard it said," Shvager admitted, "that dampness caused the writing to disappear, and that by chemical means it can be restored. But we hasidim have a different view of the matter, a very different view."

Whereas the hasidic book dealer saw this as a mystical omen, Ansky's interpretation was analogical. The episode reminded him of something else he had seen on his first mission to Galicia: the desecrated synagogue in Dembits in which all that remained of the Ten Commandments over the Holy Ark were the words *tirtsaḥ*, THOU SHALT KILL, and *tin'af*, THOU SHALT COMMIT ADULTERY.

According to Ansky, the situation in 1915, in the immediate wake of the pogroms and atrocities, had been one of superficial destruction.[2] Though no Jewish household in the path of the advancing Russian army had been left intact, Jews had withstood the suffering stoically; the tragedy had not broken their spirit. It was as if the tablets of the Law, proud symbols of a Jewish collective united under God, had been shattered, the pieces remaining as testimony. Destruction could not shake the pride of a people who had once been given such tablets and who lived by their commandments even as the shards lay scattered. But now, after two full years of occupation, epic grandeur had given way to routine degradation; a heroic people had been reduced to a motley of professional beggars. The letters of the holy scroll had flown off, leaving the parchment naked.

In Hadrianic times, as Ansky remembered from his heder years, the martyred Rabbi Hanina ben Tardion had counseled his daughter that the Torah scroll might be consumed together with his flesh, but that the spirit of the Torah was indestructible. Ansky invoked the image precisely to contest the notion of spiritual inviolability. Once the letters were gone, the sanctums vanished too.

To view the pogrom victims with anything but reverence was a radical departure from the traditional Jewish responses to catastrophe. To make sense of the immediate event in terms of ancient texts, to seize upon the symbols of past holiness to highlight the present sacrilege was, on the other hand, the very essence of tradition. Ansky's was the third generation in a succession of Jewish intellectuals in eastern Europe whose basic loyalties were challenged in the crucible of destruction.

SO long as there were Jews faithful to their hasidic masters, the old myths, heroes, and strategies were never abandoned. To the masses of traditional Jews, history was still the hieroglyphic of the holy. In hasidic thought, especially, the mediation of the tzaddik guaranteed the preeminence of transcendent experience in human life. Whenever a tzaddik was implicated in "real"—that is, verifiable—historical events, his powers of intercession dominated the plot.

In 1753, twenty-four Jews were charged with the ritual murder of a Christian boy. Half of the suspects were tortured and executed and the rest converted to Christianity. The hasidic imagination recast this grotesque occurrence into a perfect hagiographic tale.[3] The date or details of the trial and execution were of no concern to the storyteller, who simply recounted that "there was a blood libel in the holy community of Pavlysh" and conveyed the news third-hand, through the narrator, who heard it from Rabbi David, who received a letter written by someone in Pavlysh. Rabbi David escaped in time and came as far as the Baal Shem Tov's residence in Medzhibozh (a town in the Ukraine). "The Besht [Baal Shem Tov] told him several times that the people would be saved. But they were killed, and afterward a letter reached Rabbi David telling him about the horrible and painful tortures that each of them had suffered." Such an oblique telling shifted the focus away from the event, leaving the Besht and his dramatic foil, Rabbi David, to sort out its meaning.

The time frame of the story now switches from the undifferentiated past to the specific moment when the news arrives. Our attention is riveted on the Besht's reaction, for on the surface his prophetic and intercessionary powers appear to have failed. The letter comes on Sabbath eve, normally the time of great rejoicing. Everything the Besht does that evening violates the norm: he cries bitterly in the ritual bath; he prays the Reception of the Sabbath prayer and the Maariv (evening service) with a bitter heart; he weeps as he sanctifies the wine; he retires to his room before partaking of any food, lies down on the floor and instructs the members of his household to eat without him. The Besht is greatly grieved over the death of the martyrs.

The transition to darkness signals the third act in the drama. The candles have burned out; it is midnight, and the Besht is still stretched out on the floor. His dutiful wife is lying on her bed and Rabbi David is fighting off sleep on the other side of the bedroom door. In this appropriate dream state, all three characters are ready to experience the visitation of the martyrs.

The anonymous martyrs of Pavlysh, headed by Rabbi Akiva, tell their story with the requisite tripling effect of the folktale. They describe the three ascending levels of the heavenly palaces they have visited and the three levels of suffering that a human soul can endure: man suffers on earth in his daily life; martyrs suffer under torture; and the dead suffer in Gehenna (hell). Say the martyrs: "That half hour in Gehenna makes all other suffering seem like the skin of a garlic clove in comparison."

Coming back to the initial puzzle, the Besht's inability to foretell and annul the decree, the martyrs hasten to assure him: "You, sir, are not aware of your power. When you, sir, upset the Sabbath, there was a great tumult in paradise." That is to say, the Besht's intercession had an overwhelming impact not on the transitory plane of history but on the ultimate domain of heaven. The Besht remains the unrivaled intermediary between God and man; his prayers and sorrows are felt throughout the worlds and heavens. His is not a private but a cosmic personality. In the layered world of Hasidism, the heavens and the earth are fluid, though only the tzaddik can remain on earth even as he rises on the ladder of holiness up to God, or receive visitors from the true world even as he lies prostrate within the world of illusion. The blood libel in Pavlysh takes its place alongside the martyrdom of the Ten Rabbis, whose death sentence, according to the Eileh Ezkerah prayer recited on Yom Kippur, likewise withstood the intercession of the great Rabbi Ishmael. The balance sheet of heaven and earth is sometimes better kept if the tzaddik holds his cosmic powers in check.

The hasidim viewed every act of outside intervention as an evil decree. Each time government action threatened the religious and social autonomy of the Jewish body politic, a delegation of hasidic and other orthodox leaders headed for the capital while the loyal flock at home crowded into houses of prayer. One such delegation met in Warsaw in 1790 to appeal the reform plans of the Polish parliament, which were then under consideration. Local hasidic legend later told of the visit by delegate Rabbi Levi Yitskhok of Bardichev (born c. 1740) and pointed to a pillar in the study house on Bagna Street next to which the great master had stood as he bestowed a threefold blessing on the house: that the students studying there never suffer from the cold; that they be spared from the hands of the Gentiles (that is, from the draft); and that there never be any fires in the surrounding courtyard.[4]

Competing with the religious and communal leaders for the government's attention at the end of the eighteenth and beginning of the nineteenth century were a tiny group of maskilim, Westernizing Jews who increasingly looked to intervention and even coercion as a necessary means of achieving progress in the eastern European backwater. Mendl Lefin (born 1749) was among the pioneers, a friend of Moses Mendelssohn and a man with powerful connections in the Polish Sejm (Parliament). He too was in Warsaw in 1790–91, where he issued a French brochure advocating a number of moderate reforms. In it he mentioned the recent visit of Rabbi Levi Yitskhok and compared his attempt at intercessionary prayer to a similar episode in Christian hagiography: "Mais comme le rôle de St. Simon de sa colonne ne lui reussisoit pas ici bien il decampa" (as his playing at St. Simon on his pillar was of no avail here either, he left).[5] Polyglots and superb propagandists, the maskilim knew how to address each audience in its own idiom. To burlesque the hasidic leader, Lefin had only to invoke a famous Christian saint of the fifth century who had once intervened successfully in church affairs by standing atop a pillar in the desert. For hasidim, the pillar on Bagna Street remained proof of the tzaddik's true powers—the study house, after all, had not burned down even a century later. For the maskil appealing to his gentile audience, who presumably believed that Simon was miraculously successful, the true efficacious pillar of Christian lore would cancel out the counterfeit pillar of hasidic faith.

The levity of this literary face-off between Mendl Lefin and Levi Yitskhok should not obscure the radical nature of the maskilic agenda: the maskilim accepted non-Jewish thought and mores as at least equal in authority to the teachings and practices of Jewish tradition, and they threw their weight behind the fundamental reform of Jewish life in line with Western ideas of progress.[6] When tsarist rule was imposed upon the majority of eastern European Jews following the dismemberment of Poland at the end of the eighteenth century, the stakes in this contest rose significantly. The draft decree of 1827, dreaded for so long, was the first great test of collective will, and as the Jewish polity reeled under the blows, the maskilim, for the most part, stood by and applauded.

In and of itself, the draft would have met with resistance on the part of a people who had no stake in Russian society, let alone in its military enterprise. Because minors were drafted into Cantonist battalions (special military training units) followed by a full, twenty-five-year term of service when they reached majority, the period 1827–1855 was the most divisive in the history of Russian Jewry in the nineteenth century, reaching a crescendo of anarchy in the last three years of Tsar Nicholas' rule. Nicholas, a great believer in the military as an agency of social control, in the case of the Jews was additionally motivated by missionary zeal. Of the estimated 70,000 Jews conscripted during this period, about 50,000 were minors, many under twelve years of age when they were caught, and at least half of this latter group were forcibly baptized.[7]

Under Russian feudalism, Jews were still treated as a corporate entity: taxes were levied against the group, not against each individual, and draft quotas were to be filled by the *kahal* (pronounced *kool*), the Jewish community council. For reasons of its own, the kahal preferred drafting children to drafting their fathers and filled the rest of the adult quota with the poor, the unemployed, and the generally undesirable. The quotas were enforced by a new breed of men, some Christian, mostly Jewish, who kidnapped the children in broad daylight on their way to school or, if need be, from their mothers' arms in the dead of night. The kidnappers were called *khapers* or *lovtshikes* (from the Russian); in fairy tales, these names replaced the wicked witch or the devil himself, and there could be no greater insult among adults than to be taunted with a khaper's name.[8] When the law of 1853 allowed the kahal to induct any Jew traveling without a passport, there was nothing to stop roaming bands of professional khapers—not even a valid passport. Yekutiel Berman (born 1825) remembered traveling in this period with a loaded revolver.[9]

The community was torn apart: khapers preyed on the populace; the community railed against its leaders; the rich exploited the poor; one region kidnapped Jews from the next (a Jew from Congress Poland who happened to cross into the Russian provinces on a visit was fair game); military might was pitted against civilians; Christians were set against Jews. The home became a battleground as parents tried to fight off the kidnappers. Captured recruits were sometimes kept prisoner in their own town until the draft quota was filled and the army ready to claim its victims. Even those exempted by law weren't safe, since the communal lists were doctored in such a way that the only sons of the poor were drafted in lieu of the several sons of the well-to-do. Like the *Judenrat* a century later, the leaders of the kahal oversaw this demoralization, forced to choose who would live and who would never return.[10]

A keen sense of desecration pervades the songs and memories of this period. On the simplest level, the songs convey the degree of common despair through discordant rhymes. One famous song tells of a draft dodger who finds refuge on the outskirts of town with strange Jews, who hide him in a pit. After three days, weakened by hunger, he reappears in their home. The mistress of the house puts a piece of bread on the table, and as he prepares to eat, with proper ablution and blessing, he hears ominous noises outside:

> Vi er hot genumen dem ershtn vort bentshn,
> Zaynen arayngekumen a fule shtub mentshn.[11]
>
> He'd gotten so far as the first word of the prayer
> When in came a mob after his head.

The bread remains and the lad is carted off to town where his mother rushes before the council members to plead on his behalf:

> Vos iz dos far a velt,
> As me nemt an eyntsikes kind un m'farkoyft far gelt!
>
> What kind of world can this be,
> When an only child is sold for money!

From the folk perspective, soldiering in and of itself was an act of apostasy. Soldiers were called *yevonim* (literally, Ionians or Greeks) in Jewish code. This immediately conjured up the ancient polarity between Jerusalem and Athens. To sing of Jewish yevonim, therefore, was itself a contradiction in terms, underscored by the rhyme *isur derabonim* (a rabbinic prohibition):

> Isureynu—isur derabonim,
> Lomir zingen a lid fun yidishe yevonim.
> Bord un peyes tut men undz opshern,
> Shabosim, yontoyvim tut men undz farshtern.[12]
>
> The prohibitions we follow are the prohibitions of our Elders,
> Let us sing a song of Jewish soldiers.
> They cut off our beards and our sidecurls,
> Violate our Sabbaths and festivals.

The religious freedom of the Jewish recruits was flagrantly violated. Many were subjected to torture until they agreed to convert, and the tsarist regime would not allow converts to return to their despicable faith. Greater yet was the listener's sense of outrage when it was the *rabonim* (rabbis) who rhymed with the crime:

> Kleyne oyfelekh rayst men fun kheyder,
> Men tut zey on yevonishe kleyder.
> Undzere parneysim, undzere rabonim,
> Helfn nokh optsugebn zey far yevonim.[13]
>
> Little children are torn from their lessons
> and pressed into coats that have soldiers' buttons.
> Our rabbis, our bigshots are in cahoots,
> teaching our kids to be recruits.

For a recruit faced with exile and apostasy, even the most trying aspects of life at home seemed jolly by comparison:

> Beser tsu lernen khumesh mit rashe
> Eyder tsu esn di soldatske kashe.[14]
>
> Better to study Bible and Rashi
> Than eating the soldiers' mush.

Jewish parents reaffirmed the traditional value of learning *khumesh mit rashe* by intensifying the religious education of their sons as a buffer to conversion and in the hope that the kahal might spare the better students.

All this served effectively to undermine the authority of the kahal, which was soundly attacked from all sides: by the government, which held it accountable for an ever-growing number of recruits; by the common folk, who sometimes rioted and sometimes denounced its misdeeds to the authorities;[15] and by the maskilim, who argued that conscription, even in so harsh a form, was a necessary prelude to emancipation and that only the kahal and the rabbis were to blame for any excesses in its operation.[16]

In the scheme of maskilic memory and artistic persuasion, the scene of desecration, the place where the laws of the land and of the Torah were violated with impunity, the locus of evil, was not St. Petersburg but the local kahal chamber and synagogue. It was here, according to Isaac Baer Lebensohn writing in 1851, that twelve pious Jews were forced to swear falsely on the Torah.[17] Knowing that a poor man in town had an only son eight years of age, the witnesses swore that the son was really twelve, was one of seven sons of the rich man in town, and was therefore eminently fit for the draft. In Cantonist times, the practice called *ikuv hakriye*—in which anyone, rich or poor, man or woman, could interrupt the reading of the Torah to demand redress for a wrongdoing—was put to dramatic if ineffectual use. The aggrieved mother whose only son had just been drafted would now be shouted down from the platform and the reading would continue as if nothing had happened (this is what the maskilim A. I. Paperna, Judah Leib Gordon, and Jacob Dinezon later remembered).[18] The synagogue Jews were deaf even to the woman in Minsk who cried: "Lord of the universe! You take pride in our father Abraham, because he readily sacrificed his son on the altar. Order me to slaughter my only son and I will do it at once, but could you prevail upon Abraham to give Isaac up for conversion?"[19]

Both the folk and the maskilim of that generation, for very different reasons, turned their anger and their energies inward and absolved the higher authorities (God or the tsar) of responsibility. The rhymed couplet of this chapter's epigraph, which dates from around mid-century (Ginzburg-Marek, 52), reflects the common man's perception that the tsar would intervene if only he knew what evils were being perpetrated in his name. It was the internal authority structure, in other words, with its ethos of communal solidarity, which had been so badly shaken by the draft decrees. If Cantonism was a central link in the chain of Jewish suffering, it was because, in the words of one grandmother, not even the Tokheḥa listed among its curses the possibility of Jews being kidnapped by other, pious Jews.[20] The maskilim, for their part, had everything pinned on the good graces of the government, which alone could promote the linear progress of history. Had not the government proved its noble intentions by opening two rabbinic seminaries for the training of a new, enlightened leadership, and were not the teachers and pupils automatically exempt from the draft? No wonder, then, that in their topical works of fiction the maskilim could safely disregard the contradictory evidence. A. B. Gottlober (born 1811) supplied a happy ending to a story of Cantonist times—in violation of what he actually experienced. In the story version, the maskilic hero was freed and the evil kahal deputy was drafted in his stead. Similarly, Gottlober made no mention of the popular uprising against the kahal which he witnessed in person; and, for lack of a better scapegoat, he blamed the institution of kidnapping on the hasidim![21]

From anarchy the pendulum swung to unbridled optimism at the beginning of Alexander II's reign, in 1856. Cantonism was abolished, though khapers continued to round up the able-bodied until 1874. The serfs were freed, and a limited number of Jews were permitted to settle the interior of Russia. With the easing of censorship, a Jewish periodical press came into its own: in Hebrew (1856), Russian (1860), Polish (1861), and finally in Yiddish (1862). Through the press, secular literature became institutionalized and diversified. Novels were serialized; feuilletons on topical issues were featured "below the line" (that is, on the bottom half of the page); writers learned to differentiate their audience according to language; and literary personae made their first appearance. The writers of this second generation made their name in the Jewish press: Judah Leib Gordon (born 1830), Sholem Yankev Abramovitsh (born 1836), Peretz Smolenskin (born 1842), Abraham Uri Kovner (born 1842), and Moses Leib Lilienblum (born 1843). Smolenskin even published and edited his own newspaper.

As a generation attuned to contemporary Russian thought, these writers closely monitored the apparent groundswell of liberalism and heeded the call of the Positivists that art be connected with real life and that literature seek to redress the ills of society. More sharply than before, the maskilic pen aimed inward, at the cultural backwardness of the nation, the ossified religious practices, and the lack of effective leadership. The central problem of the 1860s, as the Jewish intellectuals saw it, was how to preserve a rational form of Jewishness within a framework of gentile acceptance.[22]

Only much later, when tsarist reaction and reform had already gone through more cycles, did a Russian-Jewish intellectual of the third generation—Ben-Ami (born 1854)—discover this analogy:

> The inquisition perpetrated terrible things; it subjected the body of the adult Jew to torture, but he was able to laugh proudly at his persecutor while keeping his soul and his conscience free of defect or fear, and in order to save his body, could don the filthy skin of his persecutor and executioner. The *khapers* tore little children from the arms of their mothers and gave them over, not to the inquisitors, but to drunken soldiers, so that they be raised as Christians.[23]

Ben-Ami's leap from the recent to the distant past necessarily overlooked the difference between the zeal of the Inquisition to enforce absolute religious purity and Tsar Nicholas' single-minded pursuit of converts. But who could bother with the fine points when the age of the Cantonists was taken into account? Young boys ages eight to eighteen hardly stood a chance against forced marches in mid-winter, brutal military discipline, a diet of pork, and permanent exile. The Cantonist era left a legacy of 50,000 lost children.

THESE guinea pigs of modernity, the maskilim and the small group of Russian Jews who won acceptance by society in the 1860s, were also the first to feel its rod of chastisement. The carrot and the stick were administered in the remote setting of Odessa, the El Dorado of the south, where God Himself, as the folk put it, lived the life of Reilly. There, at the end of May 1871, a pogrom of major proportions gave Russian Jews a preview of things to come. The 1.5 million rubles in property damage was bad enough. Worse was the fact that the Greek rioters—angry at being displaced by Jews in the city's economic and political life—preferred to destroy property rather than steal, for this was a measure of their anti-Jewish hatred. Worse still was that the police stood by and watched. And finally there was the sense of betrayal—local non-Jewish intellectuals and progressive public opinion blamed the pogrom on the Jews themselves.[24] The shock waves of Jewish destruction would always register strongest among those who hoped for goodwill and common sense among their Christian allies.

The timing of the violence remained unchanged from generations past. April and May would continue to be the cruelest months for the Jews of eastern Europe, whether by virtue of the Easter festival and its proximity to Passover, or by virtue of some demonic force that exacted its human sacrifice with the coming of spring. "The [Christian] rabble," remarked Peretz Smolenskin, "needs Jewish blood to mark the festival of Passover."[25] The springtime of ritual murder would blossom again in 1881, 1903, and 1943.

The peculiar interplay of history and myth, of violent time that somehow conspired to fit a larger pattern of natural time, was only one reason the moderns would seek long and hard for effective secular means to take in the theme of Jewish catastrophe. The liturgical models of prophecy, midrash, piyyut (synagogue poetry), and chronicle had placed greater stress on the repeatability of the pattern as it confirmed the archetypes and had ignored the time-specific location of the catastrophic events. The moderns reversed the emphasis, stressing the event itself, its social and political context.

Within a very few years of the Odessa pogrom, two very different literary approaches emerged from the ranks of the eastern European intelligentsia. One applied modern methods rather mechanically to produce the first pogrom novel ever written; the other, obviously more important for my thesis, revolutionized the liturgical model to treat the pogrom as metaphysical allegory.

The novel would have seemed an obvious choice—first, because it encouraged reportorial accuracy in the writer; second, because of the greater leniency of the censors, who read works of fiction more carelessly than journalistic treatments of the same theme; and, third, because the plot of the novel was tailor-made for adventure in the metropolis. Murder and intrigue were the stuff of all Hebrew novels at the time, regardless of their subject matter, so no one would look askance at myriad subplots, complete with forged letters, attempted poisonings and romantic triangles. The pogrom novel, as understood by its popularizers, made order out of chaos by imposing a single, schematic plot: murder and mobs in the big city gave dramatic weight to an otherwise predictable love story of an exemplary Jewish woman and a (com)passionate gentile man, a pattern later to be followed by Yiddish novelists from Sholem Aleichem to Sholem Asch and by continental movie makers from Jiri Weiss to Vittorio de Sica.

Yekutiel Berman, last seen traveling in khaper country with a loaded revolver, serialized the first pogrom novel ever written in Smolenskin's Vienna-based newspaper before issuing it in book form.[26] The actual contours of the Odessa pogrom allowed Berman to enlarge upon the details of intrigue, such as the Greek merchants sending to the homeland for reinforcements and especially lethal stones. But such exclusive focus on the perfidy of the Greeks, all of whom got their just deserts, localized the event and neutralized its implications. And then there was the biblical prooftext. Calling the pogromists *The Ravagers at Noon,* he applied the words of Joel 4:6—"And you have sold the people of Judah and the people of Jerusalem to the Ionians"—in a literal sense: *Ionians* meant Greeks, unlike the way in which *yevonim* meant Russians.

Smolenskin, Berman's publisher, took a bolder approach, using the Odessa pogrom to issue a call for self-defense; but the protagonist's heroic stance in the pogrom, coming as it did at the end of a tortuous four-part novel, could not seem to be anything but a convenient way of killing him off.[27] Thus, modern novelistic means, which placed such a premium on immediacy, factuality, character, and plot, did not necessarily guarantee a more adequate, contextual understanding of the emerging crisis in Russia than did the traditional laments, sermons, and sacred tales.

Allegory proved a far more effective method, especially at the hands of a master at camouflage. In *The Mare, or Pity the Poor Animal,* S. Y. Abramovitsh alerted readers with an epigraph from the Song of Songs (itself the subject of allegorical interpretation at least since the times of Rabbi Akiva): the steed in Pharaoh's chariots (1:9) was none other than the people of Israel.[28] Only the censor failed to identify this book as the most far-reaching, intellectually challenging, and subversive work in all of nineteenth-century Jewish literature, a mistake not to be repeated eighteen years later when a Russian periodical ran a translation of the novel by the author's son. Publication was stopped after the third installment and the journal was forced to close.[29] By then, *di klyatshe* (the mare) had become a household word.

The pogrom sequence was the least of it. *The Mare* was a study in exploitation—the major theme of maskilic satire, which was now expanded to encompass the social inequalities in Jewish society, the political repression in the empire, and ultimately the dualistic struggle between the forces of good and evil. Satan-Ashmedai (in Jewish lore the king of demons) appeared in person to represent the tsar; political repression throughout Europe; and the energy for evil in the cosmos. Not too long before, Abramovitsh had shared in the euphoric hopes for a new era of reform and enlightenment. By the 1870s some of his generation were beginning to break faith with the Haskalah (Enlightenment), often under the impact of Russian Positivism;[30] but nowhere was the indictment of society so global and the despair so inescapable as in this masterpiece of allegorical persuasion. Among the Haskalah's central tenets that Abramovitsh repudiated was the political realignment of the Jews with the forces of liberalism, a thesis originally advanced by Moses Mendelssohn in 1783 in his political tract *Jerusalem.*[31] Abramovitsh despaired first of the enlightened despotism of the tsar and then, more radically, of the Russian liberals (the Society for the Prevention of Cruelty to Animals, in his allegorical code) whose duplicity toward the Jews was second only to their powerlessness. The enlightenment, according to Abramovitsh, had produced a class of Jewish intellectuals like Yisrolik (the hero of *The Mare*) who were now left with no alternative but to return home. The maskilim were cut off from both worlds; at best, they could be prevailed upon not to perpetuate the cycle of exploitation.[32]

The hero's madness was Abramovitsh's vehicle for pointing to the maddening effect the world was having on the Jews.[33] Ashmedai took special pride in the pogroms, blood libels, and Jewish hate literature of his creatures down below, but never to the exclusion of other, more universal forms of evil. In the early version of *The Mare,* written in the year of the Odessa pogrom but referring nowhere to it by name, the description of bloodthirsty mobs wrecking Jewish homes and murdering Jewish infants appeared alongside other instances of inhumanity. "If you've tired of seeing the misery that others inflict upon you," Ashmedai says to the hero at the end of the original pogrom chapter, "I'll show you the great misery that you inflict upon one another."[34] The final version, written during the first decade of the twentieth century, had Ashmedai extend his tour to include an apocalyptic landscape of industrial blight and military devastation. Abramovitsh defined the problem of conflict ever more globally, and in this work at least, began to posit the impossibility of leading a moral existence in a world predicated on exploitation.[35]

The Mare was as far as Abramovitsh ever dared go. He dropped his ambitious plans for a Madman's Library and abandoned his crazy narrator for being too bleak, too negative, and too "modern."[36] Meanwhile, the devil's work proceeded brilliantly, transforming Russian society into a veritable madhouse of reactionary rulers, rioting peasants, and frenzied revolutionaries, with the Jews caught totally unprepared and unprotected. The pogrom wave of 1881–82, the first in the history of tsarist Russia, took a far greater toll than loss of life (negligible by later standards) or extensive property damage (in over 200 different locations in the southeast): it destroyed the faith of three generations of Russian Jews and created a groundswell of unprecedented discontent.

Abramovitsh's equilibrium, already readjusted several times over, was badly shaken; but unlike Smolenskin, Lilienblum, and others, he had no new political programs to offer on the ruins of the old. Unique among the writers of his age, he stopped writing. "This period of tribulation for Jews," he explained in a letter from Odessa in 1882, "that has called forth so many scribblers and petty patriots from among our ranks, has had an opposite effect on me, and set upon my lips the seal of silence."[37] The push and pull of catastrophe, which sent estranged Jews like Leo Pinsker rushing back to the fold and sent others running for cover—to America, to Palestine, to the soil, to social revolution—all this struck Abramovitsh with a mixture of sorrow and scorn. The writer laureate of the Pale was reduced to temporary silence.

An innovator of such talent who had already tried just about everything—the sentimental and picaresque novel, romance and the novel of education, drama and verse, allegory and essay—might have been expected to reemerge, if at all, with something new, something commensurate with the radically changing times. Instead, in what proved to be a cultural development of paramount importance for eastern European Jewry of the nineteenth century, Abramovitsh resurrected his old standby: the cantankerous, unpredictable figure of Mendele the Bookpeddler.

Here was a character (invented back in 1864) who had none of Yisrolik's higher aspirations, who was too busy hawking his Jewish books and religious objects to be bothered with ultimate questions of chaos and cosmos. In compensation, he was far better equipped than Yisrolik to deal with the internal dynamics of Jewish life. The peddler was on intimate terms with his clientele; in the Pale of Jewish settlement he was as well known "as a counterfeit kopeck."[38] Despite a penchant for traveling, Mendele was no picaro; he was a dutiful husband and father and a caring, considerate master to his long-suffering horse. If nonetheless his money bounced in the marketplace of tradition, it was mainly because he took rather perverse pleasure in the seductions of nature and because among the "newfangled" books in his wagon, there were some that he himself had discovered, edited, rewritten—even authored.

Still, the question remains: Why Mendele? Why, at a time of upheaval, should Abramovitsh have returned to that which was so familiar? Precisely because others had the answers and Abramovitsh did not; because traumatic though the pogroms were, he was unwilling to isolate the present course of history from that which had come before; because despite his earlier indictment, he refused in the name of Jewish nationalism to discard modernity out of hand, to spit in the well of enlightenment which he and the other young men of his day had drunk from so thirstily; because, when all was said and done, Jews remained "one great contradiction,"[39] and no one, as we shall see, embodied that dialectical passion better than Mendele. As a consummate artist and arbiter of Jewish taste, Abramovitsh preferred updating the old to generating something entirely new. From now on, his best efforts were channeled into a grand literary enterprise of recasting and translating his entire earlier corpus: his spectacular comeback in Hebrew was built on twenty years of prior achievement in Yiddish; the new *Mare* became a midrash on the old; Mendele was reborn to retrace his own steps.

OF the three main stops on Mendele's normal route—Idler Junction, Pauperville, and Foolstown—the last endured through the years unscathed: "Pleasurable laughter hovers over my lips at this moment, when I call the name of Ksalon before you, a laughter ANNOUNCING PEACE AND HERALDING GOOD FORTUNE (Isa. 52:7) . . . LET my brothers, THE FAR AND THE NEAR (Isa. 57:19), AT SEA OR ON LAND, be informed that Ksalon our mother still lives, praised be His Name!"[40] Like Second Isaiah announcing to his sorely tested nation that the redemption of Zion had begun, Mendele brought word five years after the pogroms that Ksalon had survived the ravages of time. And a good thing, too, because no place was more central to Abramovitsh's fictional geography than the commercial metropolis of Foolstown, ingeniously derived from the obscure biblical place-name Ksalon (Joshua 15:10) but also playing on the Hebrew word for fool, *ksil*. The Hebrew reader was meant to recognize the town from its earlier incarnation as Glupsk (notably in such works as *Fishke the Lame* and *The Travels of Benjamin III*). The change to Hebrew allowed for a density of allusion that Abramovitsh would henceforth reserve for openers and other special occasions. In this passage, the pseudobiblical parallelism and the repetition of verbs of the form *b-s-r* (to herald, inform, announce) tell the male reader of Hebrew (since women did not read Hebrew fiction in those days) that Ksalon is being measured on a scale of absolute holiness. Prophetic language elevates Ksalon to the City of God, the celestial Zion, whereas the description that follows bespeaks a crowded, filthy, gaudy, dilapidated, and stagnant reality—in short, business as usual.

Pauperville-Kabtsiel-Kaptsansk, on the other hand, has suffered greatly, and in the second part of the story, written in 1887, we meet Mendele coming from the synagogue in a particularly spiritual frame of mind, only to have his penitential mood cut short by the sudden appearance of a peasant making off with his one and only horse. Mendele cries for help and is knocked unconscious. On recuperating several days later, he tries to get a sense of what has happened. What disturbs him most, driving him virtually into a state of frenzy, is the pathetic attempts of his family and friends to put on a happy face. Mendele deals with their passivity in the wake of the pogrom by invoking a hallowed response and turning it on its head. He wishes that he could take up one of the harps by the waters of Babylon and play an ecstatic tune mixed with sorrow, so that suffering Jews might dance until they dashed themselves in madness against the rocks. "When I saw the unfortunate members of my household holding back their pain with friendly smiles in order to calm me down, I turned my face to the wall—and I wept."[41]

The local peasantry had staged a pogrom and the Jews of Kabtsiel were helpless to retaliate and too passive even to shout. Denied their cathartic protest, they were robbed of their reparations as well. Nothing could be done to prosecute the rabble, since the crime had been redefined as a revolt of the peasant masses rising to do battle against the exploiting class, the Jews. The spoils of war were not proscribed by law, and the victims were lucky not to be prosecuted instead.

In this story, enigmatically titled "In the Secret Place of Thunder" (after Psalms 81:8), Mendele was made to confront the futility of sorrow and sentiment. The standard repertoire of laments, like Psalm 137, could be used only if turned against itself. Nothing but parody could do justice to this grotesque "war" waged against the penniless by the equally downtrodden. Only parody could burlesque the facile rhetoric of those "official poets" who had sprouted like mushrooms in this time of national penance to compose the requisite dirge on the destruction of Kabtsiel. And then there was Gimpl, the local savant, who could channel the rhetoric into pipe dreams of national revival.[42] Mendele found himself torn between tirade and tears.

Yet to stifle one's feelings led to madness; witness the fate of Yisrolik, whose anger was always misdirected. Mendele's equilibrium was restored, thanks to his open anger, his ability to give free rein to sacrilege, to unleash the darker side of himself. Mendele's underlying optimism was fueled by his outrage.

In Abramovitsh, as in no other writer before him, the tension between contempt and compassion became not only the subject but the very substance of his art. The shattered tablets and flying letters were the sole remains of Jewish life. Abramovitsh came to see all of existence in terms of binary oppositions, of the acute tension between the sublime and the ridiculous, flux and stagnation, the human-in-animals and the animal-in-man; between "me" and "them," nature and nation.[43] From where Abramovitsh stood, the pogroms had intensified the screaming contradictions of human and Jewish existence, making the swing between "pathos and parody"[44] ever more sudden and extreme.

Mendele was the master disassembler. Because he was not a full-blown, psychologically definable character,[45] his very unpredictability mediated the most diverse perspectives. Abramovitsh reinlisted his services in these later stories because only a Mendele who embodied the contradictions of Jewish life could negotiate the political sloganeering coming from one side and the stifled sobbing coming from the other, then see his way clear to a reasonable course of action. Abramovitsh had made his most radical political and existential statement in *The Mare,* in rebuttal to the reigning optimism of the 1860s. Now, in the third and fourth decades of his career, Abramovitsh reacted to the secular messianism of the new generation by steering a moderate course between apologetics and skepticism. Whatever platform Mendele advanced in Abramovitsh's name—a conciliatory view of the gentile lower classes as victims of circumstance, or an outright rejection of Zionism—did not distinguish him from other spokesmen of Russian Jewry. Rather, it was the *way* Mendele operated that mattered—that precarious, outrageous blend of the sacred and profane; that double edge that burlesqued the greatness of Israel even as it affirmed it in the most hallowed terms; his ability, at the end of "In the Secret Place of Thunder," to sing a psalm of return, "Here I will make my home, for such is my desire" (Ps. 132:14), to extol not the virtues of Zion but those of Ksalon-Glupsk-Foolstown, the debased center of Israel in its Russian diaspora. This was the vital link between the traditional and the modern Jewish literary responses to catastrophe.

With Mendele we leave the faithful mime behind forever and enter into contract with his cynical counterpart. Whereas sacred parody had a limited, thoroughly ritualized place in the medieval and rabbinic periods, sacrilegious parody becomes dominant in the modern age. Several reasons can be deduced for this, all of which have direct bearing on

Mendele's achievement. As the Russian Formalists discovered[46] and as recent Israeli criticism has reconfirmed,[47] parody comes to the fore whenever literary norms atrophy and become routine. Writers use parody to unmask the artificiality in the accepted conventions and to argue for radical change. Moreover, as we learn from Israel Davidson's pioneering survey of Jewish parody,[48] nothing was considered too sacred for nineteenth-century Jewish reformers east, west, and across the ocean. It was as if Purim, with its sanctioned call for parody and drunkedness, were now being celebrated all year long. But most important for the subject at hand is the setting in which sacred parody originally appeared in Lamentations. There we saw the individual survivors whose suffering pulled them away from the collective just long enough to be freed of its patterned response. It was then that they felt the betrayal most acutely and were able to express their sense of outrage by doing violence to the sacred texts. Even after the survivors rejoined the ranks, the parodied text would never be the same. Henceforth it would always carry with it the pain of that momentary defiance. Thus, by absorbing the experience of atrocity in the present, the text could also anticipate the future: the Akedah as mass martyrdom; the giving of the Torah as its desecration; the prayer for rain as the poisoning of the wells.

Mendele clearly operates with a different set of rules. He is out to attack everything that is stagnant and clichéd in Jewish society, whether traditionalist or modern. Mendele's norm, as Miron has shown,[49] lies outside the system, in nature or in the freedom of individual movement, not in any sacred source or in Jewish society as presently constituted. After Mendele is through with the attack, there will be nothing left but shards—and a mandate to regroup and rebuild on the basis of *new* and *different* norms.

Mendele, like the paradigmatic survivor, is also a loner, but with an eastern European Jewish twist. He never retreats into solipsism or isolated rage for too long. How else could he earn a living, after all? Dependence on the very customers who so infuriate him is precisely what sets him into action. He speaks their language(s) better than they do. He knows them inside out and can take them by surprise. He joins them in order to wreak havoc from within and stands apart in order to recoup for the next round. Mendele is the quick-change artist par excellence whose variety of parodic roles singles him out among the unambiguous voices of nineteenth-century eastern Europe and define his pivotal position among the writers of following generations.

Abramovitsh sent his bookpeddler back into action following the "silent years" of the early 1880s because he wished to capture the tragicomic circumstances of Russian Jewry in the figure of this wandering old-timer doing the circuit year after year, trapped by his trade and his creed in a closed and self-destructing world. Within these strictures, Mendele thrived on the freedom to question everything that came his way, to work against those whose words he presumed to report and to subvert the very works he was supposed to be promoting. If anything, his field of activity had been greatly expanded by the altogether revolutionary feat of his speaking in Hebrew, in a new, synthetic prose style combining all strata of the language. Abramovitsh turned the limitations of a classical idiom to his advantage by allowing Mendele to subvert the allusive qualities of biblical, rabbinic, and liturgical phrases. Every word was potentially explosive if properly abused. In Mendele's hands, talmudic hairsplitting and sacrilegious wordplay became prerequisites for self-emancipation.

For eleven years, from 1886 to 1897, Mendele's travels took him back to the old haunts but also along routes never taken before. If anyone could, this man would find a method in the madness of history. In 1890 Mendele decided to travel for the first time by train and in so doing tested his wits against two of the most radical *isms* of the modern age—nationalism and political anti-Semitism. The trip was portentous from the start: "IT IS NOT THE VOICE OF THEM that flee from a fire, NEITHER IS IT THE VOICE OF THEM that run from armed bandits—IT IS THE NOISE of Jews, THAT CONGREGATE UPON the train station of Ksalon, THAT IS HEARD ON HIGH."[50]

Capitalization does not begin to convey the shock of recognizing in Mendele's opening words Moses' famous outcry as he descended from the mountain to find the children of Israel dancing around the golden calf (Exod. 32:18), as well as bits and snatches from Isaiah (29:8) and Jeremiah (31:15). The art of quotation in this passage works to overturn the original sacred text. The sacred language of God and man is here applied to the grossly physical reality of men and men so that the latter may cancel out the former.[51] This highly allusive wordplay, which was deemed impossible to translate, actually sets the metaphoric stage: the Jews with bundles in their hands and on their shoulders, push and shove for a place in the third-class train compartment "while the Gentile passengers are strolling up and down the hallway in front of the station with their luggage and waiting until the bell rings for a second or even a third time, when they will mount the train at leisure, and each proceed to his appointed place"—all this can be likened to an unredeemed rite of exile. The sense of desecration is carried further by prophetic echoes denouncing the idols of Baal that BOWETH and STOOPETH (Isa. 46:1–2); the wealthy, who exploit the nation, thrusting WITH SIDE AND WITH SHOULDER against the weak (Ezek. 34:21); and the sound of Rachel's weeping THAT IS HEARD ON HIGH (Jer. 31:15). Still more disturbing are the counterechoes, those memorable phrases that recall God's glories and the Exodus in particular: THE BUNDLES they carry UPON THEIR SHOULDERS (Exod. 12:34); their fighting for places in the congested train WITH A MIGHTY AND OUTSTRETCHED ARM (Deut. 4:34); and finally the bundles and bedding that mount up on either side of the compartment FORMING A WALL FOR me ON my RIGHT AND ON my LEFT (Exod. 14:22), like the waters of the Red Sea.

The weight of this bleak analogy is by no means carried by allusions alone, though they certainly provide much of its power. Travel is a metaphor for history. The old coach ride that Mendele so much preferred represents the traditional journey of a people in the world, whereas their modern experience can be likened to the class distinctions on board a train. Even before boarding, Jews and Gentiles are automatically distinguished, the ones worried and always pushing to get ahead, the others slow and dignified, as befits their privileged status in society. Once inside, they submit to the social segregation of classes and sects. The change of travel from coach to train has brought about commensurate changes in human behavior. "The majestic sweating of a free man" on board a coach is the very image of natural man who retains his basic goodness, his freedom of choice, his sense of oneness with others and with nature. Train travel upsets the harmonious balance. Nature is fragmented by speed, which blinds the passenger to the handiwork of God. Confined within the artificial boundaries of a train, man becomes alienated from his own sweat.

Miraculously, however, Jews are able to thrive in this moving, deafening, overcrowded prison, transforming their seething environment into a kingdom of sorts, a huckster's market. Mendele, too, gets drawn into a feverish barter on the train, and as one form of contract gives rise to another, he begins to take notice of his neighbors—exiles, he discovers, from Prussia via Lithuania. And so the innocent trip from Ksalon takes on several layers of meaning. Mendele's discomfort is the anomie wrought by industrialization; the plight of Reb (Mr.) Moshe and his family represents the fate of defenseless minorities in the modern nation-state; and all those Jews crowded into the third-class compartment en route to nowhere and vying with each other along the way are the symbolic equivalent of an exodus dead-ended.

The perverted prooftexts start to fly whenever Mendele runs afoul of the Jews acting as a collective—which is to say, wheeling and dealing. But when faced with instances of individual sorrow—his family in Kabtsiel trying to cover up the pogrom or Reb Moshe and his family fighting off their hunger—he is moved to tears. It is now Mendele's turn to act as the foil for others. He abdicates in favor of Reb Moshe as soon as discussion turns to foreign relations. This points to another reason for the train's being such an ideal fictional setting: the friendship born of reciprocal need that binds Reb Moshe to the Polish Catholic cobbler could not have been found on Mendele's normal route,[52] just as the politics of anti-Semitism that came between them lay as yet outside the Pale.

As a man of simple faith, Reb Moshe uses prooftexts only in support of his arguments, whether to unmask political anti-Semitism as a throwback to antediluvian times or gently to rebuke his Bible-quoting friend Japheth with appropriate wisdom from Proverbs.[53] True to his name, Moshe-Moses, the pious Lithuanian tailor eventually delivers a new Torah which Mendele then commits to writing. The homiletic logic of this story requires that everything be anchored in the biblical past, in the best rabbinic tradition of paring history down to its constituent archetypes: train as exile, Shem and Japheth as Jew and Pole, modern anti-Semitism as the evil that brought about the Flood. Like Moses, Reb Moshe has struggled with God after being rebuffed by those to whom he looked for brotherhood. The revelation comes when Japheth, too, is cast into exile, making him a ready candidate to receive a debased but utilitarian Torah of Survival, handed down from those who were schooled in adversity since Second Temple times. Now that some Gentiles, members of superfluous minorities, are also reduced to traveling without tickets in the third-class purgatorial compartment, Jews have something useful to teach them. They can once again be a light unto the nations. On disembarking, Mendele finds out that Japheth has indeed learned his lesson well—it is he who bribes the railway official not to collect fares for the remainder of the trip.

Two competing time schemes vie in the course of this momentous journey. It seems at first that the inexorable movement of history has turned the tables on Mendele, reducing him to a naïve observer, ignorant of the social and political developments that stare him in the face. Never having heard the name before, he thinks Bismarck is some quack doctor, and when asked about the age we're living in, Mendele pulls out his trusty Jewish calendar. By trip's end, however, Mendele's naïveté and Reb Moshe's faith have undercut the evil pretense of modernity. Scripture and Halacha, albeit debased, triumph morally over the exercise of raw power in the name of false science. Mendele has never been more optimistic than when he takes leave of Japheth studying Torah in the tents of Shem, at the end of this great ironic midrash on survival in a divided world.

"Shem and Japheth on the Train" works as a sermon because the alien surroundings cramp Mendele's normal, argumentative style and hold his anger in check. So long as he plays the foil, Mendele's satiric voice gives way to Reb Moshe's voice of ironic consolation. Once on native ground, Mendele resumes the task of portraying "his" Jews in a grotesque light, scoring his best points against their most common traits and activities. But uncommon things are beginning to happen to make even his own turf seem as alien as the inside of a train. Not too long before, a lone adventurer like Benjamin of Tuneyadevke-Btalon–Idler Junction had set out for distant places, but whole Jewish communities were now on the move, driven by fires, expulsion, and the fear of pogroms. Was this real change? Was the Jewish monolith finally being toppled, to be replaced by a healthy, responsive body politic? Could the new prescriptions put Humpty Dumpty together again or would the inertia of generations resist any new redemptive claims put forward in the people's name? Mendele was sent by his author to find out, assuming in each case the appropriate role to parody both sides in the controversy.

It was a time of fly-by-night messiahs, of prodigal sons who returned from their worldly pursuits with elaborate schemes for the redemption of their benighted brethren. What better place to enter the fray than in the preface to one such success story, *The Wishing Ring, or In the Vale of Tears,* by Hershele of Pauperville. Mendele announces Hershele's arrival on the scene in the crowning invocation of his career, couched in the most hallowed words of consolation, from Isaiah and from the kaddish:

> Praised and revered be His Holy Name, for the great privilege he has conferred on me, poor sinner that I am, to be His messenger and hasten to bring these Holy Congregations the good tidings.
>
> Mazl-tov to you, Kabtsiel! Congratulations to you, Btalon! Best of luck to you, Ksalon! How fortunate and how happy the three of you are, FOR YOUR INIQUITY IS EXPIATED (40:2), FOR LO, YOUR DELIVERY IS COMING (62:11), God willing, SPEEDILY AND SOON (*ba'agala uvizman kariv*).[54]

Raised high above his flock, Mendele the harbinger sees the grand design behind their suffering. These three Holy Congregations have endured trials born of love and deeds of great courage that will redound to their glory forever. They have undergone a martyrdom of hunger, and by conquering their passion for food "and similar gross appetites, without which other people, ordinary mortals, cannot exist," they have proved themselves worthy descendants of the original triad of martyred communities—Speyer, Worms, and Mainz.[55] In what has aptly been described as a "gigantic messianic farce,"[56] Mendele unmasks the fallen, indeed monstrous reality of Jewish life: the Kehillah Kedoshah is nothing more than a starving bunch of Jews; the notion of their martyrdom only sanctifies their passivity.

These last appearances of Mendele's were made at a time when much more was at stake than ever before. This was not Mendl Lefin, spoofing the naïve hero-worship of the hasidim; not the maskilim of the

1850s using their privileged status as partners in tsarist reform plans to attack the feudal structure of the kahal; not the writers of the 1860s and 1870s crying, after the fact, over the fate of the poor children—this was a struggle for the soul of a nation that for the first time was faced with a real choice between exodus and revolution.[57] Abramovitsh remained skeptical to the end. The Positivist in him rejected both the old and the new pieties that barred a rational understanding of the root causes and militated against effective action. Chief among these surrogate structures were a newly revived messianic myth, attacked brilliantly in his preface of 1888, and a recent surge of interest in the annals of the past, the cult of history, which he challenged with equal vigor in 1897. In the same way that messianism legitimated the intolerable status quo, the traditions of Jewish response to catastrophe were themselves at fault for providing Jews with a ready answer for every catastrophic occasion. Just as Mendele entered the messianic fray in the guise of Isaiah, he approached the *Leidensgeschichte* (the history of suffering) of Russian Jewry as something of an amateur historian:

> What I am about to relate to you now, my friends, took place in the very year after the great conflagration in the Holy Congregation of Pauperville.
>
> The fire was recorded for all ages to come in the community chronicle, and the Jews of Pauperville began to reckon each and every event in their life according to the year of the calamity. Thus, for example, they say that a man was born, was married or buried so many years after the fire. The ban against yarmulkes, the decree requiring the certification of teachers, the death of the children because of the sinfulness of the town, the epidemic, the forcible cleaning of the ritual bath and of the polluted river—all took place so many years after the tragic fire. There are still some old folks around from the time of that fire, and whenever they sit around at dusk behind the stove in the study house and tell about it, youngsters thirstily drink in their words while tears flow from their eyes.[58]

What Jews string together in the chain of catastrophes turn out to be little more than benevolent tsarist decrees designed for the improvement of their lot. They ascribe the death of their children to laxity in religious observance, and the epidemic gets lumped to civic ordinances to clean up the bath and the river, a not-too-subtle indication of how the epidemic got started in the first place. The reckoning of births, deaths, and marriages according to a local time scheme is indeed characteristic of traditional societies, and one would expect the Ukrainian peasants living around Pauperville to do the same. What Jews have added is the stamp of literacy—everything is recorded for all ages to come in the *pinkes*, or community chronicle—and the legacy of destruction is passed down to link generations in one saga of shared experience. The nature of the primal event is still unknown; but judged by the company it keeps, it may prove to be less than cataclysmic.

Mendele now pulls out other tricks to buttress his own authority in anticipation of the face-off: as a perpetual wanderer and child of the shtetl, he is an expert on Jewish life; as a litterateur he can pass judgment on the newspapers which capitalize on death and suffering, filled as they are with reports of deserted wives, eulogies of this one and that, and heart-rending descriptions of the latest fire. Finally, as a man of nature, he and his Jewishness are one, for a change, on this day of Lag b'Omer, the late spring festival that allows the mourning period between Passover and Shavuoth to be interrupted with weddings and the enjoyment of fresh air. On such a day it is all right for him to respond to the forest he is passing through, and on such a day he is even inspired by the sights and sounds of the Jewish festivities taking place back home. Suddenly, he comes upon the inhabitants of his hometown; they are on the march—hungry, thirsty, tattered, and torn.

> "What happened to you, my brethren?"
> They replied with one voice: "Our city is no more! We are the citizens of Kabtsiel but Kabtsiel is no more!"
> "DESTRUCTION FROM SHADDAI HAS COME!" A VOICE OF WEEPING was heard from the women. "A visitation from his Holy Name!"
> "THE LORD WAS VERY ANGRY with Kabtsiel," others added with a sigh.
> "Because of our many sins," men took up the refrain, "because of our sins the soot in the chimneys took fire."[59]

In addition to these direct quotations from Isaiah (13:6) and Zechariah (1:2), there follows a barrage of biblical echoes that raises the local fire to mythic status. When Mendele interrupts them for the facts, it emerges that abominable sanitation and cramped housing were the actual causes. Undaunted, the Jews of Kabtsiel conclude with an unbeatable combination of prooftexts to justify their negligence: "The truth is in accord with the biblical verse, IF THE LORD WATCHETH NOT THE CITY, VAIN ARE THE EFFORTS OF THE WATCHMAN (Ps. 127:1)—if the Lord HATH SENT A FIRE FROM ON HIGH (Lam. 1:13), MANY WATERS CANNOT QUENCH it (Song of Songs 8:7)," to which Mendele can only bow his head in temporary defeat. "NO WISDOM, NO UNDERSTANDING, NO COUNSEL CAN PREVAIL AGAINST a biblical passage (Prov. 21:30)."

The Jews of Kabtsiel have won the first round. Mendele meanwhile is drawn into the pathetic panorama of dissolution that unfolds before his eyes; but no sooner do the Kabtsielites begin squabbling over the territory to be staked out for their begging than Mendele resumes his adversarial role, and the biblical echoes clash with the context once again. As the Israelites apportioned their tribal inheritance, the people of Kabtsiel plan their conquest. Even those who never had any property consider themselves eligible for reparations.

As deft as this sparring between Mendele and the Jewish collective may be, it is but a warm-up for the last round. Mendele, feeling the full force of the tragedy when he is confronted by a helpless infant, rises from his sudden anguish to deliver the final blows. "I WAS DRIVEN MAD BY THE SIGHT OF MY EYES," he exclaims in the words of the Mosaic curses, and then launches into a passionate appeal for self-help and self-respect.

For Mendele, the Jewish body politic is more than a figure of speech: "WHO IS LIKE YOUR PEOPLE ISRAEL, A UNIQUE NATION ON EARTH (2 Sam. 7:23), whose members are like limbs of a single body entwined one with the other," but what good is this solidarity when it extends only to the act of suffering? Everyone wants credit for having been a victim of the fire, everyone wants a place in the grand pageant of Jewish martyrology. Thus prophesies Mendele, mustering the concluding words of Jacob (Gen. 49:1) and of Moses (Deut. 32): for not coming forth with immediate, substantive aid, the Jewish communities will pay double later; the victims will not recover and the communal kitty will be milked dry, until, "in the end of days, the whole house of Israel will raise a great lament over the conflagration."

His words have no effect. The truth of his prediction comes home to him years later when he meets a lone survivor from his town, none other than Leyzerl the madman, rushing about the streets of Ksalon with the children in fast pursuit, laughing at him and screaming.

In Mendele's final analysis, the life of the collective dragged everyone down with it. The surfeit of tradition made it harder to act effectively. Destruction and dislocation would not bring about a substantive change because Jews knew too well how to exploit their suffering. Any momentary gains for group solidarity—the children sitting by to take in the words of past tribulations, the paupers leaving en masse to recoup their losses—were more than offset by the centrifugal forces that catastrophe unleashed—greed, self-interest, parasitism.

Though the fire had taken place sometime in the hoary past, its lessons were very much of the present. The new generation of Russified intellectuals, men like Ben-Ami (born 1854) and S. Frug (born 1860), were especially prone to invoke "the judgment of history," as if the record of past persecutions and the doctrine of historical progress were the only moral reference points against which the behavior of Israel's enemies could be called to account. Rebutting them in his own voice in 1902, Abramovitsh had this to say: the history of Jewish persecution could not be the basis for a modern Jewish identity because, among other reasons, the preoccupation with death and destruction would backfire sooner or later and turn Jewish youth against its bloody heritage. The vision of Zion, similarly stripped of its spiritual dimensions, was equally barren ground.[60] Abramovitsh by this time was launching a rear-guard action to reaffirm the essential unity of God, Israel, and the Torah. Alas, without Mendele to effect the union, these words carried little rhetorical weight.

The balancing act, it seems to me, could no longer be sustained. Like so many later innovators, Abramovitsh was forced to succumb to the pressures of history. He himself took to writing works of consolation and lament sans equivocation and sans reproach. When asked by Sholem Aleichem to contribute to a special fund-raising volume for the victims of the Kishinev pogrom, Abramovitsh came out with a stylized chronicle, "The Discovery of Volhynia," designed to comfort his readers with the record of a prior migration to the south of Russia when conditions in the north had become intolerable.[61] And when the pogroms hit home, in the sixty-ninth year of his life, Abramovitsh experienced all the terrors of hiding in a cellar and of counting the dead and wounded who were assembled in the Jewish school that he ran in Odessa. Abramovitsh took ill immediately thereafter and, on the advice of his doctors, left for Switzerland. It stands to reason that the drastic revision of *The Wishing Ring,* done in Switzerland, reflects the change that Abramovitsh underwent as a result of the pogrom.[62] The celebrated prologue in which Mendele mediated most brilliantly between Hershele the traveling messiah and the sorely tested folk was moved to the end of the story, an openly sentimental epilogue in which the traveler returned to his devastated home of Pauperville. His spirit broken by what he saw, Hershele could do little more than recite kaddish for the pogrom victims while Mendele stood by in silence.

From the temporary to the terminal silence of Mendele the Bookpeddler, Russian Jewry was turned inside out. The centrifugal forces that had been gathering momentum in the Cantonist era were now scattering millions of Jews across the globe and driving those who remained to seek ever more radical solutions to the nation's plight. Very little of this revolutionary turmoil comes through in works of nineteenth-century Jewish literature because there were so few available forums (no Yiddish newspaper appeared in all of tsarist Russia in the 1870s and 1890s) and viable literary forms, not to mention the absence of freedom of the press. Most intellectuals were too embroiled in politics to be bothered with fiction and poetry. It was a time for bread and not for books, as Hershele put it.[63] That is precisely why Abramovitsh looms so large: it is he who established the intellectual agenda and artistic repertoire of the modern Jewish literary response to catastrophe.

Thanks to Abramovitsh, parody came into its own as a preferred mode of response. Henceforth, the more closely linked a concept was to the central articles of traditional faith—to retribution and redemption—the more likely it was to be subverted, inverted, mimicked, and mocked in the face of catastrophe. In addition, those writers whose medium was Hebrew would find themselves positively tyrannized by Abramovitsh's linguistic achievements, so much so that parodic allusions would creep in even when uncalled for. And the figure of Mendele, the lone and learned critic of his people, would serve later writers for opposite ends: some would make him into a visionary and prophet and some would remove him further from the crowd so that he might see the panorama of Jewish life in all its radical nakedness.

Abramovitsh's point of departure was the collective: its mores, its past, and its economic structure. Despite everything—and this is what characterizes the second generation—Abramovitsh held to his belief that if the root causes were exposed, Jewish society would weather the storm. So long as Mendele traveled the roads, the hazardous landscape could still be negotiated. The next generations, including writers like Peretz, Ansky, Berdichewsky, and Bialik, began with a search for personal transcendence, and then pitted the heroic ideal against a society that they perceived as hopelessly fragmented, cowardly, and corrupt.

CHAPTER FOUR

The Pogrom As Poem

When the first shots were fired in the Great War, the Heavenly Tribunal convened to decide on the victor. The angel for Russia placed all of Krupp's military arsenal on the scale to show what Germany was about to let loose upon innocent people. The angel for Germany calmly placed no more than two Russian nails on the other end of the scale. The nails tipped the balance. It turned out that they had been used in the Kishinev pogrom. The outcome of the war was thus decided.

A Yiddish folktale from World War I

IN a landscape of violence all values are under siege: justice, civility, and privacy; love, beauty, and nature; freedom, form, and reason. Each catastrophe threatens the sustaining structures. Violence was a built-in feature of Jewish life, a permanent albeit unpredictable part of cyclical time, and Judaism therefore developed sophisticated strategies of containment and contrition. In the nineteenth and twentieth centuries, these strategies broke down just as the violence became more endemic and extensive. Class conflict and political anti-Semitism were new factors to be contended with as Zionism and Jewish socialism arose to rationalize the violence. Each successive wave of pogroms, expulsions, and mass destruction then either vindicated or challenged the secular ideology that claimed to have all the answers. Literature likewise took on a secular, ideological slant, displacing in both the literal and Freudian sense the earlier traditions. Parallel to the subversive fiction of S. Y. Abramovitsh, who pitted the new myths of salvation against the old tactics of passive acceptance, Hebrew and Yiddish poets began their own campaign to challenge their readers. But since the traditional domain of poetry, at least among Ashkenazi Jews, had been the synagogue, and effective liturgical responses to catastrophe had accrued over millennia, the kinot, piyyutim, and historical songs could be dislodged only by a sensibility more radical than Abramovitsh's responding to more radical kinds of violence.

Meanwhile, the medieval legacy was reinforced in Yiddish folksong. The liturgical impulse of locating the catastrophe on a scale of archetypes was carried over into the folksong. Song was the perfect vehicle of group expression, for as Alan Lomax pointed out, the content of song communication is social and not individual, normative and not particular.[1] And so, while in the everyday realm of work, play, love, and child-rearing, the standard repertoire was supplemented by ever more topical songs under the impact of the Yiddish theater and of Jewish political action, when it came to moments of national crisis—to pogroms—the oldest liturgical strategies came to the fore to reorder the outrage into fixed phrases and stock images:

Misfortune, terror, and fury
We've never been without—
Now as in each century—
And where they come from we know not.[2]

In the timeless scheme of Jewish misfortune, the response, as always, was to protest the destruction directly to its source:

So loud your shout reaches on high
And wakes the Old Man.
His sleep is just a lie.
What's He trying to put over?
What are we, flies in the wind?
Is there nothing in our favor?
Enough! It's got to end!

This plaintive song was as conventional as its theology. With proper intercession, God could be awakened to reassume control of history. It was therefore important to present Him with the stigmata of the pogrom in order of ascending sanctity. After appealing to the undifferentiated audience of Jews in stanza one, the singer focused on the blameless children sundered from their mothers in stanza two, and the torn feathers in stanza three; the climax was reserved for the *sheymes*, the torn pieces of holy script that bore the Name (*sheym*) of God. The desecrated scrolls were the sacred counterpart of the torn feathers:

Everything is torn to pieces
Brides, canopies, and clothes.
Of bedding and pillows
They left not even a feather.
Fly, you feathers, fly aloft
Fly higher to the One Above;
You can wake the Old Man up.

Sometimes the feathers were called on to act alone, as when Khashke from Vilna, doubtless a pseudonym, composed an entire pogrom song

"To the Jewish Feathers."[3] Besides being part of the realia of every pogrom (for destruction was still measured in terms of property, not life), the feathers of torn bedding symbolized the desecration of the hearth. The security and basic comfort of one's home was scattered in white all through the streets of Odessa and Balta and Kiev and Yekaterinoslav.

Even when the singer invoked historical facts, the relics of the violence were organized into public symbols and thematic formulas, so that the details were applicable anywhere and only the place-name would have to be changed:

> Ver s'hot in blat gelezn
> Vegn der barimter shtot Ades.
> Vos far an umglik s'hot getrofn
> In eyne tsvey-dray mesles.
>
> Plutslung hot men oysgeshrien:
> Shlog dem yidn vi vayt ir kent!
> Pulyes in di fentster hobn genumen flien
> Der pogrom hot zikh ongefangen in eyn moment.[4]
>
> Oh, have you read the papers
> About the famous city of Odessa?
> What a calamity befell it
> In the course of two or three days.
>
> Suddenly someone cried:
> Hey, beat the Jews with all your might!
> Through the windows bullets began to fly.
> In a moment the pogrom was at its height.

There is no appeal to God, to Jewish history, or to any symbolic construct in the next four stanzas; but neither do the descriptive details of the pogrom—broken windows, a murdered bride with her murderer at her side, an infant nursing at the breast of a dead mother—allow us to determine which of the three Odessa pogroms (1871, 1881, or 1905) is being eulogized. In another variant,[5] the scene was moved to Bialystok (1906), which rhymed with *eyne tsvey-dray teg* (line 4); and in the song about the much bloodier Proskurov pogrom of 1919,[6] the street balladeer simply sacrificed the rhyme. The rhyme, rhythm, melody, and topoi (thematic formulas) remained unchanged from one singer to the next, from one onslaught to another.

But Jewish poetry now had other avenues beyond the prayer book and popular lyric, and the modern Jewish poet could view history from more than one perspective. Even before widescale violence disrupted the lives of eastern European Jews, the study of the past had begun to preoccupy the minds of the intellectuals, thanks in large measure to the pioneering efforts of Heinrich Graetz, Leopold Zunz, Moritz Steinschneider, and other German-Jewish scholars. The newly discovered history of the Jews provided the poets with alternative myths, with nonrabbinic and even antirabbinic paradigms of greatness. When Judah Leib Gordon, Abramovitsh's contemporary and counterpart, began in the second half of the 1860s to explore the theme of national catastrophe, he chose as his protagonists the least exalted king of Judea (who did not hearken to the voice of the prophets) and a leader of the failed rebellion against Rome. Blinded Zedekiah in prison[7] and Simeon bar Giora dying in the Colosseum "between the lion's teeth"[8] were Gordon's mouthpieces to challenge the notion of sacred history.[9] The isolated individual facing imminent death could find no meaning either in traditional concepts of retribution or in history itself.

The publication in 1892 of the Hebrew Crusade chronicles[10] enabled a poet of the next generation to identify with models of individual heroism from the Middle Ages. Saul Tchernichowsky (born 1875) raised Baruch of Mainz[11] to epic stature by conflating two historical characters, who would then embody a new concept of Kiddush Hashem. Baruch cried out at the grave of his murdered wife that he had sacrificed their two daughters "on the altar of man's inhumanity" (line 629), and to avenge the crime against his people he had set fire to the monastery. Hailed as a prophetic response to the Kishinev pogrom, this most accessible of Tchernichowsky's narrative poems, written in Heidelberg in 1902, soon occupied a central place in the secular liturgy of the Zionist movement.

While the past was being ransacked for usable paradigms, contemporary events sent out contradictory messages. On the one hand, each pogrom was worse than expected, creating what Paul Fussell has aptly called an "irony of situation."[12] Destruction to life and property increased enormously in each successive outburst of anti-Jewish violence, and these came with ever greater frequency. In all the pogroms of 1881–1883, fewer Jews were killed than in Kishinev during Passover of 1903; the forty-nine casualties of Kishinev, in turn, paled before the 800 dead in the pogroms of 1905–1906 (over 300 in Odessa alone). And in the 726 pogroms that broke out in 1905–1906, fewer than half as many Jews were murdered than in Proskurov on February 15, 1919. After that, the numbers hardly matter; we may accept Simon Dubnow's figure of 60,000 dead in the Ukrainian civil war of 1918–1919 or go as high as the 250,000 of other estimates.[13]

To compound this irony, each wave of violence was preceded by a period of hope: the pogroms of the 1880s followed the liberalization under Alexander II; the Kishinev pogrom ushered in what was supposed to be a century of promise; the pogroms of 1905 followed by one day the granting of civil liberties to all citizens of the tsarist empire; Jews mobilized in unprecedented numbers to fight for their countries in World War I only to return home to communities ravaged by expulsions and pogroms. No group welcomed the Bolshevik Revolution as fervently as the Jews, but before it established its rule, military pogroms claimed anywhere from tens of thousands to hundreds of thousands of Jewish civilian lives. And the cruelest irony of all was that in 1939–1941, when there was still a chance to flee eastward, many Jews stayed put in the face of the advancing German armies, because they recalled the benevolent German occupation in the previous war.

On the other hand, Jewish poets were overprepared for catastrophe, and nothing could really take them by surprise. The Jewish poet responding to national upheavals labored under a surfeit of tradition, whereas his non-Jewish counterpart, to judge from Fussell's research,[14] often lacked the requisite language, poetic mode, and imaginative framework to deal with disastrous defeats and a landscape of violence. For the Jew, history conspired with literature to repeat the old archetype over and over again. After all, a pogrom was a pogrom, and a drunken Cossack bent on plunder and rape was the same whether he swore allegiance to Khmelnitsky, Tsar Nicholas II, or Simon Petlura, the Ukrainian nationalist chiefly responsible for the massacres of 1918–1919. And so the Jewish poet was caught between acquiescence to an inherited tradition of response, which seemed only too viable—and rebellion against it, if only to break out of the vicious cycle. The turning point, moreover, was not Sarajevo, but Kishinev.

FOR the most part, the tradition emerged from Kishinev intact and renewed. S. Frug's thoroughly conventional poem "Have Pity"[15] was the first response to appear in print:

> Streams of blood and rivers of tears
> Deep and wide they flow and roar.
> Our misfortune, great and timeless,
> Has laid its hand on us once more.
> . . . . .
> Brothers, sisters, please have mercy!
> Great and awful is the need—
> Bread is needed for the living,
> Shrouds are needed for the dead.

This poem, designed to raise funds for the victims of Kishinev, was set to music and revived for similar purposes during World War I,[16] revived again during the pogroms of 1919,[17] and invoked as late as March 1942 in a private appeal for aid written in the Lublin ghetto.[18]

In a curious way, tsarist censorship helped perpetuate the literary tradition. The less said about the (officially sanctioned) rioters, the better; hence the pogrom was depicted, as it had always been, from a purely internal vantage point, against a backdrop of historical parallels: Daniel in the lion's den, the zealots who fought against Rome, the medieval martyrs.[19] The pogrom had also given rise to its own legend, the death of Moyshe-Tsvi Kigl, a synagogue attendant in Kishinev, said to have been murdered in front of the Holy Ark. As one correspondent put it: "I saw this saintly man with my own eyes. His head of grey and his long silvery beard reminded me of one of the Ten Harugei Malkhut, of Rabbi Hanina ben Tardion."[20] In fact, as Nachum Sokolov later ascertained, the old *shames* was killed *outside* the synagogue by a mob of rioters who happened by.[21] Two contemporary poets nonetheless seized on the patriarchal figure dying in defense of the Torah.[22] It was martyrdom in the only context the tradition would allow: one heroic death to expiate the involuntary death of many; the desecration of the inner sanctum redeemed by the supreme act of self-sacrifice. Thus transfigured, the *shames* of Kishinev was to reappear as an icon of Jewish suffering and valor: in Ephraim Moses Lilien's memorial drawing for Kishinev (Figure 1); in the fourth act of David Pinsky's programmatic play *The Last Jew*;[23] in Asher Barash's martyrological tale "At Heaven's Gate."[24]

So far, nothing in the songs, poems, plays, and newspaper accounts that were generated by the Kishinev pogrom would suggest a change, much less a watershed in the Jewish response to catastrophe. The new strategies that had been evolving since the 1880s were, however, implemented in the spring of 1903 when a group of third-generation intellectuals met in Odessa to plan effective action. Born under the sign of history, these writers were responsive to all the pressures around them; they were one of the most eclectic, ecumenical, and diversely talented groups of Jews that had yet thrown in their lot with their eastern European brethren. And so it was that Ben-Ami (born 1854), Ahad Ha'am (born 1856), Simon Dubnow (born 1860), and Chaim Nachman Bialik (born 1873) came out with a proclamation written in Hebrew rather than Russian, calling for a radically new agenda: the establishment of a secret bureau of information to gather and disseminate all the pertinent documents of destruction, and the organization of armed self-defense units in all the Jewish communities in danger of attack.[25] Ben-Ami, it should be mentioned, was a veteran defense organizer, having pulled together an ad hoc group of Russified Jewish students back in 1881,[26] though nothing of national scope had ever been tried before and nothing like it would succeed—until forty years later in the Warsaw ghetto.

The politicization of Jewish life had already come so far as to produce

1. Ephraim Moses Lilien, "To the Martyrs of Kishinev," 1903.

an unbridgeable gap between the Zionists and the socialist internationalists. The former sought their legitimation in the past, in the national sovereignty of the people on their land; the latter looked to the rising proletariat for support in the common struggle for social revolution. And so, whereas the Odessa group began its proclamation by invoking the memory of the Cossack insurrectionists Khmelnitsky and Gonta, a counterproclamation put out by the Jewish Labor Bund[27] set Kishinev against the promise of the enlightened twentieth century but hastened to assure Jewish workers that anti-Semitism was merely a function of certain socioeconomic factors. Both groups organized for self-defense, and, in addition, the Odessa group dispatched Bialik to Kishinev to collect eyewitness accounts of the massacre, to photograph the damage, and to assemble whatever documents would stand up in a Russian court.

This time, the world at large took heed of the Jewish destruction, and Bialik's notebooks were superfluous, not to be published until sixty years later.[28] It is never the public record, however, that tells the story. Having come to expect the subjective reality to set the norm and give rise to new responses, we should look to Bialik's creative effort before and after the visit to see how one man writing at a critical moment in Jewish history was able to provoke action by transforming the poetics of violence.

FROM the opening line, "Heavenly spheres, beg mercy for me!"[29] it appears as if Bialik had fallen back on a purely liturgical stance in response to news of the pogrom. The more learned reader, however, might already recognize in these words the echo of a famous fornicator, Rabbi Eleazar ben Dordia, "who did not leave out any harlot in the world without coming to her" (B. Abodah Zarah 17a). After crossing seven rivers for the sake of one who commanded a purse of denarii for her hire, Rabbi Eleazar was told that he would never be received in repentance, at which point he sat between two mountains and cried out: "Heaven and earth beg mercy for me!" "How shall we pray for thee?" the heavens replied; "We stand in need of it ourselves." Who is it then, that shouts in Bialik's poem: the one who sleeps with harlots or the one who is slaughtered? No matter—God is deaf in either case, and the speaker concedes the impossibility of prayer: "My own heart is dead; no prayer on my tongue" (line 5).

Upon the Slaughter

Heavenly spheres, beg mercy for me!
If truly God dwells in your orbit and round,

And in your sphere is His pathway that I have not found—
Then you pray for me!
For my own heart is dead; no prayer on my tongue;
And strength has failed, and hope has passed:
O until when? For how much more? How long?
(lines 1–7)

Since God is deaf and prayer is stifled, the speaker turns to the only active force around, the hangman, whom he apostrophizes with a travesty on Psalms: *lekha zro'a im-kardom* (line 9)—you have the arm and the ax, instead, of *lekha zro'a im gevurah,* YOU HAVE THE ARM OF MIGHT (Ps. 89:14).

Nape me this cur's nape! Yours is the axe unbaffled!
The whole wide world—my scaffold!
And rest you easy: we are weak and few.
My blood is outlaw. Strike, then; the skull dissever!
Let blood of babe and graybeard stain your garb—
Stain to endure forever!
(lines 8–14)

The replacement of the heavens with the hangman resonates with an even more startling repudiation, that of God's glory in the day of Creation as proclaimed each Rosh Hashanah in the majestic hymn of Kallir:

Melekh azur gevurah
Gadol shimḥa bigevurah
Lekha zro'a im gevurah.[30]

King girded in power
Great is thy name in power
Powerful is thy arm.

Whereas Kallir, inspired by midrashic sources, depicts the Lord clothed in each of His ten garments, one of which is the robe of vengeance, Bialik follows through with his description of the hangman:

Dam yonek vasav 'al-kutontekha—
Velo' yimaḥ lanetsaḥ, lanetsaḥ.
(lines 13–14)

The blood of nursling and of aged on your garment—
It will never be erased, never.

The crimson and white garments of the Lord are here replaced by the indelible stain of the victims' blood on the hangman's clothing, and even the rhyme word of the piyyut, *lanetsaḥ* (forever) is outrageously paired with *retsaḥ* (slaughter) in line 12. As for God's robes of vengeance—

> Who cries *Revenge*! Revenge!—accursed be he!
> Fit vengeance for the spilt blood of a child
> The devil has not yet compiled . . .
> (lines 22–24)

The plain meaning of the poem, as such lines indicate, was readily accessible, even if the foregoing allusions were open only to a very few. The countercommentary added rhetorical and theological weight to the repudiation of the sacred order signaled by the triumph of the hangman over the heavens. The short-circuiting of Scripture perfected by Abramovitsh to convey the fallen state of Russian Jewry was radicalized by Bialik into an outright rejection of divine justice and therefore of the possibility of retribution in a world devoid of God.

Since, as we saw in Chapter 2, the language of prayer admits travesty too, Bialik's choice of paradigms argues for hidden continuities. A people defiled by the unavenged blood of its children is indeed analogous to the scholar permanently defiled by his harlotry, and Gideon's despair over the Midianite oppression—echoed, as E. L. Strauss has shown,[31] in lines 2, 15, 16, and 20 of the poem—can justly apply to today, even if Gideon received a positve response from God and Bialik's generation did not. Put to subversive use, the language of prayer can subvert that very subversion. Bialik's antiliturgical outburst, written on the eve of his trip to Kishinev, preserved the radical tension between atrocity and the hallowed texts.

Bialik arrived about a month after the pogrom, to join the most systematic effort yet undertaken to document a Jewish catastrophe. With this sudden interest in facts, one would expect a writer who had spent five weeks inspecting the ruins and interviewing the survivors to exploit his authority as best he could. The nineteenth-century Hebrew poets who preceded him appealed to observable reality with "real" characters who acted in a historical setting and who narrated their experience in the first person—Zedekiah awaiting execution in prison, and Baruch standing before the mass grave in Mainz. Bialik, heeding the mandate of the Odessa group and the narrative conventions of modern Hebrew verse, introduced into Jewish literature the actual, physical landscape of violence—after the fact, to be sure, but with all the debris very much in evidence. The failed petitioner of "Upon the Slaughter" became the outraged reporter:

> Arise and go now to the city of slaughter;
> Into its courtyard wind thy way;

> There with thine own hand touch, and with the eyes of thine head,
> Behold on tree, on stone, on fence, on mural clay,
> The spattered blood and dried brains of the dead.[32]
>
> (lines 3–5)

Bialik's reportage is at once more and less accurate than what he actually witnessed. As Menachem Perry noted, we are shown a synecdochic landscape—that is, scattered fragments of the whole, the last vestiges of the pogrom soon to be erased.[33] But by the time of Bialik's visit, he could not have seen the beheaded Jew and his dog lying together on a mound (lines 23–24), or smelled the blood or heard the cries. To be sure, the survivors he spoke to remembered that and much more. Bialik's special method, however, was to pick out the standard poetic formulas: the streets covered with feathers, desecrated Torah scrolls, the infant crying at his dead mother's breast. As Israel Halpern was the first to observe, Bialik also omitted any mention of the sporadic resistance to the pogromists, data that appear in the recorded interviews.[34] Clearly, what Bialik had in mind, was a higher truth than could be gleaned from mere eyewitness accounts.

Bialik's higher purpose was to desacralize history in God's own name. A third of the way through the tour of the courtyards, attics, and cellars, the speaker of the poem turned his attention to the hiding places

> where the heirs
> Of Hasmoneans lay, with trembling knees,
> Concealed and cowering—the sons of the Maccabees!
> The seed of saints, the scions of the lions!
> Who, crammed by scores in all the sanctuaries of their shame,
> So sanctified My name!
> . . . . .
> *Now wherefore dost thou weep, O son of man?*
>
> (lines 87–92, 97)

God himself has been leading the tour, and it is the prophet's steps we have been following! Suddenly we are thrust back in time to the God of the midrash on Lamentations, who descended to earth with Jeremiah in the lead to inspect the ruins of the Temple. What began as a detailed accounting of places and events has been revealed a divine monologue, the exploration of God's pathos in a world gone mad.

God's last and bitter charge on earth is to deny the victims their symbolic victory and the survivors their consolation. All His anger turns inward, to "the seed of saints, the scions of the lions," coded references to the martyrs of 1096 and 1648, and to His own inability to act. He descends to the latter-day valley of dry bones (lines 99–137), but except for a dark Shekhinah (divine presence) choking on her grief, nothing else stirs. In the burial ground, the Temple sacrifice is abrogated for all time as the Lord announces His capitulation:

> See, see, the slaughtered calves, so smitten and so laid;
> Is there a price for their death? How shall that price be paid?
> Forgive, ye shamed of the earth, yours is a pauper-Lord!
> Poor was He during your life, and poorer still of late.
> When to my door you come to ask for your reward,
> I'll open wide: See, I am fallen from My high estate.
> I grieve for you, my children. My heart is sad for you.
> Your dead were vainly dead; and neither I nor you
> Know why you died or wherefore, for whom, nor by what laws;
> Your deaths are without reason; your lives are without cause.
> (lines 146–155)

When finally we come to the abode of the living, we find them solely preoccupied with death. Given that they bartered their lives for the price of the dead whose death had no meaning either, nothing could be more obscene than to run through the standard litanies.

> Regard them now, in these their woes:
> Ululating, lachrymose,
> Crying from their throes,
> *We have sinned!* and *Sinned have we!*—
> Self-flagellative with confession's whips.
> Their hearts, however, do not believe their lips.
> Is it, then, possible for shattered limbs to sin?
> Wherefore their cries imploring, their supplicating din?
> (lines 186–191)

What is left after the unredeemability of death and the obscenity of life is a powerless God calling for His final deposition:

> Speak to them, bid them rage!
> Let them against me raise the outraged hand—
> Let them demand!
> Demand the retribution for the shamed
> Of all the centuries and every age!
> Let fists be flung like stone
> Against the heavens and the heavenly throne!
> (lines 191–194)

How cautiously the rabbis of the midrash had imputed feelings of compassion to their Lord, hedging the boldest anthropomorphisms with "were it not for the biblical verse black on white, it would be impossible to say." Even in folksongs two millennia later, the singer of the Balta pogrom would insist upon the pretense of a sleeping God. "His sleep is just a lie," he claimed in 1881. For Bialik, who was steeped in traditional sources, the absence of God was too terrifying to contemplate but too real to dismiss. Such a state of separation was second only to those stemming from the loss of one's parents and of the innocence of youth, themes central to Bialik's other work.[35] Only such a poet as Bialik could deliver the ultimate protest through the mouth of an abdicating God. The commanding voice of Kishinev could be no other than God's, just as the slaughter could be linked only to His failure. The Jews' powerlessness was a measure of His; His incomprehension was equal to theirs.[36]

Thus, whatever action followed could not follow from God. The equation that was once upheld between God's sanctity and the people's mandate to sanctify His name, to die for Kiddush Hashem, was now replaced by a negative sum. A new level of commitment could be achieved only on the ruins of the old value system. The political message, which everyone but the censor was quick to grasp, was a call to armed resistance. "In the City of Slaughter" did more to agitate for Jewish self-defense than any proclamation of the Odessa Hebrew writers or the Central Committee of the Bund.

These two poems, the pseudo-prayer and the pseudo-reportage, instantly raised the thirty-year-old Bialik to the status of "national poet," a mantle he wore with great misgivings.[37] Though not without its critics from within the ranks of the Jewish intelligentsia,[38] "In the City of Slaughter" was soon recognized as having established for the pogrom genre a new model against which all subsequent efforts would be measured.[39] In Bialik's Yiddish translation,[40] which appeared two years after the Hebrew, the poem could appeal to young Jewish readers of both sexes who were searching to identify with a national cause. Bialik, therefore, mustered greater authority than any modern Jewish poet before or since, by virtue of having been in Kishinev himself and of having reported the event in both Hebrew and Yiddish with a voice that resonated with biblical echoes. Through this major poem, Kishinev became a symbol of national ignominy—and of something more. For with one hand Bialik built the pogrom up into an archetype based on a support system of martyrdom, resurrection, retribution, confession, and mourning—while with the other hand he severed the link to God and called for His abdication.

Once the pogrom poem was freed from its theological foundations, it took on a life of its own, independent of time, place, and personal witnessing. Some of Bialik's successors democratized his prophetic seer into an average citizen in order to internalize the pogrom—to render its psychological, even sensual impact. Others took the scene of destruction and abstracted it further, depicting the pogrom as a metaphysical, rather than a national, event. Only when the pogrom became coterminous with history, when the entire Jewish people was marked for destruction, did Seer and Scene reunite to exhort, to extoll, and to lament. In the end, poetry itself became an act of faith.

THE strewn feathers of the 1880s had given way to the nails of Kishinev,[41] cited in the epigraph to this chapter as the storyteller's shorthand for a new level of violence marked by brutality and murder. During relatively tranquil times it was still possible for a lone pogrom to stand out, and Kishinev did, in fact, release a floodgate of artistic response in European and Jewish languages, in the visual and verbal arts, in America and in Europe.[42]

Then, on the very eve of the Great War, Russian Jews were treated to a replay of the hoary past. To be sure, there had been the Damascus blood libel of 1840, which had mobilized public opinion world-wide, but European Russia in the twentieth century was something else. In that particular dialectic where one people's taboo becomes another's obsession, Mendl Beillis was accused in 1913 of murdering a Christian child to use its blood for ritual purposes. That Beillis won the case in a Russian court offered very little solace. There was a pattern of persecution at work that seemed to defy historical change.

Nor was the situation any different when World War I broke out a year later, for the locus of Jewish suffering was not the battlefield but the cities and market towns of eastern Europe, and the scenario was all too familiar: the Russian government began the wholesale expulsion of Jews from the Russian war zone, and 600,000 were dislocated before the advance of the German army brought this to a halt; the Germans, in turn, deported 70,000 Lithuanian Jews to Germany for forced labor; the Cossacks orchestrated a reign of terror over the civilian Jewish population of occupied Galicia, while the Poles rallied under the flag of anti-Semitism and staged their own pogroms whenever the opportunity arose.[43] Zalmen Schneour's prediction in 1913 that "the Middle Ages draw near!" seemed to have been borne out in fact.[44]

The kind of face-to-face violence, blind hatred, and persecution that Jews were subjected to during World War I was such native ground that the selective recording of history came into play once more and the Jewish tragedy was kept separate from world events. While leftist non-Jewish writers like Maxim Gorky[45] and John Reed[46] drew attention to the special plight of the Jews, Jews themselves began to speak in terms of a *khurbm*, a national catastrophe. *In Sackcloth and Ashes*[47] and *The Tragedy of the Jews in the European War Zone*[48] were the English-language equivalents of the "black books" that appeared in Yiddish[49] and Russian.[50] The coding of catastrophe into archetypes naturally followed. In Zvi Cohn's *Black Book,*[51] published in Lodz, no doubt with the blessings of the occupying German army, the Russian atrocities were documented under the standard headings of Eichah (Lamentations), Martyrs, and Marrano Women (marranos being the secret Jews of late medieval Spain and Portugal). Ansky was to title his war memoir *Khurbm Galitsye* (The Destruction of Galicia), while Sholem Asch combined his war stories with tales of medieval martyrdom in *Dos bukh fun tsar* (The Book of Anguish).[52]

The Jewish dimension of the war was not lost on the American Jews who could read of the massacres and expulsions in the Yiddish and Anglo-Jewish press. The combination of their own profound hatred of the tsar and the neutrality of the American government inspired a national revival among the East Side immigrants of New York, which in turn was bound to affect the new generation of Jewish writers.[53] In the words of one historian, "Whatever his cosmopolitan illusions, the café radical, like the synagogue Jew, saw the *shtetl* aflame."[54] News of the destruction gradually transformed the Yiddish writers and poets from immigrants to exiles, though most of them had arrived on America's shores of their own free will. Suddenly they felt the loss of their homeland.[55] By 1916, the full extent of the destruction was known and Zishe Landau could begin his lament "for our shattered Jewish life" with a traditional litany of place names:

Now, for our shattered Jewish life
I kneel, and pray to you for grace;
I weep for our old mother Vilna,
For Brod, for every holy place;

I weep for Warsaw, Kovno, Lemberg,
For every large and little town
Whereon the foe of old has fallen,
And which the foe will fall upon.[56]

He drew from cities north and south, not from his native region of Plock, Poland, in order to convey the scope of the disaster. But even a *khurbm* could not erase the memories of the underside of Jewish life in eastern Europe, the corruption born of poverty that had propelled so many to the shores of the New World. And so Landau went on to weep

For every dirty Jewish alley,
Each dingy hole with goods for sale;
For every pawnshop, tavern, alehouse;
For our false measure, weight and scale;

For every merry Jewish brothel,
That on a Gentile street seemed gay;
For all that ever has been ours
Now vanishing in smoke away.

These feelings of anger and remorse found their resolution, however, in a prayer for physical restoration and spiritual renewal, the latter to be achieved not by divine or political means but through something peculiar to the poet's craft—an otherworldly (*nitdoik*) charm that would soothe the people's grieving soul:

> There's goodness in whatever's Jewish;
> Rebuild this poor life, do restore!
> And rock to sleep the souls dispirited
> With an unexisting word.

Among the ranks of the café radicals, there was one at least who felt the contradictions so deeply and who so despaired of redemptive slogans that the pogroms became for him the center of apocalypse. And at the center of the center was the mind of the poet acting out the madness of history in the feverish privacy of his dreams. This artist was Moyshe-Leyb Halpern.

Halpern's "A Night," first published in 1916 and reworked in 1919, broke with poetic tradition in several ways: it explored the impact of violence on the individual psyche; it viewed the pogrom in terms of broad historical categories; and it achieved all this in an innovative form that avoided a sequential narrative.[57] Instead of being constructed as an ordered tour in which God leads the reader through the desecrated city, Halpern's poem followed the structure of a dream.[58] The descent of wild horsemen into the fiery abyss preceded the appearance of the dreamer himself and represented his fall from reality into the closed system of a nightmare.

> Oh-ho, ho-ho—
> Who calls so? Who is the man who came
> Down from the mountain at midnight?
>   In the wildest gallop
> He descended with outstretched arms.
> (1:1–4)

The images and sounds owe more to the Revelation of John and to the poetry of Heine[59] than to anything in Jewish apocalyptic sources, though Daniel too saw dreadful beasts in his nightly visions. When a biblical cadence and formula are introduced in the third chapter, the thematic direction pulls in opposition to the weight of tradition:

> And a king, who comes on a snow-white horse
> Will bring peace and rest to the earth.
> Whether a blessing, or whether a curse—
> Thus it is written in the holy verse:
> *And it shall come to pass in the end of days.*

It then emerges that the rider king is himself responsible for the holocaust perpetrated in his name, a destruction so total that there is no one left to be redeemed.

Two nightmares are portrayed in "A Night"—one personal, the other historical—and the interpenetration of the two constitutes Halpern's great achievement. The personal nightmare begins with the appearance of the poet's double, a sadistic creature referred to as *dos mentshele* (the little man) who emerges in the dream and quickly disabuses the dreamer of any hope of salvation, taunting him eventually into self-torture. *Mentshele* is the actor who parodies the dreamer and his dream.[60] Like the Mendele persona who fulfills similar functions in Abramovitsh's fiction, *mentshele* exposes the false morality of the collective; and like the reporter-prophet in Bialik's "In the City of Slaughter," he confronts the dreamer-survivor with the relics from the latter's ravaged homeland: a dead man's head, a *tsholnt* pot (containing the traditional Sabbath stew) and a blood-spattered prayer shawl (chapter 4). The double's cynical and grotesque treatment of the tragedy reaches its climax in chapters 8–15, in which the dreamer is made to relive painful scenes of childhood, to see his father dangling from a rope, and to witness the rape and mutilation of other family members. In chapter 14 *mentshele* describes the pogrom as a wedding dance:

> Harp and song sound rhythmically—
> All are dancing, I dance too.
> Ho-lo-lo, ho-li, ho-li—
> They break the door down to the house,
> The window-panes they smash to bits,
> Door and glass fly higgledy-piggledy—
> Ho-lo-lo, ho-li!
>
> (14:1–7)

If the individual has been subjected to such a psychic nightmare, it is not because of a failure of national nerve and not because of God's capitulation, but because of the perversions wrought by false credos. "A Night" is a blanket indictment of all redemptive movements. That is why the horsemen of the apocalypse are fused with the white-robed messiah in the opening segments of the dream. In the second half of the poem, Halpern treats the nightmare of history and the history of false redemption—those collective constructs that shape and inform the individual's psyche.

The section begins with a blasphemous parody of the Sermon on the Mount. Instead of calling for brotherly love, *mentshele* prescribes an eye for an eye, a tooth for a tooth. In a world bent on destruction, one must destroy others in order to survive, and whatever booty is salvaged may then be shared with one's brother. As for one's sister,

And if your sister bears a bastard,
Shout that its name is Holy Ghost the soldier
And that the bastard is a god-to-be
Who, like Jesus, brings us only love and mercy.
And if they don't believe you, take the cross from your heart
And also take the prayer shawl—half white and half black—
And place them together and spit on them both.
And then order all the flags of the world brought to you
And braid them all together in a rope
And hang yourself at your father's side,
And with him swing back and forth
Until the rope rots through,
Until a gentile buries you two
In the ground with his dead horse.

(16:13–26)

All the redemptive ideologies—Judaism, Christianity, and socialist revolution—are equally discredited and share equal blame for the suffering perpetrated in their names. The prayer shawl is interwoven with the crucifix and the flag. One is simply the extension of the other. In chapter 19 this suffering is traced from the Egyptian servitude to Christian martyrdom under the Romans to Jewish martyrdom under the Christians. The history of Western civilization is summed up in the lines "Tsit zikh a levaye-gang, / Iz er toyznt mayln lang"—"a funeral cortege stretches for a thousand miles" (19:19–20).

Since all visions in this poem are translated into individual experience and since role reversals are the reigning logic of the dream, the dreamer himself is acclaimed as the messiah in chapter 20 and as such is laid to rest in his grave. The circle of private grief and collective suffering is closed when the dead victims of past redemptive struggles pour their own version of the Tokheḥa upon the head of the dreamer-messiah:

"Forever ravaged shall the earth be
Where you have spun your dream.
Without why or wherefore, every night
A man shall be hung from your tree.

"And if you reach out beseechingly,
Your hand shall wither away.
And you shall choke on your every word
When you remember this place."

(20:33–40)

The dreamer's "hand shall wither away" when he longs not for Zion but for his shattered homeland of Galicia.

The very last vision of the poem, added in 1919, is of annihilation both physical and psychic. As did El Cid, the dreamer asks that his dead body be tied to a horse; in this way his physical remains will blend into the earth, just as the memory of the nightmare will be completely erased. The new ending brings together the horseman and the dreamer, the "I" and the world, emphasizing that the irreconcilable polarities can be resolved only in death. The human being is both redeemer king and apocalyptic horseman. In apocalyptic time, individual striving is everywhere subverted by the idolatry of the people who worship the flags and the crosses and the empty promises. The pogrom signals the loss of previous logic, the moral bankruptcy of civilization, just as the poet's nightmare objectifies his own disillusionment. Trapped in the prison of his mind and despairing of all man-made solutions, the individual can hope for salvation only through oblivion: "That was, is gone. I disappear / In death. In life I was never here" (chapter 25).

Halpern's apocalypse was heralded by social and psychic anarchy. Nowhere did God enter into this scheme, for His absence was no longer a question for Halpern—or for any of the other café radicals. Even in his tirade against the messianic heresy, Halpern's argument was with man and not with God. Man is the measure of all hopes and disappointments in "A Night." The vision and the visionary are both erased at dream's end.

Bialik's Seer, like Elijah before him, was commanded to flee the wretched human abode and cast his cry into the storm. It was a tactical retreat from a Jewish community that still sustained itself on a doctrine of divine retribution. Halpern's redeemer-horseman, in contrast, leaves all human civilization behind, and the *mentshele,* coming from within the Seer himself, leaves no room for escape, save self-annihilation. The degree to which Halpern deviates from Bialik is an index of how the pogrom was gradually becoming emancipated from Jewish history.

THE October Revolution completed the transformation of politics and literature begun by the Great War. Those Jews who saw the Red Army as their protector rallied to its flag, whereas those who saw the oppressive regularity of Jewish suffering even in the wake of the revolution were drawn to nationalist ideologies. Meanwhile appeared European modernist trends which defined violence as the substance, not merely a subject, of art. Aestheticism, classical forms, and even syntax were proclaimed dead by the Futurists in Italy and Russia and by the Expressionists in Germany. Myth was revived as a way of expressing the horror. Christian and anti-Christian myths resurfaced in the folklore and literature of the trenches, informing two of the most celebrated poems of the postwar era: Aleksandr Blok's equivocal hymn to the revolution, *Twelve* (1918), and T. S. Eliot's *The Waste Land* (1922).

Now that chaos had become fundamental to the modern consciousness, it was no longer possible for Jewish poets automatically to appropriate catastrophes solely for their own or for their people's use. Pogroms could no longer be seen in isolation; Jewish iconography was no longer deemed adequate to mediate upheavals of such magnitude. Jewish poets now wrote their own requiems to the war and hymns to the revolution. Blok's apostolic revolutionaries made their appearance in Yiddish and Hebrew, both in translation and imitation.[61] Then, in 1922, Yiddish Expressionism made its formal debut in Warsaw with the first in a series of manifestos titled "The Aesthetics of Struggle in Modern Poetry," by Peretz Markish.[62]

Markish came of age fighting on the Russian front in World War I and was later rumored to have perished in the Ukrainian pogroms. *Di kupe* ("The Heap," 1921), his major poem on the pogroms, begins with a dedication that ostensibly provides a historical anchor:

> To you, the victims of the Ukraine,
> Where the earth is filled with your remains,
> And to you as well, the slaughtered in a heap
> In the town of Horodishtsh at the Dnieper,
> —Kaddish![63]

The opening poem also includes the date "11th of Tishrei 5681," confirmed by historical sources as the actual date of the pogrom in Horodishtsh in which 216 Jews were murdered.[64] Name and date notwithstanding, only figurative events are described here, with a metaphoric density that is sometimes impenetrable.

"The Heap" is a quintessentially expressionist work in which the outside world exists only to the extent that it is reflected within the poet himself. As a result, the poetic voice changes in each chapter. Sometimes the poet addresses the heap of corpses; sometimes he identifies with it; sometimes he prays to it and stands guard over it; at other times he madly blasphemes against it. The tone of the poem changes from tragic reverence to grotesquerie to sentimentalism to satire—not infrequently within the same chapter. The egocentric vision allows for no temporal development. Each chapter captures a single moment, and even the poetic "I" has no biographic past: he is society at large or every "I" reading the poem.

Markish, as does Halpern, pits the pogrom against Christian as well as Jewish symbolism. By the end of "The Heap," all covenants have been abrogated and all sanctities have been defiled. The corpse heap now vies for authority with Mount Sinai, and the Ten Commandments are cast into the mud. The heap is crowned "queen of mountains" and occupies the highest heaven, while Sinai is relegated to the marketplace below where God too can be found, bloody and recrucified. But Sinai and the cross should be understood rhetorically, not literally, for as much as the poem is a response to tradition, it is also an attempt to mediate between the sensation of the pogrom and its meaning. Markish is overwhelmed by the physicality of the pogrom—by the revolting smell of decomposing bodies, the landscape of violence left in its wake. Bialik's and Halpern's rebellion against the tradition of discovering meaning in the pogrom is replaced here with the attempt to link sensation with a higher meaning. The opening chapter, written in sonnet form, begins:

> Nit! Lek nit, kheylev himlisher, mayne farpapte berd,
> Fun mayne mayler khlyupen broyne ritshkes dzyegekhts,
> O, broyne roshtshine fun blut un fun gezegekhts,
> Nit! Rir nit dos gebrekh oyf shvartser dikh fun dr'erd.
>
> Don't! Heavenly tallow, do not lick my pasted beards,
> Brown streams of grease run from my mouths,
> Oh, brown leaven of blood and of sawdust,
> Don't! Do not touch the puke on the black thigh of the earth.

Candles, lit perhaps in memory of the dead, burn in heaven while the pasted beards of dead Jews lie in heaps below. The dialect words with their unmistakable Slavic sounds, the harsh colors and consonants, all help create the illusion of specificity though the images themselves are indeterminate.[65] The "black thigh" makes the earth suffer as a person.

In the second quatrain, the metaphors of the first are realized as the heap of corpses becomes a swamp:

> Avek! Se shtinkt fun mir, se krikhn oyf mir fresh!
> Du zukhst dayn tate-mame do? Du zukhst dayn khaver?
> Zey zaynen do! Zey zaynen do! Nor s'shtinkt fun zey an aver!
> Avek! Zey loyzn zikh tserepete mit hent tseboygene vi mesh . . .
>
> Away! I'm stinking, frogs are crawling over my ass!
> Looking for your parents here? Looking for a friend?
> They're here! They're here! But they're giving off a stench!
> Away! They're delousing themselves clumsily with hands like disfigured brass.

The corpse heap is alive, not only with the slowly rising leaven but with frogs and moving human hands.

This is *real* history, evoked through the medium of sensation, which leaves little room for the transcendental. Horodishtsh thus emerges as an antisymbol. The heap of corpses in its marketplace is the ultimate expression of anonymity—the fathers, mothers, and children have no individual identity whatsoever. We are not even told how many they are. A hundred? A thousand? Nor are the perpetrators of the crime mentioned directly. All we see is the church sitting near the corpses "like a skunk at a heap of strangled fowl" (line 11). If anything, the corpse heap stands as a monument of condemnation against a world that has destroyed the Jews in the name of God and against the Jewish victims themselves. The kaddish itself is a travesty. The opening sonnet ends with an outburst of profanity:

> O, shvartse dikh! O fayer blut! Oyf tents, oyf tents—aroyf di hemder!
> M'hot undz do oysgeleygt di gantse shtot—a kupe—ale,
> Yud-alef tishrey tarpe.
>
> O black thigh! O fire blood! Lift up your shirts—to dance, to dance!
> We've been laid out here, the entire town—in a heap—all, all,
> The eleventh day of Tishrei, 5681.

Yet even of Markish it can be said that the liturgical framework creates a construct as timeless as the texts it sets out to subvert. Twenty-five chapters later, when the poem concludes the way it began, but with a resounding liturgical flourish, "tsu Gots nomen, / Omeyn!" (to God's name Amen!); when bits and snatches of the High Holiday liturgy—the Kol Nidre, the Reader's Meditation "Hineni he'ani mima'as," the Neilah—punctuate the expressions of revulsion; and when every archetypal structure (the Tower of Babel, the Tabernacle of the Lord) and every sacred mount (Ararat, Sinai, and Golgotha) have been eclipsed by the Heap, the pogrom is that which remains, rescued from the oblivion of a world apocalypse. The act of rescue was Markish's purpose in writing the poem; he had just returned from the eastern front, where the dead were numbered in the millions and the living shared their quarters with vermin.[66] The rotting flesh of Jews was that much cheaper because pogroms had become commonplace and the Jews themselves, not to speak of the world at large, had become inured to the spectacle. Markish's choice of date and town are arbitrary—there were so many hundreds of pogroms to choose from. Once chosen, however, the sacrilege of the corpse heap would forever challenge the abstraction of mass death with its stench.

Needless to say, "The Heap" provoked a storm of protest in conservative Jewish circles. The attack was led by philosopher-poet Hillel Zeitlin in the pages of *Moment,* the leading Yiddish daily in Warsaw.[67] Those who shared Markish's radical sympathies, however, were not shocked by his blasphemy and expressionistic hyperbole. On hearing Markish declaim the poem publicly in Vienna in 1921, Manes Sperber was reminded of the street ballads of an earlier era;[68] and in an important critical essay, I. Nusinov recognized this "most revolutionary work of our entire pogrom literature" as a self-contained cry of national grief, a kaddish.[69] Perhaps the ultimate paradox is that even the poet who used the pogrom to revile his audience, to express his revulsion, was addressing only other Jews. The very act of writing a pogrom poem placed him within the same continuum he had set out to renounce.

NEVER before had the memory of past destruction resurfaced with so much force as during the Ukrainian civil war of 1918–19, for no other area of eastern Europe was so steeped in Jewish calamity. Jews of every ideological persuasion were filled with an overwhelming sense of déjà vu. Khmelnitsky and Gonta, figures out of the seventeenth and eighteenth centuries, were universally invoked, not as a way of circumventing the censor, as when Bialik's great pogrom poem had originally to appear under the guise of "The Oracle at Nemirov," but because the analogical mode of thinking still reigned supreme. Even Markish, in a mood of national defiance,[70] lashed out in fury at the heirs of Gonta and the Haidamaks (Cossack bands). In truth, the pogroms were staged by many hands, including anarchists, Bolsheviks (briefly), and White Army counterrevolutionaries under the infamous General Denikin; but it was the specter of Ukrainian forces under Petlura and mobs of armed peasants destroying town after town—some of the very same places memorialized by the medieval chronicler Nathan Nata Hannover in 1653—that called forth the Jewish dialectical response to catastrophe. Sholem Asch, always an accurate guide of public taste, came out with *Kiddush Hashem,* a novel set in the time of Khmelnitsky;[71] and somewhat later, Asher Barash used the figure of Gonta as a fictional overcoat for Petlura.[72]

The modernist response pulled in the opposite direction, away from notions of continuity and group solidarity. As much as eastern European Jewish writers, whether living in Kiev, Berlin, Jaffo, or New York, could not escape the theme of catastrophe, their desire to subvert the tragic claim of history was equally pervasive, and this subversion took many forms. In New York, the café radicals were divided among the aesthetes, like Zishe Landau, holding out for the "unexisting word" that would conjure away the ruins; the antiromantics, like Moyshe-Leyb Halpern, who debunked all pretense, beginning with their own; and the neoromantics, who abstracted the great historic themes back into their constituent myths.

This last form of subversion is the hardest to catch because it seems to adopt the liturgical mode at face value. Thus, with H. Leivick and A. Leyeles, we return once more to the pogrom as crucible of heaven and earth, as final arbiter of free will and divine providence. In reviving the epic, moreover, they chose the most hallowed paradigm of destruction—mass martyrdom. Both Leivick and Leyeles described mass suicide as the inevitable and most exalted response of the pogrom victims. Whether such a case actually occurred is not at issue, for it was the recollection of the Crusades and perhaps of the Khmelnitsky massacres that inspired the poets. This was the stuff that epics were made of.

Leivick was a unique figure among American-Yiddish poets and was in many respects the forerunner of the Holocaust survivor. Few events of the recent past loomed quite as large in the minds of New York's East Side immigrants as the revolutionary upheaval in Russia, and few people had had experiences as emblematic of that event as Leivick's years of tsarist internment. Escaping on foot from Siberia, Leivick came directly to the Lower East Side, there to write of his experiences in an impressionistic style quite new to Yiddish literature:

Even now
on the roads of Siberia
you can find
a button,
a shred of one of my shoelaces,
a belt,
a bit of broken cup,
a leaf of Scripture.[73]

This was a synecdochic landscape with a difference, for the relics of his flight were really stigmata of individual suffering:

Even now
on the rivers of Siberia
you can find
some trace:
a scrap of one of my tattered shoes;
in the woods
a bloodied swatch dried stiff;
some frozen footprints
over the snow.

Purification through suffering was a notion close to the heart of the Russian-Jewish intellectuals raised on Tolstoy. But unlike most of the other café radicals, Leivick was not content with impressionistic lyrics. As he widened the search for individual redemption to take in a vast historical panorama, Leivick came to see destruction as the sinister twin of redemption, power as the evil counterpart of powerlessness. And so, whereas in his visionary drama *The Golem* he focused on the destructive forces of redemption,[74] in his narrative poem "The Stable" he looked at the redemptive possibilities of destuction.[75]

He began with a single act of desecration from which the poem derived its title. "German soldiers turned our Cold Synagogue into a stable—for their horses." So read the first of two epigraphs to the poem, ostensibly an excerpt from a letter. The second, in Hebrew, was the inscription commonly painted on synagogue ceilings (from Ethics of the Fathers 5:23): "Be swift as a deer, strong as a lion, bold as a leopard, and light as an eagle." The synagogue-turned-stable, therefore, represented the sacrilege of war, while cosmic harmony was symbolized by the painted animals. These were the opposing forces that Leivick sought to reconcile.

"The Stable" (1920) is the story of Joseph and his brothers, survivors of the pogrom. Early on, the brothers have resigned themselves to their fate, but the youngest longs to return to the synagogue in the hope of redemption. "We too have all heard / the oracular voice of the stable, just as you did," they say, countering his plea, but *they* see no escape, "for night is here and there and everywhere" (7:19–20, 30). The youngest brother cannot accept their verdict and returns to the devastated town.

The pogrom has disrupted the accepted order in heaven as on earth. Everyone and everything is now in search of new meaning and new contexts within which to exist. Just as the youngest brother directs his search to the moon and stars, the stars address their sorrowful questions to him:

> It makes no sense to us
> We do not know when
> Nor what.
> Nor what.
> (18:21–24)

Finally, the youngest brother achieves his desired revelation:

> Nakhtgebet—
> Geveyn on reyd,
> Far dem vos zet
> Dem tsar fun freyd.
>
> Shtumgebet
> In toytgefar—
> Far dem vos zet
> Di freyd fun tsar.
> (19:1–8)

> Night prayer
> Speechless lament
> For him who stares
> The joy in grief.
>
> Silent prayer

In danger of death—
For him who stares
The joy in grief.

In answer to his silent prayer, the painted animals of the synagogue—the deer, the lion, the leopard, and the eagle—come to rest at his feet, and the forest comes alive with fantastic sights and sounds. This answer makes clear that it is the Temple of Beauty, not of God, that has been desecrated, leaving the survivors on earth as in heaven without a sanctuary. Freed from their moorings by the violence of the pogrom, the celestial survivors reveal to the youngest brother the exaltation of his suffering—that life is beauty and life is horror.

Having failed to accept or understand this revelation, the older brothers find solace in the song of the blue ritual slaughtering knives:

Victory and blade
Victory and blade of slaughtering knives,
Victory and blade and song of slaughtering knives.
(32:67–69)

Theirs is a collective victory, a path of purification through death rather than through suffering. It is a far cry indeed from Bialik's "Upon the Slaughter," where the blessing alluded to in the title was totally inverted. Instead of the ritual slaughterer it was the slaughtered victim in Bialik's poem who pronounced, in effect, this: "Cursed art thou, O Lord, our God, former king of the universe, who hath commanded me to be slaughtered for nought." And it was a farther cry still from Halpern's "A Night," which vehemently denied that anything beautiful or redemptive could follow from the senseless murder of Jews.

Leivick's purpose was to reverse this modernist trend by stressing the sublime: the interface of beauty and atrocity, redemption and death. Unfortunately, neither the aesthetics of mass suicide nor the revelation of cosmic harmony is particularly convincing. Extremes of good and evil are too easily come by in a poem that is so removed from history as to be credible only in the poet's private scheme of things. But the fact remains that in the Yiddish secular community Leivick's was a moral voice comparable to Bialik's, whether because Leivick's status as "survivor" gave him added authority or because the notion of purification through suffering, as indirectly borrowed from Christianity, had a special hold on a powerless group of Jews. In either event, Leivick's effort to transmute the horror into beauty was as blatantly nontraditional as the modernist penchant for outright blasphemy.

The final abstraction of the pogrom was achieved by A. Leyeles, who maintained, as did Leivick, an active political profile and treated the themes of history and redemption with broad poetic gestures. In "The Story of the Hundred" (1921), Leyeles introduced biblical parallels and imitated the "adding style" of the epic in order to stress the archetypal nature of the pogrom:

> On that day a yellow crazy sun emerged over the earth
> And scorched the earth with a yellow blaze.
> On that day a hot indifferent heaven
> Stared in dazed heat at the earth,
> And at the grasses,
> And at the creatures,
> And at the people.
> On that day the blood of the people
> Turned to poison.
> And mixed together
> With the copper sea above.
> And the whole world
> The seething yellow world
> Hissed and hissed
> Like a huge snake before the catch .[76]
>
> (lines 1–15)

Two biblical promises clash here. Instead of proclaiming a redemptive eschatology, the opening words introduce the dreaded Mosaic curses (Deut. 28:23–24). These curses, moreover, unlike those in the Bible, do not follow a moral inducement or indictment. It is an unmotivated vision of the end-time. All we know is that the End will somehow be connected to the Beginning, to the serpent of Creation.

Not the pogrom but its after-effects are described. Of the victims, only a mere hundred have survived. Since disorder is the order of the new day, those who are weak have now become strong. God, in His heavenly palace, sets about reversing the order of Creation. First, He destroys His myriad angels in all the seven heavens; then He comes down to earth to grovel at the feet of the hundred. *He* is the serpent creeping on its belly. His purpose in coming to the hundred is to have them revoke the covenant. "Free me," He implores them (lines 258–261),

> You who have survived
> From the responsibility for each new day,
> From my debt to the last [day].
> Redeem me!

The hundred fulfill His wish; God dissolves Himself and the world returns to primordial chaos.

We recognize the scenario of God's capitulation from Bialik, only there is no historical reality to the pogrom in "The Story of the Hundred." For Leyeles, as N. B. Minkov correctly noted, the pogrom is a philosophical and not a national category.[77] The pogrom, like the atomic bomb, is a possibility in human existence, one that threatens to overthrow all foundations—theological, natural, and social. The power of the poem derives from its epic passages which depict the dissolution of the universe with a detached, carefully controlled poetic exposition that reads like a latter-day Tokheḥa.

THE pogrom poem, which for centuries had been the embodiment of traditional values and poetics, became in the twentieth century a central vehicle for subverting the tradition. Whereas there had previously been only one paradigm of equivalences, the pogrom lament and the Purim thanksgiving, numerous alternatives were now put forward: the pogrom as prophetic indictment (Bialik); as personal nightmare (Halpern); as pornography (Markish); as pastoral (Leivick); and as philosophical postulate (Leyeles). Each new interpretation, moreover, was calculated to rescind another tenet of tradition: Bialik destroyed the type by desacralizing history; Halpern countered the collective eschatologies with individual despair; Markish, the transcendental with the grossly sensual; Leivick, the sacrilegious with aesthetic exaltation; and Leyeles, the national with the metaphysical. Left to its own momentum, the modernist revolt might eventually have expanded this genre beyond the knowable realm—had it not been for the intervention of history.

Twenty years after Kishinev, it did not seem as if a pogrom or even a mass suicide could again be a call for collective action, until someone discovered an ancient archetype that the rabbis had deliberately suppressed and that the ravages of time had long since demolished: Masada. Here was the perfect myth that mediated (to use the word in Lévi-Strauss's sense) the polarities of defeat and defiance. Through Isaac Lamdan's famous poem, and through later archeological discoveries, the mass suicide in that desert fortress became an emblem of the Zionist revolution.[78] Two years later, the Arab riots of 1929 (*me'ora'ot TaRPaT*) provoked a major schism among the Diaspora intellectuals, giving further evidence that catastrophe past and present would continue to structure the basic loyalties of Jews the world over.

Halpern joined Leivick, Lamed Shapiro, and other Yiddish writers who broke with the communist daily *Frayhayt* for hailing the pogroms in Hebron and Safed as a justified revolt against Zionist colonialists. These writers began producing their own publication, *Di vokh,* which claimed to tread an independent path. Yet the redemptive claims of the

Left continued to exert an enormous pull on all of Yiddish secular culture, and the voice of the independents merged with that of the party on all the issues that mattered: the choice of Birobidjan (the so-called Jewish Autonomous Region in Eastern Asia) over Palestine; Yiddish over Hebrew, the Red Army over the bourgeoisie.[79] There was no possible bridge between Masada and Moscow.

In the first two decades of the twentieth century, the pogrom had been relegated by modernist poets to the rarified realms of psyche and symbol; in the late 1930s it returned to its point of departure. Like the plaintive songs about scattered feathers and a sleeping God and like the street ballads of the Odessa, Bialystok, and Proskurov pogroms, there appeared a pogrom poem written by Mordkhe Gebirtig—a folk bard, not an intellectual. The backdrop was as real and immediate as could be. Following the death of Polish statesman Józef Pilsudski in May 1935, anti-Jewish boycotts in Poland took on a new momentum and on March 9, 1936, a pogrom broke out in Przytyk (pronounced *Pshitik*). Jews fought back, and one rioting Pole was shot dead. The courts then meted out the punishment—against the Jews. In response, on March 18 the Bund called a general strike which was supported by an overwhelming number of Jews.[80]

Thus, the one pogrom that claimed but three Jewish lives became, like Kishinev, the focal point of resistance and the catalyst for Gebirtig's rousing hymn:

> Fire, brothers, fire!
> It all turns to you.
> If you love your town,
> Take pails, put out the fire.
> Quench it with your own blood too.
> Show what you can do.
> Do not look and stand—
> With folded hand.
> Brothers, don't stand around, put out the fire
> Our town is in flames.[81]

What Gebirtig did, in effect, was reabsorb Bialik's anger and turn the earlier revolt into a source of consolation. The negative became positive. The attack on Jewish passivity became an open cry for solidarity. And this integration was far more important than any specific program that Gebirtig might have offered. By 1938, with the whole Jewish polity under attack, in Germany as well as Poland, Gebirtig could not hope for anything more than a holding action to save what little could be saved. Yet the very fact that the pogrom poem could still be the bearer of a message—be it self-defense, blasphemy, purification through suffering, or suicide as metaphysical epic—was testimony that the efforts of the modern Yiddish and Hebrew poets had not been in vain.

THE modern pogrom poems, for all their subversions, did not establish a new archetype or paradigm of destruction. On the contrary, they progressively reinforced the timeless import of the collective catastrophe—on the individual, societal, and even cosmic scale. To be sure, the old sustaining values of redemption and retribution had been totally disavowed, but that simply freed the response to pogroms from its traditional constraints. The new poems, moreover, were interchangeable; with no references to time or place, none of the specifics had to be altered. The abdication scene could be read either from Bialik or from Leyeles; Halpern and Markish could blaspheme in unison. Uncannily and unpredictably, the modern pogrom poem had rehabilitated the rabbinic strategies of favoring the subjective reality to the facts, the timeless configurations to the temporal details, the sacred texts to the historical context. With this script in hand, the Jews of eastern Europe would enact the crucial transition from pogrom to Final Solution.

CHAPTER FIVE

The Rape of the Shtetl

"And where is this dead town? On the other side of the moon?"
"No," he said smiling, "it's right here, in Poland."
I. L. Peretz, ca. 1895

UNTIL November 1940, the Jews of eastern Europe had never experienced ghettos per se. Attempts to restrict Jewish settlement to certain quarters in the crown cities of Poland had invariably met with failure. Even when excluded from a city, Jews simply moved nearby where they could pursue their livelihoods unimpeded. They always felt that there was safety in numbers, and when urban conditions deteriorated at the end of the fifteenth century, for reasons of economic competition and religious intolerance, Jews jumped at the opportunity to establish new towns and to settle the territory annexed by Poland in 1569. Within a century, under the aegis of the nobility, whose power rivaled that of the king, there sprang up hundreds of new "private towns" where Jews were welcomed and protected. These were the typical *shtetlekh* (market towns) of eastern Europe, based on a nonagrarian feudal economy, owned by a squire, and run in large measure by the Jews. Some of the oldest shtetlekh came complete with stone synagogues, built like fortresses, where Jews could take refuge and defend themselves in the event of attack. After major catastrophes, like the Khmelnitsky massacres of 1648–49, they returned to their towns to rebuild the ruins and reconstitute the community.

The real decline of the shtetl began in the mid-nineteenth century when its two foundations—the feudal economy and the power of the nobility—were overturned. The freeing of the serfs in 1861 coincided with the coming of the trains. Thousands of landless peasants flocked to the cities, where there was no work to be had. Meanwhile, the shtetl was left high and dry as big manufacturers bought their raw materials directly from the villages and easily underpriced the local artisans. The weekly market was rendered obsolete except for the exchange of basic commodities. Those shtetlekh with no direct access to the trains were left to stagnate, arrested in time. With the failure of the Polish uprising of 1863, members of the nobility, in addition, were stripped of all their powers and the shtetl came under the direct and intrusive rule of the tsar. Cantonism was a case in point.

When I. L. Peretz was dispatched in 1890 to report on the shtetl economy in the province of Lublin, what he found was proverty so pervasive that it had effectively destroyed the social and religious fabric of Jewish life:

> But what about the statistics? Can they answer: how many empty stomachs, useless teeth; how many people whose eyes are drawn out of their sockets as with pincers at the sight of a piece of bread; how many people who have really died of hunger—rely upon a speak-easy, a crook and a horse thief?
>
> . . . Do statistics record the anxious heartbeats that thumped in the breast of the grandson of the descendant from Spanish ancestors, or the son of the author of the *Tevuas Shor,* before they committed their first illegality? Do they measure how their hearts bled *after* they committed it? Do they count the sleepless nights before and after? Can they show how many were the days of hunger? How many times the children flung themselves about in convulsions, how often hands and feet shook when the first glass was filled by the unlicensed brandy-seller?[1]

Purportedly of Spanish ancestry, Peretz built to this rhetorical crescendo in order to drive home the message that Polish Jewry was a proud nation with a glorious past, but a nation that had been reduced by hunger to bootlegging and theft. Writing in an allegorical vein somewhat later, Peretz concluded that the shtetl was a dead town whose inhabitants had lost the will to live.[2]

Long before this first organized attempt to collect data on the shtetl, two generations of eastern European maskilim had already composed its epitaph. The attack on the shtetl, as Dan Miron has shown, was as old as its image in Yiddish and Hebrew fiction.[3] The earliest writers, Yisroel Aksenfeld, Ayzik-Meyer Dik, and M. A. Shatskes, anatomized shtetl folkways in expectation of their progressive decline. The classic literary image of the shtetl took shape, according to Miron, in the late nineteenth and early twentieth centuries along a three-dimensional axis. Incorporating the mimetic, panoramic approach of the earlier writers, Abramovitsh, Spektor and Peretz exploded the myth of the shtetl, the notion that it was a Kehillah Kedoshah with a direct link to Jerusalem. Mendele's farcical address to the martyred triad to towns—Idler Junction, Pauperville, and Foolstown—was Abramovitsh's way of attacking the false messianism of the shtetl. Peretz's pointed references throughout "The Dead Town" to the *agunah,* the abandoned widow, parodied the figure of Fair Zion as portrayed in Lamentations. These were but two instances showing that, in the eyes of the intellectuals, the shtetl could no longer claim mythic grandeur.

From an ideological standpoint, finally, each of the writers "discovered" the shtetl in the name of ideals gleaned in the far-away cities of Warsaw, Vilna, and Odessa. Armed with notions of progress and utility, the maskilim viewed the shtetl as a provincial backwater that would never evolve into a rational society. Peretz, for instance, selected for scrutiny those aspects of shtetl life which were of special concern to the Polish Positivists: the state of the artisan class and the plight of women.[4] The mission that brought him face to face with the collapse of the shtetl economy was financed by Warsaw industrialist Jan Bloch, a convert who maintained close ties to the Jewish community.[5] The tension between the big-city intellectual and the benighted shtetl masses, between the romantic vision of past glories and the observation of present squalor, between myth and reality was perhaps never so sharply drawn as in Peretz's *Travel Pictures,* the fictionalized reportage quoted above. That Peretz then did a complete about-face and began to extol the virtues of traditional piety in his neohasidic tales and stories makes sense in light of the prior revolt: the myth of the shtetl could be revived only when the actual, historical shtetl was presumed dead and only if said revival were informed by ideas foreign to the shtetl itself.

Of the writers such as Peretz and Asch who were responsible for the reaffirmation of the shtetl myth, the one most relevant to the theme of catastrophe was Sholem Aleichem (see Chapter 7). Readily acknowledging his debt to Abramovitsh, whom he deemed the grandfather of Yiddish literature, Sholem Aleichem created his own geography of eastern Europe with such fictional place names as Mazepevke, Khmielnitsk, and Gontoyarsk—each derived from another Ukrainian warrior—to suggest an unbroken tradition of enmity, a sense of past and of bloody legend.[6] In line with standard maskilic thinking, he was at first highly critical of the shtetl and its mores, but with time and distance, he came to appreciate its potential as a fictional shorthand for Jewish collective survival in exile. The fictional town of Kasrilevke emerged, in the first years of this century, as a place of hidden treasures, a Jewish mini-empire that would weather the winds of change through group solidarity and stubborn faith. Sholem Asch followed suit with a full-blown shtetl romance, an exercise in pure entertainment which enjoyed enormous popularity among young urbanized readers hungry for a sentimental myth of origins: in the beginning was the shtetl, home and haven for all.[7]

This literary transformation came just in time to register the major assaults about to be unleashed on the Jewish body politic. As the Jews of eastern Europe were increasingly shaken by dissension from within and attacked from without, the writers squared off over the fate of the shtetl. From their competing vantage points and rival languages, the intellectuals subjected the shtetl to the acid test of history. No longer the scene of satire and comic action, the shtetl became the setting for violence and existential despair. It evolved into a perfect metaphor for the rape and rehabilitation of the whole collective enterprise that was eastern European Jewry.

ABRAMOVITSH'S rebound after the pogroms of the 1880s and Bialik's indictment in the wake of Kishinev were calculated to shock Jewish sensibilities at a time of national emergency. By the same token, I. M. Weissenberg's polemically titled work *A Shtetl* hit its readers like a bombshell.[8] Less than a year had passed since the events described in the work had shaken Russian Jewry to its core: labor unrest, brutal government reprisals, and revolutionary terror had culminated in a general strike, the granting of Russia's first constitution, and then a wave of pogroms and political reaction in October of 1905. Like Abramovitsh before him, Weissenberg resisted the temptation to reflect the broad spectrum of events as they had unfolded in the cities and chose instead the limited focus of the shtetl. That even the great Sholem Aleichem succumbed to this temptation shows that the choice of novella over novel and of shtetl over city was not an easy or obvious one. With its contrived plot, its romantic triangle, and its attempt to mock the very conventions it was exploiting, Sholem Aleichem's *The Deluge* was hardly an advance over Yekutiel Berman's pogrom novel of the 1870s.[9] Weissenberg's success would prove a lesson to future writers, showing that great catastrophes were best refracted through the prism of the small town.

Since the shtetl had only recently acquired its romantic splendor, to begin the story, as Weissenberg did, with the men gathered in the house of study "between afternoon and evening prayers" was to conjure up images of a Jewish community united under God, especially as "the air was filled with anticipation for the approaching holiday" (page 29). But when, from the undifferentiated mass of men, there emerged identifiable clusters of shopkeepers, tailors, shoemakers, butchers, teachers, and finally "a knot of young men," "caps pushed to the back of their heads, oblivious to everything around them" (page 30), it was the last, surprisingly, who commanded attention. Low men on the totem pole of shtetl values, these carpenters and cobblers suddenly took a stand to protest the imposition of a monopoly on flour for the approaching holiday of Passover. Yekl, the ringleader, was shouted down and sent flying from the study house, "bareheaded, his nose running blood."

A Shtetl was a study of violence through radical politics, the first of its kind in Yiddish and Hebrew fiction. Written to challenge the romantic revival of the shtetl, Weissenberg's novella was more profoundly an all-out attack on notions of communality, on the hegemony of learning and respectability that was said to characterize traditional Jewish society, on the supposedly inexorable bond that tied Jews to other Jews, analogous to the covenant that tied them to God. In stark and carefully selected detail, *A Shtetl* documented the centrifugal forces that turned workers against the bosses, poor Jews against rich, carpenters against butchers. Once before, as we have seen, the shtetl had been torn apart, but the conflict between the kahal and the community had been induced from without and had lasted only as long as the tsarist draft decree. Class conflict and social unrest, in contrast, arose out of conditions endemic to Russia as a whole: rapid industrialization, economic instability, and political repression, not to speak of the specific disabilities enjoyed only by the Jews. For this reason the socialist revolution had an irresistible appeal to Jewish workers, first in the big cities and then in the industrializing shtetlekh. The economic base of Weissenberg's unnamed shtetl, probably patterned on his native town of Zelechow, was a type of mass-produced boot made to be "exported" to the nearest city. In return, the shtetl "imported" Marxism from Warsaw in the form of leaflets, strange-sounding slogans, and the first bona fide organizers.

Carefully balanced as to structure, the novella ends as it began, in the house of study, with Yekl claiming victory by shouting down the rabbi with a cry for pistols and revolvers instead of psalms.[10] In between, the *tshayne* (the combination teashop and tavern where the young workers congregate) becomes the nerve center of the shtetl and even its court of appeals. Within a few months of Yekl's ill-fated debut, the whole shtetl is torn by strikes. "Not for a moment that summer was the marketplace empty. One strike followed another; not a workshop or factory was spared" (page 40). The rise of the movement has been anything but smooth, however, and its future is by no means secure. Twice, the abuse of the movement's powers has led to the death and even murder of other Jews, and during the second outburst, when the socialists were in low ebb, their beating of a traitor had disastrous repercussions: "Then blows echoed through the streets for fair, as workers were pulled from their benches and dragged from their lofts. Inflamed and bloodthirsty, the men chased down their victims, and soon blood began to spurt afresh from heads already steeped in gore. The cobblestones were bathed in blood. The sky shuddered. The sun burned red, the air was thick and red. Like a great slaughterhouse, the marketplace lay smashed and bloodied" (pages 66–67).

All this is told by a dispassionate narrator who dwells on bits and pieces of external detail, on observable reality alone. A shuddering sky is as far as poetic license ever takes him. There is no room here for history or myth.[11] Individual identities dissolve into broad categories of "workers," "men," and "blows." The only moral judgment in the story is confined to a rather simple-minded cobbler named Itchele who has trouble choosing between loyalty to the PPS (Polish Socialist Party) and the Jewish Labor Bund. Limited though his consciousness might be, it is Itchele who protests whenever the movement oversteps its bounds and it is he who is privy to the following revelation:

> He started back to town, heavyhearted, but once back in the shtetl he felt even worse. Looking around the marketplace at the peaceful little houses with their windows half open, he sensed something he had never sensed before: there, beyond the shtetl, lay such a vast multitude, and here everything was so small, so puny, held together by just a dab of spit . . . It occurred to him that if the thousands out there suddenly decided to have a bit of fun—just a simple bit of peasant fun—if each of them took from the houses of the Jews no more than a couple of rotting floor boards apiece and carried them off under his arm, nothing would remain of the shtetl but an empty plot of land. (page 55)

Prompted by the sight that Sunday morning of a procession outside of town—a procession that combined the splendor of Christian pageantry with the fervor of Polish patriotism, Itchele's startling insight reaches far beyond the specific resolution to this story. Because the literary shtetl functions as a form of shorthand, its lessons carry over to the fate of eastern European Jewry as a whole. Whatever choices made and whatever bloody victories won *within* the shtetl are overwhelmed by the larger forces that descend upon it from without. At story's end, the movement is quashed overnight by a contingent of Russian soldiers who arrest all the workers and drag them off in chains. This last procession, of political prisoners, recedes into the morning mist like "a wandering black smudge," fulfilling the spirit if not the letter of Itchele's premonition. For the time being, the floor boards still remain.

Through a sleight of hand, all the violence that went into shaping modern Jewish history can be made to vanish, not by a benign presence—the way in which, let us say, the adult world steps in at the end of William Golding's *Lord of the Flies* to rescue the young pagans from one another—but by the overarching enmity of the gentile world, sometimes dressed in uniform, sometimes brightly clad in peasant garb. This is not a Zionist critique, mind you. Weissenberg's loyalites are clearly on the side of the workers, and his portrayal of the shtetl fat cats borders on caricature. Yet, although workers' solidarity is certainly an advance over the old feudal system and although the new shtetl image is predicated upon the "radical flattening of the shtetl myth," as Miron puts it, Weissenberg is also alive to the precariousness of the whole endeavor. By choosing to depict "the revolution in a glass of water," he lets two forces of destruction play themselves out: the one that disassembles the community by pitting young against old, workers against bosses, and the other that regards all classes and age groups within that community as rabble.

WHEN the Great War broke out, Jewish settlements all along the front were subject to pogroms, mass expulsions, and total destruction, whether at the hands of enemy forces or of the Russian army. The Russians, backed by local Poles, were convinced that every Jewish cellar harbored a secret telephone, that every Jewish windmill relayed messages to the Germans, that every synagogue and house of study had a secret arms cache, that every well contained hidden gold. Kangaroo courts took care of the rest. In Galicia and Bukovina, Gentiles prepared for the Russian onslaught by placing icons and crucifixes in their windows. These homes, in a grotesque reversal of Passover, were left unharmed.[12] When, for example, the Russians retook Zaleshtshik, a town in Bukovina, the icons were still in place from the pogrom of nearly two years before. Only Jewish property had been laid waste and only Jews had been expelled. The Christians now intervened with the Russian military to prevent the return of the Jews.[13] Unlike the troglodyte world of immovable trenches in the west, vast areas were won, lost, and regained in the east and each time the shtetl population paid the price.

As the war dragged on, however, ruins and refugees became a commonplace and Jews learned to live under abnormal conditions. In 1915 Ansky already sensed that apathy and degradation had become a way of life, at least in Galicia. The broken tablets of the Law—emblems of a heroic struggle—were replaced by routine degradation, as symbolized by the vanished letters. Whereas poverty had destroyed the façade of shtetl respectability when Peretz had come for a visit, and the exercise of raw power had showed the shtetl to be morally and politically vulnerable in Weissenberg's day, actual ruins lay before the next generation of writers.

Those who came of age during World War I, who spent their adolescence and young adulthood under German occupation or under the shadow of Russian terror, were filled with an overwhelming sense of sacrilege. And not, in this case because of Russian barbarity and German cruelty, but because of what had been irrevocably lost in the war—that final claim to Jewish sanctity, intimacy, and security. When all the bonds—between Jews and God, Jews and other Jews, Jews and Gentiles—seemed to have been severed, there was nothing left but to chronicle the loss.

Covenantal claims were the first to go. In Leyb Olitzky's collected war stories, the lone rabbi who lamented that the present destruction was worse than in Second Temple times because now "we're left without Torah and without good deeds, heaven help us!" was himself the butt of the author's satire.[14] The rabbi's own children had gone astray and he was portrayed, in true maskilic fashion, as a man involved in arcane halachic questions, a model of exaggerated piety with his two pairs of phylacteries. Olitzky drew an explicit link between the religious desecration and the collapse of shtetl morality: "And if we, their daughters, have become whores? And if God turned the Rebbe's house of study into a stable?" (page 268).

There is scarcely a Jewish prose account, fictional or autobiographical, that does not dwell on the pornography of the war. At best, wives and especially daughters were sent to the local commandant to finagle a permit for flour, salt, lumber, or what have you, invoking nothing more than their feminine charms. This was jocularly known as "delivering a *bitoy*," a pun on the Hebrew for "daughter" *(bat)* and the German for "petition" *(Bitte)*.[15] But to behold the most respected merchants, those who prayed in the hasidic *shtiblekh* or commanded a privileged seat in the house of study, indulging in even so innocent a form of seduction was demoralizing enough. And the thin line to outright prostitution was easily crossed. Jacob Mestel, an officer in the Austrian army, told of twelve- and thirteen-year-old girls serving the officers' needs; of a mother trying to stop her seventeen-year-old daughter from selling her body for a piece of chocolate; of a rich merchant's daughter who allowed herself to be "seduced" in her store while her husband was away at the front.[16]

The profit motive reigned supreme. In the words of Fishl Bimko's schlemiel narrator: "The war, you see, is different from an earthquake, for in an earthquake, all are swallowed up together, and in a war, this is not the case; a war doesn't do harm in equal measure—it misses some."[17] Though profit making was invariably followed by inflation, as Kalmen-Yankl the narrator-hero was quick to learn, and expulsions could come at any time, slap-dash Jewish entrepreneurs were making good on wartime scarcity as never before. And those who didn't speculate or smuggle could profit by informing on those who did.[18]

In addition, therefore, to the collapse of the religious and moral order, the ascendency of a new class of wheelers and dealers brought about a total upheaval in the accepted social order. Merchants of long standing lost all in pogroms and expropriations while former artisans, peddlers, and especially teamsters rose to instant wealth. And since the young were normally more fearless and adventuresome than the old, the patriarchal structure collapsed as well. Olitzky's *In an Occupied Shtetl* showed how the war disrupted the last vestige of family unity.[19] The novel began as one family abandoned its crazy daughter to the advancing Austrian army—only to return home to her. The father proved to be a selfish, ineffectual, and inflexible man: he denied help to his own father caught in a pogrom, but was afraid to go into partnership with his brother in smuggling. The sensitive young hero discovered half the shtetl living off *heymishe parnoses* (domestic livelihoods)—that is, selling their daughters to the Germans for whatever favors they could offer. In another episode, a father fled without his son when the two of them were caught threshing stolen flour.

The entire medieval structure collapsed as fathers turned against sons and daughters, wives against husbands, and, most startling of all, Jews against peasants. Since the mandate of the critical realists was not to lament the external persecution as much as to unmask the process of internal decay, the most damning bit of evidence Olitzky could bring was to show Jews preying upon their Christian neighbors:

> Jews cleaned up the abandoned property after the goyim, who were torn, like deeply rooted trees in a hurricane, from their settlements of long standing by their exaggerated fear of the enemy:
>
> "Why, they cut your tongues out, those damned Germans!"
>
> The Jews had a good laugh at this gentile credulity. Serves them right! And as they busily collected the inheritance that was left to them involuntarily, they shook their heads half in sympathy and half in jest:
>
> "If Esau only knew how things would turn out!"[20]

The war, it seems, had made the shtetl more Jewish—and less so. The truly indigenous, gentile population fled, leaving only the most debased specimens: the thief, the Goy-for-the Sabbath, and their ilk; but Jewish greed for their abandoned wealth turned to total demoralization. From hoarding food, stealing furniture, stripping gentile houses bare, and hauling wheat on the Sabbath, the shtetl Jews worked themselves up to robbing the Greek Orthodox Churck. A delegaton of lowly peasants finally appeared before the rabbi to protest this sacrilege, pleading their case in broken Yiddish. Gentile faith, in case the reader missed the point of this grotesque story, proved more constant than that of Jews who resumed their criminal activities once Yom Kippur was over. As far as Olitzky was concerned, Jews had forefeited their claim even to being victims of catastrophe.

Choice of genre and the earlier literary attack on the shtetl dictated much of this condemnatory tone. Olitzky's shtetl was Mendele's geography revisited. In a story called "Off to Work," Olitzky contrasted the obscene intimacy of the shtetl bathhouse, the wild pleasure Jews took in the cacophony of voices and the intense heat, with their total inability to do physical, albeit forced, labor.[21] The scene was reminiscent of the bathhouse of Glupsk. Bimko's Kalmen-Yankl was a poor imitation of Sholem Aleichem's arch-schlemiel Menakhem-Mendl, the one who left Mazepevke-Kasrilevke never to return. It was Weissenberg's example, however, that inspired the most outstanding shtetl novella of the First World War, Oyzer Warshawski's *Smugglers.*[22]

If Weissenberg's shtetl strikers were reduced to faceless mobs propelled by the cycles of growing violence, Warshawski's smugglers were examples of raw sexuality: every action emanated from their physical desires. As in Weissenberg, the grand scheme of destruction and redemption was relegated to the background, and not till story's end did history intrude upon the best-laid plans of very mortal men. Warshawski can also be located within the larger tradition of critical realism, with his focus on the animal in man, his transcription of vulgar speech, his focus on a spectrum of three characters in lieu of a central hero, his beginning *in medias res* during the German occupation (rather than beginning with the Guns of August or with a Jewish soldier returning, or deserting, from the front), and, finally, with his Naturalist determinism that saw heredity and environment governing all of man's behavior.[23]

Both the structure of *Smugglers* and its image of the shtetl are defined by the rise, consolidation, and decline of smuggling.[24] We begin modestly enough, in the muddled brain of Pantl the Teamster, who hits upon a plan to smuggle basic commodities to the starving capital of Warsaw. Eventually this burgeons into the mainstay of the shtetl economy (with bootlegging as an important sideline). A change of such magnitude does not come easily, of course, and Warshawski leads us through the transition with a brilliant eye for significant detail, picking up at the very point where Peretz left off back in 1890.

"That's what things were like, once," ruminates a patchwork tailor, who ranks even lower than a cobbler or carpenter on the social scale of the shtetl.

> In the good old days, when there was peace on earth and a pound of fine rye bread cost just five kopecks . . . "Once upon a time . . ." That's all disappeared like a dream, a nightmare, since the war's broken out—"Because of our many sins," as Yitskhok-Yoyne the tailor would add. Nowadays! Who does any work nowadays? Who orders any clothes? Business has just died off. Everybody's into buying and selling . . . It's as bad as can be. So what can you do about it? (page 48)

These thoughts on the shtetl economy present and past—the only sense of the past the shtetl still harbors—inspire the tailor to start an illegal distillery.

The same economic considerations that drive Yitskhok-Yoyne to bootlegging and motivate Pantl the Teamster to take up smuggling affect the old moneyed class as well; the daughters of tailor and salt merchant alike are pressed into service as sexual bait. The movement, in other words, is toward greater similarity among all strata of shtetl society as smuggling erases the line first between classes, then between the sexes. When Fayvke, the leader of the young smugglers, pays his girlfriend Reytshe a visit, he is met with this unforgettable tableau:

> Reytshe stands naked, facing away from them, and wraps herself with pieces of bloody meat. She wraps them around her breasts, around her stomach and around her legs. The flat pieces of cool wet meat stick to her warm skin and steam forms instantly . . . It is a horrible sight: a naked person, wrapped with strips of raw meat; it looks like someone is being flayed alive . . .
>
> "Reytshe!" cries out Grunem [her brother], and to Fayvke: "Look, do you see what a moneymaker she is?"
>
> And Fayvl begins to respect Reytshe, and she seems to him somehow different, on a higher plane than he: "Who would think of looking [for contraband] on a body?" (pages 86–87)

What makes this scene so disturbing, beyond its obvious shock value and the analogy it suggests between the exploitation of the human body for profit and the outright forms of prostitution soon to be introduced into the shtetl, is the curious contradiction between the fatness of the meat and the image of being stripped beyond the skin. The new realism of writers such as Warshawski carries with it a modern emphasis on sensation (as opposed to mind), on the touch, smell, sight, and sound of violence. The truest image, in such a scheme, is the one whose very extremity—of a nakedness beyond the skin, of animal passions in human garb—upsets the façade of civility. This brings us to the ultimate merger effected by the new culture of smuggling: the merger of Jews and Gentiles. Three Polish whores are brought in from Warsaw to divert the German guards along the road, and soon these "business partners" displace the wives of the Jewish smugglers in bed.

Smuggling is the great leveler, an almost cataclysmic force that breaks down old barriers and inhibitions. With a stroke of artistic genius and a sly nod to Abramovitsh (whose *Wishing Ring* contained a similar scene), Warshawski telescopes the entire transformation of the shtetl into a single image: Pantl's wagon on its way from the shtetl to Warsaw.

> Smuggling engulfed the shtetl like a flame, taking hold everywhere, crawling, sniffing and cleaning out every nook and cranny. Among those now making the

trip you can find not only such [innocents] as Dovidl and Shayke, but also a student. Say he needs to exchange or buy a textbook in Warsaw. He packs, covering the contraband with his books and breaks even in the process. As soon as he sees that textbooks are a good business, he starts making the trip three times a week. Otherwise he would sit home all day—"the studies aren't going well" . . . And the shtetl's only private tutor also makes the trip. He's a salaried official of the kahal, who used to keep the books for the credit union that doesn't exist anymore, since the war broke out, so his wife has to mend underwear to supplement their income. And even the dayyan's [rabbinical judge's] daughter makes the trip—an unmarried girl . . . It's really not proper. Such a fine specimen—how does she come to Pantl's wagon? But what can you do about it? (pages 171–72)

All the members of the shtetl intelligentsia—sometimes after tortuous rationalizaton—swallow their pride to join with the low life and the local peasants.

And not only Jews make the trip, the goyim do too, not to mention them in the same breath. In the beginning, the gentile women traveled alone and left their daughters to clean house, to cook meals for the toddlers; but later, when things looked good, and the more hands the merrier, they started taking their daughters along and they would carry the goods in groups of two or three. The mothers had in mind only the business, but no sooner do the daughters set out on the road than they jump down from the wagon, adorn their hair with flowers and things, so frivolous they are, and when they jump back on, their eyes meet the lusty glances of the Jewish and gentile boys, the way things always work on Pantl's and Kopl's wagons. (pages 172-173)

But all is not harmony en route to Warsaw. Parental bonds are easily severed in this licentious atmosphere, and peasant mothers soon find themselves estranged from their daughters. "And so they do their smuggling separately. They even hide their profits in separate places. A daughter has no knowledge of her mother, nor the mother of her daughter" (page 173).

Of all the new institutions that have risen from the ruins of shtetl society—the cultural club where young Jews gather for lectures and dances, Yitskhok-Yoyne's speakeasy, the cellar that doubles as a whorehouse—the wagon represents the shtetl's great triumph, worthy of the Polish anthem the Jewish smugglers have composed in its honor. For it is the shtetl that now feeds Warsaw, not the other way around, and shtetl wagons have supplanted the trains where the risk of confiscation is so much greater. But like the culture clubs and speakeasies, the wagon contains within it the seed of its own destruction. Sexual anarchy, generational dislocation, and the rule of passion are the price of economic success.

Pantl's son Mendl turns against his father when both take a fancy to

Natshe, the youngest of the three whores from Warsaw. The cellar resounds with their blows which poor Natshe is helpless to stop, and even the Polish militia is shocked by what it sees. On the following Sabbath the air in the study house is thick with vicarious sexuality: "Some of the [more observant] young men, with pale faces and blue rings under their restless eyes, would give anything to know who this broad was, exactly . . . could it be the tart with the blue eyes and blond curls? And at the very thought of her the corners of their mouths grow moist and they begin swaying with great fervor, each time banging up against the lectern in front of their noses" (page 140). Father and son are finally reunited by their mutual hatred for the shtetl fat cat, and the study house explodes with violence—dividing the shtetl along the more familiar lines of old money against new. Similarly, when the rabbi tries to close down the cultural club as a hotbed of heresy, he succeeds only in turning the young against the religious establishment.

Despite Yitskhok-Yoyne's defiant cry "To hell with the honest groschen, hurrah for the crooked ruble!" (page 237), and despite the fact that the leadership passes from Mendl to his younger brother Urke, signaling the regeneration of the smugglers, the new shtetl order is soon to be destroyed by events in the world at large. Exactly as in Weissenberg's account, the Gentiles gain the upper hand and shatter the illusion of Jewish power. Russia sues for peace, the Germans evacuate and suddenly a Polish Military Organization is formed—exclusively from the ranks of the local Christian populace. Try as the smugglers may to dispel the gloom by staging a wedding and reviving their anthem, the sexual, moral, and political contradictions leave little doubt as to their ultimate fate. Once again, the shtetl has won a Pyrrhic victory.

WHAT form the final collapse of the shtetl would take was now guided by the political misfortunes of eastern Europe. In postwar Poland and Galicia (annexed to Poland after 150 years of separation), the slow economic strangulation of the shtetl contrasted with a breathless activity in the political, social, and cultural life of the Jews. On the eastern side of the Polish-Soviet border, the attack on the shtetl was brutal and swift. Since the Bolsheviks had signed the death warrant of the market economy and since the Ukraine had become the revolution's Armageddon, the destruction of the Ukrainian shtetl was both inevitable and irreversible. Even if the Red Army were to step in at the eleventh hour and avert the pogrom, the shtetl and all its concomitant values of group solidarity, traditional hierarchy, and transcendental faith were marked for destruction from within. This sabotage could not be resisted with bribes, sexual or otherwise; would not be resolved when the bosses granted a ten-hour day; would not be relieved if some of the more destitute emigrated to America. The revolutionary assault would be carried out by the sons and daughters of the shtetl. They would know best how to add insult to injury, how to combine inner and outer dimensions of sacrilege. Never were the sides so unevenly matched, with the young, free-thinking, armed proletarians pitted against the old, starving, traditionalist "bourgeoisie." The only question was: Who would destroy it first, the native sons or the Ukrainian nationalists?

Just as the fate of the shtetl was divided between east and west, no single voice would speak for its future. It is fair to say that by 1920 the cultural hegemony of Jewish eastern Europe had broken down once and for all. The great bilingual and trilingual writers were rapidly fading from the scene—Peretz (1915), Sholem Aleichem (1916), Abramovitsh (1917), Ansky (1920), and Berdichewsky (1921)—to be replaced by a fourth and then a fifth (postwar) generation whose politics also dictated its choice of language. The result was a strict division of labor between Yiddish and Hebrew letters of the interbellum period, the former preoccupied with the economic collapse of the shtetl and the latter with its crisis of faith. Yiddish writers, following the example of Weissenberg and Warshawski, were firmly lodged in the marketplace; Hebrew writers, picking up on Bialik and Berdichewsky, were reluctant to venture beyond the houses of prayer and study. As the distance between the writer and the shtetl increased, these differences became more pronounced. From Berlin and Kharkov came the Marxist critique of the shtetl, led by Bergelson and Markish respectively, while the Hebrew-Zionist writers Hazaz, Yaari, and Agnon looked back in anguish from the remove of Paris, New York, and Jerusalem. Neither side, however, doubted the final outcome. Whether one believed in imminent world revolution or hoped for Jewish national sovereignty—either way the old center was doomed to extinction.

By coding catastrophe through the image of the shtetl, the novelists arrived at results analogous to those of the poets. At the poets' hands, the pogrom had been divested of its convenantal trappings, but its sense had been expanded to include the aesthetic, sensual, psychological, political, and philosophical realms. The pogrom, in effect, regained its archetypal stature, no longer needing a specific terrain or cast of characters to be operative. Similarly, the fictional attack that aimed at cutting the shtetl down to size revealed, paradoxically, its ongoing relevance. The smallness and self-containment of the shtetl, that which made it such a perfect vehicle for the exploration of the Diaspora Jew acting as a collective, alerted the novelists early on to its essential vulnerability, and they, in turn, became the first to chart the ultimate disaster. World War I, the Russian Revolution, and ensuing civil war created a triptych of destruction, redemption, and destruction which brought the question of Jewish survival to the fore. When the shtetl was focused on, to the exclusion of the cities or the larger geopolitical scene, total destruction suddenly became a real possibility.

The focusing process, as already noted, took many years to perfect. Abramovitsh had fixed his unrelenting gaze on the inner dynamics of the traditional community and predicted that when Pauperville burned to the ground, the centrifugal force of Jewish catastrophe would bring ruin to the entire Pale of Settlement. Weissenberg, writing a decade later, saw class conflict as the catalyst of disorder, wreaking havoc while greater danger gathered on the sidelines. Another decade passed and the shtetl was overrun and abandoned. To recoup its losses under German occupation, the shtetl reunited in a common front of greed and depravity, giving even the peasants a run for their money. Built on quicksand, Warshawski argued, this solidarity needed but a sudden jolt, such as the German retreat, for the whole shtetl underground to be swallowed up—smugglers, bootleggers, informers, and all. Then came the long-awaited revolution, which drove a permanent wedge between the vanguard of the new and the enemies of progress. The shtetl found itself cast in the role of villain.

If the shtetl stood in the way of progress, there was no point to mourning its loss. Those Jewish writers who welcomed the revolution, for reasons too complicated to enumerate here, had to weigh the fate of the shtetl against the universal class struggle. How they floundered, trying to find some rationale for the destruction!

In the anti-Bolshevik stage of his career, David Bergelson once fell back on a mythic scheme, sketching the pogroms in one of his stories as a timeless conflict between Gentiles and Jews;[25] but he later disavowed this story and never collected it.[26] Instead, the shtetl appeared almost as an afterthought at the end of his unfinished novel *Civil War,* the saga of a Bolshevik peasant named Botchko.[27] As Petlura's armies closed in, "the desperate town sought someone in the cold skies and found nothing, just a vast emptiness," while down below, "Alexandrovka repudiated Leyzerke [the local Jewish Bolshevik] and let it be known in the strongest terms that Leyzerke was no longer one of them" (page 118). Not until Botchko had driven the enemy off did the shtetl turn to Leyzerke, "the bonesetter's son," for help. And if the Revkom (the Revolutionary Committee) resorted to extreme measures, as in "A Tale about Rich Men," when it demanded a five million ruble tribute from the town it had just rescued from destruction, there was surely a lesson to be learned.[28] The poorest shtetl Jews threw in their last to stay the execution of evil Reb Vove, the rich man who had exploited them, proving that solidarity could be found only among honest labor, while the Revkom, for its part, was only kidding—proving, in this heavy-handed Purim farce, that the ends justified the means. By 1926, when Bergelson was firmly "locked into step" (the name of a pro-Soviet journal he edited), he portrayed the shtetl as a haven for smugglers and for counterrevolutionaries over whom "the firm hand of justice" would ultimately prevail.[29]

Peretz Markish, who joined up before Bergelson, tempered the scenario of destruction with a curious blend of Jewish and revolutionary romanticism. In the first part of his novel *The Generations Come and Go*, the father, Mendl the Miller, intervened on the shtetl's behalf in an apotheosis of self-sacrifice.[30] The feast he catered for the Ukrainian commander saved the shtetl from destruction but did not save him. Ezra, his son, arrived too late with the Red Army contingent. And so, it was the generational scheme of martyrdom that assured continuity even as the social, economic, and religious bases of Jewish life were laid waste.

Bergelson, who turned Jewish solidarity into a Marxist joke, and Markish, who would make of his "folk Jew" a hero at any price, hit close to home despite their professed ideology. Beneath the rhetoric of revolutionary supremacy lay the horrible, irreducible truth—that only catastrophe would reunite the shtetl on the eve of its actual destruction. Hayim Hazaz, a thirty-four-year-old Hebrew writer on his way out of this self-destructing universe, was the first to see it in its true apocalyptic light:

> "THE UNCLEAN SPIRIT . . . SHALL he make VANISH FROM THE LAND (Zech. 13:2) . . . THROUGH THE GREAT FIRE SHALL THEY PASS, AND MAY THEY PASS THROUGH THE SEA OF AFFLICTION (Zech. 10:11)! AND HE SHALL MAKE THE EARTH SHAKE AND THE PILLARS THEREOF TREMBLE (Job 9:6) . . . YOU SHALL BE A DESOLATE WILDERNESS (Joel 4:19) AND THE NAME OF ISRAEL SHALL BE REMEMBERED NO MORE (Ps. 83:5)! Long live the International!"[31]

Except for the final note of affirmation, it would be impossible to identify as a young shtetl revolutionary the person uttering these prophetic denunciations in their original Hebrew. It couldn't be Mendele up to his old tricks, because Mendele never sallied quite so directly. Then again, Mendele never had a gun, whereas Motl Pyekelne, the young revolutionary whose last name means the back part of a stove, took the mandate of the revolution into his own hands and aimed it against his own people. Ordering the pious Jews of the shtetl to sweep the streets on the first day of the Passover festival was hardly what Zechariah had in mind when he railed against the false prophets, and Motl's perverse application of Scriptural authority was aptly rebutted by a counterquotation. The shtetl Jews reaffirmed *their* allegiance even as they were forced to desecrate the holiday: "MY VOWS TO THE LORD I WILL PAY IN THE PRESENCE OF ALL HIS PEOPLE, IN THE COURTS OF THE LORD'S HOUSE, IN THE MIDST OF JERUSALEM, HALLELUJAH (from the Hallel; Ps. 116:18–19)."

In this face-off between perversity and traditional piety, unlike in the earlier rounds between Mendele and Pauperville, the reader's sympathy goes out to the embattled collective, not to the embittered rebel. Yet Hayim Hazaz rigged the fight to make it more interesting. In his story, Motl is only one—among the least sympathetic, in fact—of a number of rebels who read the words of revelation as an apocalyptic code, whose certainty in their own election gives them license to transform society in anticipation of the imminent end. Like the Jews of Qumran or like the kabbalists of Safed, this small group of initiates devises its own sacred texts. Unmarried men and women live together, their bathhouse lodgings or their communist club becoming the center of religious fervor, a surrogate *shtibl* and Temple in one; they drink late into the night, singing revolutionary anthems, and then go carousing in the snow. The formerly sleeply, neglected shtetl is suddenly turned into a battlefield for competing messianic stategies. The protagonists include Polishuk, the uncompromising Bolshevik, who in a moment of ecstasy throws himself into the frozen river, like a fervent kabbalist; Sorokeh ("the magpie"), who acts on the coming anarchy by burning down all the squires' mansions; Henia, the tip of the romantic triangle, who celebrates the revolution as the "total redemption"; and Shmuel Frankfurter, the apostle of brotherly love. Even Jews still rooted in tradition are not immune to the redemptive fever: Motl Privisker the hasid will spout Lurianic kabbalah and prophetic eschatology, inspired by his ever more frequent bouts with the bottle; and Reb Ber joins up with the young revolutionaries out of a deep affinity for Shmuel Frankfurter. Nature, too, invokes the language of tradition in order to proclaim the total revocation of the old:

> The storms spread out—long, dangling, crooked, blinding, and round—and they blasted and blew [*tak'u veheri'u*] about freedom on earth and about the end of the redemption; about Amens once answered with voices loud and joyous that had since grown silent; about the trilling song and psalm with which congregants, once upon a time, backed up their leader of prayer; about festival feasts that had been disrupted; about grooms and marital honors that had been abrogated—about the Jewish pulse that had gone dead.[32]

Until now, nature presided over the rites and ceremonies of the eternal people, joined in its celebrations and confirmed its cyclical rhythms. The fact that nature still speaks in a Jewish idiom, something it has been doing on the record at least since Mendele's day, is highly deceptive, for nature is now throwing her malevolent force behind global renewal. It will be a clean sweep, regardless of Judaism's former splendor; witness the fate of Motl Privisker, who at that very moment is using the cover of the storm to hide his merchandise and will eventually be exposed and uprooted.

However interpreted, the liturgical echoes augur ill. Pulsing beneath the rhetorical surface is the ancient drumbeat of hunger, desecration, expropriation, and eternal present; in this small-scale revolutionary battle raging within the confines of each family within each shtetl, older patterns reemerge and reaffirm the terrors of the past. At the end of the first story in Hazaz's trilogy, Motl Pyekelne discovers an enemy who does not honor the distinction between proletarian and bourgeois Jews, between the living Communist International (recall his opening words) and the threatened name of Israel.[33] To save his own skin, Motl perforce becomes the savior of the shtetl. In "Chapters from the Revolution," a Jewish militia organizes to meet the common enemy—only to be demobilized by the Russian Army in retreat.[34] The story ends with the Germans' sudden return and the shtetl helpless to act in its own defense. At the very moment the revolutionaries achieve their highest pitch of self-transcendence in "Shmuel Frankfurter," Reb Ber proposes a toast to Petlura, "who irrigated the land with the blood of Israel, the blood of old and young, men and women, all of them saintly and pure!"[35] None of those assembled is then able to drink.

In Hazaz's scheme, the shtetl and its revolutionary cadres become more archetypal the closer they come to catastrophe. Ukrainian peasants kill two of Shmuel's friends before the pogrom is called off, and the shtetl fears the worst. "Like bound calves lying in the darkness, the houses of the shtetl stood bound by the winds, the terror, and the sadness. An ancient fear, this terrible garb of Israel, covered the town from the day of the funeral onward" (page 122). Each night its sleep is marred by symbols of martyrdom, such as the heavenly altar on which the souls of the righteous are slaughtered; and by signs of the apocalypse, such as Armilus, the Wandering Jew—fearful apparitions, all. And the hero of this story, the apostle of brotherly love, is predestined to die in the final act of terror, just like his ancient archetype.

Everything else then falls into place. The Bolsheviks abandon the shtetl just before Passover, assuring a massacre at the proper hour. The White Army general, an expert on Jewish sources, acts in accordance with Jeremiah's prophecy and decimates the town, so that Rachel may properly weep for her children. Shmuel Frankfurter, guilty of being both a Jew and a Bolshevik, is crucified outside the town.

Looking back on the brave new shtetl world, Hazaz concluded that Jews had failed once more to hasten the global redemption. Their selfless struggle had been for nought, and in their haste to throw off the burden of the past—the Pharisaic law, the forms of Jewish joy and celebration—they had laid their own helplessness bare. So the trilogy closed on a bitterly ironic note, with the local peasants—unwilling partners to that redemption—creating a new syncretistic religion around the altar of Jewish self-sacrifice. They transformed Shmuel's gravesite into a holy shrine, hailing him as the messiah. Beyond that, the Jews had lost the shtetl too. It would no longer house either the old Temple or the new. All its dreamers, prophets, and profaners had been abandoned to the storm.

AS the end drew nearer, Jewish writers harked increasingly back to the beginning, until ends and beginnings started to blur. Even though, as we have seen, the response to catastrophe no longer implied—in its use of archetypes—the same theological arguments or the same redemptive faith, the old archetypes continued to resurface with new meanings attached. The novelists, whose point of departure was the actual, observable community, discovered the great importance of the covenantal claims of Jewish catastrophe. After Weissenberg and Warshawski, one would not have expected ever to hear the shtetl referred to in mythic terms again. But the redemptive promise of revolution, followed so swiftly by the fear of total destruction, gave the old symbols a fearful new vitality. What the class struggle did not split asunder with apocalyptic fury, the wrath of the Gentiles would finish off. Even if all the shtetl's wayward children were to close ranks in the face of destruction, its last stand would be theirs too.

Once disabused of the great revolutionary hope, Jewish writers found pitifully few options still open. The attempt to create a surrogate shtetl on the ruins of the old way of life—to build, say, a Jewish commune on Polish soil—was no more likely to succeed than the ideal communist state, a lesson I. J. Singer's hero learned the hard way.[36] Abstracting the revolution into radical messianism, younger brother I. B. Singer showed how the Sabbatian heresy transformed the shtetl into a seventeenth-century Polish Sodom. If we read *Satan in Goray* as a shtetl novella of the 1930s,[37] surely one possible interpretation among many, we see how the revolution, born of postwar chaos, gave free rein to violence, hatred, raw sexuality, and self-destruction, until all that could save the shtetl from itself was the imposition of God's will, the rigid conformity to religious belief and virtue.[38] "For the impulse of man's heart is evil from his youth" (Gen. 8:21) was Singer's working hypothesis, and if Stalin didn't clinch the case, Hitler surely would.

Those who were trapped in Poland discovered exactly how forsaken the shtetl really was. In the short span of six years, between his first shtetl novella and his last, Mikhoel Burshtin charted the shrinking universe of Polish Jewry. *Over the Ruins of Ployne* (1931) ended with the hero's father leaving the shtetl for Palestine to the sounds of Hatikva interrupted by a Bundist anthem, while the hero himself reserved judgment as to which of these alternatives would save the collective.[39] Framed by two cemeteries, *By the Rivers of Mazovia* (1937) began with the brotherhood of man in the rows of crosses, the mass graves, and the stars of David in the military graveyard of World War I, and ended with the two protagonists swearing to rebuild the shtetl as they stand by the graves of their beloved, killed in a pogrom. This pitiful graveside ritual, this attempt to consecrate the living by venerating the dead, could hardly dispel the overwhelming sense of impending doom. Writing the second novel partly in response to the recent pogrom in Przytyk (1936), all mention of which was banned by the Polish government, Burshtin was not even free to call it by its name. Thus, in what may be the most bizarre instance of "persecution and the art of writing,"[40] Burshtin referred to his fictional town of Smolin as Sa-ma-lin, the pogrom as a "typhoon," and the Polish rioters as coolies!

Smolin was actually quite a funny place, where, for instance, the rabbi's daughter was an expert on Freud who busily psychoanalyzed her own and her father's inhibitions. "At the edge of the abyss," wrote Itsik Manger in 1939, "even laughter becomes desperate."[41] With an eye for comic discrepancy, Burshtin noted how things got better fo- the world at large, while shtetl Jews reverted of necessity to their old way of life:

> There are many things in town which the Smoliner [Jews] make do without. They make do without radios, which every Smolin official has in his home. They make do without the public baths that City Hall put up. Even the young people who once stopped at nothing to institute a new order in Smolin, now make do without books, because the library they assembled over these eighteen years is taking a rest in some cellar or other. The Smoliner, who tasted worldly pleasures for so brief a time, became avid penny-pinchers once more. A Smoliner learned to live on a gulden a day, on half a gulden, even on no gulden at all. And in other areas too: in their clothing, their food, and in their walks (only on certain streets . . .) there are two Smolins.[42]

What Burshtin could not have known is that this retrograde movement back to preindustrial time, back to a ghettoized existence, would culminate in total destruction, in the eradication of the shtetl from the map and its Jews from living memory.

Zionism was the last hope, and it is to Zionist writers that we must look for any visible assurances of continuity. For in their personal attempt to retrieve the shtetl out of distant childhood memories, Hebrew novelists Yehuda Yaari and S. Y. Agnon were also acting on a central impulse of Zionist ideology: the desire to resegregate the Jews, to translate medieval notions of corporate autonomy into a modern nation state, to rehabilitate the Kehillah in the face of renewed anti-Semitism and the failure of emancipation.[43] A mysterious line links the medieval ghetto to the shtetl and thence to the Yishuv (the Jewish settlement in Palestine). Each is a construct of collective survival and each is built upon the one before. Thus, the shtetl novella circles back on itself, as one corporate entity gives rise to another; thus, the pogrom poem by dint of progressive expansion, comes to encompass the possibility of an all-out pogrom. Literary continuities seem to have some bearing on historical reality.

The Zionist image of the shtetl is the more attenuated from reality for its being a deliberate projection on the part of the author—but is also the more precious because it is the only thing left of the past that can be preserved for the future. When Yaari and Agnon measure their respective towns in terms of Jerusalem, their purpose is not to deflate or deprecate, but to redeem the shtetl for themselves and for their people. The measure is fairer now than it was in maskilic times because Jerusalem too is earth-bound, finite, open to attack. Both writers read their lives as a map of Jewish history, and cutting through the center of both is the great divide of World War I. "This war has changed the world's order," Yaari's narrator explains to his father. "It has separated us by a thousand generations."[44] Agnon's narrator returns to a home he can barely recognize, so vast is the damage to life and property wrought by the war. Here the similarities end. Yaari works backward in a sweet retrospective from the springtime of rebirth—his adult life on the outskirts of Jerusalem—to the "autumn" of his childhood in the burning shtetl.[45] Agnon's persona, in contrast, is caught between "nostalgia and nightmare," between the town of Shibush in its glory (his lost childhood and youth) and Shibush in decline, precisely mirrored in his midlife crisis.[46]

Nothing in Shibush (the name means "trifle" in Yiddish and "confusion" in Hebrew) has escaped the trials and traumas of World War I. All roads lead back to those terrible years: "But even when they do not mention the pogroms or the war, they do mention things that had happened to them in those days, for instance, how a man succeeded in snatching some sleep in the middle of a battle, or bringing a jug of milk to a child whose mother had been hit by a bullet while she was nursing him."[47] Much of the narrator's book, his ostensible reportage of a year spent as "a guest for the night" in the shtetl of his youth, is a chronicle of human suffering. Everyone has a horror story to narrate, whether it be Mrs. Bach and Freida (nicknamed the Kaiser's Wife) telling their Jewish mother's saga, or Daniel Bach who lost his faith and his leg during the war. The memory of sacrilege is reinforced by the landscape. The holy places have been plundered and left desolate. Mosses red as blood have sprouted on the King's Well in the center of town, "as if the Angel of Death had wiped his knife on them" (page 2). No one can forget the gratuitous hatred and cruelty of the Gentiles toward the Jews and of men toward men. The narrator, too, sees his life as sandwiched between two destructions. "The first destruction was abroad and the second in the Land of Israel; but when my house was destroyed abroad, I accepted the justice of the verdict and said: It is my punishment for choosing to live outside the Land" (page 207). Few can claim Shibush as their home, for "in these days, the towns of Poland are used to shedding their inhabitants by stealth, a few today and a few tomorrow, and one group does not grieve for the other; nor, of course does one group envy the other" (pages 20–21). Those who stay remain there to be buried, and while they live they do not procreate. Dispersed, exhausted, and traumatized, the people of Shibush have allowed the destruction to take its toll.

Shibush is all the dead towns in Yiddish and Hebrew fiction, including Agnon's own fictional construct from the very beginning of his career.[48] The graveyard is the only place that really thrives. "Grave literally touches grave—not as in the town, where there are many places free between one house and the next" (page 82). Given Agnon's concern for the moral and religious crisis of eastern European Jewry, the market makes only a perfunctory appearance, in chapter 32, as a place that is always empty. The surface panorama of Jewish folkways, the so-called mimetic layer of the shtetl's image, is totally fragmented. Two chapters (34 and 35) devoted to "the houses of prayer in our town" actually expose the extreme divisiveness and petty squabbling among the various hasidic dynasties, the schisms upon schisms that produce a plethora of competing quorums. The inhabitants know all about the myth of their shtetl as Kehillah Kedoshah, even without the proddings of their penitent sons: "These tourists stay in fine great cities, and travel about all over the world, and they tell us to stay here where we are, where our fathers prayed, so that we should have the privilege of dying as holy martyrs and win the world's praises by showing what fine people the Jews are, who willingly accept suffering and die for the glory of God" (page 13). And as for those modern ideologies, including the author's own, that inform the making and debunking of the shtetl myth, socialists and Zionists present an unbroken record of failure.

Shibush has its share of political parties, ranging from the anarchists, socialists, and myriad brands of Zionists to the ultraorthodox anti-Zionists. "It cannot be said that Shibush lacked idealists," the narrator concludes with his usual tongue-in-cheek, "but between ourselves, how much did it cost" (page 326). Zionism occupies a middle ground by virtue of its dual character—its call for revolutionary change was couched in the most familiar terms of faith and solidarity: Jerusalem, Erets Yisrael, the Return to Zion. This was both the source of Zionism's appeal to the Jews of Poland [49] and the source of its weakness; anyone could espouse the cause without actually lifting a finger. Examples of such armchair Zionism abound in Agnon's Shibush.

It is the young, of course, who respond to the revolutionary call of Zionism, though here, too, Shibush's record is mixed. The fate of the two Yeruhams, both of whom settled in Palestine, fairly sums it up: Yeruham Bach was killed in the Arab riots of 1929, whereas Yeruham Hofshi (Freeman) returned home in anger. Early in the story the narrator visits his "comrades in the Diaspora"—the members of the Gordonia group, whose clubhouse, appropriately enough, is raised above the shtetl streets so that one must "ascend" to its portals. "The ascent is not difficult, for after all there are only five small steps, but the top one is shaky, and you must take care not to be alarmed, for alarm can lead you to stumble" (page 100). Their clubhouse, like every other pretense in Shibush, actually points to the shtetl's decline, with its rickety staircase, its dark interior, its windows that look out only on ruins. It is not a house but a warehouse; not even that, but a converted warehouse, and those who use it long to see something that lies far beyond the shtetl.

This tragicomic description is followed by a lead passage that brings together the oldest and newest shtetl institutions:

> There are pious men in this country who have built themselves Houses of Study, and they boast that when our holy Messiah reveals himself he will come first to their House of Study. These young men, on the other hand, do not boast that the Messiah will come to them first; they do not mention him, but most of their thoughts are devoted to going up to the Land of Israel and cultivating the soil. I do not know which are the more worthy of love: the pious in the Diaspora who wish to trouble the Messiah to come and visit them abroad, or these young men who take the trouble to go up to the Land of Israel to prepare it for him. (pages 100-101)

Eventually the narrator *will* choose, but not before he rescues something of the House of Study to take back with him to the Land of Israel. For according to Agnon, Zionism in and of itself cannot sustain the people, even on the Land (witness the fate of Yeruham Freeman and of the narrator himself, who has twice left the Land). Therefore the ruins of the Diaspora that stand as an emblem of loss also intimate a holiness that must be salvaged at all costs.

At the center of the shattered image of Agnon's shtetl is the old house of study. In the language of Jewish literature, ever since Bialik, the Beit Midrash, or *besmedresh,* was the requisite backdrop whenever a writer wished to explore the individual's struggle with God and the crisis of tradition.[50] We have already seen what Weissenberg and Warshawski did to burlesque that convention. Agnon's narrator makes his way there on the morning of Yom Kippur, soon after his arrival. Like the Great Synagogue he prayed in the night before, the Beit Midrash is a shadow of its former self. Denuded of its sacred books, it is gradually losing its population too. But in contrast to Bialik's "Eternal Student," who was drawn to the light outside the House of Study, to nature and beauty, Agnon's narrator perceives a wonderful luminescence emanating from *both* directions, "a light such as you have never seen in your lives, one light made up of many luminosities" (page 11) that draws him back to the deserted room and inspires his efforts at renewal. For the narrator's return to Shibush on the eve of Yom Kippur signals an act of *teshuvah,* of penitence and reaffirmation, and the serenity he finds only in the House of Study eventually grows into a love for his people in exile. Similarly, the key to the Beit Midrash, which the narrator receives by default, the key which is misplaced and replaced, given, and finally locked away, become the narrator's sole means of salvaging the Torah, the core of meaningful human existence. Midrashic layers underlie the allegorical message. The Temple keys, which the priests had returned to heaven during the Great Destruction and of which (in my understanding) multiple copies were reentrusted to synagogues in Kehillot Kodesh throughout the lands of the Jewish dispersion were now, in the aftermath of the Great War and on the eve of a still greater destruction, to be transported back to their original home and locked away for safekeeping in Jerusalem, until such time as the Temple was rebuilt.

The hope of spiritual rehabilitation through a duplicate key to an Old House of Study in a fictional shtetl in Poland is not much in the way of consolation. But Agnon's method is midrashic, bringing Torah and catastrophe, Israel and Poland, the narrator and the shtetl, into bold juxtaposition. Each pair is reciprocally enlightening: even as the Torah, Israel, and the narrator's sense of personal identity give new meaning to the life-and-death struggle of the Polish shtetl, so in turn does the shtetl live on through the Torah, the Land, and the few repatriated Jews. Who, in 1939, could promise more?

CHAPTER SIX

The Self under Siege

And I, a person who for years had been removed from everything, thought to myself: A generation of iron men will arise, and they will rebuild what we permitted to be ruined.
Lamed Shapiro, 1909

IF neither God nor His surrogates had any say in the course of Jewish history, as the modernist pogrom poem made amply clear, and if the community no longer provided refuge in times of war and revolution, as demonstrated in a variety of shtetl novellas, then the last and only holdout was the individual, emancipated from God and community. Yet in eastern Europe, where the claims of tradition and community were so much stronger than in the west, the course of emancipation never did run smooth, especially as the path led through landscapes of such vast destruction. Nor would the community give up its claim on the individual so easily. Ever since the first Jew tried to remove himself from the crowd of exiles mourning by the waters of Babylon, the presence of the one still implied the presence of the many. For if the self desired to bear witness to the destruction, it then became the symbolic survivor of the community (and thus, the community in miniature); or if, as a result of ideology or devastation, it wished to detail its willing or unwilling departure from the community, the rejected group loomed just as large as the self; and if, despite all odds, the self succeeded in negating the group, the self was invariably lost as well.

Paradoxically, the impact of catastrophe in the twentieth century was not to emancipate the Jewish individual from his collective base but to open him up to his other, female half. Throughout the premodern period women had been given minimal attention in Jewish responses to catastrophe, except to occupy the most stereotypic roles: Jerusalem a grieving woman in mourner's clothes, mother Rachel weeping for her children, women dying as they nursed. In martyrological accounts, from Second Maccabees until Hannover's *The Deep Mire,* heroic women had usually remained nameless. The most famous woman martyr, who had sacrificed her seven sons and then herself, was known alternately as Miriam and Hannah. Men had been so much in control of the liturgy that even when they had written special *tkhines* (prayers) for women, such as the "New *El Malei Raḥamim* Prayer" published in Nowi Dwor in 1813, there had been but a passing reference to "Hannah's" martyrdom, whereas all six of the rabbis and communal leaders killed in the slaughter of 1656 had merited special mention.[1] How the liturgy would have been different if women had written the prayers is difficult to tell—perhaps there would have been a greater emphasis on the lost children, or *agunot,* or perhaps women would have enjoyed a greater share in the world to come.

Not until the last decades of the nineteenth century did the status of Jewish women in traditional society become a serious issue, thanks to the influence of Russian and Polish Positivism. It was in the next generation, however, that writers began to explore the individualization of the self and attempted, for the first time outside of kabbalistic literature, a psychological integration of male and female aspects. With the coming of revolution and world war, men were all being torn from their homes, and it was time, at last, to give up the image of the male rescuing the weeping (female) community of Jews in eastern Europe. Consequently, writers were freer to work with images of destruction that might make more sense to or appeal equally to women. The fragmented texts written in response to modern violence were actually attempts to bring together on equal footing male and female retrojections of catastrophe and trauma. In literature, if not in life, women could now bear witness both for themselves and for the men.

IN the classical Jewish memoir, such as it was, the author was expected to dwell on the collective or moral significance of the past, not on its personal dimensions. This was because the careful plotting of the soul in search of perfection, the core of the confessional genre since the days of Saint Augustine, was foreign to Jewish tradition outside of the Kabbalah. Typically, the stimulus for the writing of a Jewish memoir was the precipitous end of an era, usually as a result of catastrophe.[2] Jews sat down to write with a sense of longing, once the foundations of society as they knew it had been fundamentally altered; or they tried to restore a sense of equilibrium in the face of a new caststrophe by recalling the bitter experiences they had withstood in the one before. At each breaking point—the Spanish expulsion, the Khmelnitsky massacres, the incursion of modernity into western and eastern Europe, the pogroms, the revolutions—the rescue operation was launched anew. As Jacob Shatzky put it with a touch of irony, only that which was lost forever was of interest to Jews.[3]

The will to bear particular witness had to be cultivated. Nothing in my research suggests that it is an innate faculty of humankind, Jewish or otherwise. The impetus within the Jewish community came from a small group of intellectuals, such as historian Simon Dubnow, who called on former Cantonists to record their saga for publication in his Russian-language journal; or from the Yiddish writers Peretz, Dinezon, and Ansky, who, in a long-winded manifesto issued on New Year's Day 1915, warned their readers: "Woe to the nation whose *history* is written by foreign hands and whose own writers are left to later compose only songs of lament, penitential prayers, and threnodies."[4] At least one young woman, Anne Kahan,[5] heeded their call by keeping a wartime diary. What did come naturally to Jews, once engaged in the memorial enterprise, was to include the culture as a whole—the town, the community.

This parochial, collective, and liturgical slant on historical experience was radically challenged by the Great War and the Bolshevik Revolution. The Great War occupied a unique place in the annals of Jewish suffering because, in addition to reasons given in earlier chapters, it was the first catastrophe that Jews in vast numbers experienced as soldiers and as enemies to one another. Throughout the war zone, for instance, Ansky recorded numerous variants of a single story, always told as an actual occurrence.[6] Two soldiers supposedly met in hand-to-hand combat, and one stabbed the other with his bayonet. "Shma Yisroel!" the dying soldier called out with his last breath, and the enemy realized in horror that he had killed another Jew. Ansky recognized this legend as the symbolic kernel of the tragedy: a nation caught up in a world torn apart.

Jews suffered from two distinctly different forms of violence in the Great War: the familiar violence of pogroms, expulsions, and forced labor, and the impersonal, mechanized violence of the trenches. This duality is clearly reflected in the literature. For one thing, translations into Yiddish of the best-selling European war novels focused on the devastating effects of trench warfare. Andreas Latzko's *Men in War* (1918), one of the first important antiwar narratives, appeared in Yiddish a year after its original publication in German. Then followed Henri Barbusse's *Under Fire* in 1924, Jaroslav Hašek's *The Good Sol-*

dier Schweik in 1928, Erich Maria Remarque's *All Quiet on the Western Front* in 1929 and 1930, and Ludwig Renn's *War* in 1930–31. (Significantly, Ernst Junger's *The Storm of Steel,* which accepted the war as a necessary, higher reality, was never translated.) All this challenged the Jewish writer to confront the universal dimension of violence, to apply the vocabulary of Jewish suffering beyond its particularist setting. The tension between the universal and the particular was perhaps most acute in a new genre produced by the war: the memoirs of Jewish medics,[7] officers,[8] ordinary soldiers,[9] and prisoners of war.[10] Punctuating the exposé of army life with its cruelty and corruption were revelations of anti-Semitism and of the uniquely tragic fate of the Jews. Out there in the trenches and field stations, there was no community to mediate the assault on one's body and soul. The brotherhood of the trenches, where all classes of French, German, British, and Italian doughboys discovered their common bond—be they poets, miners, peasants, or clerks—was less attainable in the multinational armies of the tsar or of the Hapsburg monarchy. The Russian- or Polish-Jewish soldier who hoped to achieve a degree of acceptance denied him in civilian life discovered, more often than not, that he shared a deeper bond with his Galician- and German-Jewish enemy than with his comrades-in-arms. Hatred from one's fellow soldiers was reinforced by a growing alienation from friends and family back home, who might not even be there at war's end. The armistice would not restore plundered Jewish property or reinstate exiled Jewish populations.

To be a Jewish soldier, therefore, was to feel uniquely vulnerable. Thrust, with his comrades-in-arms, into a mechanized warfare that was rapidly transforming the physical, political, and cultural landscape of Europe, the Jew was no better equipped to respond than anyone else. Certainly the output of Jewish war poetry was meagre and unexceptional, be it that of Jacob Mestel and Nokhem Oyslender writing in Yiddish, Avigdor Hameiri and David Shimoni writing in Hebrew,[11] or Uri Zvi Greenberg writing first in one language and then in the other (see Chapter 10). Once off the battlefield, however, the landscape of familiar destruction awakened the old patterns of response. Like Gershon Levin and S. Ansky, who recognized the ancient signs of destruction as they stood before the ruins of Jewish Galicia, twenty-six-year-old Isaac Babel, recently joined up with Budyonny's First Cavalry brigade, reaffirmed the truth of Lamentations even as he violated the commemorative fast:

> We devour the cooked potatoes like wolves, and each one has five glasses of coffee . . . the ninth of Av. The old [Jewish] woman howls, sitting on the floor, her son who idolizes his mother and says that he believes in God, in order to do something pleasant for her—sings in a pleasant small tenor and tells the story

of the destruction of the Temple: the frightful words of the prophet—they eat manure, the girls are raped, the men slain, Israel destroyed, angry, wailing words. The lamp smokes, the old woman howls, outside is [the shtetl] Demidovka, Cossacks, everything like the time when the Temple fell . . .[12]

Perhaps there were Jewish Cossacks once before in history, but none ever kept a diary or ever fashioned the memory of that impossible alliance into lasting works of art. Babel's *Red Cavalry,* as we shall see, represents one limit in the spectrum of Jewish behavior *in extremis,* whereas the moment of midrashic recall, facilitated by his knowledge of Hebrew, illustrates the recurrent norm.

Despite the total and terrifying isolation felt by Jewish soldiers fighting in the Great War, the quintessential Jewish war memoir, the text that was later to inspire Ringelblum, Kaplan, Kruk and other ghetto diarists, remained Ansky's *Khurbm Galitsye,* precisely because the author submerged his personal experience so as to highlight the broad panorama of Jewish suffering. Only once in its four volumes did the author let down his guard, with an outburst of joy at being alive.[13] A diary was nothing if not subjective, and Shatzky, for one, faulted the author for his myopically critical view of Galician Jewry;[14] but the collective was kept so consistently in focus that the reader forgot how central Ansky himself was to the events described. The diary told of a mission, interrupted during the four-month breach in the Russian front, to aid his brethren in the occupied territories. At a time when Galicia was totally off limits, when those of its Jews not yet banished or murdered were banned from traveling or from engaging in commerce because all of them were viewed as traitors in the eyes of the Russian occupiers, Ansky raised the necessary capital and carried the relief effort single-handedly from place to place.

Since his was a self-appointed mission, though subject to the vagaries of war, Ansky's memoir enjoys a narrative flow that is lacking in most diaries of soldiers sent to do battle first on one front and then on the other. Ansky, moreover, was retracing his steps—that is, revisiting some of the same towns where he had collected religious artifacts and had recorded folksongs, stories, sayings, and jokes during his celebrated ethnographic expedition prior to the war. *Khurbm Galitsye* is therefore replete with anecdotes and ethnographic observations, a veritable encyclopedia of popular response to catastrophe.

There is another, equally impressive side to Ansky's memoir. If one may characterize his generation, as I did in Chapter 4, as thoroughly at home in Jewish and general culture, as intellectuals who served universal causes with Jewish pride and who returned to serve their people in a spirit of universalism—examples being Peretz, Sholem Aleichem, Dubnow, and Berdichewsky—then Ansky surely stands out as the proudest of them all. When he returned to Russia in 1905 and threw his energies into revolutionary politics and Jewish cultural causes, he could boast of a career as a Russian Narodnik, as private secretary to Peter Lavrov, as secretary of l'Ecole Internationale in Paris, and as a cultural anthropologist. With his Russian liberal contacts, his flawless accent and his uniform (see Figure 2), Ansky had access to the whole military establishment, from the general staff to the raw recruits, and his portraits of Count Dolgorukov and Igor Demidov offer extraordinary insights into the misconduct of the war. At one point, Ansky even undertook a secret trip to St. Petersburg to alert the government as to the true conditions at the front. Here was the ultimate "traveler disguised," whom the shtetl population greeted as a kind of Elijah figure[15] and who, dressed in officer's uniform, could lay bare the passion for bloodshed and the pathological hatred for Jews of his Russian compatriots. The ability to pass undetected from native to enemy turf would later become the essential ingredient of Jewish survival.

Ansky's sense of mission carried over to the act of memory itself. A few months into the war he, Peretz, and Dinezon had issued their appeal against allowing strangers to write the history of the Jews during this tragic period. Soon Ansky gave way to a deeper, more drastic fear—the fear that this history might not be written at all. The Russian press, including its liberal wing, believed the accusations of Jewish treason; accounts of Jewish heroism were systematically censored and a blackout was imposed on news of pogroms and expulsions. After July 1915 no Hebrew or Yiddish printed matter was allowed to pass through the Russian mails, and the Jewish press was forced to close. Thus, Ansky's task of rescuing lives and property was compounded by the need to make the story public, to use his access and authority to reveal what was happening to a whole tribe in Israel—the destruction of its eastern kingdom.

One may generalize and say that in modern times the conspiracy of silence was directly proportional to the scope of Jewish catastrophe. Whereas the Kishinev pogrom was documented, publicized, and protested throughout the western world, the vastly greater destruction to Jews in World War I was noted by very few outside observers, and the holocaust of Ukrainian Jewry in the civil war that followed would have been all but erased from memory were it not for the efforts of a handful.

In May of 1919 a terse appeal was issued by the Editorial Board to Collect and Research Materials on the Pogroms in the Ukraine.[16] "Jews!" it read, "a terrible pogrom disaster [Tokheḥa] has befallen our cities and towns, and the world does not know; we ourselves know nothing or very little about it. The deeds must not be suppressed!" In order to ensure the preservation of the data that started pouring in, at a

2. S. Ansky in the uniform of a Russian relief official, 1914.

time when Petlura's forces, later Denikin's, later the Poles, and still later the Soviet regime tried to confiscate and destroy the archive, multiple copies were made and deposited for safekeeping. In September 1921 the whole archive was smuggled out of the Soviet Union and brought to Berlin. Reporting on these "five crates of Jewish woes," Hirsh Dovid Nomberg contrasted the Jews' task of documentation with that of the Gentiles.[17] "We Jews are fated to another kind of glorification. Like dogs we lick away our own blood! We collect and collect and collect: blood, tears, and sorrows." But even in the freedom of Berlin, only two volumes of the planned seven-volume history were published, and the third would not appear until 1965. In addition to this major monographic series, local histories were commissioned, creating a new genre—the documentary novel of destruction. Weaving a seamless narration out of eyewitness accounts, Rachel Feigenberg, a survivor herself, focused on the fate of a single shtetl in *A Chronicle of a Dead Town (The Destruction of Dubove).*[18] Here, the anatomy of mass murder was laid out in agonizing detail, complete with reconstructed dialogues, and among its most horrifying accounts was the martyrdom of the rabbi, the father of Micah Joseph Berdichewsky.

Despite all precautions, the archive was to share the survivors' fate. The major part was shipped to the YIVO (the Yiddish Scientific Institute) in Vilna when Elias Tcherikower, its director and moving force, left Berlin for Paris in 1933. When the Nazis caught up with him in Paris, he fled to southern France, leaving behind his own manuscript on the pogroms and the remainder of the archive. At the end of 1940 it was rescued by Zosa Szajkowski, historian, soldier, and resistance fighter, whose history of the archive forms the basis of this discussion.[19] As for the bulk of the archive in Vilna, including documentary film footage, the Nazis saw to its destruction in 1942.

If Tcherikower's archive looked ahead to Ringelblum's Oneg Shabbat in the Warsaw ghetto, and Feigenberg anticipated the documentary novels on the Holocaust, then Eliezer David Rosental's epic list of destruction was the last successor to Hannover's *The Deep Mire.* Sixty-three-year-old Rosental, a maskil of the old school, survived a major pogrom in Teplik and then proceeded to collect everything he could on the Ukrainian pogroms, to order the data alphabetically by town, to translate it into Hebrew and mail it, letter by letter, to Berlin where Bialik, Ravnitsky, and Druyanov oversaw the publication.[20] Only three volumes of *The Scroll of Slaughter* were published in his lifetime,[21] reaching the letter *tet,* and *yud* was published a half-century later.[22] Rosental died in Odessa in 1932 in the most desolate conditions imaginable. And so the creation of an archive of destruction was a modern refraction of an earlier response, for the archive was an anonymous endeavor in the same way that Jewish lamentation was meant to be at once personal and anonymous. Yet even with institutional backing, heroic feats of rescue, and the collaboration of trained historians, statisticians, journalists, and an army of anonymous collectors, everything conspired against the documentation of Jewish catastrophe.

THE fashioning of a personal identity is usually predicated on the possibility of choice and of making moral decisions. The soldier who volunteered to fight his way through the rubble was therefore in a much better position to impose his view and memory of things than the hapless disoriented recruit. Ansky's memoir could be the most "Jewish" of them all because it was the most self-determined. Modern Jewish writers who were in search of a contemporary hero worked under a double constraint: eastern European society at large did not offer the Jew that many choices and human behavior was itself subject to inherent limitations. In literature, as in life, the real test of character came in extreme situations.

Whereas writers of Peretz's generation had entered the twentieth century unsure of what the future would bring, and had therefore looked increasingly to the past to find instances of Jewish greatness—to hasidim, water carriers, Cantonists, hidden saints, and rabbis' daughters—writers of the next generation, born in the 1880s, developed three distinct character types to cover the scope of individual behavior under stress: the heroes of action, reaction, and inaction.

To find models of bravery and physical prowess, these writers turned quite deliberately to the margins of Jewish society. Here they came upon the *ba'al-guf*, an inarticulate boor who lived by his passions and responded not to the dictates of Law but to the varied calls of nature. He and his fellows were a motley group of thieves and roughnecks, but when Jews were in danger they fought back, and when the draft board called them up—they went.

Since the literary history of this intriguing character has yet to be written and since he occupies a role in the Jewish fictional gallery no less prominent than that of Mendele or the shtetl, I should mention something about his pedigree. Anyone, Jew or Gentile, could be *ba'al-guf*, provided he was relatively well-endowed physically, economically, or both. The greater the deprivation in the society at large, the easier it was to qualify. Thus, a tavernkeeper and a peasant farmer were suitable candidates if no one else around could eke out a living.[23] Philosophically, the character can be traced to primitivist notions about the noble savage who gives vent to his "original, natural, but subsequently repressed, desires";[24] or, closer in time but different in teleology, to

Nietzsche's superman, unfettered by moral scruples. Be that as it may, his appearance marked a radical departure from anything ever called a Jewish hero before.

Bialik, who launched the *ba'al-guf's* literary career, played so skillfully on the character's inherent ambiguities that critics are still arguing about whether *Arye Ba'al-guf* (1899) is to be read as a positive or negative type. With Sholem Asch (born 1880) we come to the first *ba'al-guf* story with an explicit ideology. The "Kola Street" irregulars are noble men of passion, bound to the rich Polish soil, just like the peasants and the horses of the region. The passivity and false pride of Scholars' Street where money and learning make their unholy alliance, is clearly no match for Kola Street which "was not in the Diaspora, as it were: there no Jew was ever beaten. If it happened that recruits passing through the town in the fall began to riot, members of the congregation would take matters into their own hands: armed with shafts torn from carts and iron bars wrested from shutters, they would go out into the streets and teach the hooligans a lesson."[25] Reb Israel, the oldest and most respected inhabitant of Kola Street, bridges the two with a deep sense of the past on the one hand and a code of frontier justice on the other, but Notte, his son, lives only in the present and only for his animals. Everything about Notte suggests his deviant status: in Jewish folklore, *Notte ganef* is the equivalent of Robin Hood; and Notte's hobby, flying pigeons, is considered so despicable that since mishnaic times it disqualified people as witnesses (Mishnah Rosh Hashanah 1:8). The pigeons, in the end, mediate the violence that they provoke—a small-scale pogrom in which the gentile baker is killed and Notte is badly wounded. The community exacts its guilt offering by killing off most of the birds, and the hero exorcises his rage with the blood of the last surviving fledgling.

Thanks to Asch, Kola Street became a generic name, the place in shtetl geography where the ne'er-do-wells hung out, where Jews and Gentiles worked in close proximity, where blood flowed freely and muscle was valued over mind. The street had been there before, but not until the transvaluation of values, when a new generation of Jews took history into their own hands, organizing strikes, self-defense units, and revolutionary cells, did the Kola Streets of Eastern Europe present a model to be emulated. Before he could become a striker, fighter, or collective farmer, the new Jew was expected to shed the inhibitions of shtetl propriety, bourgeois respectability, and arid intellectualism. The *ba'al-guf* represented this new Jew in his earlier, rudimentary state: a man who acted alone, on impulse, but remained fiercely loyal to the tribe. Neither he nor his surrounding culture was yet responsive to history. What can be said about Benya Krik and company, Babel's glowing contribution to this rogues' gallery, holds true for the *ba'al-guf* as a generic type: his actions sprang from his individual will, whereas the society around him was presumed to be static and outside history.[26]

To live unencumbered by the past or the future—that was the *ba'al-guf*'s mandate. The whole community could quake in its boots each year in the spring when the recruiting officers came round and posted the list of draftees, and by early autumn every self-respecting Jewish youth dreaded the thought of the impending three-year stint; but now writers' sympathies shifted to the side of those who made the best of it, who thought less and did more:

> The younger generation split in two: One half, the soft pantywaists, who could be kneaded like clay figures—they went to synagogue to pray. And the other half, with Berl the Lout at their head, the roustabouts, they went to Leyzer's tavern. The crowd was made up of tough tailor lads, apprentices, who couldn't read or write, and who had always regarded the military as "bullshit."
>
> "We'll get used to it soon enough—Sewing tunics . . . making boots . . . baking bread—who cares? . . . And the three years'll be up before you know it. We'll bring back a few hundred rubles, we'll see the world, and that'll help us make a decent match. Thirty-six months—that's nothing . . . So—live it up, boys, live it up like there's no tomorrow!"[27]

The point not to be missed about these foul-mouthed Yiddish-speaking rowdies is their essential conservatism. Their highest aspiration is to return home with enough money to make a good match—with a Jewish girl, to be sure. And though Berl the Lout, the leader of the pack, feels free to prey upon the local moneybags, whose sons are off in hiding, in a later episode of Fishl Bimko's *Recruits,* Berl's sense of honor sends him rushing to save some elderly Jews from peasant hands.[28] The *ba'al-guf*'s behavior does not effect change; his behavior is society's barely sanctioned release mechanism and guarantee that everything in the end will return to what it was.

The schlemiel, who may be said to represent the normative type in eastern European Jewish fiction, likewise makes no dent in the world, for he becomes a hero, as Ruth Wisse put it so memorably, when real action is impossible and reaction remains the only way a man can define himself.[29] Sholem Aleichem immortalized a whole town of schlemiels, a town called Kasrilevke, where the people use verbal aggression to fight off the forces of destruction (see Chapter 7).

This leaves us with the characters who agonize so long and hard about their place in the world that their confrontation with society, when such occurs, leads nowhere. They are alienated urban intellectuals, perennial students who recently returned from some place in Switzerland, or self-taught philosophers who mercilessly expose their own motives and those of others. They are called *telushim* (dangling men) and have no place to go, caught between the lost world of tradition and inaccessible worldly pleasures. They are a new breed who live on the periphery of politics and culture, knowing too much and doing too little. They are close cousins of characters in Peretz, Bershadsky, Chekhov, Maeterlinck, and Hamsun, whose story is typically told in monologue form, in short sketches or entries of a diary—that is, in a form that closes out any but their own solipsistic and passive view of life.[30] What happens to such tortured souls in the face of catastrophe mirrors more directly than anything we have seen the collapse of normative behavior, the denial of meaningful choices, and the crippling burden of memory.

Unlike the *ba'al-guf*, who is very much rooted in a physical environment, and unlike the schlemiel who holds fast to a belief in the basic goodness of God and His world, the *talush* is not bound by any place, and having no transcendental faith to uphold, he is utterly defeated in the end. He may, like Zalmen Schneour's student, return home immediately from Switzerland on receiving news of the pogrom and when the actual death toll surpasses his most feverish imaginings, he may raise a great cry of revenge. But the *talush*'s world is always fragmented, no more so than in periods of catastrophe, and the enemy is everywhere. "Where was this monstrous pogrom-beast?" he may ask. "I haven't seen her, I had seen only fragments of her."[31] So all the pent-up anger will be vented instead on the shoemaker's dog, his "childhood enemy," and even this pathetic act of vengeance will leave him trembling, fearing that the gentile neighbor overheard. Or he may, like I. D. Berkowitz's "young man with blue-tinted glasses in a sheepskin coat and a finished collar" fancy himself the God-given leader of his suffering flock.[32] "In the dark and terrible night" of 1905–6, with a group of panic-stricken Jews behind him, he will seek refuge from the pogrom in a charity hospital and be totally unmanned by the gentile janitor. The illiterate janitor lording it over the educated Jews will be one of two reversals, the more grotesque occurring inside the hospital among the Jews themselves. The dying Jews rebel against the living who intruded on their space, and off in a corner the tubercular girl who is the object of our hero's fantasies promptly rejects his advances. Order is restored only by the fear of the common enemy.

Halfway across the world, in Palestine, the situation is no different. The old pioneer teacher in Yosef Hayim Brenner's story, a *talush* in khakis, begins each day paralyzed with fear:

> They were sure to come. They could be expected any day now.
>
> They would be on that little train that came to fetch the wood. They would be arriving from back there, from that nightmare-ridden waste, where the soil lay desolate, the trees hewn down and the dwellings in ruins; from that dead region where the handful of farmers who were left paid the soldiers billeted in

their houses to chop the remaining almond trees into firewood; from the place where the only food was unground millet, to fill the belly and still the pangs of hunger; from the place where damp huts, infested with mice and vermin, soggy with filth and permeated with the accumulated stench of months, gave sorry shelter to women and children who were chilled to the marrow and contorted with disease; from the place where out of the surviving hundreds, half a dozen dead were carted away daily for burial.[33]

With a war between the Turks and the British raging in the background, what the teacher dreads most is the impending arrival—of Jewish refugees! It is they who are about to invade, bringing the apocalyptic landscape of starvation, disease, and death that much closer. His indirect interior monologue is an incantation of terror in which death, detailed and specific, draws near from an indeterminate place. In this instance, the educated hero is impelled to take on the establishment, the cynical bureaucrats of the Evacuation Committee; he even violates one set of rules, those of hygiene, in order to act on a higher, biblical standard of morality, but in the end, his energies sapped and with still newer arrivals expected at any moment, he settles on a purely individual solution, the only "way out"—succumbing to his own death.

And if once there was a young man in whose eyes "two bright sparks were burning . . . like the flames of memorial candles lit early in the evening," and if this young man appeared before the celebrated Yiddish writer David Bergelson in Berlin with a specific plan in mind—to assassinate the infamous Ukrainian pogrom leader—the result is a foregone conclusion.[34] The narrative frame undermines the heroism of the hero even before he opens his mouth. He was "a stranger . . . sort of . . . seemed . . . as if"; his cheeks were crooked, his left one "looked as though it were . . . at war with the world." Once he takes over the narration (in monologue), the young man's fixations with his grandfather's clocks, with the Pinskys of his childhood who lived across the boulevard, with room number five across from his in the pension where he and his would-be victim live—all reveal a profoundly disturbed mentality. The assassination that seems to rivet his vacillating mind is in fact motivated by petty and personal concerns—to show Pinsky's beautiful daughter that he is really a man capable of action. In an attempt to procure a gun from a Jewish relief agency, the hero is provoked to his penultimate act of violence—slapping the psychiatrist assigned to help him. Suicide is left for last.

The historical reality of which the *talush* was a distillation was by no means one of passivity. Young Jewish men and women were joining the ranks of revolutionary and Zionist parties in ever-growing numbers and organized resistance was high on their agenda in Russia, Poland, and Palestine; so much so, in fact, that pogrom victims were now listed by their party affiliation.[35] The published list for the Zhitomir pogrom of

1905 also included, probably for the first time, the name of a Christian student, Nikolai Blinov, who died defending the Jews. It was an uncanny instance of life imitating literature. Ansky recalled[36] that shortly before Blinov's death, the two had starred in an amateur production of Yevgeni Chirikov's *The Jews* in which Ansky had played Leyzer and Blinov had played the Christian student Berezin, who had died protecting Leyzer's family in the pogrom. Forty years later, Lamed Shapiro vividly recalled the services held in Blinov's memory: "Perhaps for the first time in our history, [Jews] recited Merciful God in Heaven *(El malei raḥamim)* for a 'goy'—not under duress, as for the hated tsar, but with ardent love and bitter sorrow."[37]

Also unprecedented were the assassination attempts. Hirsh Lekert, a Vilna shoemaker and member of the Jewish Labor Bund, shot at the governor in retaliation for the flogging of a group of workers who had taken part in a May Day rally. A year later, in the spring of 1903, Pinkhes Dashevsky, a Zionist student from Kiev, avenged the Kishinev pogrom by shooting at a leading anti-Semitic agitator named P. Krushevan. Both attempts failed. Lekert was hanged and revered forever after. Dashevsky was released after serving two years at hard labor; he later took part in the search for the murderer in the Beillis trial and finally perished in a Soviet prison in June 1934.[38] The unsuccessful assassin in Bergelson's story of 1924 turned up in the person of Sholem Schwarzbard, who actually shot and killed Simon Petlura, the infamous leader of the Ukrainian pogroms in May 1926. At the trial in Paris, the atrocities were brought to light and Schwarzbard was acquitted.

The same writers who drew the *talush*'s portrait so convincingly were not only aware of these new developments—the organized resistance, the solidarity between Gentiles and Jews, the acts of revenge—but were also aligned with many of these causes. In the aftermath of the Zhitomir pogrom, Brenner, an active revolutionary and pioneer-to-be, cried out for vengeance in a famous monologue in which he spoke as a son to his bereaved mother,[39] and Lamed Shapiro composed a hymn to self-defense.[40] "Writers . . . are the conscience of a nation," said the young man at the end of Bergelson's "Among Refugees." "They are its nerves, they present their nation to the world, people read a writer's works because they want to find out how the nation lived in his time." Was it because revolutionary heroes made for bad literature that the writers presented their nation to the world as a bunch of schizophrenics and abdicated dreamers? Or was it because, once they began to explore the life of the educated young Jew, they could not help but see the countervailing forces of fragmentation? The pogrom-beast was everywhere and nowhere. When disaster struck, the community, a loose coalition of interest groups, would fall apart altogether. In the charity hospital the dying would turn against the living, and in the pioneer settlement the living would repulse the dying. The elite group of Jewish intellectuals thus had no one to attack and no one to lead. And since their own identities were none too secure, these dangling men caught between tradition and a thousand versions of modernity, between loyalty to parents and past and an unfulfilled craving for love and life, could barely hope to save themselves, let alone any larger constituency.

The *talush* represented the embattled mind of the modern Jew, who had no recourse to either creed or community. At the other extreme were the mindless, brawny *ba'al-gufs* who never thought twice before picking up an iron bar—or the first available woman. The very fear or contemplation of violence was enough to incapacitate the *talush.* But what if the violence, when it actually struck, defied the neat categorization of types and shattered the boundary between victim and executioner? What if the pogrom were something so irreducible and elemental that no political platform, however sophisticated, would explain it away? What if its victims were children with no acquired defenses, and what if the violence descended with such speed and brutality that it robbed even adults of their power of speech and severed their ties from family and friends? What if it could happen anytime and anywhere and make its wounds felt long after the danger had passed? These were the questions that no one dared to ask until Lamed Shapiro (born 1878) appeared on the scene and placed the subject of catastrophe at the center of his work.

To make the pogrom beast unassimilable, Shapiro adopted an impressionistic style, analytically dispassionate. He stripped his characters of ethnic trappings and intellectual baggage, then thrust them into the vortex of pogroms, and, as in premodern accounts, he omitted real geographic names and topical references so as not to bracket the violence within a specific time and place.[41] In lieu of ethnic and geographic detail, Shapiro anchored his descriptions in carefully wrought psychological portraits linked in a mysterious and altogether untraditional way—to nature.

In Shapiro's story "In the Dead Town," nine-year-old Beylke lives among graves, where serenity and closeness to nature contrast sharply with the pain and suffering in the nameless shtetl in the valley below.[42] From her vantage point atop a willow treee on the edge of the Jewish graveyard, Beylke sees humankind as puny, breakable dolls, mechanical beings who bring nothing but misery and senseless violence into the world. Free to roam about in a world of eternal present, Beylke responds only to the stimuli of nature, but there, in the natural cycle, she finds the link to her past. Beylke's suppressed memory of the pogrom lies dormant, exactly like the snow-covered river which died an agonizing death with the onset of winter. As surely as the river will rush back to life with tremendous violent spasms in the springtime, so will Beylke's memory reawaken with elemental, terrifying force.

The storm-pogrom equation was the key to Shapiro's radical agenda. Nature, he believed, was the life force, the main source of regeneration.[43] Yet nature could harm as well as heal. A survivor such as Beylke, cleansed by prolonged communion with nature, was then "raped" by the storm, which is to say, made to relive the trauma. If the cycle continued and the trauma were thus "worked through," transmuted, then the beginning of self-renewal could be traced, paradoxically, to the act of destruction itself. Similarly and more radically, Shapiro implied that the violence of the pogrom, like that of the storm, could itself be liberating, even as it drove its victims to madness. Both through nature and through physical violence, people could purge that weaker part of themselves, break those civilizing shackles called humanism, politics, and culture to become "iron men."[44]

"Lean, towering, broad-shouldered . . . with dark, suntanned skin, protruding cheekbones, and black eyes," the hero of Shapiro's next story, "The Cross," is the picture of well-being, a strong silent type who travels the prairies on the roof of train cars—a *ba'al-guf* on American soil.[45] The only give-away is the crucifix on his forehead, "two knife gashes, one across the other." When the story finally unfolds, after the hero's symbolic purification in a river, it emerges that he is a Russian-Jewish intellectual transformed—and transfigured—by the pogroms.

Judging also from his detached manner of speech, he is a true-believer-turned-cynic. "It was a trivial matter," he says of those days, "our desire to reshape the world—first Russia, then the other nations. Meanwhile, we were still working on Russia" (page 117). As a member of a Russian revolutionary cell, he dismissed the news of pogroms as mere manifestations of the counterrevolution, with no bearing on him as a Jew. Stirred, however, by his love for Minna, the reticent and beautiful (Gentile) leader of the group, he is ready to sacrifice himself for the greater cause. None of this stands up in the face of the pogrom, which catches him totally off guard in his own home. He fights back ineffectually, is forced to witness the torture of his mother, a woman he always hated, and then, "to save his Yid soul from Hell," is branded for life with a crucifix on his forehead.

At that moment, his ties with the past are broken forever. His prior life now appears like the slavery of Egypt, a form of bondage from which he has to break loose at any price.[46] With a single blow, he finishes off his dying mother and then steps out into a world in chaos. At one point, upon meeting his tormentor, he does not lift a hand to kill him: that would be too logical and too puny a form of revenge.[47] In the supreme illogic of the streets, a Jewish student with a revolver shoots himself instead of the pogromist whom he has trapped in an alley. The hero's final act of "liberation" is to rape Minna and to strangle her to death.

The pogrom instantly transformed a *talush* and victim into its very antithesis—a man of action, a murderer, freed of inhibitions, emancipated from all that ever tied him down. In Shapiro's scheme, the pogrom released the pent-up animal in man. Like preyed-upon beasts, the victims bit and clawed at their attackers: in "The Kiss," Reb Shakhne died biting the foot of Vasilenko, the peasant;[48] Beylke lost herself "in wild, intoxicating joy" as she sank her teeth into the foot of the Cossack who was raping her mother; men, women, and children alike "gritted their teeth" whenever their back was to the wall. This raw animal aggression had nothing to do with heroism, just as the man with the cross never acted upon his revolutionary ideals. Cut off from language and from a living community by the violence of the pogrom, the survivor-animals found their habitat in nature, the purging ground of memory, and only there did they gain the strength to start over. Nothing captured the paradox of freedom-through-coercion and liberation-through-violence as well as the symbol of the cross. Was the hero a victim, a suffering Christ, or Cain, the murderer marked for life? Was it a grotesque mandate for remembrance, this frontlet between his eyes (a question posed by the hero himself), or was the cross to be construed as the Crusader's badge of zealous action? The scar remained, any way you looked at it, and the transformation was complete. Victims became victors or turned the violence back on themselves. Love turned to hatred, hatred to madness, and madness to health. Nothing would be what it was; no one would return to the person he had been.

On a programmatic level, the man with the cross represented a new kind of hero—an "iron man" who would, in the words of the story's narrator, "rebuild what we had permitted to be ruined" (page 130). Here was the first *talush* ever to be reborn as a *ba'al-guf*, though his later fate was an open question. Someone so brutally disabused of politics could not very well return to lead a strike or drain a swamp. Secular humanism, Shapiro's argument went, did not stand up to primal aggression, nor had all attempts, as old as civilization itself, succeeded in taming and rechaneling that aggression. In order to reverse a time-honored legacy of denial, Shapiro knew that he would have to look beyond the self under siege and take on God as well. To make the pogrom into the ultimate parody, a repudiation so total that it canceled out all prior notions of man created in the image of God, he had to subvert the myths of both Judaism and Christianity and launch a "countercommentary" such as no one since Bialik had yet attempted.

Taken in sequence, Shapiro's abuse of Scripture and liturgy shows a definite progression. Reb Shakhne could have avoided a violent death if he had agreed to kiss the swollen, filthy foot of his tormentor, or have died a martyr's death by refusing. Instead, he sank his teeth into the foot—in open rebellion against the enemy and in hidden defiance of the death reserved for the righteous—to die, as did Moses, with the kiss of God.[49] In the same way, the Passover saga of redemption celebrated in the freedom of New York was eclipsed by the father's savage cry for revenge, "Pour out Thy wrath," signaling to the nine-year-old hero that, having survived the pogrom, he and his family were to suffer its consequences as long as they lived.[50] Soon after Passover, his mother would give birth to a bastard—the fruit of Old World violence that God had done nothing to stop. In "The Cross" (1909) it was the Christian God who showed His true colors, when there came a peasant to make the sign of the cross, literally and figuratively, over his victim. With this single act, brotherly love was converted into sadism, remembrance into oblivion, pogromist into Jew. In telling Beylke's story (1910), Shapiro had to step out of the prose narrative to deliver the parting words. The fatal determinism of mechanical beings dancing to the tune of death was all the doing of

> God in a striped and spotted robe
> And trousers—half yellow, half red.
> He's playing a comb and blowing a flute—
> And Life goes dancing with Death.
>
> (page 23)

So long as humans took their cues from the clown-God, instead of from nature, they would never rise above the pathetic and the grotesque. In each case, therefore, acts of primal aggression, of biting, screaming, mutilating, and murdering, repudiated other items in the catalogue of Western spirituality: quiescence, redemption, salvation, and providence. But these subversions were still pot shots compared to the sweep of Shapiro's last two pogrom stories, published in 1919.

From the opening tableau of "The Jewish State," the Kehillah Kedoshah, bound to God by divine law, seems perfectly intact.[51] The face of the rabbi's daughter-in-law, a recent bride, is visible in public only when covered with a white silk kerchief and only through the arch-shaped wicket in the oaken door to the women's section of the synagogue. It is Yom Kippur, the holiest day of the year. With each carefully chosen detail, another strand is added to the web of sanctity that surrounds the rabbi, his son Menachem, Menachem's new wife, the rabbi's wife, and the absentminded cook, Slove. Whatever the signs of sensuality—Gershon the slaughterer's secret passion for the daughter-in-law, or Menachem's strong baritone voice when he studied out loud—they are held in check by the normative structures; perhaps overly so, since Menachem is too bashful to sleep with his wife. Then, three weeks after Sukkoth, comes the pogrom, which is bypassed entirely by the author but whose after-effects are immediately visible. "All of Krivodov gathered in the large synagogue. The oaken door had been opened and both sections joined into one—men, women, and children—all sitting together" (page 16). The adults are fasting voluntarily, in a penitence very different from that of Yom Kippur. Gershon the slaughterer's hand is in a sling; the rabbi's wife is mortally wounded. Despite the losses, the community has reconvened in the house of prayer, and it is time to record their tribulations in prescribed liturgical fashion: "*Re'ey adonoy, meh hoyo lonu,* See, oh Lord, what hath befallen us, we were led like sheep to the slaughter and they plundered our possessions and they profaned thy name among the nations" (page 18).

But once the oaken door in the synagogue of Krivodov (which means "crooked oak") has been thrown open, then someone is bound to enter the breach, and that is none other than Menachem, whose name ironically means "the one who brings comfort." Smoking a thin cigarette, he suddenly appears to deliver the Great Denunciation, to spell out the sacrilege, to repudiate the meaning of Jewish catastrophe. Noticing the book of records, he cries out to the community scribe: "Shmaye! Don't forget to record the Martyrs. Khone the porter, after all, died to sanctify God's name, and Berl the thief too, and Gitl the Hussy took on eight goyim—all for the sake of heaven!" (page 19). The rabbi only adds to his son's blasphemy by quoting God's answer to Job from out of the whirlwind: "Is that right! And who created the world and the ocean and the seven heavens—was it you perhaps? Was it you?" "So who created the bath and the bathhouse attendant?" comes Menachem's angry rebuttal. "Was it me, perhaps? And who created the bean stew and the goats' beards and grandma Trayne's cotton breeches—was it me, perhaps? Oh, Lord of the Universe, Master of the World, you mighty creator of Trayne's breeches—take under your wings the souls of these saints who suffered for the honor and love of your holy name—Jehovah!" (pp. 19–20). The congregation protests, shouting that for their sins and for the likes of Menachem they are being punished by the Lord. "For *your* sins!" he laughs. "Do you have the strength to sin? Do you even have the brains to sin?" Denouncing the Jewish God in terms perhaps borrowed from Bialik, Menachem goes on to proclaim the dominion of the enemy god: "Now *there's* a god for you—a true God of Love. He wouldn't even hurt a fly, yet look what he can do. Just look how he runs the world—the whole world belongs to him. A god, my dear Jews, has got to be *good* for something. A god, dear brothers and sisters, has got to be able to *do* something. After all, you too could be gods when it comes to not doing" (page 21). So much for the impotent God of Israel. Menachem then rejects his defiled wife, kept virginal for nothing, denounces his own cowardice and vows to extirpate the whole Jewish collective. Once the bearer of comfort, the natural leader, has broken loose from the fold, it is only a matter of time before the crooked oak is felled completely.

In the years that follow, the lull between the pogroms and the Great War, the rabbi's home is reduced to a shadow. Old Slove still mans her post but Gershon suffers a crisis of faith: he stops slaughtering. Rumors circulate about a renegade Jew turned priest—someone with an extraordinary voice and a bizarre talent for mimicry. He is inciting the peasants with stories about blood for Passover. The shtetl might dismiss these rumors out of hand, except that "it was reminiscent of the Middle Ages. Of Gonta, Khmelnitsky, the Haidamaks. Half-forgotten but familiar names, a strange sort of property, that—once it was in their possession—Jews were loath to give away" (page 30). Their suffering has become a commercial enterprise, a cynical covenant, so why should they give up their part of the bargain? For precisely these reasons, the renegade son is mobilizing the enemy from without.

The war thrusts Krivodov into the abyss. Catastrophe strikes during the forced march of refugees: families are trampled underfoot and the rabbi is left to die alone. Gershon, too, is singled out. The animal in him springs forth in a moment of rebellion that we have come to expect in Shapiro's landscape of extremity, but once his tormentors are routed, he turns the aggression inward and throws himself off a precipice. Menachem reappears, with shaven head and sunken cheeks, for a last act of defiance against the Gentiles, to follow through on his earlier defiance against the Jews. As Menachem cries out, in the agony of death, his voice is recognized by Slove, now old and senile, who survived all the pogroms, the torture and the killing, and who traveled on the Lost Train until it was left stranded in the middle of nowhere. It is she who takes over in the end—the blind life force, nature personified, the only thing left, asking no questions and expecting no explanations.[52] The Jewish people are back in the wilderness of Sinai, complete with fiery columns dancing through the sky, but with a very old woman in the lead, not a divinely inspired man.

Just as nine-year-old Beylke was the quintessential pogrom survivor, able to purge the violence through prolonged communion with nature and to stand as a symbol of nonmechanical, vitalistic being, so is the ultimate resource a very old woman named Slove in Shapiro's story of world war and revolution. Slove's loyalty and service contrast with the rebellious acts of Menachem and Gershon the slaughterer (presumably modeled on a real person of that name who perished near Kiev in 1919).[53] Since in Shapiro's view the "Jewish state" began to self-destruct even prior to the war, the rebelliousness of the Gershons and Menachems, first against God and the Jews and then against the goyim, produce no lasting results. Both of them meet a self-consuming end, Gershon by committing suicide and Menachem by dying so unheroically—defending a Jewish wheeler-dealer who was asking for trouble. All along there were forces at work defining the hidden essences of life—Gershon's baritone and Slove's blind capacity to survive—but neither answer to history or ideology. After the destruction of the kingdom, only primal energies are left: a mythic struggle without heroes, a metaphysics without God.

The world as a place of sheer destruction was the vision that Shapiro saved for last, for a story that dealt ostensibly with "white chalah" and pogroms.[54] To force the apocalypse on his readers, Shapiro did something that no Jewish writer had ever done before: he portrayed from the Gentile's point of view the violence perpetrated against Jews. Previously relegated to stereotypic roles, the goy was suddenly thrust center stage. Through Vasil, the speechless, historyless peasant, Shapiro traced the dehumanization of the "average man" from his first exposure to pain to his resurrection as a cannibal.

Vasil is not born without feelings. "One day a neighbor broke the leg of a stray dog with a heavy stone, and when Vasil saw the sharp edge of the bone piercing the skin he cried" (page 325). He still has a chance to develop human responses, but "he did not utter a sound." He is all mouth, but has no language, so everything good has to be embodied and everything bad is suffered in silence. The best thing in life is food, particularly white chalah. "He once stole a piece and ate it, whereupon he stood for a time in a daze, an expression of wonder on his face. He did not understand it at all, but respect for white *chalah* stayed with him" (page 325). Beatings, in contrast, become the sole guide for human conduct; wherever he goes, there is a pecking order of brutality—at home, in the army, and later on the front.[55] Once the war breaks out, food and fighting become the essence of his being.

In war, the cycle of nature works totally at odds with its accustomed rhythm in peace time. When the soldiers fight in winter, there is food aplenty. In the spring, with nature in bloom, the army suffers its first major defeats; the officers give orders to withdraw, and mutiny ensues. The "enemy within" then takes the blame.

Vasil knows about Jews from home. They are "people who wore strange clothes, sat in stores, ate white *chalah* and had sold Christ. The last point was not quite clear: who was Christ, why did the Jews sell him, who bought him, and for what purpose?—it was all as though in a fog" (page 325). The army is to teach him the plain meaning of that "last point"—namely, that Jews are the enemy; but everything else about them eludes Vasil completely. There is Nachum Rachek, for instance, a Jew who fights valiantly on the front. Why then does Rachek vomit green gall after the battle in which only he and Vasil remained alive? And why does Rachek admit to him, after those leaflets were handed out among the soldiers, that yes, Jews were responsible for everything? In the slaughterhouse of war, Jewish sensibility and sarcasm clearly have no place.

A full-scale rout comes in the summer, completing the reversed cycle of death-in-life. Though the army is back on native ground, the fields are unrecognizable, so totally have they been wasted by the war. "And while the armies crawled over the earth like swarms of gray worms, flocks of ravens soared overhead, calling with a dry rattling sound—the sound of tearing canvas—and swooped and slanted in intricate spirals, waiting for what would be theirs" (pages 330-331). The apocalypse unfolds—freed, for the time being, of Vasil's limited consciousness—with heightened imagery, macabre sounds, and terrifying echoes from the Jewish past. "By night burning cities lighted their path, and by day the smoke obscured the sun" (page 331). This obvious inversion of the Exodus is followed by a list of imaginary place-names that creates the illusion of specificity, of an actual eastern European landscape, while invoking the memory of earlier catastrophes. "The swift, narrow Sinevodka River was entirely choked with human bodies a little below Lutsin and overflowed into the fields" (page 331).

Abandoned by God to a nameless army that has already suffered massive annihilation in a nameless war and in whose ranks all moral and even military discipline have collapsed, the Jewish collective—chosen for its weakness, its age-old culpability, and its civilized norms of behavior—is doomed. Even resistance is entirely futile against evil of such magnitude: "Young [Jewish] men tried to resist and went out with revolvers in their hands. The revolvers sounded like pop guns. The soldiers answered with thundering laughter, and drew out the young men's veins one by one, and broke their bones into little pieces" (page 332).

Progressively brutalized by forces beyond his control, swept into the inexorable evil of war and goaded by an ancient enmity sharpened for the present onslaught, Vasil is now ready to act as the messenger of death. He breaks into a Jewish household demanding food, strikes out at the woman when she resists, and suddenly discovers the equation that has eluded him all his life: "His eyes were dazzled, almost blinded. Half a breast, a beautiful shoulder, a full, rounded hip—everything dazzling white and soft, like white *chalah*. Damn it—these Jews are *made* of white *chalah*! A searing flame leaped through his body, his arm flew up like a spring and shot into the gaping dress" (pages 332-333). He kills the husband, strangles the woman, and, after she is dead, bites into her flesh, discovering further, in this moment of cannibalistic ecstasy, that "white *chalah* has the taste of a firm juicy orange." Others before him, when pushed to the brink, gritted their teeth and bit their attackers. Vasil does more because his needs are so much greater. Killing is not enough; he has to suck the life-giving juices from his enemy in order to gain her strength. "In a circle, in a circle, the juices of life went from body to body, from the first to the second, from the second to the first—in a circle" (page 333). For Vasil, all circles are now closed. Haunted since childhood by the Jewish enemy and yet hungry for their food, he refuses, in this ultimate act of rebellion, to accept anything less than his due. But the circle of his victimization has closed as well. *He* is the victim of rape, not the Jewish woman with her flesh of white chalah.[56] It is he whom society has utterly brutalized. Vasil is the antithesis of the man with the cross who, purged by the pogrom, could begin again. By revealing the other side of man, Vasil's act of cannibalism also reveals the Other Side of God: "Pillars of smoke and pillars of flame rose to the sky from the entire city. Beautiful was the fire on the great altar. The cries of the victims—long-drawn-out, endless cries—were sweet in the ears of a god as eternal as the Eternal God. And the tender parts, the thighs and the breasts, were the portion of the priest" (page 333).

Both levels of the story, the real and the symbolic, come together in the double meaning of *korbones*: "victims" as well as "ritual sacrifices."[57] Vasil thus takes his rightful share—not the substitute shewbread of the Temple, but the flesh of the human sacrifice. Besides the Mosaic cult that failed to humanize the animal instinct in man, it is Christianity that stands condemned in this parting tableau of desecration, for Vasil, acting on a central article of Christian faith, has inverted the priestly rite of substituting the Host for the flesh of Christ.[58] There is no better substitute for the man on the cross than the flesh of another Jew. In the Revelation of Lamed Shapiro, therefore, man reverts to beast, the Judeo-Christian heritage is replaced by a cult of human sacrifice, nature revokes its life-giving capacities, and the beast of the apocalypse reigns supreme.

BOTH physically and philosophically, Shapiro was in a better position to convey a sense of the universality of evil than were many of his younger colleagues with first-hand experience of the war and revolution. From the safety of New York and Chicago, where all his pogrom stories were written, Shapiro recognized that politics and culture had done little more than camouflage the collapse of society and that with this collapse, man's primal aggression came increasingly to the fore. Through his use of an impressionistic style that focused on individual male and female perceptions of violence, Shapiro could suggest the existence of hidden realities and point to metaphysical themes that extended far beyond the confines of a given pogrom.

Those, in contrast, who actually survived the battles, who were wounded and captured, who manned the barricades for the revolution, who defended their towns against the Ukrainian nationalists, and who later came out with memoirs or fictional accounts of their experience often remained insular in their approach. The very title "Memoirs of a Jewish Army Officer" or "Prisoner of War" or "Political Commissar" announced an experience bracketed in time when the writer had been thrust head first into the maelstrom of history, had come out of it alive, and had been anxious to tell all. Rarely did the memoirist render the trench or barricade as emblematic of the age. He did not see the violence as something inescapable that was rapidly encroaching on all of mankind; he did not perceive that not just the self but all of civilization was under siege. Even Avigdor Hameiri struggled so hard with Greek mythology and binary oppositions in *The Great Madness* that this fictionalized war memoir appeared far too studied to make its case effectively.[59]

In "straight" fiction, where there was much more room to tamper with reality, ideology intervened to ensure an insular perspective. Hebrew writers, by virtue of the fact that they wrote in Hebrew and that the revolution proved inimical to their national aspirations, translated their lost faith into a recurrent plot: their Jewish revolutionary heroes were brought back to the fold by story's end; all of them discovered, sooner or later, that claims of blood ran deeper than love, ideology or class.[60] The Hebrew fictional soldier who returned from the front—Grisha Sokolov in Eliezer Steinman's "The Jewish Soldier," Solomon Stufashkover in Avraham Freiman's *1919*, Daniel Singer in Yitzhak Shenhar's "Chapters from a Novel"—began by embracing the Gentile world and its women and ended, however ambivalently, by defending the Jews.[61] The one plot that revealed the degree of total estrangement of individual Jews was the one that told of the most heinous act of betrayal—Jews joining in the slaughter of other Jews. Shenhar dealt with this theme in "Flesh and Blood," and for many years Shapiro tried in vain to exorcise it through his art.[62] But the plot of return and the plot of betrayal were still ways of delimiting the violence, of making it manageable.

Only writers who were willing to see violence as the decisive and paradigmatic element in modern life, regardless of politics or place, could achieve a universality of vision comparable to Shapiro's. In the immediate wake of World War I and the Bolshevik Revolution, Shapiro came as far as projecting an image of the world through the eyes of Vasil. The next step was to portray a world full of Vasils where every human being, whether peasant or rabbi's son, was rendered capable of perpetrating violence, and where ultimately the only choice that mattered was for the Jew willfully to become the Other.

WITH Isaac Babel (born 1894) and Israel Rabon (born 1900) we come to two writers who, in drawing a universal landscape of extremity, broke with the mold not only in terms of form but also in terms of language. The tradition was no longer confined to Hebrew and Yiddish letters, for through acculturation and displacement eastern European Jewish writers had adopted Russian, Polish, German, French, and English as their media. This happened at a time when the symbiotic relationship between Hebrew and Yiddish had also come to an end. A cosmopolitanism of style confused matters even further, making it possible to write in one language as if one were writing in another. There was nothing recognizably Yiddish in the style or world view of Israel Rabon, and the similarities between Babel and Shapiro owed as much to their adoration of Chekhov and de Maupassant as to their common Ukrainian-Jewish heritage. A Yiddish writer schooled in cosmopolitanism could abstain from using Jewish cultural symbols even when treating the theme of catastrophe, just as a Russian writer feeling thoroughly at home in his medium could make the Jew into Everyman. Defying the limitations of language, culture, and audience, both writers pressed their vision of the universality of violence.

Rabon served in the Polish army in 1920, the same year that Babel was fighting on the other side as war correspondent in Budyonny's First Cavalry. Rabon's approach was to make *The Street* into a landscape of modern violence.[63] In this picaresque novel, a precursor to Céline's *Journey to the End of the Night,* Rabon operated with two opposing sets of analogies: animal comparisons that reduced all human actions to those of dogs, tigers, horses, and the like, and crucifixion scenes, which he saw as the only mythic symbol that did the terror justice. Since the hero alternated between nightmare and reality, each took on the character of the other and in the confusion lay the eloquence that enforced factuality.

Rabon's hero returns from the front with nowhere to go and no profession to speak of. He settles in Lodz purely by chance, lodging sometimes in a dark cellar, sometimes in a park, and sometimes in a flophouse. His only past consists of memories of pain and humiliation from childhood and of four years spent in the war. The crazy cobbler from whom he rents a room is fond of playing war games, and once, so drunk that he becomes the Polish general incarnate, he forces an impoverished Swabian child to play the role of the kaiser. With other cellar children helping out, the cobber drags the "kaiser" kicking and screaming off to be hanged—literally hanged—and only the hero's intervention prevents this combination of murder, animal sacrifice, and war game from being carried out.

Not surprisingly, the circus and cinema are the most life-like places in town, and here the hero meets a panoply of clowns, wrestlers, crazy poets, and loose women in whose company he feels almost at home. In the midst of his street life he recalls a central episode of the war, prefigured as a fantasy. Out of hunger more real than imagined, he fantasizes being baked alive in a huge oven, lying "crucified" on the baker's trough, and being devoured. Later, as he (actually) lies feverish in the dark and empty circus tent, he remembers an experience from the last days of the war. He was wounded in battle and awoke at night on a snow-covered steppe with no refuge from the extreme cold and nothing to eat or drink. At the end of his tether, he stumbled over the body of a dying horse. "Like a famished child senses the smell of his mother's breast at night, that's how I sensed the presence of something warm" (page 110). It was a question of survival. With his last bit of strength he slashed open the stomach of the beast, pulled out its innards, and crawled in. "Oh, how warm I felt, how warm!" (page 112). This double reversion—man becoming beast and man returning to the womb—is shocking enough, but Rabon wishes to convey the extremity of war in other than naturalistic terms alone. And so, on awakening, his hero crawled out into the cold morning air and was immediately frozen to the spot: "From head to toe covered in a bloody red armor made of frozen Bordeaux-red blood. I couldn't let my arms down. They were spread out. My feet stuck to the ground and I looked like a crucifix. My God! I had become implanted in the ground like a red, bloody crucifix! . . . I, a bloody crucifix on a White-Russian steppe!" (page 113).

This bloody tableau is reminiscent of Warshawski's red meat wrapped around the female smuggler's body, an image of radical nakedness that goes beyond the skin. Rabon, however, takes the image of man-as-bloody-beast much further than Warshawski. Here, in the battlefield sequence, it is an image sufficently real to suggest the end point of human transformation and sufficiently eloquent to paint the war as the crucifixion of mankind. The fact that this man also happens to be a Jew adds force to the equation but is not central to its meaning, for the thrust of Rabon's postwar vision is of humanity stripped naked, of an urban jungle where only that which is imagined—the fleeting glance of a woman, the silent movie pageant, the laughter of a dying clown—is real, and all meaningful human interaction lasts only as long as the circus or the movie runs.

In Babel's view, the universality of violence could be apprehended only through history, in the texture of local dialect, ethnic idiosyncrasies, and religious passions. His very first story, inspired by events of that year (1913), told of the expulsion of Jews from the villages, the same theme that Sholem Aleichem picked up for the last two episodes of the Tevye stories. Babel's lifelong attraction to extremes of peripheral intelligence was already evident in the character of "Old Shloime," deaf and dirty, who tapped a hidden source of defiance when he learned of his son's plan to avert expulsion by converting to Christianity.[64] Rather than submit to the forces of history, Old Shloime hung himself in the middle of the night. Though not a practicing Jew, he would " 'tell God how they've hurt him. After all, God exists. God will accept him.' And of that Shloime was convinced" (page 20).

The deeper Babel treaded in the landscape of violence, the tougher his prose became. Gorky, so the story goes, sent him out into the world to experience history first-hand, and when he came back from serving on the Rumanian front, he wrote for Gorky's virulently anti-Bolshevik paper, *The New Life (Novaya Zhizn).* With a matter-of-fact style, Babel chronciled the chaos and the abuse of revolutionary power as he saw it unfold in the streets and state institutions of Petrograd. These slice-of-life reports invariably ended on a sardonic note: "All this I have seen myself: the sullen, barefoot children, the puffed, pimply faces of their gloomy mentors, and the broken sewage pipes. Our poverty and wretchedness are truly unsurpassed" ("A Fine Institution"). "A stunted kind of life that will be. We've seen enough of that kind of life, the stunted kind" ("Premature Babies").[65] To further hone his spare, ironic, and amazingly compact style, he rewrote someone else's *Observations on War* and made of their flowery French original something almost on his own.[66] Then he joined the Cossacks.

The diary he kept that year reveals both the factual basis for many of his *Red Cavalry* stories—the real life models for characters such as Gedali, the Rabbi, and Grishchuk, not to speak of the commander, Semyon Budyonny himself (who later denounced the collection as erotomaniacal garbage)—and Babel's despair at being "unfit . . . for the work of destruction" (entry for 13 August 1920).[67] The challenge was not simply to convey "the layers of worthlessness, daring, professionalism, revolutionary spirit, and bestial cruelty" that characterized his comrades-in-arms (entry for 21 July), but to purge his own revulsion, his "rabbinic sensibilities," so as to transmute the horror into a higher level of reality. Nothing could have been more difficult. On August 20 he recorded an episode in which ten Polish prisoners of war, including one Jew, were shot in cold blood. That made Babel an accomplice to the murder, or so, at least, it appeared in the story version he wrote, in which the Jewish prisoner, a clerk from Lodz, pleaded with the narrator for mercy:

> "You are a *Jude,* sir!" he whispered, frantically fondling my stirrup. "You are—" he squealed, the spittle dribbling from his mouth, and his whole body convulsed with joy.
>
> "Get back into line, Shulmeister!" I shouted at the Jew, and suddenly, overcome by a deathly feeling of faintness, I began to slip from the saddle and, choking, I said, "How did you know?"
>
> "You have that nice Jewish look about you," he said in a shrill voice, hopping on one leg and leaving the thin dog's trail behind him. "That nice Jewish look, sir."[68]

However much he might dissociate himself from a fellow Jew by describing him as a wounded dog, the murder weighed so heavily that the narrator felt compelled to make notes about each of the ten prisoners. "Nobody else but me would do this in the Red Cavalry." While he, the man of conscience, was busy taking notes, the Cossacks were plundering the beehives nearby. "And I put aside my pen. I was horrified at the great number of memorials still to be written" (page 133).

Now this was a story that Babel himself expunged from the collection. Only squadron commander Trunov, who ordered the execution, was deemed worthy of a memorial, not as a murderer but as the heroic protector of his men.[69] For the men of the Red Cavalry came to represent to Babel a new code of behavior in which nothing but the exercise of extreme power could soothe a man from the terror that he suffered—an honor code in which not to kill a wounded comrade was the highest act of immorality and selfishness.

In *Red Cavalry,* unquestionably a central work of modern fiction, Babel raised his conversion to the Cossack code of violence to a choice of universal significance.[70] The Bolshevik campaign to occupy Poland took Lyutov, the narrator, through a mutilated landscape of absolute extremity, a world in which sensation was all that ultimately mattered. Amid the ruins of ancient cathedrals, nobles' estates, and countless shtetlekh, Lyutov was initiated into killing, the victim being a goose that was to be served for dinner. Lyutov's heart, "stained with bloodshed, grated and brimmed over" (page 77). Later he discovered "the rapture of first possession"—to have a little cart called a *tachanka* all his own with a driver named Grishchuk thrown in for good measure (page 85). Meanwhile, he came upon people of his faith, birdlike Gedali, for instance, visionary of a joyous revolution, who challenged Lyutov to choose between "the turbulent winds of history" and "the passionate edifice of Hasidism" (page 77). And even when the hasidic rabbi Motale came out on top, with clever jibes at the narrator's expense, this only made the contest more interesting; whether wanting to or not, the reader found himself rooting for Lyutov to become more extreme, more masculine, more like a Cossack. Toward the very end of the quest, in the story "The Rabbi's Son," Babel gave the Jewish-Christian reader one last chance to identify with the Torah as the preferred symbol of humanity, before he, Lyutov, chose horses instead, renounced his past and his Judaism, surrendered his particularity to embrace the strangely beautiful Cossack code of violence. "Months passed, and my dream came true. The Cossacks stopped watching me and my horse" (page 200).

Life, in Babel's scheme, was a series of initiations into violence, whether one lived at home with one's parents ("The Story of My Dovecot," 1925) or set out from home on a journey ("The Journey," 1932). And if one had the good fortune to grow up in Odessa, the southern outpost of the Russian sun, then one knew of a clan of Moldovanka *ba'al-gufs*—Mendl and Benya, Froim and Lyubka, Jew-and-a-Half and The King—for whom the exercise of violence was no more than the full-blooded passion for life. The Red Cavalry was the fullest expression of a life in which every human being, including the son of a rabbi, was made a partner to violence and in which the bespectacled Lyutov prayed fervently to God to grant him "the simplest of proficiencies—the ability to kill" his fellow men (page 187). To kill: to be as real as everything around him, to be like the universe, like history.

No less important than Lyutov's conversion to the Cossack code of violence was Babel's apparent success in purging his "rabbinic sensibilities" in order to write about catastrophe and destruction in the modern age. Despite the temptation nowadays to rehabilitate "Babel the Jew" in light of his tragic end and the end of all Jewish culture in the Soviet Union, one must take his writing in context and appreciate the extent of his radical break with the Jewish past.[71] It is crucial to understand the precise nature of the traditions that stood in his way, that he as a Jew felt he had to overcome.

Playing the role of dutiful son intoning kinot and rehearsing the Destruction in the shtetl of Demidovka as his mother sat howling on the floor was the surest means of rendering the Cossack violence transtemporal. Babel would dissociate himself from the use of such archetypes, from the characters who employed them, and most certainly from their attendant theology of sin, retribution, and redemption. Even Gedali's syncretistic messianism was not his. Instead Babel would push the historical context, the here-and-now in all its specificity, with an eye for strategic detail almost unsurpassed in modern fiction. Though rabbinic midrash and medieval chronicles were not devoid of atrocity stories, Jews were reticent about referring explicitly to physical violence. More often than not, violence was done *to* things (sanctuary, Torah scrolls, pillows, and hearth) in lieu of detailed mutilation, rape and murder. In Babel, everything from the moon to a man's horse could suffer violence. "He talked about the stars and about gonorrhea in the same tone of voice," wrote Victor Shklovsky.[72] For images, Babel drew equally upon the "odor of crucifixes" and the "carved gray stones" of the old Jewish cemetery. In his famous requiem to the rabbi's son, he listed "the portraits of Lenin and Maimonides" lying side by side, "pages of the Song of Songs and revolver cartridges."[73] Just as Babel mixed symbol systems, he refused to make the Jewish destruction separate from the rest of the world's. Rather than the communal dislocation insisted upon in Jewish sources, Babel would insist on individual dislocation—physical, social, emotional, and psychic. In his work, there was a modern emphasis on sensation (as opposed to mind) in the encounter with disaster. And only when the individual was finally cut off from the sustaining archetypes, from the exalted messianic schemes, from the insular perspective on destruction, from the communal saga, from the past, from his own set of inherited symbols, could he then hope to enact his will *in* history and *through* history. This was the generation of iron men that Shapiro had called for. Whether such men—and women, too—would rebuild the ruins was the question that only history could answer.

CHAPTER SEVEN

Laughing Off the Trauma of History

But as they say, if it's fated to be a disaster, you lose your tongue.
Sholem Aleichem, 1915

"I talk, therefore I am" is a fitting motto for the Jews that people Sholem Aleichem's fictional universe. Even their silence speaks a thousand words. In Sholem Aleichem's work the Jews of eastern Europe appear first and foremost as a speech community in which three or more languages are used simultaneously. Sholem Aleichem's wordplay depends entirely for its success upon a milieu sensitive to nuances in Yiddish, Hebrew, Ukrainian, Polish, Russian, German, and English. That in itself is culturally and historically unusual, especially because his audience—the audience that best appreciated his genius—was not a cultural elite (such as Christian clerics able to deal with Greek, Latin, and vernaculars, or similar priestly and academic mandarins) but the general population. The anomaly of this interplay of languages is much greater at a time of catastrophe. When we might anticipate obscenity, muteness, syntactic failure, neologism, and autistic repetition we have instead a community of argumentative Jews—traveling salesmen, market women, upstanding householders, fathers, mothers, and sons—talking their way out of disaster in an orchestrated cacophony of voices.

A systematic reading of Sholem Aleichem provides, perhaps uniquely, an appreciation for the textures of languages within a cycle of destruction. These textures, in turn, challenge the notion of any one language as the embodiment of truth, or of silence as the only adequate response to the abdication of truth. To begin with, the Jews of eastern Europe considered *both* of their central languages the bearers of truth. Taking Hebrew in all its nineteenth-century polyphony (its biblical, rabbinic, medieval, and maskilic layers) as the mythic vehicle and Yiddish as the concurrent mythic commentary, Sholem Aleichem shows that the daily life of eastern European Jews stood as commentary on biblical life. Just as for the Revivalists, the late eighteenth-century American Protestants, daily life became the allusion *for* the Bible, their experience *became* the text—so Yiddish in the works of Sholem Aleichem does not allude to the original Hebrew but informs it.[1] Moreover, as Hebrew lost its prophetic or redemptive character (except for the orthodox and the Zionists), Yiddish too was in danger of losing its mythic base; in response to this secularization process, Sholem Aleichem attempts through Yiddish to create a separate myth, a perfect linguistic medium that would shield the community from all the forces of history.

Increasingly, cryptic language takes on a central role in the lives of his fictional Jews. There is a High Cryptic Style, all in Hebrew, used by the learned and semi-learned to send messages through the mail, and a Low Cryptic Style used on the streets when there are policemen around. Since the police too can be expected to know a smattering of Yiddish (after all, they are invited every Friday night for chalah and gefilte fish), nonstandard Hebraisms are used to talk over their heads, to communicate coded messages in the language of Jewish learning. Both High and Low Cryptics are recognizably cryptic derivations of the *central* tongue, an ideal and idealized form of spoken Yiddish which is as much the creation of Sholem Aleichem as his discovery.

When compared to Yiddish folk locution "in the raw," to the extent that such records have been preserved, Sholem Aleichem's version thereof is strikingly devoid of obscenity, especially the scatalogical kind, and uses Slavic and regional forms with great precision. The absence of *really* low language—which is the true index to the extreme "liminal" states into which the Jews were eventually put, for example, in the Nazi ghettos and camps—reveals what Sholem Aleichem is about: he is using language, a richly variegated form of Yiddish, to protect his characters from historical disruption. It is entirely likely that the "common Jew" also used language in this way and that Sholem Aleichem simply (as if this were simple) exaggerated what he heard. What is even more likely is that Sholem Aleichem wanted to resurrect a failing Yiddish, one that was polluted, too Hebraized, Germanized, and Slavicized, too vulgar or too flat, as a way of maintaining Jewish inviolability.

He lived just long enough to see his art of the incongruous tested to the limit. His was a comic paradigm that could be followed by very few because so few could sustain a vision of human inviolability. Against a historical field of disarray and destruction, his characters used their colloquial speech as a protective sheild.[2] Working against the resilience of language was history, a permanent vehicle of destruction.

History was relentless and inscrutable. To the extent that the Old World characters were people of faith—such as Tevye, the comic Job, or Reb Yuzifl, the schlemiel rabbi of Kasrilevke—they could still accommodate history to a divine scheme; but the moment a character was thrust into the contemporary world—Menakhem-Mendl the jack-of-all-modern-trades, or any of the travelers in a third-class train compartment—they experienced a world in which miracles, if they happened at all, were a result of human error, not of divine will. Tevye, in the end, was forced to pack up and leave his village, and even Reb Yuzifl died without benefit of the Old Age Home he had fought for so bravely.

Sholem Aleichem began his Yiddish career shortly after the first series of tsarist pogroms in 1881–82. Whether for reasons of external or internal censorship or because his youthful enthusiasm compensated for the trauma of history, the pogroms did not figure directly in his early writings.[3] He was certainly not alone here, for the *pogromshtshik* hardly appeared at all in Yiddish and Hebrew fiction until the Kishinev pogrom.[4] Sholem Aleichem's optimism in this period derived from his faith in a Jewish-liberal alliance in tsarist Russia, the dream that Moses Mendelssohn had been the first to espouse. This faith was not shaken by the Kishinev pogrom. Unlike some Jewish intellectuals who despaired once and for all of the Russian liberal sector, Sholem Aleichem initiated a project designed not only to raise funds for the pogrom victims but also to mobilize support from within Russian society. To these ends he published *Hilf* (Aid), subtitled *An Almanac for Literature and Art,* which was, from an aesthetic point of view at least, the most impressive Yiddish publication of its time.[5] In addition to the work of major Yiddish and Hebrew writers, it contained three parables by Tolstoy written especially for the volume and a story by Vladimir Korolenko, all in authorized translations by Sholem Aleichem. Obviously, the censor was especially zealous: David Pinsky's realistic drama *The Zvi Family* was expunged altogether, and Korolenko was represented by a rather sentimental story—in marked contrast to the stark eyewitness account of the Kishinev massacre, which circulated underground.[6] In line with these constraints and with his optimistic agenda, Sholem Aleichem's own contribution to the volume focused on peripheral phenomena—on the petty rivalries fueled by the arbitrary rule of the tsar.

"A Hundred and One" was a fairly benign example of how, under tyrannical rule, "the comic results from the fact that all normal laws are suspended and the arbitrary reigns."[7] Within such a world of arbitrary rule, the language of intervention can never work to one's benefit, either because cultural differences are exacerbated or because one branch of government can overturn the decision of another. What happens here is that administrative fiat severs the bond of two neighboring towns, Bohopolye and Holte, under the "Temporary Rules" of 3 May 1882. Henceforth, Holte is decreed a village where the presence of Jews is no longer desirable (because they supposedly corrupt the morals of the peasants); thus, no Jews are allowed to settle there anew. But since Holte is the more prosperous place, the inhabitants of neighboring Bohopolye will do anything in their power to steal across. With the local police waiting to turn them back at the bridge, Jews must meet the challenge with special rhetorical skills and with a working knowledge of Ukrainian:

> "How can that be!" he argued. "I've lived in Holte for many years: *Ja maje sobstvene gorod uv škole* [I have my own city in the school]! *Ja maje skilke rodiči na kladbišče* [I have my several relatives in the cemetery]!"
>
> But the entreaties were as efficacious as yesterday's snow. (page 104)

The Jewish claim to ownership is so spiritual and otherworldly and is expressed in terms that are so culturally specific (having a "city in the school" means owning a seat in the house of study!), that rendering them into another language, even that of the native peasantry, only heightens the Jews' vulnerability. Their manipulation of various codes will be an index to the way in which Sholem Aleichem's characters negotiate the perilous terrain of history.

Government intervention does not fare much better than face-to-face negotiations with the local police. After years of personal anguish and animosity, Yerakhmiel-Moyshe's case is finally taken up by the Russian senate, which allows him to return home to Holte, across the bridge; but the victory over his archrival, Nakhmen-Leyb, proves utterly meaningless when, at exactly the same time, the tsar revokes the "Temporary Rules" as symbolic restitution for the excesses of Kishinev. As of 10 May 1903, 101 localities that had previously been barred to Jews are opened up for "free domicile" and Holte, of course, is on the list.[8] Yerakhmiel-Moyshe, we are to understand from the story's finale, goes mad and remains in Bohopolye, while Nakhmen-Leyb is the one to make the coveted move.

And so, for Sholem Aleichem the meaning of Kishinev was that Jews would continue to be the butt of diabolical tsarist jokes, though perhaps mutual aid and cooperation—across cultural barriers far more formidable than those between Bohopolye and Holte—could soften the blow. Help came in small doses in a crazy world bent on destruction.

As towns, Holte and Bohopolye could be shuffled around with impunity, just like their hapless inhabitants. As fictional settings they were accordingly indistinguishable, all the more so in the revised version of the story. Their fate was too tied in with the grimmer aspects of tsarist fiats to make for a timeless work of fiction. Immortality, though, was already on its way in the form of Kasrilevke, the "Town of Little People." It was many years in the making before it emerged as Sholem Aleichem's shorthand for Jewish collective survival in exile. In his stories about this town, Sholem Aleichem mined the most popular of Yiddish folk motifs, the foolstown of Khelm, as well as the core of maskilic satire to produce a normative community of such faith and language that it could transform defeat into victory.[9]

The finest episodes in the Kasrilevke cycle are deceptively simple. They use well-worn plots and a gallery of recognizable types. As these stories were serialized in the Russian-Yiddish press, readers grew familiar with the stock characters: Fishl the Correspondent, Zeydl Reb Shayes, the only man in town who subscribes to a newspaper, and a Hebrew one at that; Reb Yuzifl the Rabbi and—pardon the proximity—the town's two or three domesticated goyim. Many plots were lifted straight out of folklore and nineteenth-century satire, sometimes with a title that revealed the probable source. Thus, when Sholem Aleichem in 1904 published one of his longest Kasrilevke narratives, "The Great Panic of the Little People," the word *behole* in the title invoked a forty-year tradition of spoofs on shtetl hysteria.[10] Sholem Aleichem followed the standard three-part plot of these works: (1) the arrival of news from the outside world sends the isolated shtetl into a state of panic; (2) all normal activity stops as the entire shtetl prepares feverishly for the imminent event; (3) when the truth is finally revealed, everyone is disappointed, duped, or disgraced.[11] The same pattern could be used for any number of stories because the anticipation of destruction was structurally parallel to the anticipation of salvation.

So long as the shtetl was viewed as a provincial backwater fanatically resistant to the changes that enlighteners or the tsar had designed for its own benefit, the shtetl Jews could do no right and their every reaction was an overreaction. But once the enlighteners grew disenchanted with their government's intentions, they came to view the shtetl's resistance as a quixotic struggle against malevolent forces. Straddling the two positions in 1890, Sholem Aleichem could joke about the shtetl running scared over a blood libel that didn't come to pass, but he also concluded with a stern warning not to take anti-Semitism too lightly.[12] Fourteen years later, with Kishinev a reality, Sholem Aleichem began to see the shtetl's prime act of resistance as rhetorical.

In "The Great Panic," Kasrilevke gets word of the pogrom by means of a letter, written in ornate and clichéd Hebrew and addressed to a ritual slaughterer from his semi-learned son-in-law: "With trembling hands and quaking knees do I write these words to you. Know that the weather here has undergone a severe change. No pen can possibly describe it" (chapter 2). A direct, terse, and unambiguous message in plain Yiddish would have conveyed the imminent threat of a knowable danger. A string of fixed phrases and circumlocutions makes the event at once more ominous and less so. For as the narrator, a native son himself, informs us: "Sages and savants have long noted that the Jews are incomparable at the art of reading between the lines," and as the son-in-law's letter passes from hand to hand, each (male) reader adds his own terrifying interpretation to the coded lines. On the other hand, the son-in-law might have gotten carried away with his own eloquence, as so often happens to this type of semi-learned correspondent. Indeed, the inhabitants of Kasrilevke swap jokes at his expense, trying in this manner to dispel the gloom, until Zeydl, the sole subscriber to the Hebrew paper *Hazefirah*, corroborates the news and they are duly thunderstruck.

The letter illustrates the High Cryptic Style, or at least a faint echo of the original flowery Hebrew as rendered by the author into *prost zhargon* (plain Yiddish) and as translated into English. Jews would find this funny because they would recognize the discrepancy between the profanity of the times and the biblicism of the language, whereas we readers, whoever we are, should realize that Sholem Aleichem is trying to play with language in such a way that events change as the language in which they are reported changes.

Within the narrative frame of a pogrom scare, Sholem Aleichem provides us with an anatomy of Jewish language, a compendium of speech patterns from the cradle to the grave, in the home, marketplace, and houses of prayer. Perhaps this is what he meant to signify when he subtitled the work a *poema*, a Russian loan-word for a long narrative poem. Language, as we shall see, becomes part of a lyrical statement.

From early childhood, the Kasrilevker learns that the world is divided into Gentiles and Jews. In answer to the Gentile children's taunts, their *Tatele-mamele* ("daddy" and "mommy") imitation of Yiddish speech, and the pig's ears they form with the corners of their jackets, Jewish children respond in kind with a well-rehearsed rhyme:

Kishkes kokhn
in der vokhn!
Mir a broyt,
dir a toyt!
Mir a vogn,
dikh bagrobn!
Mir a shlitn,
dikh bashitn!

Kishka cooks
In our pots.
For me a bread—
You drop dead!
For me a wagon,
For you a hearse!
Pant and rave,
Dig your grave!

Even at this early stage, life in the shtetl bears out the meaning of the biblical passages they learn in heder. When young Makar Kholodny ("the cold one") beats them up for singing this ditty, they learn the true meaning of the passage THE VOICE IS THE VOICE OF JACOB, YET THE HANDS ARE THE HANDS OF ESAU (Gen. 27:22), and when a band of Gentiles gangs up on them, they understand the plight of the Israelites fleeing from the Philistines (chapter 4).

As the Kasrilevker Jews and Gentiles grow up, the language of mutual abuse loses its innocence. Thanks to a little church learning, Makar, apparently modeled on a real-life anti-Semite from Sholem Aleichem's childhood,[13] rises in the municipal hierarchy and knows enough to call the Jews by their generic names—*Itska, Berka*—and to taunt them with their favorite words, *ay-vay, shabes kugl.* They, in turn, address him with mock respect in High Goyish (Russian) instead of Low Goyish (Ukrainian). In the tavern, store, and market the divisions become even more pronounced because there the Jew is in control, and with strategically placed Hebrew words he can ensure his economic and moral superiority. "Can one possibly explain," wonders the narrator with tongue in cheek at the very end of the story, "why it is that a Kasrilevker Jew will throw in all the Hebrew he's ever learned the moment he starts talking about a non-Jew?" This super-Hebraized form of Yiddish, which I have dubbed the Low Cryptic Style, is a legitimate defense in time of danger, but in normal business dealings it represents unfair advantage. "Place a BEAKER OF VINTAGE into the HANDS of the UNCIRCUMCISED ONE," says the Jewish tavern keeper to his Jewish help, "but don't EXCEED THE BRIM, and a slice of the STAFF OF LIFE, for he hasn't PARTAKEN OF NOURISHMENT all day, and CHARGE him two SILVER PIECES and BID him SALLY FORTH, but SCRUTINIZE him that he doesn't APPROPRIATE a thing." All the key words—here set apart by diction and capitalization—are nonstandard Hebraisms that the poor peasant would never have heard in spoken Yiddish.

Economic advantage makes the Jew so self-confident that he abuses his non-Jewish customer to his face in a Hebrew-Yiddish-Slavic argot. "Please don't take it amiss, my lord," says the Jewish storekeeper in Ukrainian, "*sholem babayis mashkn bakeshene*"—which means "when the promissory note [Hebrew-Yiddish *mashkn*] is safe in my pocket [Yiddish *keshene*], there will be peace between us [Hebrew *sholem babayis*]" (chapter 8). These are the words of Mordkhe-Nosn, the merchant and community *macher* (wheeler-dealer). He is portrayed by Sholem Aleichem, in a rare instance of Marxist caricature, as a boor and a sycophant, the worst that the shtetl "bourgeoisie" has produced. The market, therefore, is seen as a breeding ground of animosity and its language as the language of deceit and distrust.

In the home, the relations between Jews and Gentiles are altogether different. The Goy-for-the-Sabbath "knows well and good that what *they* eat, he, Khvedor, can also eat, but what he, Khvedor, eats—they are forbidden to eat" (chapter 3). He asks no questions, just goes about his business blowing out the Sabbath candles and carrying a prayer book to the synagogue, actions his employers must abstain from on the holy days. Except when drunk, Khvedor is docile and obedient, and on those occasions when he does go overboard, the Yiddish-Slavic curses heaped upon him by the Jews put him in his place. Thus, communication with Khevdor reflects his partial integration into Jewish life. It consists mostly of commands, curses, and key words like *shabes* (Sabbath), *bulke* (roll), *khazer* (pig) and *kapore* (scapegoat).

Hapke the Maid represents the total integration of Gentiles into shtetl society, behaviorally and linguistically.

> Hapke speaks Yiddish like a Jew. Her speech is peppered with a profusion of [mispronounced] Hebrew words, like *mirtshen* (God willing), *nakhteyse* (all right), *kenore nisht* (no evil eye), *losate* (for now), *lavdl* (to differentiate [between the sacred and profane]), *gutyonte* (good holiday), *makhreynvaser* (water for ablution) and many more. And when Khvedor's back is turned, she can think of no better appellation than *kaporenik* (good-for-nothing). (chapter 4)

So great is the shtetl's love for Hapke and its absolute reliance upon her services that it saves her good name after Makar seduces her. This is not easy for Kasrilevke to do, for it means forgoing the pleasure of taking revenge upon its long-standing enemy.

Whereas the home can provide a setting of perfect integration between Gentiles and Jews, the house of prayer can be turned into the scene of bitter rivalries between Jews and other Jews. A legacy of religious schisms has left at least one vestige in the order of prayer. The Jews of Kasrilevke, following hasidic practice, recite *Hoydu* ("Give thanks to the Lord") before *Borukh sheomar* ("Blessed be He who spoke") in the morning service, whereas the Jews of neighboring Kozodoyevke retain the prehasidic order of the misnagdim (chapter 14). Lest we think this verbal one-upmanship is but a quirk or a historical curiosity, the narrator has assured us earlier that speech and wordplay are the

Kasrilevker's main arsenal of attack and self-defense. "As is well known throughout the world, a Kasrilevker will stop at nothing for the sake of one good jibe; he will walk for miles, risk his livelihood and even his life" (chapter 5). Nothing can douse the verbal fireworks, not his fear of the goyim or even his fear of God.

Only the cemetery and bathhouse remain untouched by strife, for they are the mythic centers of the town. Unlike the market, a place of corruption and monopoly, and unlike the synagogue, where street animosities permeate as well, part of Kasrilevke exists in ecological balance: since the old Jewish cemetery is the only grazing area in town, it feeds the Jewish goats, who in turn provide Jewish children with their much-needed milk. And part, the bathhouse, exists in a state of nature: Adam and Eve, the bathhouse attendants, live in perfect innocence; virgins (the rabbi calls them *kinderlekh,* "children"), they go around naked most of the time, sleep out of doors, and commune with the frogs in summer. Not surprisingly, the bathhouse is the locus of a special, Adamic language: "And Adam rises very early, when God Himself still slumbers, and with his healthy pair of arms he draws pail after pail of water, belting out by heart whole chunks of Psalms with a melody, and his voice sounds and resounds, you can hear it from inside the bathhouse, and it carries with the wind over the banks of the river and is lost somewhere far off in the distance" (chapter 11). Living with the bathhouse attendants on the premises is the aged Reb Yuzifl, whom the community has entrusted to their care. He is "a pure soul in a broken vessel," a pathetic Job who justifies God's ways with a parable for every occasion. His is a language of faith, though the only ones he can still move with his piety are Adam and Eve.

In their whole lives they never heard so many words of Torah as they now heard in a single day from the old rabbi Reb Yuzifl. And everything they heard was new to them. In their eyes he was like a traveler from distant lands who told exotic tales which defied the imagination . . . [Winter and summer] they heard the rabbi talk on matters of the spirit, telling them the wonders of the Lord, of men in this world and angels in the world to come, of the earth and all its creatures, of the heaven, sun and moon, the stars and all the galaxies. (chapter 12)

Thus, the bathhouse is the locus of language in its purest form, a language of perfect faith and harmony, a language upon which and through which the Jews of Kasrilevke should be able to maintain their psychological and social balance, a language which is their ultimate resort and ultimate resource. But this is a language that is too isolated from the forces of history, which can now penetrate the borders of the town through rumors and lies spread by means of cryptic Hebrew letters and anti-Semitic Russian newspapers. Makar Kholodny, now a ranking official in the town administration, has access to one such paper through which he learns about the Protocols of the Elders of Zion and the most recent case of Jews baking matzoh with Christian blood. When he questions Mordkhe-Nosn on the matter, it is enough to drive even this obsequious, power-hungry merchant into a fit of rage. Makar is thereby convinced that the accusations are true. All this adds to Kasrilevke's panic, until one fine day the whole town packs up and runs.

Reb Yuzifl alone stands fast. "Harken and know," he says to Adam and Eve, "that the Guardian of Israel doth not slumber or sleep. Let me tell you a parable about a king . . ." (chapter 13). Though absolute, his faith is ineffectual. By sheer coincidence, not by virtue of the inhabitants' faith or creativity, it is Kasrilevke's language, more acerbic, argumentative, and cryptic than Reb Yuzifl's, that more directly weathers the storm. Whom should the townspeople meet on the road but their traditional enemy, the people of the neighboring town of Kozodoyevke. Confronted with a comedy of errors—each town having sought refuge from the imagined pogrom in the other town—the two shtetlekh are reconciled to each other by talking through their fright and embarrassment: "and they talked away, talked themselves full as a barrel and talked their hearts out . . . then they shook hands, took leave of each other nicely and embraced" (chapter 14).

Nothing has really been solved. The faith of mythic Kasrilevke wins only by default over the fear of mercantile Kasrilevke, and the existence of two Kasrilevkes points to dangers ahead. For as the shtetl falls apart, its central tongue also seems to do so, creating a possibly unbridgeable gap between faith and pragmatism. However delighted we may be to see the neighboring towns make up their old differences, it is not they who are endangering each other but an enemy lurking on the outside and its agents working from within. In the face of *real* danger, *all* speech may become ironic and cryptic, at which point comes loss of community and the resultant terror, hysteria, and anarchy, or, at the opposite extreme, Reb Yuzifl's brand of transcendental faith divorced from any social context. And real danger does in fact lurk on the horizon.

FOR many, Kishinev shattered hopes that a new enlightened era would be ushered in by the twentieth century. For Sholem Aleichem, the faith in political reform lingered on until the revolution of February 1905—until, that is, there came a cycle of military pogroms, more brutal and widespread than before. Sholem Aleichem lived through the 1905 pogrom in Kiev and, almost as the atrocities were unfolding, he recorded the events in his own city and throughout the Pale for the American Yiddish press: "Brothers! Did you once weep over the Kishinev disaster? Forget it! Listen instead to what happened in Nyezhin." "Jews, throw out your old laments. Cry for Odessa!"[14] With the pogroms came exile. Sholem Aleichem left Russia by train at the end of 1905 and never returned except on tour.[15]

From Abramovitsch, Sholem Aleichem learned that the third-class train compartment could serve as symbolic shorthand for the plight of exile: all those Jews, en route to nowhere, crammed into a few filthy cars and telling tales along the way. But Sholem Aleichem's *Train Tales*, written mostly in 1909 and 1910 when the author suffered a near-fatal attack of tuberculosis, made Mendele's train ride of 1890 seem like a field trip. An anonymous traveling salesman presents tales of insanity, blind ambition, reckless gambling, white slave trade, apostasy and self-hate, pogroms and anti-Semitism. Each train provides a different setting for the telling of a tale; on a busy commuter train the story may begin and end abruptly, in accordance with the storyteller's schedule.

Of all the trains that travel the Jewish route, the Straggler Special *(der leydikgeyer)* is the one most conducive to traditional, long, drawn-out stories, because just as you can wait on the *platzform* and go crazy with boredom until the interminable ritual of switching and fueling the train is completed by a band of inebriated goyim, once on board, you have the rare privilege of stretching out "as in your father's vineyard" and of sharing in a story. Seldom do more than two passengers travel in a car at any one time on the Straggler Special. The kind of story that this train inspires has much to do, in fact, with its sudden stops and starts, its long periods of repetition, its infrequent runs, and its unpredictable schedule. The Straggler Special, in short, becomes the hero of a miracle tale for the age of technology.

Judging from its title, *A khasene on klezmer* (a wedding without musicians) promises, at worst, to be a domestic tragedy, unless *khasene* is to be construed in its patriarchal slang meaning of "misfortune."[16] Indeed, in the spirited narration that follows, every upbeat statement is qualified to mean its opposite. First, the tale is introduced in mock storybook fashion: "*Vayehi biymey,* this took place, heaven help us, *ha-konstitutsye,* during the days of the Constitution, that is to say, when the salvations for the Jews began. Though I must tell you that we Jews of Heissin have never been afraid of pogroms. Why weren't we afraid? Simply because there was no one in our town to beat us up" (page 130). Not that the addressee, the worldly traveling salesman, and by extension each one of us, would be taken in by such a ridiculous boast: "Of course you can imagine that if we looked very hard we could find one or two volunteers who wouldn't deny themselves the pleasure of ventilating us a little, that is to say, breaking our bones." Even so, for a real pogrom to take place, the hooligans would have to be imported by an embittered Polish nobility: "For the proof is, when the good news began drifting in from all sides, the few scoundrel squires in our parts sent off confidential letters to the proper places, saying: whereas it would be a good idea if 'something were done' in Heissin also, but since there's no one here to do it, would they be so kind as to send help, in other words, would they please dispatch some 'people' as quickly as possible." The more imminent the danger, the more the narrator tries to explain it away. Now the cast of characters takes its place: Noah Tonkonog, the bearer of bad tidings, and Nakhmen Kasoy, the man with connections. At each step in the drama it is Noah who carries the news "in strictest confidence" to every person in town. And that is how the whole town learns of the detailed plan for disposing of the Jews. The hooligans will be arriving by train and their approach is heralded by telegrams.

It is worth pausing for a moment, as Sholem Aleichem would do when he has us sitting on the edge of our seats, to recall that ever since the 1880s the trains had played a catalytic role in the tsarist pogroms. Most of the pogromists of 1881–82 were itinerant workers, drawn from the recently "liberated" serfs who had left their villages to work and live near the train stations, and were easily organized to raise hell along the route.[17] Lest our own visual images of cattle cars crowd out the terror that Sholem Aleichem's readers must have felt in their day, we should note that the train was aleady being transformed in his fiction from a souce of dislocation to a vehicle of death.

The Jews of Heissin marshal their scant resources against the coming onslaught of muscle and machine. The narrator here interjects his own words of sober pragmatism, which may very well reflect Sholem Aleichem's growing skepticism since the days of *Hilf.* He, too, once believed in the goodwill of the peasants and the compassion of the liberal intelligentsia.

> I was the only one in town who wasn't anxious to hide. I am not boasting about my bravery. But this is the way I see it: what's the sense of being afraid of a pogrom? I don't say that I am a hero. I might have been willing to hide too, when the hour of reckoning came. But I asked myself first, "How can I be sure that during the slaughter the friendly peasant in whose cellar I was hiding, or the Notary, or the Director of the factory himself, wouldn't . . ." You understand? And all that aside, how can you leave a town wide open like that? It's no trick to run away. You have to see about doing something. (page 132)

The course of action they hit upon—buying protection from the police inspector through the mediation of Nakhmen the contractor—is ironically undercut by idiomatic expressions that suggest the fatal inevitability of making such desperate choices. The Russian inspector is referred to as a *porits* ("Polish squire") and Nakhmen is reduced to delivering a handsome bribe, like a medieval court Jew. The inspector accepts the bribe and assures them that all will be well. But when Noah announces the hooligans' impending arrival, the hopes and fears of Heissin begin fluctuating wildly at each new turn of events—in the up-and-down pattern so characteristic of Sholem Aleichem's work as a whole. The inspector sends for the Cossacks.

> When we heard this we breathed more easily. When a Jew hears that a Cossack is coming, he takes courage, he can face the world again [literally, he shows the world a fig]. The question remained: who would arrive first, the Cossacks from Tulchin, or the band of hooligans from Zhmerinko? Common sense told us that the hooligans would arrive first, because they were coming by train, while the Cossacks were coming on horseback. (page 133)

The time-tested methods, it seems, have not kept pace with technology. Leaving aside for now the historical irony of Cossacks as saviors of the Jew, the immediate issue is whether God will perform a miracle and whether the Straggler Special, true to form, will be delayed. "But this one time it looked as though a miracle wouldn't take place. The Straggler kept going from station to station as regular as a clock." One can hardly resist the temptation to retell the whole story, if only to convey Sholem Aleichem's brilliant manipulation of suspense and the reader's cathartic laughter when the train finally pulls in—without the cars. Not God but human error has intervened. At the last station the hooligans have gotten drunk, drawing the crew in with them, and the uncoupled locomotive has left them all behind. By the time they arrive on foot, the Cossacks have had ample time to get there first, and *uksomim beyodom, mit di kantshikes in di hent*— that is, with whips in their hands—the Cossacks disperse the rabble. A more ironic gloss on the story than this Hebrew-Yiddish wordplay can hardly be imagined. When the elders of Moab and Midian came to Balaam with Balak's message to curse the tribes of Israel, they set out *uksomim beyodom*—"with divination in their hand" (Num. 22:7). Beyond the incongruity of translating *ksomim,* a word denoting magic, by the Slavic word *kantshikes,* "whips," lies a haunting analogue: to be rescued from a pogrom by Cossacks' whips is not unlike being caught between Balak's curse and Balaam's equivocation.

Notice how the narrator of this story, the traveling salesman from Heissin, has recast the entire experience into a playful, ironic, and allusive language that presupposes a listener-reader who is as well versed in Jewish rhetoric and Jewish affairs as he is himself. In this respect he is a much more effective narrator for a tale of modern terror than Sholem

Aleichem, who waxed too lyrical, was too judgmental, and therefore was too intrusive in his *poema* of "The Great Panic." Notice, too, that "A Wedding without Musicians" is also resolved by mere chance. "Miracle" and prooftext notwithstanding, the aborted pogrom was the closest call yet, closer by far than the private rage that 101 randomly shuffled boundaries could provoke, or the panic that false news unleashes in a traditional society. Now the signals are coming in loud and clear, and the margin of error grows narrower by the moment.

DURING these years of growing danger to the Jews of eastern Europe, Sholem Aleichem was perfecting three different narrators who maintained their essential character over two decades of new installments. Each member of this celebrated triumvirate used a different kind of synthetic language to mediate the tremors of history.

Motl, the son of Peyse the Cantor, is the living embodiment of adaptability and freedom.[18] His chief linguistic trait is the literalism of a child. "I can't make out what 'stealing the border' means," he says as the family prepares to steal across the Russian border into Austria-Hungary. "Are we some kind of thieves?" (page 173). Other children his age, like Kopl the emigrant, whom he meets in a way-station in Cracow, know much more about current events than Motl.

> What's this about a pogrom? I ask him. I keep on hearing the emigrants talk about "pogrom" and "pogrom" but I can't make out what it is. So Kopl says to me:
>
> "You mean you don't know what a pogrom is? Are you a ninny! A pogrom is something you can find everywhere. At the beginning, it's next to nothing, but once it starts it can last for three days."
>
> "I don't get it," I say. "Is it some kind of a fair?" (pages 212–13)

Wanting Motl to be the epitome of freedom and optimism, Sholem Aleichem later regretted burdening him with the subject of pogroms.[19]

Tevye, on the other hand, cannot escape the hot pursuit of history simply because history, usually in the guise of a prospective son-in-law, pursues him to his doorstep. All the personal tragedies that befall Tevye, ranging from bad business investments to his daughter Shprintze's suicide, he is able to withstand like a proud oak in the forest. It is by no means the tragic if conventional plot, however, that marks Tevye as Sholem Aleichem's greatest character, but the language that Tevye employs in retelling his Job-like saga. For Tevye, as Ruth Wisse points out, "is the most trustworthy of Sholem Aleichem's speakers," the one in whom all levels of the Yiddish language come into play, "high and low, old and new, indigenous and imported."[20] Unlike Reb

Yuzifl, whose language is too pure and otherworldly, and unlike many of the third-class train passengers, whose language is too corrupt, Tevye achieves a perfect balance between all components of the language, his special brilliance showing through in an ironic language of faith that fuses biblical and liturgical snippets with everyday concrete reality. It is Tevye's language, above all, that is the ultimate resort and ultimate resource of the Jewish people in extremis and the language of which all other Jewish dialects are a cryptic derivation. When history finally catches up with Tevye, he can talk his way out of expulsion from the village, though in an alternate ending to the book Sholem Aleichem did have him banished.[21] Tevye's is the language of tradition in its most fully realized form, a language deeply rooted in Torah, folk wisdom and pragmatism, a language that Sholem Aleichem believed could withstand any challenge the Jewish people would face.

If, in the best of Sholem Aleichem's work, the mode of talking about life sets up a pattern of acting it out, then Menakhem-Mendl and his wife, Sheyne-Sheyndl, represent the two most extreme cases of a fixed linguistic form versus an ever-changing reality. In the second series of letters between them, written in 1913 and only recently reissued in book form, Menakhem-Mendl is reincarnated as, of all things, a Yiddish journalist in Warsaw.[22] As in prior metamorphoses, Menakhem-Mendl absorbs the technical vocabulary of every new development with extraordinary ease and numerous malapropisms (some have called him a grown-up Motl), while his cantankerous wife remains equally true to form. What is different in book two, however, is that history now encroaches more directly on her life, though she never sets foot outside Kasrilevke.

Sheyne-Sheyndl reports back to him on the refugees from the neighboring villages—on one family whose male members perish while hiding from the police and another family that commits suicide rather than die of starvation. The formulaic pattern is always the same:

> To my dear, esteemed, renowned, and honored husband, the wise and learned Menakhem-Mendl, may his light shine forever.
>
> In the first place I want to tell you that we are all, praise the Lord, perfectly well, and may we hear the same from you, please God, and never anything worse.
>
> In the second place, I am writing to say, my dearest husband, that God came down on our Kasrilevke as He's never done before. (page 113)

What follows is a pitiless, garrulous, anything-but-pious account of the Khortovoy family: Moyshe-Nakhmen, his contemptible second wife ("some widowed butcher's wife"), and his brother Berl-Ayzik, their sole means of support. Expelled from his village, the prosperous brother is too proud to seek help from his impoverished brother in Kasrilevke.

When even emigration to America fails, for lack of funds, Berl-Ayzik plans his suicide pact. Sheyne-Sheyndl interrupts the story to ask about all the millions of dollars her husband had mentioned for the resettlement of eastern European Jews. "Don't they know," she continues, invoking her inviolable authority, "what mother keeps saying: *az meshiekh vet kumen, vet men zey badarfn af kapores*—when the Messiah comes, they'll be no good to anyone."

In short, things were really bad! What was there to do? Well, listen to what a Khortovoy can pull. So he decides, Berl-Ayzik, that is, to talk the matter over with his wife. What's the point [he says] when there's no way to make a living and no money to make a move to America, and dying is something you have to do anyway, so rather than die of hunger, why not take poison while you're still alive . . . He said it once, twice, three times. His wife probably burst into tears and pointed to the children, as if to say: "What'll happen to the children?" So he says, Berl-Ayzik, that is: "We'll poison the children first, then we'll also drink the stuff . . ." How do you like that for a crazy Jewish idea? Only a Khortovoy could come up with that one! (pages 115–16)

Berl-Ayzik is no more to blame for his plight than the Jewish relief agencies, which are slow to mobilize their funds. Yet Sheyne-Sheyndl's indignation is not as wildly off the mark as it might seem. Though she cannot offer global solutions as her husband can, neither can she accept Berl-Ayzik's way of coping with adversity. Buttressed by her mother's fatalism, Sheyne-Sheyndl stands fast in her life-affirming practicality.

Like all of Sholem Aleichem's archetypal characters, this odd couple will never change, regardless of what goes on around them. Nothing will shake Menakhem-Mendl's fantasy life. When, at the end of his adventures, he is sent to Kiev on assignment to cover the trial of Mendl Beillis, accused of ritual murder in 1913, he contrives to put even this act of barbarism to good advantage. Once the trial is over, he plans to be the agent of Beillis' American tour! Thus, for Menakhem-Mendl there will always be new words to be mustered and mastered, for he perceives life as an endless source of opportunity, while Sheyne-Sheyndl's speech—proverb-ridden, acerbic, and hyper-provincial—is the surest sign that all of life is a state of siege in which only the home can offer protection.

WHAT kind of speech, if any, could protect against the first total war in Europe's history? What forms of communication were still operative when instead of traveling together on the well-known routes, with or without tickets in the third-class train compartment, Jews were now fleeing every which way, by road, by rail, and by sea? Sholem Aleichem and his family were in Germany when the war broke out, and as Russian nationals they were none too welcome. Eventually they made their way to the seaboard and found a ship bound for America. One day, as he investigated life on the lower decks, the celebrated author was accosted by a Polish Jew from the provinces who bombarded him with "a mishmash of actual occurrences and fairy tales . . . a sampling of Jewish war folklore."[23] That was all the inspiration Sholem Aleichem needed to recast the entire Jewish collective tragedy—while still on board ship—into a highly structured and richly variegated comic monologue.

Just as he had once before fled Russia by train and the train had become a symbol of dislocation, so he now appreciated as the ultimate symbol of dislocation a refugee ship in the mined North Sea. Furthermore he knew that history needed a human focus in order to be translated into fiction, and to this end Sholem Aleichem retrieved a plot from an unused pogrom story he had wanted to incorporate into *Train Tales* in 1909. It was the story of a father with two sons, one of whom was hanged, the other of whom went mad.[24] Finally, a story needed a speaker. The father-and-sons motif, further inspired perhaps by his informant's learned style, suggested that he create a variation of Tevye.

Yankl Yunever of Krushnik, the narrator-hero of "Tales of a Thousand and One Nights," uses quotations in a more literal-minded way than Tevye—the biblical allusions support the situation at hand; he is as rooted in the shtetl as Tevye in the village, and both their stories are double-ended, though hardly to the same degree.[25] One son, after being rescued by his father's eloquence, is sent off to be killed on the front, while the other, after winning three medals for valor, is court-martialed. Gambling on the favorable report that his second son has not been shot but has managed, like his father, to talk circles around his executioners, Yankl Yunever sets out to find him in America. All this is narrated to Sholem Aleichem on board ship, with appropriate breaks for meals and rest.

Above all else, this is a story in which the old sustaining structures collapse one by one: no "good Russians" intervene to stay the execution of a peaceful, native population; Krushnik is destroyed, even after its miraculous rescue; nothing, not language, not secret codes, not even the Jewish survival instinct can prevent the slaughter. Never has finding the right code been so critical a survival mechanism, because this time the Cossacks arrive not to protect the Jews, but to murder them, aided and abetted by the local Poles. Early on in the war, the Jews of Krushnik rejoice at the Russian defeat, and Yankl even bemoans the fact that he might forget his Russian. German, he concludes, is a whole lot closer to Yiddish, and this linguistic affinity will give Jews an edge over the hateful Poles. When the first delegation of Jewish notables appears before the German authorities, Yankl's son Yekhiel, who is known for his language skills, uses the wrong rhetorical dialect, addressing the commandant in Hebrew instead of Germanized Yiddish. As a Jewish dignitary, Yekhiel is taken hostage against a huge ransom, but the commandant relents and Yekhiel is miraculously appointed mayor of the town. Just when the Jews, Poles, and Germans are on the verge of establishing a truce, the ritual slaughterer is arrested on charges of espionage and the delegation reconvenes, this time with a ready-made speech from the Bible: "We decided that I would begin and address him in the words of Moses: 'O Lord, you have begun to show your servants your greatness—that is to say, you have been gracious toward us, Herr German, from the day you set foot upon the land' " (page 234). Instead of the friendly commandant, however, they are met by "some other devil," who frightens them into silence: "But how can you say something if you can't talk? Besides I was waiting for the rabbi to start—he was older. And the rabbi was waiting for the *rabbiner—he'd* been appointed by the government" (page 235). The whole "speechless delegation" is promptly thrown into prison where, once again, the hero rehearses a biblical speech which he is never to deliver. His intuition fails him entirely when, that very night, he finds himself in the Jewish cemetery, ordered to dig his own grave: he, the two rabbis, and the Jewish "spy" are about to be shot. But since Yankl Yunever lived to tell the tale and since there are still a thousand more nights to go, they are saved by the Russian counterattack. "But for all that, we just couldn't say a word to each other, not a word! We'd lost our tongues and that was that" (page 240).

Unique to this monologue is that all the way through it the narrator admits to the possibility of silence at the critical moments of life. It is Yankl Yunever who says, "But as they say, if it is fated to be a disaster, you lose your tongue" (page 234). Thus far in the story the movement is from language as redemption to silence as terror. Every language skill that the Jews have learned in exile—adapting Yiddish to German, the language of the occupier; forging alliances with the local Slavic population after the foreign Slavic rulers have left; enlisting Abraham and Moses in the best of biblical eloquence—is inadequate in the changing fortunes of war and total destruction. Then, at the very moment that catastrophe seems upon them, "a true and genuine miracle" happens, and at the rabbi's bidding the Jews of Krushnik celebrate by giving thanks to the new moon. For a brief moment, sandwiched between reprieve and final destruction, language becomes communion, first with God and then with man.

You can imagine we didn't know where we were, whether in this world or the next, when it came to the "*Sholem aleichems*" [the climax of the Prayer for the New Moon]. I heard someone blubbering, right into my ear, *Sholem aleichem.*" I answered "Aleichem sholem!" and looked around. It was him, the

> *schlimazel*, Aba the *shochet*, I mean. How did *he* get here? Had he also been with us there at the burial grounds? A curse on it all! I'd completely forgotten—he'd been the first one! We must have been out of our minds, if you see what I mean. I only wanted to hug and kiss that *schlimazel*, and at the same time I wanted to hug the rabbi (may his memory stay with us always—he's now in another world, a better one). And the way he died! God Almighty! May it happen to all our enemies! (pages 240–41)

Like the rabbi of Kasrilevke, the rabbi of Krushnik is a man of great religious fervor. Through his example, a group of Jews under sentence of death have just learned that language is communion. He is now about to illustrate yet another possibility—silence as prayer.

The Russians have returned with a vengeance, and the Poles are quick to denounce the enemy within. Jewish Krushnik is razed to the ground, and among the countless victims is the rabbi himself: "So he hung there, the old rabbi, wrapped in his prayer shawl and tefillin, beaten and bloodied, in the middle of the marketplace, swaying back and forth in the wind, as though standing in prayer" (page 244). Moments before, he had indeed been standing in prayer as he recited the silent Benedictions, which he did not interrupt even as the Cossacks dragged him off to the makeshift gallows.

But the rabbi's martyrdom finally throws into question the possibility of achieving a resolution either through language or through silence. "He wasn't standing," Yankl Yunever concludes, "he was hanging, if you see what I mean, hanging in prayer!" *Er hengt shimenesre.* Literally and figuratively, the rabbi is suspended in time, at the moment of his most intense devotion, the *shimenesre*, or Eighteen Benedictions, the so-called Standing Prayer. This last image, the *transfixing* of prayer, suggests that neither language nor silence can redeem and that the martyrdom of the Jews consists precisely of the loss of language without access to an appropriate or effective silence.

These unredeemed moments are the very ones that etch themselves into the collective memory, for a silence beyond prayer is the ultimate dead end, a repudiation of the biblical intercessors and of the liturgical modes of repentance. Since all Jewish language is predicated on the primal act of speech on Sinai, since all communication is a version (or perversion) of the covenant, such breakdowns do irreparable damage unless they are remembered. The act of remembering draws the broken links into a chain, into a pattern of memory that preserves the moments of sacrilege against some future time when all the accounts will be settled.

This is not to say that Sholem Aleichem is engaged in the business of theology. What he does is to create versions of the primal language whose perfection derives at once from their infinite adaptability to change and their retention of memories and myths. He shows, again and again, that survival is a verbal balancing act, that too facile a recourse to patterned response is as suspect as a language too open to outside influences. The super-Hebraized speech of the Kasrilevke merchant is a cover for his greed; Sheyne-Sheyndl's parasitic speech is the last defense against despair; and the super-Russified Yiddish of a young revolutionary speaks volumes for his marginality. In lieu of theology, Sholem Aleichem gives us the laughter that results from the clash between languages and life. There is an ever-growing tension in his work between *what* is being narrated and the *way* it is narrated. The greater the discrepancy, the funnier it is.

When the system of codes, memories, and myths explains too much, when it is too fraught with meaning, the comic ambiguity is lost to high rhetoric. The story of Yankl Yunever and his sons loses its effectiveness as it becomes more overtly mythic, because the fine points of human frailty and human freedom—that which makes life inviolable, in Sholem Aleichem's scheme of things—drown in the grand pathos of myth. A second climax is reached with Yekhiel's "Akedah," here telescoped with the rabbinic martyrdom in Roman times. The Russians order Yankl to hang his son, and he begins the episode by asking: "Excuse me, Mr. Sholem Aleichem, could you please explain to me what's so special about the Akedah, that all the prayers in the siddur are so taken up with it?"[26] Yankl Yunever for the first time delivers an impassioned defense, with the equivocal result that the other Jews are hung at once while Yekhiel is sent off to die at the front. Even more disappointing is the last, apologetic, overwritten episode which treats the son who volunteered for action. Perhaps the madness of history has finally thwarted the best efforts even of the master himself to balance the what and the how.

When on the other hand, it is language itself that is the means of destruction, the hero is destroyed by the totally unfamiliar world he is forced to inhabit. This is precisely what happens in the works of Kafka, to whom Sholem Aleichem is often compared.[27] The comparison to Kafka raises the question of whether a preexistentialist, antimodernist sensibility, one in which the private person remains inviolate, can offer a viable response to Auschwitz, or, for that matter, to the Battle of the Somme.

Sholem Aleichem did not return to the subject of war, not because he couldn't but because he died, in May 1916. And there was symbolic closure to his death because he had already taken the ideal Jewish language as far as it could go, and even one step beyond—to the unredeemed silence of a martyred rabbi. There for all to emulate was a surrogate for religious faith and practice—a language that might still protect the Jews from harm.

At certain periods of transition there comes a writer—Abramovitsh in the 1880s, Peretz in the 1890s, Bialik in 1903, Ansky in 1917—who creates a neoclassical norm by bringing together the sum of all past possibilities and showing that sum to be the beginning of a radical countertradition. What further sets the neoclassicist apart is that his heirs are unable or unwilling to effect the same degree of synthesis, either because they are that much more removed from the earlier traditions or because so much has already been lost in the world at large. Such was the case with Sholem Aleichem. Within two generations of his death all parts of his language were unraveled. Itsik Kipnis, a native son of the Ukraine, wrote a Sholem Aleichem-type chronicle of the civil war in which the mythic strand was abandoned. In the Nazi ghettos and concentration camps, the communal speech act of singing became an intimation of loss rather than of shared faith. After the Holocaust, in the work of Yiddish poet Aaron Zeitlin, the monologue form signaled the death of Yiddish itself; and in the comic fiction of German writer and filmmaker Jurek Becker, language as the bearer of truth suffered its final blow. Yet the power of catastrophe was such that it could reconnect as firmly as it severed. A single strand, abandoned early on, became the sole and central resource for a Yiddish-speaking demon, the last survivor of the Great Destruction.

THE pogrom that Motl the cantor's son never experienced invaded the life of his literary cousin Isaac, the son of Leyb the tanner from Sloveshne. Narrated with the naïve exuberance of a childlike man, Itsik Kipnis' *Months and Days*, a classic of Soviet-Yiddish literature, is a study in bifurcated time.[28] Idyllic time—the quiet joy of a newlywed couple in the sleepy but prosperous shtetl of Sloveshne—is measured in months; tragic time—the terror of the pogrom itself and of its aftermath—is measured in days. "Two thousand days have passed since then—two thousand days and two thousand nights," says the chronicler at the beginning of his story as he goes on to describe the exact texture of those days and nights: "Days like brass trays worn out against the sun, and nights like pacified deer in hours of plenty. Or perhaps the reverse: days like bruised and beaten stars, and nights like cups of oleum, spilled out over leather swatches—oleum which flows and is poisonous—which bakes and is dead." The tension between two modes of time is echoed in the tension between the sophisticated narrator, capable of such richly metaphoric language, and the naïve narrator, who is taken in by surface realities.

As Isaac, the autobiographical hero, returns to the pogroms of the Ukrainian civil war some five and a half years later, he narrates the events in the present tense with the same eye for domestic detail, the same asides to an implied listener, the same naïve literalism as Sholem Aleichem's Motl: "So what's the big deal? I'm all of twenty-two. Call that young? As if it mattered! And how old do you think my Buzi might be? Oh, why, when, and wherefore! Take my word for it, I just don't know! I'd say Buzi is never old at all. You know what? If you go by Barber's Lane, stop in at her house, at her mother's, Buzi's mother, maybe she knows" (page 14). Sloveshne, in fact, bears a striking resemblance to Kasrilevke. It too, safely removed from the nearest railroad, is a model of social integration: "I go around dressed in my Sabbath best (in our town it is the only Jewish day of rest for everyone, for young and old, for all except the [Gentile] pharmacist)" (page 22).

Most of the "chronicle" is so disarmingly simple that one barely notices the gradual incursion of premonitions, fears, and actual violence. The Gentiles, seemingly nonexistent at the outset, are strategically introduced at midpoint in the narrative, and from there Kipnis builds a rise-and-fall pattern of terrifying intensity. Through it all the narrator never experiences the violence directly, and only his sense of time split in half carries the full weight of the terror. "And our streets don't have a high season look or an off-season look [literally the look of Purim or the look of the Intermediate Days]: the stores are neither open nor closed. The merchants aren't doing business. The cobblers aren't banging away. Everyone's sitting outside his house as if he were drying off in the sun" (page 118). It's the morning after the first wave of killings. Half of Sloveshne was on the road the night before, seeking shelter in the nearby villages. Everything is out in the open, yet there's no way of stopping the violence: "We already know who are the main celebrants at our party [*ver zenen di greste mekhutonim fun undzer simkhe*]: they are Kosenko (Klim's boy), the Kublinets (the head of the militia) and Maritshka Lukhtans—our neighbor (the pauper, the gypsy, the liar, and the one who loves Jews)" (page 124).

The narrative that opened with an extended holiday mood, with summer in full bloom and the newlyweds irrepressibly in love, draws to a close with the desperate hope for an end to the festivities—to the carnival of murder and theft. The narrator, always so acutely aware of time, loses track of it on the third and final day of the pogrom, just as his extended family is about to perish:

> Can anyone tell me what day it is today?
> I'd say no day of the week has the color, the name of today!
> But others say that today is Friday, just Friday.
> What a joke!
>
> And where are Jews off to on a Friday in such high spirits? Thrown together in a herd—men and girls, women and children. But maybe they're not in such high spirits? That's number one. And number two—where are they headed?

They're headed someplace. But they don't know yet where that someplace is. (page 153)

Except for a single outburst of passion, the narrator's language retains its childish incredulity till the very end. This serves to heighten the tension between the what and the how. The desecration of time also peaks on the Sabbath, the day of rest. Buzi's mother and nearest of kin are murdered just hours before the Red Army enters town.

Revenge and rebirth mitigate the tragic finality of the book: revenge is exacted measure for measure, thanks to the Red Army's intervention, and rebirth compensates for some of the victims, as Isaac's beloved Buzi has a little girl. It is especially significant that in restoring the moral order, in what is otherwise a faithfully accurate account, Kipnis deliberately avoided closing on a far more bitter note: the "real" Buzi died of typhus soon after the pogrom.[29]

Myth and the language of faith play no mitigating role whatsoever, whether because Soviet Yiddish politics would not allow for them or because Kipnis himself rejected the mythic component of Sholem Aleichem's legacy. No one quotes Scripture or in any way seeks to connect the present to the mythic past. Instead, the constant references to sacred and natural time—to festivals, holy days, and seasons—take the place of direct quotations, and the overall effect is of a traditional community violently uprooted from its natural cycle. That this is also a community with an active commitment to a covenantal order is a claim that can no longer be made.

MELODIES, too, can form a subtext when people communicate with one another in song. A familiar melody or musical mode can bring a group even closer together by lending force to the lyrics. But sometimes the melody and lyrics can work against each other, and then the listeners must choose which side to respond to. If the tune evokes nostalgic memories, liturgical echoes, or festive moments and the lyrics bespeak something else, something brutal and unexpected, the listener is torn between the remembrance of things past and the new reality. This kind of juxtaposition verges on parody in which the verbal tenor threatens to overwhelm the musical vehicle. Here the older stratum of the culture is invoked in order to be repudiated, or, at the very least, to unhinge the melody from its familiar meaning, to intimate a sense of loss.

Within the large repertoire of songs produced in the ghettos and concentration camps, these so-called contrafacts, primitive lyrics set to well-known melodies, represent the most conventional and stylized form of communication among Jews. Some say that these songs came into being because the supply of melodies could not meet the demand for new lyrics, and so old tunes were expediently pressed into action.[30] According to another theory, the melodies served as a mere mnemonic device.[31] Neither theory, however, accounts for the special power of these songs, the hidden meanings that emerge out of the essential disparity between the melody and lyrics. For just as the melody serves to mitigate the horror by recalling the shared memories of the group, the lyrics insist on the radical break, on a reality so cruel that it almost defies language itself.

Avrom Akselrod, an otherwise unknown poet in the Kovno ghetto, was the author of several such songs. The crushing life of the Jewish work brigades and their return home through the checkpoint—the only way of smuggling food into the ghetto—provided him with material for a song he set to Mark Warshawski's *Afn pripetshik,* the melody par excellence to evoke nostalgia for one's childhood:

Baym geto-toyerl
Brent a fayerl
Un di shrek is groys;
S'geyen yidelekh
Fun di brigadelekh
Un s'gist zikh fun zey shveys.

Tsi zol ikh vayter geyn?
Tsi zol ikh blaybn shteyn?
Kh'veys nit, ven un vu.
Der komendantele
In grinem mantele
Nemt dokh ales tsu.[32]

At the ghetto gate
a fire burns.
Inspection is fierce.
Jews are coming
from the work brigades
sweating buckets.

Should I go ahead
or stand still?
I don't know what to do.
The little commandant
in his green uniform
takes everything away.

The only thing left here of the cosy familiarity of the heder, with the teacher initiating his young charges into the wonders of the Hebrew alphabet, is the use of diminutives—the *little* commandant in his *little* coat—which makes the discrepancy between the tune and text that much greater, for the same *komendantele* wields absolute power over life and death.

In the ghetto, the use of codes *was* a matter of life and death, especially since the enemy spoke German. Many of these code words are themselves studies in incongruity. From the Yom Kippur liturgy comes the climactic call *ya'aleh,* "may our prayer ascend to heaven." In ghetto parlance, the word denoted those who ascended to power at the expense of other Jews—those such as the Judenrat and the Jewish Police.[33] This bizarre code word inspired Akselrod to compose another song:

Zog mir, zog mir du geto-yidl,
Ver shpilt in geto dos ershte fidl?
Ver fun di yales mer oder veynik
Vil do regirn punkt vi a kenig?

Tumbala, tumbala, shpil geto-yidl,
Shpil mir fun yidishe yales a lidl—
Fun ale "shefn" un "inspektorn"
Vos zenen in geto mentshn gevorn.

Ver fun di yales ken a karte gebn
Un a shayn tsum blaybn lebn?
Un vifl darf men derfar batsoln
Kdey a brigade a gute tsu hobn?[34]

Tell me, oh tell me, you ghetto Jews,
who plays first fiddle here in the ghetto?
And which of the *ya'ales*
hands out orders just like a king?

Tumbala, tumbala, play ghetto Jew,
play me a song of the Jewish top brass—
About all those bosses and inspectors
who rose to fame here in the ghetto.

Which of the top brass can issue a card
and permit to save your life?
And how much do you pay
for an easy work brigade?

The sole reference to the liturgy is the code word *ya'ales* itself, since the tune in no way echoes the prayer. The melody plays instead on the riddle quality of the ghetto: How can a people trapped in a ghetto produce some Jews who exploit others with impunity? Unlike the original song, Akselrod offers no solution to the collapse of Jewish solidarity.

The consummate satire must surely be an anonymous song from the

Vilna ghetto. In the first winter of the German occupation, fur coats and fur collars were confiscated for the German soldiers fighting on the eastern front. At about this time, October 1941, the diabolical system of working passes was instituted whereby the able-bodied recipient was guaranteed the right to stay in the remaining ghetto, as were his or her spouse and two children. Young workers registered total strangers as husband, wife, or children. People gave away all their valuables to buy into somebody's pass. In the first registration, the Nazis issued only three thousand permits (for twelve thousand people), condemning the other sixteen thousand of the surviving Jews to certain death. The round-up and murder of non-pass-holders began promptly. In the two Aktionen of the Yellow Passes, five thousand men, women, and children were dragged off to Ponar and shot.[35] From these multiple tragedies came the following song:

Hot zikh mir di shikh tserisn,
Vey tsu mayne yorn,
Di kragns hot men undz opgerisn—
Ver ikh dokh farfrorn.
Tants, tants tants a bisele mit mir,
Oy, ir groyse fresterlekh,
Ir kumt dokh fun Sibir.

Gele shaynen, roze shaynen,
Alerley kolirn.
Ven vel ikh mayn vaybl Zlate
Tsu zikh aheym shoyn firn?
Tants, tants tants a bisele mit mir,
Hostu a geln shayn,
Hob ikh khasene mit dir.

Broyt afn sentimeter
Holts afn deka,
Hot undz farzorgt der Yudnrat
Der Yudnrat fun geto.
Tants, tants tants a bisele mit mir,
Hostu a geln shayn
Hob ikh khasene mit dir.[36]

Woe is me,
My shoes are torn,
My collar's ripped off,
And I'm freezing to death.
Dance, come dance a bit with me.
Oh, you miserable cold winds,
You must be from Siberia.

Yellow passes, pink passes
Every kind of color.
When will I bring
My wife Zlate home again?
Dance, come dance a bit with me,
If you have a yellow pass
I'll marry you instead.

Bread measured by centimeters
And wood by decimeters,
provided by the Judenrat,
The Judenrat of the Ghetto.
Dance, come dance a bit with me.
If you have a yellow pass
I'll marry you instead.

The melody, recognizable to all, was that of a popular prewar wedding song. The original lyrics went:

Woe is me, my sieve's worn out,
Today it broke in two.
Dancing in your stocking-feet
Is better than in shoes!

I will dance with you, my dear,
And you will dance with me.
You can have the son-in-law
The daughter-in-law's for me![37]

The original tune and text evoke a backdrop of harmony and familial well-being, of dancing until your shoes are worn thin. Thus, through a song of celebration, revelry, and joy, the ghetto responded to the total disruption of the love bond, of family, security, and life itself. It transformed a wedding dance into a *danse macabre.* The tension between the memories of the past and the terror of the present is almost unbearable. To sing that tension is to keep the dialogue going in a world reduced to its basest essentials.

Whether such irreconcilables mitigate the horror or magnify it—whether the ghetto text cancels out the older, popular associations or whether the familiar context makes the unprecedented experience more manageable—depends in large measure on the performance style. The song takes on a ghostlike, mournful quality in Emma Schaver's rendition, sung to a slow waltz rhythm, whereas Ruth Rubin sings it in a lively 4/4 tempo.[38] Neither approaches the one interpretation that in many respects is the most appropriate, most nearly commensurate to the horror described—a raucous, Brechtian, cabaret style that would make of this song a cynical repudiation of hope. To the best of my knowledge, Yiddish song tradition never went that far.

SO long as there were living bodies, there was speech. After the war, when the remnants regrouped, the most audible sign of what they had lost consisted of the languages they had left behind. "Jewish is badly off by us mister," says a *landsman* from Warsaw to Yiddish journalist Aaron Zeitlin in the heavily Anglicized Yiddish of the New World.

> You can have the brains of a government minister—
> It's no good and *det's all.*
> Your line isn't worth a dime.

This conversation was recorded in 1945, when Zeitlin was safe in New York, the lone survivor of an extraordinarily talented family of writers, thinkers, and poets. In his "Monologue in Plain Yiddish" he captures the vulgarity, the despair and the longing of an immigrant Jew who speaks English now "because of the business and because of the children."[39]

> Sure, as greenhorns we spoke different.
> But now—
> We speak a plain Jewish and a plain English.
> Everything plain.

Though he disparages the unprofitable "line" of a Yiddish journalist, the Jew from Warsaw has come to unburden his soul, in much the same way as Tevye and Yankl Yunever did in the presence of Sholem Aleichem; and, like his precursors, the immigrant bears a tale of tragedy that cries out for resolution:

> They say: Maidanek . . . everything destroyed . . .
> Really,
> I can't understand, I can't!
> Simply plain destroyed?
> And I, old fool,
> A fool with a swimming pool,
> I remember something
> And long for something.
> For what—for women in wigs
> And bearded Jews,
> For horse-drawn trams,
> For homemade grits,
> Even for my teachers and their pointers
> and their blows;
> Even for my father's slap:
> "Smoking on *Shabes,* you brat!"
> I long even for windows and walls,
> Just for windows and walls—

Everything burned?
Like plain and simple burned?
Do *you* understand this landsman?
Not me!

In the sudden shifts from sentimental banter to rhetorical amazement, the homesick speaker reveals the extent of the break which no amount of talking will ever bridge again, because the language itself is too heavily tainted, too corrupt and self-indulgent. For Zeitlin, traumatized by his losses, America is the last burial ground for Yiddish and speech is an act of grotesque memorial. Speaker and listener may be the only ones left who still get the joke.

Even so, they at least share a normative framework and a common tongue. Language and truth both suffer a blow when Yiddish words and intonations are all that survive in a German echo chamber whose sole inhabitant is a young German-speaking Jew, formerly from Lodz. Just as he crosses linguistic boundaries with impunity, East-German novelist Jurek Becker blurs the distinction between truth and implausibility by depicting a world of the Big Lie intent on murder—a world in which lying can also become the supreme act of resistance.

Since Becker can no longer assume that he and his German-speaking audience share a familiar landscape of streets and sights, much less a common fund of trilingual Jewish word games, and since all humor is predicated upon a sense of what is normal, Becker begins his novel *Jacob the Liar* by invoking a stereotype of normalcy: a world of small shopkeepers and petty squabbles where the only run-in with officialdom comes when one has to pay taxes.[40] Against these memories of a placid mundane life, Becker paints a nameless ghetto, similarly lacking in culture-bound specifics: there is no Judenrat, no political, cultural, or religious life to speak of. With the real inner workings of the ghetto stripped away, Becker is freer to highlight and neutralize the uncanny aspect of the Holocaust. The uncanny, in Freud's classic formulation, "is that class of the frightening which leads back to what is known of old and long familiar."[41] The Nazis took great pains to set back the clock: they reinstituted the Renaissance ghetto, the medieval yellow star, and the seventeenth-century Jewish Council and thereby created a world that was both utterly terrifying and strangely familiar.

Becker's ghetto (modeled on Lodz) resembles nothing so much as Kasrilevke. The ghetto is cut off from the outside world; only one man purports to have a radio. This total isolation makes the ghetto Jews susceptible to anything but also helps them develop a sense of higher truth in the face of adversity. And this is where Becker goes beyond anything that Sholem Aleichem ever imagined. In the ghetto, words still defend those on the inside, as they did the Jews of Kasrilevke, only now they're conscious lies, not words of unblemished faith, and they save one from despair but not from death.

Jacob Heym ("Home"), a former café owner, accidentally comes upon news of the approaching Russian front, and in order to impress the news upon his friend he resorts to a lie—that he heard it on his secret radio. Eventually Jacob discovers that lying is about the only way left of instilling hope: " 'Of course, I know myself that the Russians won't arrive any sooner,' says Jacob half way through his cigarette. 'And even if I tell it a thousand times, their route will be the same. But I want to draw your attention to another little detail. Since the news reports have circulated in the ghetto, I know of no incident where anyone has taken his life. Do you?' " (page 181). Through ever more fabricated news from his imaginary radio, Jacob is able to maintain a viable community, united in the hope of imminent liberation. As it happens (and as Becker must surely have know,) monitoring foreign broadcasts was the major form of organized resistance in the Lodz ghetto. There was no other access to the world outside. As one ghetto diarist wrote in May 1944: "The little bit of news that reaches us here in the ghetto is a form of support that prevents people from giving up altogether."[42] In Becker's version, the existence of a radio is itself a lie, an improvised cover-up that eventually becomes a studied act of consolation.

In this arbitrary world where truth and implausibility are always inverted, no one ending can do the story justice. Besides, the narrator is no more to be trusted than anyone else in the story. And so Becker provides us with two endings: Jacob dies a tragic but heroic death trying to escape the ghetto; or, more incredible by far than the fabricated plot, all the remaining Jews are shipped off in boxcars to be gassed. Of all the ambiguous endings we have looked at—the belated reprieve of 101 towns, the thwarted pogrom in Kasrilevke and Heissin, Menakhem-Mendl's high hopes for the Beillis trial, Tevye's verbal victory, Yankl Yunever's search for the son who was probably killed—Becker's ending pushes language to its most precarious and paradoxical state. I talk, therefore I lie, and therefore I live.

YET the ideal language is not dead either. It survives in an attic in Tishevits next to a Yiddish storybook that dates from before the great catastrophe. "The stories in the book are pablum and duck milk, but the Hebrew letters have a weight of their own." The speaker in this monologue by I. B. Singer is a demon—the last, in fact, of all the demons: "I don't have to tell you that I'm a Jew. What else, a Gentile? I've heard that there are Gentile demons, but I don't know any, nor do I wish to know them. Jacob and Esau don't become in-laws" (page 300).

Like the storybook from which he draws his sustenance, the tale he is about to narrate could not be more conventional. Its title, "Mayse Tishevits," suggests a martyrological (or otherwise medieval) plot.[43] Yet how simple can it be, in view of the fact that we've already been seduced by an urbane, witty, learned, and loquacious Jewish demon, the perfect speaker of the perfect language, who, for lack of anyone else to talk to, had drawn *us* into this extraordinary speech act? Even on its simplest level, the story cannot be read as a typical exemplum of a righteous rabbi who is tempted by the devil and does not succumb, for it emerges that Tishevits is the last outpost on earth for such a stubborn individual. "Tishevits," the demon tells us, "is a God-forsaken town. Adam didn't even stop to pee there." As for the rest of the world, "it has reached a point where people want to sin beyond their capacities. They martyr themselves for the most trivial of sins" (page 302). Thus, as we await the rabbi's third and final test, there is ample evidence that his moral victory will carry no greater weight than the place in which he lives. But before the test can happen, the enemy destroys the town and murders the Jews of Poland.

The demon sees it all. Returning to his time frame, that of the present, we hear his final verdict:

> There is no longer an Angel of Good or an Angel of Evil. No more sins, no more temptations! The generation is already guilty seven times over, but Messiah does not come. To whom should he come? Messiah did not come for the Jews, so the Jews went to Messiah. There is no further need for demons. We have also been annihilated. I am the last, a refugee. I can go anywhere I please, but where should a demon like me go? To the murderers? (page 310)

On the scale of good and evil, the tailor-made seductions of an old-fashioned demon are fairly harmless when compared to the infinitely greater evil unleashed by human devils. For unlike demons, the human species has an ideology to justify the slaughter:

> "Enlightenment! In the two hundred years you've been sitting on your tail here, Satan has cooked up a new dish of kasha. The Jews have now developed writers. Yiddish ones, Hebrew ones, and they have taken over our trade. We grow hoarse talking to every adolescent, but they print their *kitsch* by the thousands and distribute it to Jews everywhere. They know all our tricks—mockery, piety. They have a hundred reasons why a rat must be kosher. All they want to do is to redeem the world." (pages 302–303)

The secular heresy is what brought about this disaster—man's belief in his own redemptive power. Turn man into a god and he natually becomes a devil. It is a recurrent theme in Singer's fiction, and one that works particularly well when placed in the mouth of a demon. When it comes to the hearts of men—a demon ought to know the signs of hubris when he sees them.

What is it, then, that keeps the demon going after all the demons and the last of the righteous men have been murdered by human hands? It is the very letters of the storybook that now sustain him, though the content of the book is "blasphemy rolled in piety," the enlightenment menu all over again. When all is said and done, the letters remain. Stripped of their heretical accretions, they can be recombined and rhymed as in the earliest period of one's life, as in the traditional counting-out rhyme of Jewish children in eastern Europe:

Alef—an odler, an odler flit.
Beys—a boym, a boym blit.
Giml—a galekh, a galekh knit.
Dalet—a dokter, a dokter heylt.
Hey—a hon, a hon kreyt.
Vov—a volkn, a volkn geyt.
Zayin—a zelner, a zelner shist.
Khes—a khazn, a khazn zingt.
Tes—a toter, a toter shpringt.
Yud—a yatke, a yatke shtinkt.

A—an eagle flies.
B—a tree blossoms.
G—a priest kneels.
D—a doctor heals.
H—a rooster crows.
V—a cloud blows.
Z—a soldier shoots.
Kh—a cantor sings.
T—a Tatar jumps.
Y—a butchershop stinks.

Since all language is tainted, the only purity still to be found is in children's rhymes, with their naïve juxtapositions of high and low, exotic and commonplace, imagined and real. In his own version, the demon repeats the first three letters and them completes the rhyme as follows:

Dalet a dorn, der dorn brent.
Hey a henker, a henker hengt.
Vov a vekhter, der vekhter shenkt.
Zayin a zelner, a zelner shist.
Khes a khazer, a khazer nist.
Tes a toyter, a toyter mest.
Yud a yid, a yid fargest.

D—the thorn burns.
H—a hangman hangs.
V—the watchman boozes it up.

Z—a soldier shoots.
Kh—a pig sneezes.
T—a dead man dies.
Y—a Jew forgets.

The demon's ways are devious, as always, for there is a progression at work here, perhaps even a causal link between the parts. *Dorn* and *vekhter* are the only two objects preceded by the definite article, suggesting that *the* watchman may be none other than God. In which case, working backward, it may be argued that because a Jew forgets, the dead man dies, the soldier shoots, the hangman hangs, and God is off somewhere boozing it up. Or can it be that the causal link begins with God and all else follows from His absence?

There is no answer to this question. Just as the story-within-the-story ends with the hero's being killed before he can stand up to the last temptation, so the story of the godless present can offer no solution to the problem of evil. It's a wonder the story can be told at all! The poor demon is constrained to tell stories of long ago of a place that no longer exists, with a moral that echoes in a moral vacuum, to an audience that he neither knows nor trusts. The Jews he once knew all went off to meet the Messiah. His fellow demons perished, too. And so the ultimate resort and ultimate resource of a demon storyteller living after the Holocaust are the letters of the Hebrew alphabet. These letters no longer exist in a living context to produce versions or perversions of holiness, cryptic codes, truths, or falsehoods, for the community of talking Jews has been harmed beyond repair. At best, the letters protect the lone and lonely speaker from madness and creative self-destruction.

CHAPTER EIGHT

Scribes of the Ghetto

History will revere your memory, people of the ghetto. Your least utterance will be studied, your struggle for man's dignity will inspire poems, your scum and moral degradation will summon and awaken morality.

Zelig Kalmanovitsh,
December 1942

THUS far we have heard the Jewish writers and intellectuals of eastern Europe both echo and amplify the public response to catastrophe, whether it was the movement for self-emancipation after the pogroms of the 1880s, for self-defense in the wake of Kishinev, or for the Jewish national or universal revolutionary struggle at the end of World War I. In all these cases, the scene of destruction was never more than a catalyst, a small part of the whole, and therefore its artistic representation could elucidate only so much, mobilize only so far. No writer, not even Lamed Shapiro, would dwell exclusively on the meaning of Jewish catastrophe. After 1 September 1939, however, the subject of catastrophe eclipsed all others as millions of Jews suddenly found themselves standing "at the crossroads" with nowhere to turn.

No Exit would have been a more accurate name than *Afn sheydveg (At the Crossroads)* for the journal that had begun to appear a few months before. Assembled in its pages was an impressive array of talent, from Simon Dubnow, the dean of Jewish historians, to such preeminent intellectuals as Hillel Zeitlin, Zelig Kalmanovitsh, and Elias Tcherikower, to the internationally recognized Stefan Zweig and Max Brod, to Yiddish poet Itsik Manger. Paris, the place of publication, was also a transit center of a special kind, for where else on the European continent could the Yiddish-speaking elite invite submissions from far and wide for a nonpartisan discussion of the Jewish fate and future? In a journal intended not for external consumption "but for self-exploration and internal stock-taking," Manger captured the spirit of the group when he wrote: "I do not deny the beauty of foreign myths. But now, at this historic juncture, when a nation ought to and does in fact stand at the threshold of internal consolidation, the foreign must be systematically forgotten in order to find that which is ours and thereby—that which we are."[1] The scholars, who also felt the urgent need for "internal consolidation," were far less sanguine about its ever being realized. After reviewing the evidence on Jewries west, east, and communist, Tcherikower pronounced the verdict in his essay "The Tragedy of a Weak Generation"—a generation never more divided and never less able to tolerate suffering than now.[2] Kalmanovitsh, in a prophetic essay, saw the unprecedented nature of the Nazi persecutions as the endpoint of a process in which the Jewish sense of unity as a people had been systematically destroyed between "the hammer of capitalism" and "the sword of assimilation."[3]

Because of their perfect hindsight, because they knew that the price of Jewish salvation in the Soviet Union was the loss of national identity, that the Western democracies had promoted assimilation more effectively than they had mobilized against destruction, and because they saw Palestine as a refuge for only a very few, these Jewish intellectuals working out of Paris, through a kind of projective retrospection, had an almost clairvoyant sense of impending loss. By mapping the historical origins of the present crisis, they saw all the lines converge at the very point where they now stood, at the western edge of Europe, with their backs to the ocean.

From Paris, as they could not have known, the (rail)roads were to lead them back to Poland. Yet this extraordinary self-awareness on the part of the eastern European Jewish intellectual elite reveals the full range of materials, theologies, forms, and analogies available to those writers who were soon to be rounded up behind ghetto walls, where they would create something new out of their thorough familiarity with the old. The archetypes of destruction—the burning of the Temple (the sacred center), the death of the martyr (the sacred person), and the pogrom (they destruction of the Holy Community)—were all alive in the minds of common people and intellectuals alike, even those emancipated from religious practice, due to the folk and modern literary responses to catastrophe that had evolved since the 1840s. The interplay of Yiddish, Hebrew, and Slavic languages at a time of destruction reaffirmed a sense of shared fate, of a life of daily extremity that commented on the biblical past. Though masses of Jews had been seduced away from a traditional faith in the Messiah, the new redemptive movements had spurred the search for new origins and analogies, rooted, this time, in history: Masada, the Paris Commune, the storming of the Winter Palace, the First and Second International, the Zionist Congresses, the Biluim, with a host of secular prophets and saints. And for those who stood aside from the madding crowd, the new realism in poetry and prose, with its modern emphasis on sensation, on the landscape of physical violence, on the hopelessness of the human condition, provided a means of expressing the plight of the individual.

Inside the Nazi ghettos, the walls and barbed wire that were to separate the Jews from the surrounding population were also to bring some of the internal boundaries down. The elite were brought closer to the masses, the assimilated closer to the committed, the secular closer to the religious, Yiddish closer to Hebrew. The modernists became, despite their long battles against it, part of the literature of consolation. With the ghetto's intellectuals moving closer to the people, the writers could use the polylingualism of Jewish eastern Europe to restore conceptually and socially the idea of a Jewish nation that was the penultimate consolation for the ultimate destruction. And a literature that was for centuries retrospective (including "prophecies after the fact") became increasingly prophetic—so that, in fact, analogies could be used at last not for consolation but for action, including uprisings.

IN Vilna, they were jocularly known as the "Paper Brigade"—a group of poets, scholars, and young activists employed on the so-called Rosenberg Squad to sort out rare books and documents for the Nazis.[4] The ghetto's able-bodied preferred the back-breaking slave labor of the work brigades, where one could at least beg, barter, or steal a bag of potatoes. On the Paper Brigade, one starved. No one knew, not then, in 1942, that only scraps of paper would remain, scattered about the ruins or buried deep in the ground—the legacy of a few writers who had gone about their normal business in the face of all that negated it.

The sheer quantity of paper that survived—by some estimates, about half of what was actually written in the ghettos—has much to do with the intellectuals' involvement with the "alternative community," the social, religious, educational, and political agencies that were reconstituted in the ghettos on a semi-legal or clandestine basis.[5] Nothing could be further from the truth than the image of the ghetto intellectual as loner and recluse—as we have it, for instance, in John Hersey's popular novel *The Wall.*[6] Emmanuel Ringelblum, the real-life model for Hersey's main protagonist, was most emphatically a man of the people who lived and died by the principle of *vos vet zayn mit klal-yisroel vet zayn mit reb Yisroel*—whatever happens to the People of Israel will happen to the person of Israel.[7] Ringelblum remained in Warsaw by choice, despite numerous efforts to get him out. As a key member of the Jewish Society for Social Welfare (ŻTOS), he was instrumental in setting up a network of over one thousand tenement committees (*hoyf-komitetn*), "the only licit grassroots organization in the ghetto."[8] And even when it was all over and he had already gone into hiding on the Aryan side, Ringelblum returned to the ghetto to celebrate the seder in April 1943, on the eve of the uprising.[9]

Nor did he work alone. Ringelblum handpicked the men and women to staff the underground ghetto archive (code name Oneg Shabbat): his two secretaries, Hirsh Wasser and Eliyohu Gutkovsky; the writer Israel Lichtenstein, who was responsible for the physical preservation of the archive; the veteran folklorist Shmuel Lehman; the young orthodox historian Shimon Huberband; the brilliant young economist Menakhem Linder; journalists Peretz Opoczynski and Rokhl Auerbach; and many others.[10] Each and every one was centrally involved in the ghetto's internal life, as was Ringelblum himself. When Warsaw fell, Rokhl Auerbach did not flee to Soviet-occupied Lemberg, where the rest of her family lived, but stayed in Warsaw at Ringelblum's urging. There she helped organize the Public Kitchen at 40 Leszno Street, which later became the subject of her monographic essay for the archive.[11]

Those whose names and writings have come down to us responded to their ghetto confinement by becoming more involved than before, sometimes in surprising ways. Kalmanovitsh, though not a Zionist, sent his only son to Palestine—against the protests of family and friends—where father and son spent the summer of 1939 together. Kalmanovitsh then returned to his post in the YIVO Institute and as late as December 1940 passed up a certificate for emigration to the United States.[12] When the ghetto was created, Kalmanovitsh became an observant Jew and began keeping a journal—a cross between a diary and a philosophical notebook—in Hebrew rather than in Yiddish. Along with these private acts of return, the fifty-seven-year-old scholar assumed a preeminent role in the public life of the ghetto: he helped establish and run the Union of Writers and Artists; he was the one consulted by the members of the Paper Brigade as to which rare books and documents were to be smuggled into the ghetto for safekeeping; he wrote a series of major essays in Jewish literary history; he lectured and delivered sermons.

Just as the great individual achievements of Jewish writers and thinkers in the Nazi ghettos pointed outward, to the life-and-death struggle going on all around, they also pointed to the cultural inheritance that was about to become a new legacy. "On ne part pas de zéro," wrote survivor-historian Michel Borwicz in a study of Holocaust literature that informs much of the present discussion.[13] Had those in the ghettos been convinced, as so many are today, that the war years stood outside history, that the Holocaust defied the literary imagination, and that all critical standards had therefore to be suspended, there would have been no Jewish response to speak of, and certainly no contests for the best scholarly and literary works. When the Oneg Shabbat archive sponsored an essay contest on the topic "Two-and-a-Half Years of War," its purpose was to stimulate not only excellence but hope, as stated explicitly in the subtitle: "Observations, Evaluations, and Perspectives *for the Future*." Thus, the view of the war as a culmination, as a collective and internal Jewish phenomenon, led to the search for the best and most disciplined minds—back to the intelligentsia.

This search for talent and truth, to violate yet another postwar bias, did not necessarily favor the young. One could, in fact, argue the opposite, that the beginners—writers in early or late adolescence or those who had never dabbled in literature before—were least likely to find their own voice, were most prone to clichés, to creating a patchwork of stock images and phrases.[14] Some of the central responses to the Holocaust came from a group of writers born in the 1880s, whose experience of catastrophe went all the way back to Kishinev. Chaim Kaplan (born 1880) began keeping a diary, his "only friend," in 1933, and changed its name to *The Scroll of Agony* on 29 July 1940, some four months before the establishment of the ghetto; Kalmanovitsh (born 1885) was one of the founders of the YIVO and had a distinguished career as a philologist behind him before he became known as the Prophet of the Ghetto; and Yitzhak Katzenelson (born 1886) composed his great epic poems of the Holocaust exactly as he had done all his life—by recasting the contemporary Jewish crisis in the light of the biblical past and the redemptive future.[15]

Among the host of professional talent in the ghettos—poets, prose writers, playwrights, and journalists (some three hundred writing in Yiddish and Hebrew alone)[16]—there were those who drew as a matter of course on biblical archetypes, historical analogies, and literary allusions, whereas others tried to cultivate a factual style, the kind favored by Ringelblum qua historian.[17] But whether the metaphors flowed or one eschewed "the art of comparison;" whether one kept a diary to bare one's soul (as did Chaim Kaplan) or as notes for an eventual history to be written in quieter times (Ringelblum, Kruk); whether one's poetry was cryptic and esoteric or public and rhetorical—there was always an implied audience. Writing was an act of faith. One wrote to transcend the reality of the ghetto, to make sense of it through language, to communicate, to reach out.[18] Depending on the future envisaged, one wrote either in Yiddish, Hebrew, or Polish. Katzenelson, a bilingual poet, adopted Yiddish in order to address his new-found ghetto audience; but having witnessed the annihilation of Europe's Jews, he composed his last testament, the *Vittel Diary,* in the language of the last remnant, Hebrew.[19] Similarly, while hiding on the Aryan side of Warsaw after the Great Deportation of 1942, Rokhl Auerbach kept a diary in Polish but composed her last will and testament in Yiddish.[20]

In Jewish eastern Europe, linguistic choices were never neutral. If Auerbach belonged to a generation of Polish Jews who "discovered" Yiddish in the 1920s and 1930s out of an ideological commitment either to the Jewish revolutionary or national cause, the convergence in the Nazi ghetto of the intellectuals and the masses was similarly tied to the language that both sides adopted. Once on the Aryan side, however, it was each man for himself and each woman for herself. To be writing in Polish, as Auerbach later explained it, was a sign of total isolation from her people. Writing anything was dangerous enough; writing from right to left was as good as signing her life away. Only when she abandoned all hope for personal survival did she entrust her last Yiddish message to the ghetto archive, building on a different hope—that the Jews of postwar Poland would respond to the call of a native daughter.

Culture itself became a survival strategy. Some intellectuals saw the ghetto as a historic opportunity to win back the estranged and assimilated and to involve the masses in the creation of a Jewish national culture.[21] Implied in the bleak pronouncements of Hillel Zeitlin[22] that "Polish has become the holy language of the ghetto, the holy tongue of the ghetto Jews," and of Israel Milejkowski[23] that "the chief curse of the ghetto is that there we cannot be creative" was the very opposite possibility: that of turning the catastrophe to good advantage by closing ranks, reaffirming Jewish values, and finally achieving an "internal consolidation." The Yiddish Cultural Organization (YIKOR), a semi-clandestine branch of the Jewish Self-Help in the Warsaw Ghetto, was established with the express goal of winning the intellectuals and social workers over to Yiddish.[24] Menakhem Linder, its guiding force, even coined new terms such as *aleynhilf* (self-help) and *goylim* (exiles) to capture the new reality in the language of the people.[25]

Leftist groups opposed "culturism" because they felt it lulled the populace into a false sense of normalcy. From reading Ber Mark's postwar diatribe,[26] one would think that Linder, Kalmanovitsh, and other "culturists" were Nazi collaborators, second in evil only to the Jewish Police. In fact, the line between the "alternative" and the "countercommunity," between the staying action of the communal self-help and the armed resistance, was a line often crossed by the writers themselves, a goodly number of whom doubled as fighters and partisans.[27] Katzenelson, who was too old to fight, served as resident poet for the Dror contingent of the Jewish Combat Organization (ŻOB), and Polish poet Wladyslaw Szlengel similarly put his verse to the service of the cause.[28] The Oneg Shabbat archive mobilized to aid the resistance by issuing weekly information bulletins for the underground press, by preparing reports for overseas, and by taking down the first eyewitness account of Chelmno.[29]

In many unanticipated and unprecedented ways, therefore, the intellectuals became central actors in Jewish history. As the horror unfolded with cinematographic speed (in Ringelblum's words), only the artists and intellectuals had the wherewithal to take stock, to draw conclusions, and to plan.[30] Though they managed to save more paper than lives, as Auerbach reminds us repeatedly in her excruciating memoir, there would have been no paper either—only the Nazis' films of their victims, the captured files written in bureaucratic jargon, the imperfect recollections of a few survivors, and the silent ruins. To understand the last collective response of a people in all its contradictions, one must look to the writers, who, because they shared the same fate and were intimately involved in all facets of the people's Armageddon, were able to transmute the screams into a new and terrible scripture.

THE sense of déjà vu which we have seen at work throughout the modern period was never as strong or as pervasive as in the Nazi ghettos of eastern Europe. There were three reasons for this. The first, and the most abstract, was what I have called the Jewish dialectical response to catastrophe, which always disassembled the worst disasters into their recognizable parts. It is not a trait unique to Jews, though Jews—particularly the Jews of eastern Europe, who were past masters of suffering—have a richer storehouse of analogies to draw upon than most peoples. Second, the Nazi war against the Jews was only too familiar in its outer trappings. It was fought with the imposition of yellow badges, the defiling of scrolls, the burning of synagogues, the public humiliation of rabbis and hasidim (chosen for their beards); with the establishment of labor camps (as in World War I), ghettos, and Jewish councils; with the expropriation of property and mass expulsions; with pogroms, sometimes spontaneous and sometimes premeditated. After November 1940 everyone became a historian, from forty-year-old Ringelblum to fourteen-year-old Yitskhok Rudashevski of Vilna, both of whom recognized the ghetto as a "return to the Middle Ages."[31] As in Roman times, or at least in the historical memory of those times, the Nazis coordinated their violence with the Jewish calendar, combining sacrilege with every act of destruction. The extremity of the Holocaust was such that it revived the search for archetypes: reality itself had become archetypal. And finally, there were the primitive conditions of the ghetto, which threw people back on their native resources. All lines of communication with the outside world were cut as private telephones, radios, typewriters, and printing devices were outlawed. What was left of Jewish life was either conducted in full view—in the unbelievably crowded streets of those sections of town previously inhabited by the poorest Jews—or in the privacy of one's tenement. With smuggling as the mainstay of the economy, one might as well have been back in Warshawski's shtetl.

Evidence for this overwhelming sense of recapitulation is not hard to find. On at least three separate occasions, the underground press in the Warsaw ghetto ran articles on ghettos of the past: Poalei Zion's *Bafrayung* (Liberation) in December 1940; *Yugntruf* (Call of Youth) in January 1941 put out by the same movement; and Hashomer Hatsair's *El Al* (in Polish, despite the Hebrew title) in April 1941—all assuring ghetto readers that Jews had been through this before.[32] As the observance of traditional Judaism was forced underground, the memory of the Spanish Inquisition and of the Marranos' ordeal immediately came to mind.[33] One may even say that because the Nazis launched an all-out war on Judaism, the Jews of eastern Europe responded most effectively to those forms of persecution that they recognized.

After the initial reign of terror, mass murder, and expulsion, the major ghettos enjoyed a period of relative stability—longer for some, shorter for others—during which it seemed that producing for the war effort would guarantee survival and that the Nazis were content to leave other matters to the Jews. This is when the ghettos witnessed a fantastic spectacle, a veritable "reunion of the exiles" as foretold in the Babylonian Talmud (Pesahim 88a): the gathering of Jews—including converts—from all over Europe to be governed by a Jewish Council and policed by Jewish Police. It was an autonomous existence such as even shtetl Jews had never dreamed of. "The residents of the ghetto are beginning to think they are in Tel Aviv," wrote Chaim Kaplan.[34] "Strong, bonafide policemen from among our brothers, to whom you can speak in Yiddish!"

Though we now see the ghettos only as a dark prelude, and though fixed in our minds are the flames of Warsaw and the deafening silence of Vilna and Lodz, the eastern European Jews in the ghettos saw themselves then at the sad end of an era, at the start of something "new and momentous," *and* as actors in a well-rehearsed Jewish drama whose script had been refined but not substantially revised over more than eight hundred years (since the First Crusade). The intellectuals in Paris concentrated on the loss, the intellectuals in the ghetto on the drama, and a few, as we shall see, on the messianic implications.

The bittersweet taste of Jewish self-government turned poisonous soon enough, but while it lasted, the ghetto functioned as an ironic City of God. The underground archive (whose code name Oneg Shabbat perfectly captured the romanticization-to-be of the ghetto) commissioned a major study of those areas of ghetto life that were entirely new or unprecedented in their scope: the Jewish Police (as part of a larger study on internal corruption), the tenement committees, hunger, the refugee problem, street life, and the institutional soup kitchens which also functioned as cultural centers.[35] The chronicle of collective behavior also extended beyond the confines of the ghetto to include those hundreds of Jewish communities whose surviving members (some 150,000) had fled to the capital, there to live in unimaginable squalor, even by ghetto standards. From among these refugees (or "exiles," as Linder called them) information was gathered on the life and destruction of their native towns.[36] Shimon Huberband (whose involvement in these interviews almost cost him his life when he contracted typhus) devised a plan to preserve the cultural and religious artifacts of these destroyed communities—a plan, needless to say, that could never be put into effect.[37] As paradoxical as it sounds, the destruction of eastern European Jewry had an overwhelmingly centripetal effect in some quarters of the ghetto, where writers initiated a massive (and clandestine) effort at documenting the dying communities and those still living, thus anticipating the whole thrust of the postwar memorial imperative.

The gathering of the Jews and the pooling of communal resources within the ghetto walls had their analogue in the literature of the ghettos: before the true dimensions of the catastrophe were fully revealed, the sum of all prior responses had already been reevaluated. That sum included Hebrew and Yiddish, Polish and Russian, the sacred and secular, as an increasing number of ghetto writers crossed the boundaries that had seemed so unbridgeable only a year or two before. Those who achieved some kind of synthesis between the separate domains were destined to become the major voices of the ghetto.

Private life was the first island to be submerged. Few writers could withstand the lure of the streets, no matter how insular an existence they cultivated. "There is no alternative," wrote Simkhe-Bunem Shayevitsh to his patron in the Lodz ghetto, "but to imitate the troubadours of old, the [German] Mienensinger and our Yiddish Broder Singers. To become the carriers of our own song, the preachers who bring their sermons to the people."[38] All that saved Shayevitsh from actually taking to the streets was the patronage of the man whom he now addressed so obsequiously; but, as we shall see, many other professional poets found a captive audience in the ghetto, while the venerable institution of street singers, ever viable in Jewish eastern Europe, was revived. Thanks to Mendl Grossman, the visual chronicler of the Lodz ghetto, we have a photograph of Yankev Herszkowicz, a former tailor, and his accompanist, a former traveling salesman from Vienna, performing a number in front of a youthful crowd, (see Figure 3).[39] It was nothing very sophisticated, most probably another lampoon on Rumkowski, the King of the Ghetto:

> Rumkovski Khayim git undz klayen,
> Er git undz groypn, er git undz man.
> Far tsaytns hobn yidn oykh gegesn man.
> Haynt est yede froy ir man.[40]
>
> Rumkowski Chaim gives us bran-a,
> He gives us barley, he give us life.
> Once upon a time, Jews too ate manna.
> Now each man is eaten by his wife!

When Herszkowicz ended on the obligatory note of "Our Royal Highness has already gone grey / May he live to be a hundred," the audience broke in with "May the devil take him away!"

Ghetto lyrics, whether they were actually performed on the streets or not, fulfilled two important functions: the more topical songs provided a public hungry for news with editorial commentary on the abuses of power, while the laments and rhymed chronicles made mass death and starvation an ongoing commentary on the biblical and medieval past.

More extended analogies between present and past were the province of the schools, libraries, and lectures organized in the ghetto. In Vilna, Josephus Flavius was put on trial as a Roman collaborator. Students boned up on the facts for months in advance. A mock trial—an elaborate production complete with prosecutor, defense attorney, and judges—was carried out by the history club of the youth organization.[41] The connection was obvious, for Josephus, the former soldier-turned-court-historian, was none other than Jacob Gens, the former career-officer-turned-ghetto-commandant. And according to a survey done by the Library and Reading Room in the Vilna ghetto at the end of 1942, Tolstoy's *War and Peace* was the single most popular title, despite the long waiting list for the multi-volume edition.[42] Both examples from Vilna show a heightened, modern interest in history—in the specifics of time and place and personality. This was not in the rabbinic tradition of imploding events and locating them on a preexisting scale; it was the very opposite—an impulse to understand the behavior of a Gens or the strategies of Hitler in Russia against a universal backdrop.

With a full-scale conspiracy going on between literature and life, between the memories of past persecution and their repetition in the present; with the mirage of autonomy, attended by "kings," commandants,

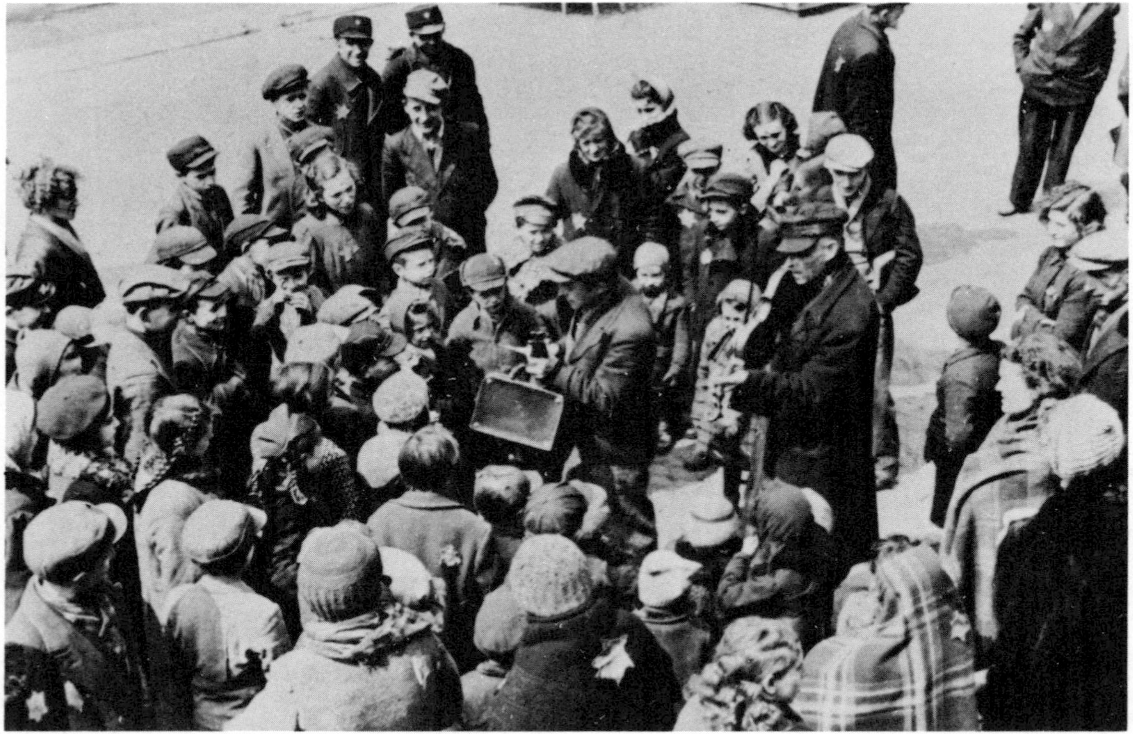

3. Yankev Herszkowitz and his accompanist giving a street performance in the Lodz ghetto.

law enforcers, mailmen, janitors, and rickshaw drivers, making the ghetto seem like an upside down version of Herzl's Jewish State; with the *landsmanshaft,* the tenement committee, the soup kitchen, the underground synagogue, school, and political party as the social base for individual survival; with life gone public and the public starved for news, writers and singers rediscovered the use of in-group codes, traditional forms, popular themes, and historical analogies. In this way they hoped to reflect the perception of what was going on and to attract an audience into the bargain.

Since ghetto Jews were misled into believing that the present was merely a replay or intensification of past destructions, then one might argue that the literary response to that misperception was no more than an exercise in repetition. The ghetto, one could further argue, was but the intermediate stage in the Final Solution, the way station to the inner circle of hell, and therefore could not, by definition, have generated a response commensurate to the Holocaust. But if instead one sees as a cumulative process the revolution in Jewish consciousness usually attributed to the Holocaust instant, then the sources of that revolution must be sought in the seven decades prior to 1942, during which a countertraditional response to catastrophe evolved, with its own hallowed texts and radical authority. Only in the ghettos was there enough time for enough Jews of similar background to test out the meaning of these past responses.

The change occurred in three stages. The first and crucial step toward apprehending the final destruction was a colossal and necessary act of misreading. Like the rabbis in Talmudic times who called on Jeremiah, Moses, and Rachel to help them weep over the Destruction and who used apocryphal and magical materials for the sake of consolation, the Jews of the ghetto, overwhelmed by their losses, began to erase all previous boundaries between the sacred and secular to reclaim the modernists in their own struggle for survival. Shayevitsh, in a remarkably muted lament, was to describe the deportations in terms of the *lekh-lekho* command to Abraham: "Go forth from your native land." The father-narrator informed his daughter that among the belongings he was packing for the unknown road were "my prayer shawl, my white robe for burial shroud, the small red-bound Bible, and Leivick's poems for moments of calm." Even to an observant Jew, Leivick's fusion of beauty and death had something to offer. And the Dror anthology published in 1940, later to be the blueprint for revolt, began with an excerpt from Asch's *Kiddush Hashem,* then interspersed the classical sources with Bialik's "In the City of Slaughter," translations of Tchernichowsky's "Baruch of Mainz," Lamdan's "Masada," and the Secret Proclamation of the Odessa Group.[43] The pogrom poems of Halpern,

Markish, and Leivick were listed in a two-page bibliography—to further steel the resolve of the young.

So great was the need for continuity in the face of the Nazi onslaught that rebuke was read as lament and subversion became part of the greater tradition. Jews drew their strength to fight the apocalypse from a new amalgam of anger, repudiation, and creative betrayal.

Second, when both the ancients and moderns proved insufficient, either because they offered too much comfort or too little, they were subjected to ironic use. The prophets of Jerusalem and of Warsaw were attacked equally for not measuring up to a catastrophe of such massive proportions. Then, in late summer of 1942, came the Great Deportation and with it the discovery that neither radical despair nor the reaffirmation of faith could in any way compensate for the end of the Jewish people. What was needed instead was some form of action, whether a last defiant stand in the ghetto or the reinvention of the Jews by the last surviving writers. This was the first apprehension of a Holocaust that marked not just the End, but a new and terrible Beginning.

OF all the boundaries, the one that lay between traditional and modern faith was more like an abyss. Though from a western perspective, eastern European Jewish writers never strayed far from the sources of their culture, and in times of destruction they hardly abandoned the old archetypes, there was no modern return to a belief in the covenant. Ghetto writers, with few exceptions, refused to identify destruction with guilt or with some divine scheme for ultimate redemption. However much the literature of the ghettos seems to be a throwback to medieval and ancient times, the surviving scrolls are not Scripture in any but the most attenuated sense.

Ghetto writings, in contrast to postwar literary responses, were overwhelmingly secular, never more so than when couched in scriptural terms. On 26 November 1940, a day before the Warsaw ghetto was hermetically sealed off, Katzenelson organized a public reading of the Bible, and, like the epic writers of old, he began the evening with a rhymed prologue in Yiddish:

> You have come to an evening of the Bible
> Broken in spirit
> And beaten in body
> With darkness in your hearts.
> You are full of sorrow, of sorrow.
> . . . . .
> Come, you unbelieving Jews,
> Come, and by your own Bible, you shall become believers!

Believe: you who have created eternity on this earth
Are yourselves eternal.
. . . . .
For a suffering made eternal
Is joy!
And grief made eternal
Is light![44]

Not God or His covenant but the Bible itself, that timeless document, established a higher reality than that of the ghetto. The Bible's message was survival, even to those who had lost their faith, for the Jewish people was as eternal as its literary creativity.[45] Poetry and prophecy were the sources of biblical greatness, and the hidden link to the present was the experience of the Jews in secular history. Katzenelson argued for the continuities—of the ghetto as a link in the chain of Jewish suffering and as an actualization of parts of the biblical past—by omitting God from the line of authority: the truth of the Book derived from the people, even as the people's survival was mirrored in the Book.

The Bible, for Zionist intellectuals such as Katzenelson and Kaplan (both of whom taught Bible before the war), was much less than the record of a covenant but much more than a clandestine code. Both men made constant reference to the Mosaic curses, to the prophets of the exile and to Job, in order to explore the historical, ethical, and even metaphysical implications of the ghetto. When forced expulsions from the towns surrounding Warsaw were carried out in the dead of winter, in January and February 1941, Katzenelson found the exact analogy which he set forth in his play *By the Rivers of Babylon*.[46] This, the first of his biblical dramas written during the Holocaust, portrayed a group of Judean exiles torn between throwing themselves into the river to escape their captivity or into a life of hedonistic pleasure. Their ultimate resolution, steeled by the words of the prophet, would be neither of these: they would sanctify life and nurture hopes for Jewish rebirth in the Land of Israel. Yet despite the lessons of biblical prophecy, including the vision of the dry bones at play's end, there was no question of accepting the attendant theology: destruction in biblical times may have been linked to human action, but in the modern Diaspora, where life itself had become perverted and persecution was inevitable (the Zionist critique), there was no causal link between sin and retribution.[47] After all, was not Job, too, the victim of senseless suffering? It was to Job, therefore, that Katzenelson turned next, in the second of his biblical plays, the only book-length publication in the Warsaw ghetto (see Figure 4).[48] Instead of what one might have expected, an allegory reminiscent of Abramovitsh's *The Mare* in which Job (Israel) was abandoned by the three friends (the world-at-large) to face the test of Satan

4. Cover design by Shloyme Nusboym for Yitzhak Katzenelson's biblical drama *Job*, published in approximately 150 copies by Dror in the Warsaw ghetto, June 1941. A contest was run for the best design, and this one was chosen.

(Hitler) all alone, Katzenelson wrote a psychological drama with heavily erotic overtones. When Job emerged triumphant he discovered not the inscrutable ways of God as announced to him from out of the whirlwind, but the vitality of death, the interdependence of joy and suffering, Eros and Thanatos, which were revealed in the very struggle for survival.[49]

As much as the biblical paradigms of collective exile and individual suffering gave some sense to the inner reality of the Nazi ghettos, modern Jewish writing had also become a source of authority to the Jews of eastern Europe—a conscious and even unconscious moral reference. If any twentieth-century writer could still claim the mantle of prophecy in 1940, it was Bialik. Though he had died six years before in Tel Aviv, his was a commanding presence in the ghettos, not only, as one would have expected, for his *Songs of Rage*, but also for his poems of hope and national rebirth. The sources of his poetry were studied by ghetto scholars; schoolchildren "welcomed" him into the Vilna ghetto; special issues of the underground press were devoted to his memory;[50] and above all his poem "Upon the Slaughter" reverberated in the minds of young and old alike. Kaplan quoted its opening lines on 5 October 1939, the eve of Simhath Torah; Katzenelson translated it into Yiddish for the poet's anniversary;[51] Zionist youth organizations reprinted its Hebrew text.[52] Bialik was the only modern Jewish poet who had successfully turned poetry into prophecy and analogy into action. Therein lay his special appeal to the young Jews of the ghetto some forty years after Kishinev, while those of the older generation with first-hand experience of Kishinev argued for Bialik's supremacy on very different grounds.

"Bialik saw our anguish, expressed it, and captured it for all times to come," wrote Katzenelson on the sixth anniversary of the poet's death.[53] "Thanks to Bialik, our most profound [experiences] have been given eternal form and this has lifted a great burden from us." It was a strange claim indeed for a professional poet to be making, for it implied that there was no further need to find the right words. What Bialik offered, according to Katzenelson, was the possibility of catharsis. The reader who rehearsed Bialik's anger against Jews and pogomists alike could achieve a personal catharsis, a victory over silence far greater than that offered by the recitation of Psalms. And since, in Katzenelson's scheme, the prophets were valued over the Psalms, the poet laureate who stood in a direct line with the prophets could allow for the fusion of past, present, and future through the literary expression of anger and grief.[54]

Others, too, measured greatness in terms of Bialik's achievements. "Poet of the people, where art thou?" asked Kaplan after invoking Bialik's name,[55] and the answer was given two and a half years later by

Mordecai Tenenbaum, a leader of the resistance, when he hailed Katzenelson as the Bialik of his generation, the one who had achieved even greater heights of prophecy and rage.[56] Meanwhile, the Zionist youth groups conferred upon Bialik the greatest honor any poet could ever hope for: they turned his words into deeds. The poet's condemnation of Jewish passivity, which had roused the self-defense movement after Kishinev, reechoed in the first call for resistance which Abba Kovner declaimed to a group of young Zionists in the Vilna ghetto on 1 January 1942.[57]

Since all forms of expression were fraught with extraordinary risks and since the psychic balance of the entire community depended on what was generated from within, the literary heritage became a vital source of meaning. The debate over Bialik and Abramovitsh, or about Bialik's poems of solace and his poems of rage (*nekhome* versus *nekome*) was a guide to action as well as belief. Whereas Katzenelson rejected the Psalms as too placid a form of response to catastrophe, Hillel Zeitlin, the religious existentialist, sat in his ghetto tenement translating them into Yiddish, and when his building was blockaded, Zeitlin went to the Umschlagplatz, the infamous roundup point for the deportations, dressed in prayer shawl and tefillin.[58] While the left-wing Jewish movements in the ghetto hailed Abramovitsh as a harbinger of the social revolution that they still believed would hasten their own redemption,[59] Katzenelson called for Abramovitsh to be deposed as an aberration from the biblical norm, as a social satirist who did not rise above the nineteenth century.[60] Only Bialik's rage responded adequately to the present crisis, said Katzenelson; but the first theatrical revue staged in the Vilna ghetto opened to a choral recitation of Bialik's sentimental *Glust zikh mir veynen* ("I feel like crying").[61] Lyricism, the organizers felt, was the best defense against despair.

The selective reaffirmation of modern Jewish literature came at a time of regrouping, during the early stages of the Nazi onslaught. The increasingly ironic treatment of the same literary sources represented a growing sense of unprecedented horror. Irony took its mildest form when Avrom Akselrod undercut the nostalgia and communality of popular folksongs with his depictions of the work brigades and of internal ghetto corruption, just as Yankev Herszkowicz's street ballad deflated Rumkowski's largesse by comparing it to the manna of the desert. But when Peretz and Bialik, the prophets of the secular age, were also called into question, a new stage had clearly been reached. Leyb Goldin's "Chronicle of a Single Day,"[62] written in the Warsaw ghetto in August 1941, began with a paraphrased epigraph from Peretz's most famous poem, "Monish": "How differently my song would sound / If I could let everything resound." So Goldin telescoped the distance traveled since Peretz's debut in 1888. The original couplet played on the supposed inadequacy of the Yiddish language to convey European ideals of romantic love. Now it prefaced the attempt of a starving intellectual in the Warsaw ghetto to chronicle his own hunger, when all he had to go on were the works of Thomas Mann and Arthur Schnitzler or meaningless phrases about the great proletarian struggle. In fact, Goldin's literary debt to Peretz, Mann, and Schnitzler was immediately apparent, down to the minutest sensory detail of a man whose entire existence hung on a bowl of soup handed out once a day at twenty minutes to one. But the weight of experiences had shifted, for now the question was no longer whether Jewish sensibilities were adequate to world events, but precisely the opposite.

The only communality that Goldin would allow was that of hunger. The most a person could hope for under these conditions was living through another day. Not only were literature and love irrelevant to the tyranny of the stomach, but they actually intensified the individual's sense of total isolation from the world outside.

At the very opposite pole of Jewish response stood Shayevitsh, whose transcendent faith only intensified during the renewed deportations from the Lodz ghetto. Yet Shayevitsh's means were ironic as well. In a poem called "Spring 5702 [1942]," he depicted the murder of the Jews as a mockery of nature itself. Once again in Jewish history, the spring had come to herald the slaughter. And so, in the next-to-last canto, the ghetto poet subjected Bialik's "In the City of Slaughter" to a point-by-point rebuttal:

> Come out with me for a walk—
> This, our ghetto, will surely please you.
> Though we are mocked and humiliated,
> You won't find a single husband—not even the most pious—
> Running to the rabbi for a ruling:
> "Can he sleep with his defiled wife?"[63]

If once the poet had railed against the useless tears of contrition, he would now find the prayer houses empty, all the congregants having been driven from the ghetto. And though Bialik's cry of revenge was never taken up (not in Lodz, at any rate), and no fist was ever raised against the heavens, even the great poet of rage would be so humbled at the sight of such suffering that he would fall to the ground three times, each time exclaiming Holy! Holy! Holy! There could be no hour of reckoning, because God Himself had been slaughtered, too. Shayevitsh had at the end only this to offer: a call to Mother Rachel and Reb Levi-Yitskhok of Bardichev to plead on Israel's behalf, though it might already be too late, and the Passover cry of "pour out Thy wrath," though there might not be anyone to hear it.

Goldin and Shayevitsh rejected the modernist response for very different reasons, the one because it fell so short of the brutal reality and the other because it offered no solace; but the questions they posed were the same: Did the individual's suffering have any bearing on the whole, and did the death of the collective leave any room for individual survival? In Goldin's anatomy of hunger, all the trappings of modern culture could not compensate for a single, watery bowl of soup; the victory of body over mind signaled the defeat of all sustaining values. Shayevitsh, in contrast, widened the tragedy of a father and child facing imminent deportation until the fates of people, God, and cosmos were also brought into focus and the central values were sustained despite an absent God. Between Goldin's extreme and reportorial individualism and Shayevitsh's equivocal affirmation of faith lay the entire spectrum of possibilities, the whole modern Jewish literary enterprise, as it was now to reemerge through the prism of darkness.

AS the people were dragged away never to return and the crowded ghetto streets were emptied of the poor and the starving, the very young and very old, there grew a need for figures that would somehow *stand for* the people, a kind of literal *in*vention. To stand effectively for the people as a whole, these figures had to be suitably adorned, had to resemble and combine various models from the past. And so other ancient archetypes were reenlisted, not naïvely, but in the push and pull between the personal and collective tragedy, now revealed in their fuller fury; between the claims and counterclaims of prior Jewish responses to catastrophe; between the strictures of form and the boundless horror. As more and more children were rounded up, Simkhe-Bunem Shayevitsh invested the greater part of his talent building up the figure of the child, and when the entire adult community was also on the verge of disappearing, Yitzhak Katzenelson retrieved the figure of the martyr within a vast epic panorama.

And now, Blimele, my child
Hold back your childish joy—
The quicksilver stream within you—
And let's get ready for the hidden road.

Don't stare at me so eagerly
With those big blue eyes of yours,
And don't ask why
We must abandon our house.

Though I, dear child,
Am grown-up and adult,
I, too, don't know why
The bird is being driven out.

You must hold them in now,
Your giggles and sweet sounds—
Like silvery chimes on old boxes of spice—
And do get dressed for the second round.
(lines 1–16)

There is life pulling in one direction and the ominous fate of the people pulling in another. Mediating the two is the father. Shayevitsh wrote or completed this poem, with the biblical name of *Lekh-lekho,* a day after the resumption of mass deportations from the ghetto of Lodz.[64] Ten thousand of the most destitute had already been taken away a month before.

Patiently the father instructs the child as to what to take along, what she may expect, how she should behave, and what similar things have happened in the past. Life and deportation cannot be easily reconciled, however, at least not in terms that are comprehensible to a child:

Don't cry, dear child, don't cry.
Life is truly beautiful and draws like a magnet
And more than ever and more than
Anywhere, it draws beyond the ghetto.

But know this—that sinful man
Must always be ready and prepared
Whether for life's noise and splendor
Or for the desolate field of slaughter.

For can't you see—I'm packing
My prayer shawl and my *kitl* for shrouds
Along with the little red-bound Bible
And Leivick's poems for moments of calm.
(lines 153–164)

By virtue of knowing the truth, that death is so imminent, the father shares a heightened awareness of life with the child. In the stanzas that follow, he takes leave not only of that which is quite real—each and every object still left in the apartment—but also that which was never quite realized: the unwritten poems that will now accompany him to the pit (lines 193–196). The ultimate desecration, he knows, is yet to come, on that early morning someday soon when someone discovers his abandoned library for use as strips of toilet paper.

The child may have less to lose, but that much less to fall back on. How, then, can she be brought into the covenant of suffering, so tersely defined in the rhyme of *mukhn-umzumen* ("ready and prepared [to fulfill God's commandment]") with *umkumen,* "annihilation" (lines 158-160)? Despite the rabbinic prohibition against teaching one's daughter Torah (B. Sotah 20a), he decides to rehearse the terrible lesson of *Lekh-lekho:* Go you forth from your native land and from your father's house (Gen. 12:1). Yet it is he who must learn the lesson all over again, for the archetype of the exile has only now been explained, in the endless road that awaits them, where still-born children will lie with their dead mothers in the snow and no cosmic force will intervene on their behalf.

Indeed, one purpose of the poem is to establish a new archetype of exile made up mostly of women and children as the chosen flock. These are images that have been seen before—the children torn from their parents (the Cantonists are invoked in line 132), women dying as they nurse, Jerusalem herself in mourner's clothes—but never placed in so dominant a position. This time, father tells daughter, Jeremiah will not accompany them into exile. Exile is an endless journey on which one's prized possessions are soap and a comb:

> Every night mother will use it
> To straighten out your hair
>
> And will watch you with great care
> And guard you from lice, God forbid,
> And sing you "Bibl, bibl,
> Little louse," and hold you in her lap.
>
> And tell you stories of long ago
> That sound like they happened today.
> And she will be our Jeremiah
> Bringing solace, though her heart is in pain.
> (lines 171-180)

Even in bleakest exile there are surrogates to be found: the mother stands in for the prophet, motherly love stands in for providence, and the chain of Jewish catastrophes stands in for the convenantal saga. Through his search for practical surrogates, Shayevitsh occupies a middle ground between the classical tradition and the modern repudiation. The archetype of exile still relies for its ultimate power on a God whose presence is implicit and whose covenant is ultimately unforsworn.

As for the father, what he can still do, since fathers are as powerless as anyone else, is to instruct his child in passive defiance, and this is what finally resolves the overriding tension between the will to live and the readiness to die:

> And now, Blimele, my child
> Put on your coat and let's be off
> The third group sways in readiness
> And we must be among them.
>
> But let us not cry. Let us not
> Moan. Rather, to spite all our foes—

Smile, just smile. Let them stare
In amazement at the power of Jews.
. . . .
For they do not know that the selfsame
Angels escort us today as of yesteryear:
On the right—Michael; on the left—Gabriel,
Uriel in front and Raphael in the rear.

And though death lies beneath our steps
God's Shekhinah watches overhead.
So child, let us go with devotion renewed
And our old proclamation of *eḥad.*
(lines 413-420, 440-447)

What is truly radical about Shayevitsh's poem is not the blatant repudiation of the covenant theology so characteristic of an earlier decade, but the creative reuse of traditional concepts such as exile and martyrdom. Did a man in whose library "Isaiah rubs shoulders with Goethe" (line 259) really expect to die with the *Shema* on his lips? If he had a son instead of a daughter, would his approach have been less syncretistic? The answer is no. *Lekh-lekho* is an unmistakably modern response to catastrophe in which the oldest and newest strata of Jewish culture come together in a ragged formation of humanism and transcendental faith, artistic self-awareness and the intimacy of prayer.

In the dialectic of Jewish responses to catastrophe, Shayevitsh's *Lekh-lekho* and the ghetto writings of Yitzhak Katzenelson (as of mid-1942) signaled a return to the substance, not only the form, of the ancient traditions. Since for both poets, however, there was no return to traditional faith except via the midrash of the moderns—Leivick *and* the Bible; Bialik *and* the Prophets—the first step toward reclaiming the past was to subvert the modern subversion. As the poet who took up Bialik's cause with greatest passion, Katzenelson was the one most likely to accept his famous equation: that the Jews' powerlessness was a measure of God's and therefore any God who could allow for a City of Slaughter had already abdicated His heavenly throne. Forty years later, now that the very existence of the Jewish people hung in the balance, and the Land of Israel was too far away to offer shelter, while the Germans had not yet met defeat in Stalingrad and the armed revolt was still a dream, Katzenelson turned back for anchor to the covenantal link between Jews, God, and Torah. Soldering that link were individual acts of Kiddush Hashem.

Orthodox Jews such as Shimon Huberband had already put forth a new definition of Kiddush Hashem.[65] Since the killing of Jews seemed to be central to the Nazi design and the motive was no longer conversion, then a new definition was needed for the exemplary martyr. Furthermore, since any act of collusion, such as handing over a list of names, could facilitate the murder of Jews, then anyone who resisted was hallowing the name of God. To save a Jew or to rescue a sacred object became supreme values; Kiddush Hashem became the way a Jew defined himself.

Recent events that Katzenelson learned about from the underground press and from personal contacts with hasidim in the Warsaw ghetto provided the real-life models of Jewish martyrdom: thirty-seven-year-old Shloyme Zhelikhovsky, a Gerer hasid who went to the gallows of Zdunska-Volya on the eve of Shavuoth 1942 exhorting the other nine victims to join him in song; thirty-three-year-old Shmuel-Shloyme Liner, the fifth rebbe of Radzin, who resisted all attempts at rescue and remained in the shtetl where he risked his life to bury the masses of dead until finally caught by the Gestapo.[66] In order to make the real into a secularized version of the religious ideal, Katzenelson demoted God, still proclaiming His (diminished) glory, and raised the standard of individual heroism. Shloyme Zhelikhovsky would have been shocked beyond words to hear his own name paired in the opening rhyme of Katzenelson's epic poem with the Ineffable Name *yud-key-vov-key* (the tetragrammaton).[67] Then, by removing the death of these two men from the temporal realm, Katzenelson could make their deification complete.

The *real* Radziner rabbi had called for armed resistance in Warsaw as early as January 1940. Once the ghetto had been established, he had tried to organize partisan units to fight in the forests, and when the Gestapo had finally caught him, back home in the shtetl of Vlodave, he had spit in their faces.[68] Of all this there was but a passing reference in *The Song about the Radziner* (canto 1, chapter 16). Instead, at poem's end, Katzenelson had him pray for a death like Akiva's, an exemplary death before God and man. The central events of the poem were atemporal, linked to the liturgical calendar (Tisha b'Av) and to rites of faith and solidarity: the burial of the dead, the recitation of the kaddish, and the preparation for martyrdom. It is no wonder that some members of the Dror-Hechalutz underground, just then preparing for the uprising, were aghast at their resident poet for writing hymns to spiritual rather than to physical resistance.[69]

Stripped of its temporality and its mortal dimensions, the story of the Radziner rabbi was then refitted with the famous triad of God-Torah-and-Israel, as first formulated by Moses Hayim Luzzatto and then popularized by the Vilna Gaon and the Maggid of Mezritsh.[70] Like Kalmanovitsh, who also expounded on this concept in his Passover sermon of 1943, Katzenelson made a leap of faith.[71] Though man, for Katzenelson, was the final arbiter of transcendence, the Torah and the people of Israel remained inviolate.

"O Rebbe!" the epic singer apostrophized in canto 1, "you are like the Torah and are something beyond . . . / The Torah is mighty; a Jew, even more" (1:15).[72] The Radziner was the most precious among men, the true guardian of his flock, no less than an equal partner to God:

And suddenly the Rebbe emits a great moan:
Lord of the Universe, I do not stand alone!
Both of us are here on guard
And thou lookest upon [the destruction of] Lublin from afar.
Thou art in hiding as I am too . . .
(1:18)

What was true on the scale of individual achievement, that the tiny shtetl of Vlodave could produce a semi-divine leader, was true 300,000 times over of the city of Warsaw. It was the rabbi himself who articulated the second article of faith, the absolute sanctity of the people as a whole:

Varshever! Alts vos ir makht, vos ir tut
Iz heylik, geheylikt, iz voyl un iz gut.

Oh Jews of Warsaw! All that you practice and do
Is holy, sanctified, wonderful and good.
(2:17)

As the city with the greatest concentration of Jews, Warsaw could be likened to the burning bush, to Sinai, to Israel Eternal, which brought Katzenelson to the heart of his radical theology:

What wilt thou do without houses of prayer
And without Jews—no Jews anywhere?
Who will recite the Psalm of the Day
And who will suffer gratuitously?
(2:19)

If the triad were destroyed, there would be no one to study the Torah, no one left to pray, and no one to endure suffering as the truest form of actualization.

The writing of this poem was interrupted by the Great Deportation, in which 265,000 of Warsaw's Jews were freighted off to Treblinka in the course of two months. After such destruction, the absense of God was a negligible loss compared to the human void. That is why Katzenelson shifted the burden of proof onto the people. Of what possible use were God and His Torah if the entire people was soon to disappear?

In the end, the rabbi was powerless to rescue his people—as powerless as God to stay the execution of Lublin. The ultimate act of faith, therefore, was the performance of *mitzvot*, the deeds prescribed by the

Torah, in a world devoid of Jews. Not far from Vlodave a trainload of Jews had been abandoned in sealed boxcars. With the money that was to buy him safe passage to Warsaw, the rabbi had peasants break open the doors and paid them so-much-and-so-much per corpse and more for any Jews who happened to survive. When all the dead of Lublin were brought to burial, he recited the kaddish (3:14).

Why? And particularly why the kaddish—of all prayers the one that, since Abramovitsh's day, had been the favorite object of abuse by those who repudiated the traditions of Jewish response to catastrophe? Precisely, one might argue, for that reason. The bridge to Bialik's desecrated landscape now led back to its original source—to the midrash on Lamentations, in which divine pathos was symbolically rendered through the figure of a disconsolate God, shown through the ruins of the Temple by the prophet Jeremiah. "Bring me Moses!" the Lord had exclaimed, "for he knows how to weep!" In the diminished world of 1943, it was the Radziner who hallowed His Name on earth, and all God could do was weep in earthly solitude. Thanks only to such lone acts of individual affirmation as the Radziner's kaddish, God continued to maintain His tie with the flock, both living and dead. God's weeping—not His living presence, not His salvation—was the missing link in the triad.[73] And so, in the first week of January 1943, Katzenelson completed one of the great midrashic responses to the Holocaust. He located God in the abandoned boxcars emptied of their Jews. In this latter-day Holy of Holies, the High Priest entered alone to hear the Almighty weeping while he, the Radziner, was silent, refusing to utter a single word of solace to the Lord (3:16).

The movement of the poem, which was also the movement of history that impelled its writing, was from presence to absence. The celebration of Vlodave as the spiritual reservoir and of Warsaw as the living Jewish metropolis gave way to the mourner's prayer for a city of Jews, to a train of empty boxcars, to a God in eclipse. Whatever leadership qualities the Radziner was supposed to represent at the beginning was not what he represented at the end. For by the end, everything had been relegated to a shadowy existence: the rabbi-without-his-flock as a stand-in for Israel; the kaddish as a stand-in for the Torah; the weeping as a stand-in for God.

LIFE and death in the Nazi ghettos brought into sharpest possible focus the nature of Jewish response to catastrophe in eastern Europe: the claim of the collective on individual loyalties; the ongoing use by that collective of ancient archetypes, buttressed over time with subordinate symbols of destruction; and the use or abuse of those archetypes by individual writers as they stood facing the void. What a detailed, sequential study of ghetto writings shows is the precise breaking point and the way in which the writers began to apprehend the Holocaust as its own archetype. It happened in 1942 when all the old strategies had already been tried: when the earlier tradition of realism and revolt allowed a writer such as Goldin to portray the extreme isolation of the individual as an all-out attack on group norms; when secular writers such as Shayevitsh and Katzenelson cast about for traditional anchor and forced new meanings upon such classical concepts as Kiddush Hashem, exile, the triad of God-Israel-Torah; when even subjecting the most recent countertraditions to irony failed to produce an adequate response.

It happened when they took away the children, because without the children there was no hope whatsoever. The forcible conversion of the children in Cantonist times, so pathetically invoked in Shayevitsh's poem, could not compare with their wholesale annihilation. "And now, Blimele, my child," he said, "put on your coat and let's be off. The third group sways in readiness and *we* must be among them." The death of the children was the decisive omen of the End.

In the process of unnatural selection, few were the writers who lived long enough to chronicle the break. Some, like Israel Rabon, wrote brilliantly about the air raids in the first week of the war but had cracked under the strain by the time the Germans came to get him.[74] Some, like Mordkhe Gebirtig, witnessed several stages of the Holocaust; but of all the songs he wrote, none gave expression to a world on fire as vividly as his prewar hymn to the burning shtetl.[75] Some sang of their hunger, then died in their ghetto beds, like Warsaw folk bard Hershele.[76] Some, like ghetto chronicler Peretz Opoczynski, were either so intent on proving the people's adaptability to suffering or so constrained by Ringelblum to stick to what they actually saw and knew, that the sketches contained no ultimate cry of anger, even those written after the Great Deportation.[77] Others, like Yiddish novelist Yehoshue Perle, are remembered for their protest alone. In the course of writing his chronicle on the Great Deportation, Perle changed the work's title from "The Expulsion" to "The Destruction/*khurbm* of Warsaw."[78] He ended it with a cry to the children, "our children, our future, our life that was to be" (page 139). Some, like Chaim Kaplan, had a fictional character report the horrible truth prior to the event. Kaplan's alter ego, a character named Hirsch, brings home the news a full month before the Great Deportation:

> My Hirsch is screaming: "Cowards! A whole community of millions of people stands on the brink of destruction, and you keep silent! You delude yourselves out of hope that the evil will not reach you; YOU HAVE EYES AND SEE NOT

(Ps. 115:5, 135:16). Are you any better than the people of Lublin? The people of Cracow? The people of Lodz? If not today, then tomorrow or the next day you will be taken out LIKE LAMBS TO SLAUGHTER (Ps. 44:23). Protest! Alarm the world! Don't be afraid!"[79]

And others marshaled evidence to prove that the trains from the Umschlagplatz did not lead to Treblinka but across the legendary Sambatyon River, where the Ten Lost Tribes of Warsaw were to live out the war years in relative security.[80]

Yet some of the Nazis' thoroughness—some remarkable fanatic thoroughness—had *no* echo in any of the earlier archetypes available. Even after the Second Temple, there had been the saga of Yohanan ben Zakkai, who had been smuggled out of Jerusalem in a coffin and who had successfully appealed to the Romans to establish a new center in Yavneh. Crusades and pogroms, however constant, were marked by scattered killing. Now, from his underground Warsaw bunker in April 1943, an unknown author admitted to this total lack of precedent:

> How limited was our understanding about what the Germans were capable of doing! We simply could not imagine that the entire inventory, all the warehouses full of merchandise, all the workshops, factories, and machines worth tens, worth hundreds of millions—that all this would be set on fire on account of us, on account of all those who buried themselves underground and found hiding places between the walls and possess nothing more than their lives and the desire, the strong desire, not to give them up. No, we simply could not imagine it.[81]

Since no amount of archetypal thinking could explain the burning of an entire ghetto to destroy its last remaining Jews, all the author could come up with was a sense of total absurdity, of playing in a Chaplinesque movie.

Against a reality that fairly screamed for an archetypal explanation, either as the culmination of all the catastrophes that came before or as a new and terrible beginning, the figures of Kalmanovitsh and Katzenelson loom above the rest. With the possible exception of Hillel Zeitlin whose ghetto writings did not survive, they were the only professional writers who seriously explored the messianic implications of the Nazi genocide.

On 27 December 1942, at a time when his own ghetto of Vilna was still enjoying a period of relative stability, Kalmanovitsh predicted that the destruction of eastern European Jewry would "steal its way into world history."[82] On that day he composed the equivocal epitaph to the people of the ghetto: "Your least utterance will be studied, your struggle for man's dignity will inspire poems, your scum and moral degradation will summon and awaken morality." It was the leitmotif of his life in the ghetto and of his death in the Estonian labor camp of Narva. "I kiss the shit of these holy Jews,"[83] the fifty-eight-year-old scholar was reputed to have said as he cleaned out the latrines in Narva. Everything this people did was rendered holy, even its uttermost degradation.

In the end, the very end, there was nothing left but the searing memory of the dead, too many to recall by name; nothing left but the rage aimed both inward and out; nothing left but to document the worst atrocities and call for revenge; nothing left but disbelief. These came together in Katzenelson's famous *Song of the Murdered Jewish People* written in Vittel, a transit camp to Auschwitz.[84] No work before or since ever tried to encompass more: the loss of wife and children as an emblem of genocide; the premonitions of destruction that had gone unheeded; the abortive attempts to flee eastward when the war broke out; the Nazi terror in the first months of the occupation; the German acts of sacrilege in every place inhabited by Jews; the internal life of the ghetto; the failure of Jewish politics; the role of the Jewish Police and the Judenrat; the armed resistance; the Great Deportation, culminating in the indescribable horror of the *kesl,* or cauldron, on Mila Street; the death of the children—"the first to go"; the gas chambers; the German people as the personification of evil; the uniqueness of the Holocaust. Similarly, no work ever aimed at greater allusiveness so as to appropriate both the ancient and modern voices of destruction—from Lamentations and the prophets to Bialik.[85] Conspicuous in his absence, however, was God, perhaps because, as Yechiel Szeintuch suggested, the Great Lament was simply a lament, unlike the works of consolation that told of martyrs and redeemers who bore witness to God's presence.[86]

In the great ninth canto, the emotional and ideological center of the poem, Katzenelson addressed the heavens, the very heavens that Bialik had once invoked in "Upon the Slaughter" and that Katzenelson had celebrated in romantic outpourings of song:

> False and cheating heavens, low heavens up on high, O how you hurt!
> Once I believed in you, sharing my joy with you, my smile, my tears—
> Who are not different from the ugly earth, that heap of dirt!
> I did believe in you and sang your praises in each song of mine.
> I loved you as one loves a woman, though she vanished like the mist.[87]

Whoever reached out to these heavens was similarly duped:

> You have deceived us both, my people and my race.
> You cheated us—eternally. My ancestors, my prophets, too, you have deceived.
> To you, foremost, they lifted up their eyes, and you inspired their faith.
> And full of faith they turned to you, when jubilant or grieved.
>
> (stanza 5)

There were still too many scores to settle—with the Bund and the orthodox, the assimilationists and the converts—and it was still too soon to know the final count, so Katzenelson could not erect anything comparable to Nathan Nata Hannover's six pillars of Jewish greatness. But one thing was certain: that no generation of Jews had ever drunk a fuller cup of sorrow, and therein lay their eternal claim to glory:

> They suffered more and greater pains, each one.
> The little, simple, ordinary Jew from Poland of today—
> Compared with him what are the great men of a past bygone?
> A wailing Jeremiah, Job afflicted, Kings despairing, all in one—it's they!
> (stanza 8)

This luminous presence made up of petty merchants and market women crowding the fairs, of old Psalm-readers and synagogue-goers, of schoolboys and radiant girls, of mothers cradling their infants, of learners and Talmud scholars, poets and writers, musicians and painters, freedom fighters and pioneers—this whole epic list would live on only in the works of Bialik, Sholem Aleichem, and Asch, each Jew a prophet in the pages of a new eternal Book (canto 15).

From the start, then, ghetto writing worked toward an exalted conclusion. The archives, with their liturgical code name and communal mandate; the overwhelming sense of déjà vu; the ironic Holy City-ness of the ghetto, seen as a community that had never been so united before, almost messianic in its "ingatheredness"; the reversion to mythic archetypes; the use of the figure of the child and the martyr in a new way to stand *for* the people (as the people disappeared, the metaphors remained, like shadows)—all this projected a composite image that was as glorified and as romantic about the ghetto dead as the subsequent literature would be about the Holocaust.

When all the psychic moorings had been pulled loose, the last remaining poet raised a great and unfamiliar cry. The people, he now discovered, had to be recreated before a memorial could be built in its memory. "I have imagined you!" he exclaimed from his last and temporary refuge. "I have invented a Jewish people!" All past divisions would ultimately cease to have meaning, for *all* of the people were now holy. Liberated from their physical reality, from the vast contradictions of their life and their death, the Jews of eastern Europe entered the realm of myth.

CHAPTER NINE

The Burden of Memory

And the dead, the dead—have they died?
Abraham Sutzkever, 1954

THERE were a few survivors, each with a story to tell about the destruction of a world: parents, children, friends, home, and homeland. The question they faced was how to retell it. Those who sought guidance in the fund of available sources found two basic ways of recalling catastrophe: by naming names or by conjuring up the apocalypse. Both the rabbis and apocalyptists of ancient times had made history emerge from the Text, but the rabbis preserved the names of the preacher and teacher, making the public sermon and study house debate the real-life setting of historical recapitulation, so that they, the rabbis, became the implicit heroes of history. The apocalyptists, in contrast, covered their tracks. Their visions were always attributed to others—Daniel, Ezra, Baruch, Enoch—with never a real person, place, or event to hold on to. And this simple pseudepigraphic device made all the difference, because it rendered the specific event alluded to in the vision that much more ominous, general, insidious. The apocalyptic omen crowded out visible reality.

These two strands were picked up again in modern times during the great flowering of Jewish literary creativity. Sholem Aleichem and others insisted on the communicability of human experience, on the one-to-one mediation of language: in their works, a named speaker addressed a known addressee. In the Nazi ghettos, Katzenelson favored the heroic epic, rooted in concrete events and revering the memory of real persons; even when he raised the great lament to encompass the fate of the entire people, each outcry was provoked by detailed recollections of cities and courtyards, friend and foe. The latter-day apocalyptists, meanwhile, worked in much the same way as their forebears. Halpern's apocalypse obeyed the logic of a nightmare; Markish's "Heap" was an undifferentiated mass of decomposing bodies; Shapiro omitted or invented place names to stretch the landscape of extremity over the entire globe; and Uri Zvi Greenberg (see Chapter 10) ranted and raged through the mouths of Jesus, Mephisto, and Shabbetai Zvi.

And so the survivors of the Holocaust, intent on communicating their incalculable losses, had basically two approaches to draw upon from the fund of ancient and modern sources: one that imploded history, and the other that made the Holocaust the center of apocalypse. There were, of course, many variables that decided which direction a writer would take, and it would be foolish to argue that cultural determinants were the most decisive. One must first of all allow for differences in age. Someone who had come of age in the ghettos and concentration camps would have a different view of the horror than would someone who had had prior life experience. And there were gradations of horror. Death in the ghettos and forests was fundamentally different from death in the camps, and it is certainly no accident that most of the literature that survived was written in the former setting and not in the latter. But in the end, all survivors faced the challenge of bearing witness in some form or other. To the extent that they were products of eastern European Jewish culture prior to the war—whether as *enfant terrible* in Warsaw during the 1920s, as pantheist poet in Vilna during the thirties, or as child prodigy in Sighet during the forties—it is fair, indeed necessary, to compare, to categorize, and ultimately to evaluate them according to a single standard.

Thus, one man's story of ghetto, flight, and imprisonment was turned into an almost unmitigated apocalypse in Piotr Rawicz's *Blood from the Sky*, and part of the achievement lay in the deliberate abstraction of events.[1] In Rawicz's rendering, the Lemberg ghetto became a "walled town" somewhere in the Ukraine; Leyb Landau, the renowned prewar defense attorney who headed the Jewish Communal Self-Help (ŻSS) in the ghetto, became Leo L., the unsurpassed spokesman for his people, a sardonic man with no illusions about the Nazi conquest;[2] and Salo Greiver, a merchant from Cracow who ran the ghetto workshops under German contract, became Garin, the "blood-smeared Golem," convinced of his power to save the able-bodied through collaboration. Rawicz compounded the abstraction of events with their deliberate confusion through a surrealistic, disjointed style of narration, interrupted by diary entries, poems, oracles, cynical outbursts, and philosophical digressions, to create a terrifying parable on hunted individuals reduced to the status of roaches.

At the other extreme was Abraham Sutzkever (born 1913) who witnessed the slaughter of Vilna Jewry in 1941 and then made Vilna the touchstone of reality. Some thirty years later, on a fantastic journey to the ends of the earth, he would still find traces of Vilna, its people and places.[3] And in the ghetto proper, he wrote lyric poems to the memory of named individuals and captured the collective tragedy in epic form. Only the Germans were consigned to verbal annihilation; they appeared, if at all, as metaphors. Unlike Rawicz's hallucinatory techniques, which discourage historical investigation, Sutzkever's work invites us to ask: Who were these people? Did these events actually happen? Catastrophe in Sutzkever's scheme was knowable and assimilable. What a verdant place was the green aquarium that would eventually house the dead ghetto Jews of the poet's memory! Sutzkever, too, was intent on imploding history; but unlike the rabbis, he rarely referred back to the revealed Text or to ancient archetypes. Instead he made Vilna the text, forcing us to look back upon a specific place at a specific time, making each reader a partner in poetic resurrection.

VILNA'S claim to be the Jerusalem of Lithuania had remained uncontested since the days of Rabbi Elijah the Gaon (died 1797). And since Vilna was perceived as the spiritual center of Jewish eastern Europe, its destructions were thoroughly documented, especially after World War I. Zalmen Reisen's massive *Sourcebook for the History of Vilna in the Years of War and Occupation*, published in 1922, was but one instance of this deep-rooted and pervasive historical consciousness.[4] And since the Holocaust was apprehended as its own archetype after the sum of all past possibilities had been assembled and reexamined, it is not surprising that the surviving Jews of Vilna, schooled in the exercise of collective memory, were among the first to map out the landscape of total destruction.

Vilna, the central repository of Jewish memory, was the first major community to experience the Final Solution. Over 33,000 Vilna Jews were systematically murdered in the first six months of the Nazi occupation, from June 24 to December 22, 1941, mostly in the woods of Ponar, some five kilometers away.[5] There was no one among the surviving 20,000 who had not lost a parent, child, or friend. "Whomever I ask about," wrote Sutzkever of his return to the ghetto after the first round of slaughter had ended, "hardly anyone remains."[6] Within a few months he was to lose his mother and his newborn child.

The Nazis were well aware of Vilna's special status. Never had the murder of Jews been so scrupulously coordinated with their cultural extermination, and nowhere was this two-pronged genocide pursued with greater thoroughness than in Vilna. As Einsatzkommando (mobile killing unit) 9 went about the business of slaughter, with the enthusiastic support of the Lithuanian militia, Hitler's professors arrived from Berlin and Frankfurt to initiate another order of business. First, a select group of Jewish scholars was pressed into service to help draw up the inventory. Noah Prylucki, the preeminent expert in Yiddish phonetics, was forced to compile a list of incunabula in the collection of the Strashun Library. When the job was complete, the fifty-nine-year-old scholar was left to perish in a Gestapo cellar. Meanwhile, Strashun, grandson of the founder of the library, hung himself with his own pair of phylacteries.[7]

Then Alfred Rosenberg, the chief Nazi ideologue, recently appointed minister of the occupied countries in the East, sent to Vilna his expert in Jewish culture, Dr. Johannes Pohl, to oversee the destruction. Pohl had been specially trained for the job, having spent three years at the Hebrew University mastering classical Hebrew sources.[8] He demanded that experts in Hebrew and Yiddish be brought in to help select which manuscripts and books would live and which would die. By his order, the 40,000 volumes of the Strashun Library and all the sacred books in Vilna's 300 houses of prayer were collected in the YIVO building located outside the ghetto—some 100,000 volumes in all—whence 20,000 were dispatched to the Frankfurt Museum for the Study of Oriental Peoples and the remainder were sold for pulp. The YIVO's treasures came next; nothing in Vilna was left unexploited. The lead plates of the Talmud in Rom's printing works, the pride of nineteenth-century Jewish publishing, were sold at thirty marks a ton. Pohl's successor, a former leather merchant, had 500 Torah scrolls made into boot linings.[9]

Among the forty ghetto intellectuals who were co-opted to work in the Rosenberg Squad, nicknamed the Paper Brigade, a few volunteered in order to save whatever could be saved. Sutzkever was one. In the YIVO building alone, some 5,000 volumes were concealed. The most valuable items—letters by Tolstoy, Gorky, Romain Rolland, and Bialik; manuscripts of Peretz and Sholem Aleichem; the diary of Peter the Great's valet and of Theodore Herzl; drawings by Chagall—were smuggled *into* the ghetto for safekeeping or parceled out among friendly Poles and Lithuanians.

And so, just as Vilna, the neoclassical center of eastern European Jewry, was chosen as the Armageddon of Jewish culture, so Sutzkever, the preeminent neoclassical poet of his generation, found himself thrust into the front line of battle. It was he, supported by his mentor Kalmanovitsh, who launched one flank of the counterattack as soon as the slaughter abated: Yiddish culture in the ghetto became a central arena of spiritual resistance.

Sutzkever's activities in the public domain—the theatrical revues, exhibitions, lectures, and poetry readings that he organized or inspired—were a symbol of hope and creative power for the powerless Jews of the ghetto.[10] For that alone, Sutzkever's name would go down in history. But what concerns us here is his activity as a poet who, foremost among Jewish poets, made the memory of the dead the nexus of his artistic expression and whose allegiance to their memory brought about three profound shifts in his response to catastrophe: from romantic exuberance to pained confession; from private grief to public exhortation; and from epic statement back to a private, metaphysical communion with the dead. These three stages are more than poetic biography; they mark the way-stations of a people whose mass murder and miraculous rebirth Sutzkever was fated to witness, internalize, and commemorate.

ON the surface, there could have been no candidate less suited for the job. In the bleak and polarized world of interbellum Poland, Sutzkever made his appearance as a "barefoot tramp" playing on his "wander flute," the romantic self-image par excellence:

> What then is left to do in such an hour,
> O, my world of a thousand colors,
> Except,
> To gather into the knapsack of the wind
> The red loveliness
> And bring it home for evening bread.[11]

As late as 1940 he published a volume called *Woodlore (Valdiks)*, consisting of ecstatic hymns to the boundless wonders of nature and beauty which he recreated through dazzling rhymes, galloping rhythms, and virtuoso inventions of language. More amazing yet were his "Four Poems in Old Yiddish," written in 1938—masterly stylizations of medieval Yiddish verse, an inaccessible body of the literary tradition which Sutzkever had spent several years studying under the tutelage of Max Weinreich and Noah Prylucki at the YIVO.

This celebration of nature, beauty, and language was totally at odds with the leftist urban cosmopolitanism of his fellow writers of Young Vilna. In a moment of exasperation, the poet Shmerke Kaczerginski (born 1908) supposedly shouted: "Sutzkever! We're living in a time of steel, not of crystal—*fun shtol un nit krishtol!*"[12] Yet Sutzkever's prior training as a poet would prove more resilient to the terror of ghetto and forest than the iron-clad faith of his comrades-in-arms. For to create in a time of catastrophe one needed an anchor in the past, and to write in the midst of total destruction one needed a living audience, whether human or not. "There is no continuity, no healthy poetic tradition," he complained in 1939 about the younger Yiddish poets in Poland and North America. "Everyone starts out from the beginning and is therefore a step backwards."[13] Sutzkever, in contrast, pursued a systematic search for precursors: Moyshe Kulbak and Leyb Naydus from among the Yiddish poets of Lithuania; Yehoash, Halpern, and Leyeles from the United States; Cyprian Norwid from the Polish neoromantics; the medieval Yiddish epics from the secular past. Who but Sutzkever in the shadow of Ponar would ever have thought of mounting an exhibit in honor of Yehoash, the great Bible translator and the forerunner of Yiddish modernism? As the past was for Sutzkever the measure of poetic excellence, nature was the wellspring of poetic creativity. His ability to defy the poverty and oppression of the prewar years with a seemingly inexhaustible fund of poetic inventiveness made him a bona fide partner to nature, a member of a macrocosmic community peopled with forests and flowers and stars. Nature, the source of his transcendent vision, would also be his judge and jury, the only addressee in a time of human eclipse. And here is the paradox we are about to explore: through a faith that drew upon sources outside Jewish tradition and that lay beyond the boundaries of the Jewish community, Sutzkever was able to establish his place in the continuum of Jewish response to catastrophe.

HE bore witness to the slaughter, then hid alone for weeks on end. He rejoined the traumatized survivors, then lost his mother and child—his past and his future. In these first few months of the Nazi onslaught, the poet's exuberant faith in himself and in his poetic powers was tested as never before. His own survival, it seemed to him then, had been bought at the price of others'. He accused himself of having crossed the narrow line between creative self-absorption and egotism by abandoning his loved ones to the enemy. Could he not be likened to Cain, the first murderer in history, whose egotism led to his brother Abel's death ("Because I Drank Wine," July 1941)? "If I am too weak to cut down your killer," he wrote after the death of his mother, "Then on my own flesh I shall have to wreak vengeance" ("From the poem *Three Roses,*" chapter 6). This self-reproach was the beginning of Sutzkever's break with the values that had so recently sustained him. His first confrontations with death were translated into radical confrontations with himself.

From a poem called "The Circus," which Sutzkever did not publish for thirty-eight years, we can see how relentless was his condemnation of personal and collective panaceas in the earliest stage of the Nazi occupation.

> Tell me, good brother,
> What is it and what does it mean,
> This dogfight we're in?[14]

The reference point in this angriest (though by no means best) of Sutzkever's poems was a "circus improvisation" that he and two other random victims were forced to play. Sutzkever, along with an eighty-year-old rabbi named Kassel and a boy named Moyskhe, was dragged off the streets (the ghetto had not yet been established). They were made to undress, to dance naked around a burning pyre, to sing Russian songs and to feed the flames with Torah scrolls looted especially for the occasion.[15] This act of sacrilege was recast soon after in a poem that consciously echoed another nightmarish carnival of shattered illusions: Moyshe-Leyb Halpern's "A Night."[16] Yet Sutzkever's anger was not against the Germans, whom he does not mention, but against God, against Isaiah's "rust-eaten consolation," against the passivity of a people who inherited "the likeness of an age-old affliction," against "all the beautiful words" he once used, and, above all, against himself for not dying the death of a martyr.

It was impossible even to write an elegy for his mother without an image of radical nakedness, a grotesque, dehumanized, and surrealistic image intruding upon his private grief:

> A pack of nerves locked in chains
> Like criminals
> And over them a purple blackjack.
> And each and every nerve
> Bites at the throat of the one beside it:
> "You're to blame, you."
> And screams in Yiddish . . .[17]

The human body is compared to a glass prison where the senses are visible in all their rawness and in their enslavement they mutilate each other. The sole glimmer of beauty is buried somewhere in the past and hovering overhead is the mark of Jewish enslavement, a yellow Star of David. All this, of course, is but a microcosm of the ghetto as a whole, where the body politic is similarly stripped and ravaged.

If the death of his friends and of his mother weighed so heavily on his conscience, how much more so the death of his firstborn child. When the child was conceived, during the Soviet occupation of Vilna, no one could have foreseen that it would be born in a Nazi ghetto. Given the new reality, each birth was a victory in itself. One ghetto child was even named Malina in honor of the dismal *malines* (hideouts) where the infant had come to term.[18] But if such a child, born in the wake of the greatest slaughter yet experienced, was put to death immediately thereafter, how was a father to be consoled? What could his poetry offer in the face of such a loss? Here is the exemplary response of a ghetto Jew:

To the Child

Out of hunger
or out of great love—
but your mother can witness to it—
I wanted to swallow you, my child,
when I felt your small body cool
in my fingers,
as if I pressed in them
a warm glass of tea
and felt it turning cold.[19]

The greater the loss, the more radical the act needed to regain wholeness. Nothing less than devouring the child will do. Accentuating his despair is the very real hunger of the ghetto which could almost provoke a father—at least in thought—to eat his child. Mitigating the despair is the wrenching union of hunger and love. Echoed in the opening lines is the Yiddish expression *Ikh vil im ufesn,* "I want to eat him up," meaning "I love him to pieces." The father's exact formulation, however, reveals that the inner turmoil cannot be resolved. The ambiguous "but" in line 3 can mean "But for your mother's presence I would have swallowed you" or "Either way, your mother was there, witness to my indecision." Just as the great love cannot explain away the hunger, the image of the glass of tea cannot fully domesticate the horror.

The poet has come to confess—something he never did prior to the ghetto and rarely did in its aftermath. The death and disappearance of his family and friends have aroused in him a complex of emotions: the need to defend his behavior before an external witness and to pass moral judgment on himself. This was a new dimension in Sutzkever's poetry. Usually he sprang from the individual experience directly to a higher plane of truth (hence his affinity to Yehoash). Even in a moment of absolute despair, the contemplation of suicide became the subject for a metaphysical poem on the hidden wellsprings of life in a broken piece of glass ("In the Cell," June 1941). Here, too, in addressing his dead child, Sutzkever tries to transcend his feelings of guilt and betrayal with a statement of faith.

Since you are no stranger, no guest,
on our earth one does not birth another:
One births oneself like a ring
and the rings link in chains together.
(lines 10–13)

Life "on our earth," he explains, is cyclical, not discontinuous. New life arises out of old. It is a principle he has upheld before, especially in the relationship between parents and children ("My Father and I," 1937). But to whom, really, is he explaining this iron-fast rule of rings and chains? The movement is illogical, for if the child is the living manifestation of the parent, this should only intensify the sense of loss. The birth-as-chain theory doesn't work if the child dies before the father. Undeterred, however, the father exclaims:

> My child,
> You who in words are called: love,
> and who without words are yourself love,
> you—the seed of my every dream,
> the hidden third,
> who from the wides of the world
> with the wonder of an unseen storm
> have made two meet and flow together
> to create you and complete our pleasure:
> (lines 14–22)

The child is no less than the life principle itself. That tiny creature already dead is the essence of everything real: the force that motivated the love and the one who presided over the very act of sexual union that brought him into being. Through an alliterative spell and a new, luxurious rhyme (*tsveyen/derfreyen,* here rendered as "together/pleasure"), Sutzkever exults in the connectedness of life, in the created being that is its own creator. Father-mother-and-child become a unity forged by the child "from the wides of the world." Love is an active, cosmic force embodied in the child.

From these heights the father inevitably falls back to the horrible truth. All the meeting and conjoining that the child effected has now been severed by its death:

> Why did you darken the creation
> as you did when you shut your eyes
> and left me outside like a beggar
> with a world blanketed in snow
> which you shook off?
> (lines 23–27)

What remains is the stark fact of death: the child who was credited with creating himself must willfully have rejected that life and in so doing has turned his back on all of creation. The child abandons not only his father but the entire universe. The father is as orphaned as the world is cold.

Nature has become an equal partner in the tragedy, replacing the mother who earlier stood by as silent witness. Until now the father's egocentricity has not allowed for an active third party: "one births *oneself* like a ring," he insists in line 12; "you—the seed of *my* every dream," he claims in line 17. Once nature is implicated, it too must witness the father's terrifying loss:

> No cradle, whose every motion
> holds within the rhythm of the stars,
> had brought you joy.
> The sun—for you have never seen it
> shine—
> might as well crack and shatter like glass.
> (lines 28–32)

He who believes in fellowship with nature acknowledges the deeper bond that exists between a child and the cosmos. It is not a faith that is traditionally found in eastern European Jewish literature, though it occupies a prominent place in Bialik's private mythology ("Imperceptibly, One by One," 1916). Even before the child smells its first flower and beholds its first tree, it rocks to the rhythm of the stars and absorbs the light of the sun. Now that union has come to nought.

The fifth stanza (lines 28–35), added some time after his years in the ghetto to an otherwise laconic and thoroughly understated poem, provides a distant echo of his rage and some indication of how the child actually died:

> A drop of poison burned out your faith.
> You thought
> it was warm sweet milk.
> (lines 33–35)

The lines recall the father's initial desire to be nurtured by the child. Now it seems that just as nature bypassed its natural partner, so too did some human hand ensnare or poison the child. Who did it and how? Sutzkever offers no further evidence either in his memoirs or in the poem. It was not until February 27, 1946, when he testified before the International Military Tribunal in Nuremberg, that the bereaved father revealed the full extent of the tragedy:

> Towards the end of December in the ghetto my wife gave birth to a child, a boy. I was not in the ghetto at that time, having escaped from one of these so-called "actions." When I came to the ghetto later I found that my wife had had a baby in a ghetto hospital. But I saw the hospital surrounded by Germans and a black car standing before the door . . .
>
> In the evening when the Germans had left, I went to the hospital and found my wife in tears. It seems that when she had had her baby, the Jewish doctors

of the hospital had already received the order that Jewish women must not give birth; and they had hidden the baby, together with other newborn children, in one of the rooms. But when this commission with Muhrer came to the hospital, they heard the cries of the babies. They broke open the door and entered the room. When my wife heard that the door had been broken, she immediately got up and ran to see what was happening to the child. She saw one German holding the baby and smearing something under its nose. Afterwards he threw it on the bed and laughed. When my wife picked up the child, there was something black under his nose. When I arrived at the hospital, I saw that my baby was dead. He was still warm.[20]

It is difficult to decide what confounds the imagination more: the savagery of the Germans, their unbounded energy for the murder of Jews, or, by radical contrast, the poet's lyricism. The father's outcry is not to be heard; there is no protest against the Germans, God, or fate. Nor does Sutzkever resort to any of the standard responses to Jewish catastrophe. This is all the more astonishing in the light of the immediate reaction among the Jews of Vilna:

February 5 [1942]

Today the Gestapo summoned two members of the Judenrat and notified them: "From today on, no more Jewish children are to be born." The officer, somewhat taken aback himself as he made the announcement, added that he had received the order from Berlin . . .

The impact of the order on the ghetto is indescribable. Everyone cited the first Sedrah in Exodus in which Pharaoh had forbidden the birth of male children. The Pharaoh of the twentieth century is far more cruel—no births whatsoever![21]

Herman Kruk, the Bundist and secular intellectual, introduces this entry in his ghetto diary not with the text of the German decree but with the relevant passages from the Book of Exodus. There is no recourse to biblical precedents in "To the Child" because Sutzkever's response is not addressed to a community of Jews who seek meaning in the hallowed texts. Nor is it God from whom he seeks to be absolved of his guilt.

With no desire to fall back on symbols of the national saga and with no tidings of comfort from God, the father returns, chastened and equivocal, to himself:

I wanted to swallow you, my child,
to know the taste
of my anticipated future.
Perhaps you will blossom as before
in my veins.

(lines 36–40)

If his body had once given life to the child, could he not do it again, after the child's death? Perhaps, but the doubts, suppressed so long, finally win out. For the father, the cycle is closed, not because such rebirth is impossible—the intimate bond between life and death is Sutzkever's main article of faith—but because he, the father, is unworthy.

> But I am not worthy to be your grave.
> So I bequeath you
> to the summoning snow,
> the snow—my first respite—
> and you will sink
> like a splinter of dusk
> into the quiet depths
> and bear greetings from me
> to the small shoots beneath the cold.
> (Vilna ghetto, January 18, 1943;
> lines 41-49)

The internal debate has spent itself. Sutzkever opened with the moment of death, the child's body still warm. Though even from the outset it was clear that the glass of tea would remain cold and undrunk, that the child's loss could never be overcome, the father rebelled against the finality of it all, fighting to renew the cycle—through himself. Now he must finally admit that the child has *willfully* rejected life and that he who betrayed his child is not worthy to be its grave, let alone its resource.

Which leaves him with the "summoning" snow, the last and only hope. The child who has never beheld the sun will itself sink into the earth *vi a shpliter zunfargang,* "like a splinter of dusk" or of "sunset light," and will bring personal greetings to the frozen shoots beneath the snow. The poem ends with this image because the poet knows that after winter comes spring, the season of rebirth. The coldness of nature, in contrast to the coldness of a glass of tea, inevitably and cyclically yields to warmth.

Snow was central to Sutzkever's poetic landscape; it was the stuff of his private mythology. "My illusion is Siberia," he explained to Shmerke Kaczerginski in the ghetto;[22] his childhood years in Siberia he associated with the birth of his creative powers, with the source of beauty itself.[23] Siberia was his paradise lost, and snow, rather than a traditional symbol of death, was for Sutzkever the symbol of clarity, charity, and rebirth. In the ghetto, however, snow carried different associations. It was on seeing snow, in the winter of 1943, that the poet was reminded of his personal tragedy—the death of his son some time between the end of December 1941 (according to Sutzkever's Nuremberg testimony) and February 1942 (according to Kruk). Thus, if the cyclical nature of life was his basic article of faith, then snow was the barometer of the cycle: it marked the childhood past ("my first respite" in Siberia); the anniversary of his son's death; the present moment (January 18, 1943, roughly a year later); and nature's rebirth in the future.

The father overcame his grief through a faith in something more ancient and elemental than the Torah. Whether Sutzkever arrived at his pantheism via the Spinoza revival among eastern European Jewish intellectuals in the 1920s and 1930s or whether it was his natural affinity for the pastoral, celestial, and regenerative landscapes that fed the wellsprings of his poetry is not at issue. For what truly amazes in the context of the Nazi genocide is Sutzkever's desire and ability to draw his experience away both from the ghetto and from the Jews by making it pertain to the whole of nature—in nature's relationship to the human species—regardless of any God or gods.

Even a poet who had no recourse to the religious tradition had to invoke some system of belief—if not from Jewish, then from pre-Jewish myths. Instead of employing national or theological constructs he described the death of his child solely in terms of natural cycles, which lie at the very heart of mythic thought.[24] This, then, is the first key to the paradox: though Sutzkever represented, at least in this poem, a complete break with traditional Jewish responses to catastrophe, the underlying pattern remained thoroughly traditional. The punctual event was transformed into something transhistorical. The discrete, actual calamity became part of an eternal cycle that transcended the fate of the individual: each martyrdom was an Akedah; each group of martyrs became the ten Harugei Malkhut; and each martyred community recalled the destruction of Jerusalem. Shayevitsh and Katzenelson operated similarly with biblical paradigms, as did the Jews of Vilna the moment they invoked the memory of Pharaoh. The crucial difference was that Sutzkever's cycle was nonhuman and that ultimately his confession of guilt was addressed to a macrocosmic community. "So I bequeath you / to the summoning snow." A man cannot absolve himself. But the lost part of a man can reenter the cycle of nature, be reborn, and thus achieve its own redemption.

The evil that violated the human sphere had no dominion in the natural realm; those cycles remained untouched. And though trapped inside ghetto walls, the poet still had access to nature, and nature in turn allowed his great personal loss to be absorbed within its cycle. Thus, Sutzkever's one response to the Nazi onslaught was to reaffirm his earlier faith. Just as at a time of political and economic turmoil he had been busy extolling the life-giving forests and the beauty of words, so at a time when nations outdid each other in the pursuit of evil, when history spared no one, the poet upheld the cosmic cycle of rebirth over the historical cycle of destruction.

Sutzkever found his answer in the snow, in the cold that purified and provoked memories. His poem's very obliqueness opened a crack into the interior of ultimate evil; its relentless egocentricity captured the struggle of one father out of millions of Jewish fathers and its private mythology revealed the mysteries that lay hidden in the dead body of a newborn child.

In the ghetto, Sutzkever's faith in nature helped him mediate the antithetical poles of creation and annihilation. But for a poet caught up in a life-and-death struggle of his own which threatened to destroy meaning and language and beauty, not to speak of the entire Jewish people, it was a luxury to dwell solely upon the memory of the dead. No sooner were the mass killings in Vilna temporarily suspended, in January 1942, than Sutzkever threw his energies into Yiddish cultural life, and on January 18 the first theatrical revue opened with a program of Sutzkever's choosing.[25] The day before, Sutzkever had written a poem that evoked, whether consciously or not, the lines of the first number, a choral recitation of Bialik's Yiddish poem "I feel like crying":

> I feel like making a prayer—to whom, I don't know.
> He Who once gave me comfort gives me no ear now.
> To whom, then?
> It holds me like iron.
>
> I should perhaps ask a star: my distant friend,
> I've lost my word; come, be its stand-in.
> But the good star,
> it too won't hear.
>
> I *must* make a prayer. Someone very near
> tortures himself in my soul and insists on the prayer.
> Making no sense, then,
> I'll babble till dawn.[26]

Now that life was constricted to a ghetto, and now that God and nature, who for Sutzkever were one and the same, had turned a deaf ear, to whom would the poet turn? Poetry was prayer, but could there be prayer without a recipient? The star, once the subject of his verse, was too removed. Nor did Sutzkever yet know or trust the Jews who would fill the high school auditorium for the following day's inaugural concert. And so, as an affirmation of solitary consciousness, the poet resorted to poetry without sense and without a known recipient.[27]

Yet inherent in this paradoxical prayer was the new direction Sutzkever was about to take. For though it described the poet as soliloquist, the poem itself was not written in an inaccessible, private, personally solipsistic language, and the inner urge to create new poetry meant that he would be a poet more committed to art than ever before. The more he experienced of the Nazi terror, the more it confirmed his ongoing trust in the redemptive capacity of art, his faith in the mystical power of art to save, literally *save,* the good singer from death.[28] In pursuit of that redemption, Sutzkever found his audience.

The opening a year later of the Yehoash exhibit, which he himself had conceived and organized, was the highwater mark in the cultural life of the Vilna ghetto. On that occasion Sutzkever proclaimed to the assembled guests:

> Death itself shrinks before this beauty,
> And drives back again
> His grimy smoking cauldron.[29]

By then there were many ghetto Jews, including fifteen-year-old Yitskhok Rudashevski, who agreed. "Looking at the exhibition, at our work, our hearts swell with enthusiasm," he wrote on March 14. "We actually forget that we are in a dark ghetto."[30] "As you read Yehoash," he had noted earlier, "you are united with beauty."[31]

In the course of the previous year, Sutzkever had reached beyond his private dialogues with the dead, and as he discovered a new audience, the community of surviving Jews, he had changed not only his style but the very axiom of his poetry. To address his fellow Jews in a language they could respond to, Sutzkever had recourse to history, both to the recent ghetto past and to the Jewish historical myths. He began to write dramatic and epic works of great rhetorical power in which the events of ghetto life were disassembled and reassembled according to the ancient archetypes. This was the natural legacy of an eastern European Jewish poet, even for such a one as Sutzkever, who had not been raised in a religious environment.

There were many poets, in Vilna and in other ghettos, who captured through lullabies and ballads terrible moments of private grief. These include some of the most poignant Yiddish songs ever written, such as Kaczerginski's "Still, Still, Let Us Be Still," Leah Rudnitsky's "Birds Are Drowsing on the Branches," and Isaiah Spiegel's "Close Your Eyes, Birds Have Arrived."[32] Sutzkever's poetic and philosophical reach extended beyond these arrested moments of private grief, as he pursued all possible avenues of regeneration. In his two most ambitious works written in the Vilna ghetto, Sutzkever linked the ghetto's tragic history to the theme of generational and natural continuity.[33] "The Grave Child," completed in April 1942, tells the true story of a lone escapee from Ponar who sought refuge in the Jewish cemetery of Vilna, there to give birth in an empty grave.[34] The victory of life over death is anticipated in the woman's last recollection of the slaughter before she loses consciousness:

A murderer
Tore me away, lacerated my hands
And threw me down to the ground.
But I kept on grasping the tree in my arms
Kissing it and biting,
And would not let go. And from above,
Along with blows and wild shooting,
There fell apples, apples—
A world of golden-red apples,
And mingled with my blood.
(lines 110-119)

It is this almost sexual union with the tree that rescues her from death, the shower of apples, eternal symbols of love and procreation, protecting her body from the bullets.

As this was a poem for public consumption, Sutzkever added to these emblems of nature and beauty national symbols as well. The heroine's name is Rachel—"Mother Rachel," as the grave-digger calls her at the poem's end, and were this not affirmation enough, Sutzkever later embellished the final sequence with a reference to the Messiah who, according to ancient belief, would be born in a grave "So as never to die again" (line 164). In recognition of Sutzkever's essential traditionalism, of his ability to dramatize the ghetto's epic of survival through recognizable symbolic constructs, the Union of Artists and Writers in the Vilna Ghetto awarded "The Grave Child" first prize for poetry in July 1942.

The hope that Vilna would be spared its final death, so perfectly conveyed in the image of the child/messiah born in the grave, was rapidly fading as the Jewish populations of the surrounding towns were wiped out one by one. In March 1943 Kruk reread Ansky's *Khurbm Galitsye* and was astonished at the negligible scale of the earlier destruction. "If that was a *khurbm,*" he said to his friend Naftoli Vaynig, "then what do we call what's happening now? . . . It simply has no comparison!"[35]

Sutzkever, too, was reaching out for ever more ancient analogies until he hit upon an actual occurrence whose outline was so archetypal as to suggest the scope of the tragedy as he now understood it, in the winter months of 1943. Two years before, during the infamous Yom Kippur Aktion, a father had murdered his last surviving son so as to prevent the son from falling into the Nazis' hands. Was this not an Akedah, which raised the question of divine intercession? If God was to be held accountable for the murderous deeds of the enemy, then history had once again become the hieroglyphic domain of the holy and it was up to the poet to decipher its code.

To this end Sutzkever made the pious father himself the narrator of "Kol Nidre."[36] In the poem, the narrator's son, Yome Kagan, has fled Vilna twenty years before and joined the Red Army to fight Petlura in the Ukraine. Now, on the night of Yom Kippur 1941, thousands of Jews are rounded up in the synagogue, and among the victims marked for execution the old father recognizes his son: he has been captured by the Germans and is now prepared to die as a Jew among his own. The father raises a great cry of protest against God for all the suffering He has heaped upon him. "Save my child!" he cries, "or else I'll stab him / stab him to death out of vengeance with a song and with a smile . . . Reveal that you are here, and hear the thunder of my skull. / Or else be damned by my exploding sorrow" (6:19–20).

Sutzkever, the aesthete and nature poet, found himself caught in the familiar dialectic of Jewish responses to catastrophe. The very search for poetic traditions that would bridge the worlds of private and public memory led him back to the point of departure in modern Jewish poetry—to Bialik. The very magnitude of the slaughter—4,000 Jews on Yom Kippur alone—made the archetype of martyrdom the only model worth taking on. As Bialik insisted on making Kishinev the crucible of heaven and earth in order to abrogate the redemptive claims of catastrophe, so Sutzkever revisited the City of Slaughter in order to force the God of History to be accountable for the murderous deeds. Thus, the pious father redirected the German atrocity into his own act of defiance which challenged every notion of holiness: the Akedah, Job's suffering, Ezekiel's vision of the dry bones, the Kol Nidre as man's revocation of unkept promises, the Ne'ilah as the closing moment of grace.

Could someone like Sutzkever carry it off? Kalmanovitsh's reaction on hearing the poem was apt: "Whoever calls God to account [ver es hot a din-toyre mit got]," he argued, "must first of all believe in God."[37] There was an element of posturing in a poet who in other contexts rarely invoked the name of God and whose most religious poem written in the ghetto, "I Feel Like Making a Prayer," actually asserted the impossibility of prayer. Then again, Sutzkever was writing not for Kalmanovitsh but for Jews like himself who had lost or who had never had any traditional faith. That audience required him to reach back to the common fund of symbols and archetypes. Whether "Kol Nidre" could also stand up to the poet's own rigorous test—whether the power of its art could literally save the good singer from death—would be proved a year later, when the poem would win Sutzkever a ticket to freedom.

His retrieval of archetypes was but one sign of the new audience

Sutzkever was addressing. Meanwhile the possibility had arisen of turning the ghetto into a fortress. It was in Vilna that the first Jewish fighting organization was established (the F.P.O.) and it was in Vilna that the greatest hymns to the resistance were written: by twenty-one-year-old Hirsh Glik, by Shmerke Kaczerginski, and by Leyb Opeskin.[38] Sutzkever's hymns celebrated the "dreamers" like himself, Glik, Kaczerginski, Kovner, Opeskin, and many others "who had to be soldiers," and the iron of guns that could be turned into the spirit of revolt and revenge.[39]

Yet Vilna was also the place where the resistance met its first and most resounding defeat: the Gestapo's discovery of Itsik Vittenberg, the commander of the F.P.O.; the subsequent manhunt which pitted the Jewish police and entire ghetto population against the resistance movement; Vittenberg's decision to give himself up; and the subsequent crisis of faith.[40] Vittenberg Day (July 16, 1943), as it came to be known in the literature, was a turning point for Sutzkever as well, "the most tragic experience for me at that time," as he scribbled in his notebook.[41] "[I] had believed too much in the holiness of arms." For that reason, he was later to omit the final stanza of his hymn to "The Fortress" and to remove the poem "Take Up Arms"[42] from his retrospective volume of Holocaust poetry.[43]

The great contradictions were thus painfully felt even before the F.P.O. decided to abandon plans for a last stand in the ghetto and retreated to the neighboring forests. Now the poet was truly torn between the fighter's contempt for the passivity of the ghetto ("a DORN zayt ir itster, nit keyn DOR—a thorn is what you are, not a generation," he proclaimed at the memorial gathering for Lisa Magun, the F.P.O.'s chief liaison)[44] and the prophet's total despair that would culminate in "And If My People Shall Remain Only as a Number."

Where was the solace that usually attended the Jewish individual's rejoining of the group? For all the public recognition that Sutzkever now received and despite the profound sense of purpose that informed his calls to arms, his intense involvement in the tragic predicament of the ghetto came at a very high price. Abandoning his lyrical tone was the least of it: once it became clear that this was a human community marked for total destruction, it left the poet completely vulnerable, cut off from *his* sustaining universe of nature with its endless sources of regeneration.

The rage at being alone within what was once a proud and vigorous community became the subject of Sutzkever's most terrifying vision:

> How and with what will you fill
> Your cup on the day of liberation?

In your joy are you ready to feel
The dark scream of your past
Where the skulls of days congeal
In a pit with no ground, without end?

You will search for a key to fit
Your jammed locks.
You will bite the streets like bread
And think: it was better before.
And time will gnaw softly at you
Like a cricket trapped in a fist.

Your memory will be like
An ancient, rubble-encrusted town.
And there your furtive glance will burrow
Like a mole, like a mole.[45]

There is nothing here that consoles. All that can be heard from the past is a "dark scream"; and it is not the *fargangenhayt*, the neutral past, but the *fargangenkayt*, the past-in-chains.[46] Inhabiting the present are trapped, starving insects and rodents scurrying about the rubble—like their human counterparts. But this poem is a poem about the future, about the liberation, no less. On the day of freedom there will be no food to quell the emotional hunger of the survivor as he scurries about the ruins of his mind. The *bafrayung* (liberation) will be yoked together with the dark scream of a past-in-chains ("dayn fargangenkayts fintstere shrayung") and the cup of liberation will be filled without the survivor's feeling any joy.[47]

Sutzkever's premonition that there would be no personal escape from the memory of death and degradation looked ahead to the last stage of dislocation wrought by the Holocaust. After every sphere had been violated—the natural, national, and generational—only fragments would remain. The human individual, however whole he or she might be on the day of liberation, would exist only as a fragment of a larger, permanently shattered entity.

Arrayed on one side were nature, beauty, and art, the stuff of personal lyric poetry, and on the other were history, ghettos, and the Jews, the stuff of epic and declamatory verse. In the middle were the dead. To the extent that these were personal dead, their loss could be overcome through the regenerative cycles of nature and through individual lyric expression. More than a quarter of Sutzkever's ghetto poems were written in the second person singular—to his dead mother and child, to his brother in Palestine, to an unnamed comrade, to the recently deceased Yankev Gershteyn, to a murdered woman, to God, to the future—in an intensely personal effort to overcome both the guilt of betrayal and the physical distance. To the extent that the dead were emblematic of the living, their loss could be mediated through symbolic constructs, ancient archetypes, and heroic action. For Sutzkever, the spiritual greatness of the ghetto was embodied in such people as Kalmanovitsh ("The Prophet") and the teacher Mira Bernshteyn, who continued her classes even as the number of students dwindled from 130 to 7.[48] But to the extent that the dead were dead-ended, that nothing would be left but the numbing pain, their loss could be overcome only by the unprecedented effort of the survivor. It would be Sutzkever's task to elevate the survivor, by personal example, making him the bearer of the burden of memory.

For an understanding both of Sutzkever and of what came to be known, somewhat inaccurately, as the Literature *of* the Holocaust, it is important to realize how far this mission had been accomplished before the war ended. Sutzkever's sense of himself as the bearer of the collective memory began to emerge while he was still in the ghetto. At the end of "Kol Nidre," the father-narrator entrusts his saga to the ghetto poet; similarly, in August 1943, a month before Sutzkever took leave of the ghetto, he ended his hymn to Kalmanovitsh with what was to become a recurrent image: a bird pecking out the eye of an exemplary ghetto Jew and implanting it in the eye-socket of the poet.[49]

Memory would be preserved by transposing the individual struggle of life and death onto a metaphysical plane and by creating a poetry of paradox. In "The Grave Child," Sutzkever had already begun the process of reading history against the cycles of natural regeneration, and in the poem on the death of his child he used a personal myth of nature to link up with the cosmic community beyond the ghetto. Increasingly, the forced contradictions of creation and annihilation, beauty and death, the individual and the collective, would be captured in the poetic shorthand of metamorphosis and paradox. White doves turn into black owls ("Faces in Swamps"); soft moonlight and instant death are reflected in a piece of glass ("In the Cell"); a coffin becomes a floating bier, then a cradle ("I Lie in a Coffin"); the poet's blood resembles a magnificent sunset in the white of a limepit ("A Day among the Stormtroopers"); tears mix with fire and with a murderous stillness ("Under Your White Stars"). Perhaps most stunning of all is the image of burnt pearls, which captures the essence of writing poetry in the midst of a holocaust:

Burnt Pearls

Though it's true my words shake violently,
Like broken hands stretched out for help;
Though it's true they sharpen themselves silently,

Stalking teeth-like, lusting after flesh;
That's not why you fan my coals of Wrath,
You written word—my world's replacer;
It's rather that your sounds look out
Like burned pearls glinting
From a smouldering funeral pyre;
And no one—even I—scraped dead by days
Can still recognize the woman washed in flame
For whom, of all her joys
Burnt pearls in ashes is the sum of what remains.[50]

The red coals of his wrath are here combined with the purest symbol of beauty that nature provides—precious white pearls, the indestructible kernel of memory. Each word the poet brings forth is charred by the fire of destruction. Each surviving object, no matter how pure, intimates the overwhelming loss of love and life.

The use of paradox preserved the tension necessary to keep the memory fresh, for too rounded an image carried with it the danger of oversimplification, of too comfortable a myth. Part of the burden of memory was the ongoing effort to lay the demon to rest, to retrieve the pearls from the fire; but as memory of the horror receded, it was sometimes necessary to rekindle the fire, to jar one's own sensibilities, even at the price of renewed pain.

Sutzkever left the ghetto on September 12, 1943, with the second group of partisans to head for the forests. As a member of the Jewish partisan brigade Nekome (Revenge), Sutzkever necessarily shifted his poetic emphasis from the heroes of the spirit to the heroes of the resistance: Vittenberg, Yankev Kaplan, Asya Bik, and Avrom Chwojnik of the F.P.O., and beautiful Golda, the Jewish partisan.[51] Underlying this ideological change was a deeper shift in emphasis, for Mira the Teacher and Kalmanovitsh the Prophet were very much alive when Sutzkever composed the original hymns in their honor, whereas the fighters whom he now glorified in heroic ballads had all been killed. The third-person ballad style, moreover, marked a step backward from the intimacy he had cultivated with the missing and the dead while still in the ghetto. By the time Sutzkever had reached the forests and had learned that the ghetto had been "liquidated" and all its survivors deported to work camps in Estonia, or sent to Maidanek, or simply murdered in Ponar, the enormity of the loss had made such individual retrievals impossible. The time had come to take leave of the city as a whole, to identify with *all* the dead at once: "But I, who was nurtured in the shadow of your splendor, / The totality of you I shall carry onward—like a bloody scroll."[52]

Though Sutzkever now dedicated himself to the task of creating memorials, he could not be certain that even his rhetorical skills would suffice to save his people from extinction:

> And if my people shall remain only as a number—
> I adjure it: that from my memory it disappear.
> And may all the graves be buried deeper
> And may no dust remain of the years.[53]

Though the ghetto was behind him, the war was still raging, and there was no knowing yet how it would end. Despite the continuing danger, or perhaps because of it, the numerous deaths were slowly losing their immediacy and the problem arose not of domesticating the horror but of keeping its memory alive. Everything that Sutzkever had learned as a poet had taught him to beware of easy recourse to lamentation:

> Don't sing a mournful song,
> you'll embarrass
> the sorrow.
> Words betray.
> Names turn themselves
> over.[54]

Perhaps the answer, then, lay in the snow, where it had lain before. Here he was, at last, back in his beloved forest. The peacefulness and clarity of the surrounding snow could do wonders: it could illuminate his private memory and release the wellsprings of new life ("Don't Sing a Mournful Song"). So the overarching question was this: whether the task of memorial was best served by the high rhetorical voice of a poet addressing the largest possible community, or whether the retrieval of private memories through the mediation of nature was the most that could be hoped for.

IN each of the five way-stations Sutzkever passed through from the day he left the ghetto until his illegal arrival in Palestine, he acted on the promise to carry—and indeed, to compose—the "bloody scroll." After the Nekome Brigade had been forcibly disbanded by Soviet partisan leader Fyodor Markov, Sutzkever (with his fellow poet and partisan Kaczerginski) became the official chronicler of Markov's brigade.[55] Meanwhile, a Jewish partisan had brought a copy of "Kol Nidre" to Moscow, where it was read at a writer's forum. When word got out that the author was alive, members of the Jewish Anti-Fascist Committee, aided by a well-known Lithuanian revolutionary, arranged for Sutzkever and his wife to be flown to Moscow.

This was an extraordinary period in the history of Soviet Jewry, a time of government-sanctioned solidarity with Jews the world over. The German invasion in the summer of 1941 had ended the enforced silence of Soviet-Jewish writers which had prevailed for two years under the Hitler-Stalin pact. Suddenly, thanks to the Common Front, the Warsaw ghetto uprising and themes from Jewish history made their way into the writings of David Bergelson, Der Nister, Shmuel Halkin, David Hofstein, Leyb Kvitko, and Peretz Markish.[56] And whatever was considered too nationalistic for internal consumption was allowed by the government, for propaganda reasons, to be published in New York and in Tel Aviv.

Even under Stalinism, then, catastrophe could act with centripetal force, allaying some of the internal fears and bringing down some of the external barriers. Perhaps no work better dramatizes the dialectic of return during this brief period of group solidarity than a tiny book of poems by the ailing Soviet-Hebrew writer Elisha Rodin (born 1888). His only son, Grisha, who had volunteered for the front at the age of seventeen, was killed near Kalinin in March 1942. Rodin then wrote a series of elegies, *To the Son*, which he submitted to the military censor with the following petition: "I request that you show these poems to a person sufficiently familiar with this language [Hebrew] who is also honest and without personal ties with the Jewish national cause in Palestine. I am sure that an exact and honest translation of my poems would permit you to transfer them without delay to Palestine, because my poems serve our common interest: the destruction of Hitler."[57] Though the poems have little artistic merit, they mark a crucial juncture in the traditions of the Jewish response to catastrophe. Coming as they do at the very end of Hebrew culture in the Soviet Union, they mark the beginning of a new genre in the emerging culture of modern Israel: memorial books for fallen soldiers. By virtue of the fact that *To the Son* was published in Tel Aviv in 1943 in a popular edition by Am Oved, Grisha Rodin's name would be hallowed alongside the names of thousands of other young Jewish men and women whose bereaved parents, also of eastern European origin, were to publish books, brochures, and albums in their memory. In Moscow, however, the one copy of the book that arrived for Elisha Rodin was withheld from him until Sutzkever intervened on his behalf.[58]

In the midst of this tenuous effort to unite the fates of all Jews everywhere, Sutzkever's arrival seemed no less miraculous for the manner in which it was made public. On April 29, 1944, Ilya Ehrenburg published an article in *Pravda* entitled "The Victory of a Man."[59] The impact of this article can hardly be overestimated, both on account of Ehrenburg's enormous popularity and prestige and because it spoke, virtually for the first time in Soviet Russia, about the singular fate of the Jewish people. Hundreds of letters began pouring in from Jewish partisans, soldiers, *landslayt*, refugees, children, and ordinary citizens all over the Soviet Union who saw in Sutzkever the living symbol of Jewish conscience and continuity. Ehrenburg also described the partisan-poet's role in rescuing cultural treasures. Sutzkever had brought from the ghetto letters by Gorky, Tolstoy, and Romain Rolland, the diary of Peter the Great's servant, and (according to the Yiddish version of the article published in New York) some drawings by Chagall.

Sutzkever became the custodian and lifeline of Vilna Jewish culture. After the war, his efforts at rescuing cultural treasures were as complicated and conspiratorial as they had been during the Holocaust. This was true not only in Moscow, in the shadow of the Kremlin, but also in Vilna. Sutzkever arrived in Vilna soon after the liberation. "For two weeks now I've been wandering through the ruins," he wrote to Ehrenburg. "I've dug out cultural treasures and visited Ponar. I found no one there. Only—ashes. They had dug up [the corpses of] the Vilna Jews and burned them. The human ash is sticky and grey. I poured some of it into a pouch (it could be my child or my mother) and I keep it near me."[60] Everything of value lay buried underground: a legacy of paper and ashes. The house that he and Kaczerginski shared became the center of an ad hoc Jewish museum. They found themselves in a race against time—to photograph the ruins of the Vilna Gaon's synagogue before the Red Army engineers blew it up; to copy the Yiddish, Polish, and Russian inscriptions on the cell walls of the Gestapo prison before the Soviets destroyed the evidence; to publish the Nazi documents and the letters of the victims before they disappeared into official state vaults; to record the songs before they were forgotten; and finally, when the true postwar situation had been made clear, to smuggle to New York the rescued remains of the YIVO and ghetto archives—the diaries of Herzl, Kalmanovitsh, and Kruk. Despite all efforts, twenty tons of salvaged Yiddish books were sent to the pulp factory by Soviet officials.[61]

The farther Sutzkever traveled, carrying the "bloody scroll" from the unredeemed ruins of Vilna to Nuremberg, where he testified on behalf of Vilna Jewry, and then to Lodz and Warsaw and Paris, the less he discovered of the life that was, and the more he felt bound to recreate it: "Have you ever seen lying over fields of snow / Frozen Jews, row upon row?"[62] This frieze, one of his earliest recollections of the horror, came to him in the heat of a Moscow summer. It was a landscape of forced contradictions, a poetics replete with oxymorons: murdered Jews who, in their petrified state in the snow, were alive; cadavers carved out of blue marble. Here was absolute horror recalled as monumental beauty. But there was more to this than a personal memory transfixed and rhymed: it was Ezekiel's vision of the dry bones rewritten for the icy climate of the north. Though it expressed the vast distance between the poet and the dead, it held out the hope of a mass resurrection in the snow.[63]

No one knew better than Sutzkever how little remained. Unlike Ansky, who on his rescue mission to Galicia thirty years before could still invoke the symbols of a grand covenantal design—the broken tablets of the Law and the flying letters of the sacred scroll—Sutzkever found little more than garbled messages scribbled on death cell walls. Both the unfathomable loss and the irreducible memory of the dead were somehow contained in the fragmentariness. Thus, a Polish poem entitled "The Trace on the Barrack Wall," written by Ilona Karmel in a labor camp near Leipzig in 1944, celebrates the vibrant, sensual life that refused to be extinguished.[64] And a much later Hebrew poem by Dan Pagis, "Written in Pencil in the Sealed Railway-Car," transposes the end of human history back to its beginnings:

here in this carload
i am eve
with abel my son
if you see my other son
cain son of man
tell him that i[65]

Sutzkever, who himself had just come from the sealed-off world where all that might remain of his existence was a poem or two, or nothing at all, was intent upon reassembling the scraps and debris. The Holocaust demanded of him a monumental response, a vast poetic gathering. And so, from a single eight-line poem written to his brother in April 1943, Sutzkever composed a series of twenty-seven "Epitaphs" which he completed in 1946.[66] Here, for the first time, the voice of the tormented poet who could neither escape nor express the will of the dead was heard along with the testaments of the resistance fighter Vittenberg, of a Jewish dancer from Paris, of a fiddler named Ariel Blank, of a gypsy awaiting execution for stabbing a German, of a father to his son in Tel Aviv, and, most symbolically, with an inscription found in a Bible in Maidanek:

Good brother in freedom
This is all that I own.
Take this Bible, carry it further
Into eternity—if you can.[67]

(Six hundred years before, as Sutzkever either knew or intuited, a Bible had been found similarly inscribed in Aix-en-Provence.)[68] Collecting these disparate messages in such a way as to yield a statement of faith was clearly an act of will on the part of a poet who, barely three years before, had envisaged the day of liberation as a day of unmitigated pain. The "Epitaphs" were each designed to be a self-contained world in miniature, analogous to an exercise in holography. As in holography, where any portion of the image has the capacity to reproduce the entire image, given the same apparatus that produced the original image, so the survivor, though only a fragment of a greater whole, had become the bearer of the collective memory. Each rescued fragment would reproduce the whole original.

This impulse to impose order on chaos reflects Sutzkever's continuing involvement in postwar reconstruction and his sense of obligation to preserve and hallow the past. Only rarely in this period did he allow the opposite impulse to emerge—the effort to reinstate the chaos, to keep the tension alive. For this reason, before examining the making of the myth which was the major thrust of his poetry in the immediate postwar decade, it is worth looking at "Poem about a Herring." Here Sutzkever remembers a child who, in the moment of his execution, grabs a herring from his mother's bundle:

> And so remained, marbled in horror,
> an image that will not yield:
> a summer day's first hours,
> a child, a bloody herring in its teeth.
> I lick for the herring's brine,
> still can't find
> its taste on my sealed lips.[69]

In order to fashion the archetypes of holocaust and national rebirth, Sutzkever had to operate on opposite ground, seeking continuities and correspondences that would bridge the living and the dead. He accomplished this task in two ways: by retrieving and inventing myths and by censoring the past. A superb example of the myth-making process is his poem "The Lead Plates at the Rom Press," which he retroactively dated September 12, 1943, the day he left the ghetto for the forest. The first known draft of the poem is dated February 18, 1944. More significant is the event that it describes: a group of Jewish fighters breaks in at night to the Rom printing works, the most venerable Jewish press in eastern Europe, and melts down the lead plates for bullets. From all available evidence, including Sutzkever's own information on how the Nazis disposed of the plates and from conversations with former members of the F.P.O. (notably Abba Kovner and Rachel Pupko-Krinsky), the event never took place, which makes Sutzkever's achievement more brilliant, because the image of sacred letters melted down into lead bullets is the perfect symbol of the Jewish resistance, a revolution in Jewish consciousness that drew its strength from the most ancient sources. To further buttress the correspondence of present and past, Sutzkever, when revising the poem for publication in 1945, embellished the scene with direct allusions to the Maccabees and to the destruction of the Temple.

Arrayed at night like fingers stretching through bars
To clutch the lit air of freedom
We made for the press plates, to seize
The lead plates at the Rom printing works.
We were dreamers, we had to be soldiers,
And melt down, for our bullets, the spirit of the lead.

At some timeless native lair
We once again broke open the seal.
Shrouded in shadow, by the glow of a lamp,
Like Temple ancients measuring out oil
For their festival candelabra of gold,
So, pouring out line after lettered line, did we.

Letter by melting letter the lead,
Liquefied bullets, gleamed with thoughts:
A verse from Babylon, a verse from Poland
Seething, flowing into the one mold.
Now must Jewish grit, long concealed in words,
Detonate the world in a shot!

Who in Vilna Ghetto has beheld the hands
Of Jewish heroes clasping weapons
Has beheld Jerusalem in its throes,
The crumbling of those granite walls;
Grasping the words, now smelted into lead,
Conning their sounds by heart.[70]

The splendid rhetoric of this poem can be most fully appreciated in the insistent and semantically loaded rhymes (*kley-zayin* / *Yerusholaim* / *blayen*—weapons / Jersusalem / leaden) of the Yiddish original, as recited in the declamatory style of Sutzkever himself.[71]

The truth of the poem obviously transcends its factuality. No one will fault the poet for writing a midrash on Jewish heroism which remains true to the spirit of the fighters. But the burden of memory weighed heavier in the wake of the Holocaust than it ever had in the past, because never had Jews been so degraded and so thoroughly annihilated and never had the odds been greater against their chances of moral and physical renewal. To rebuild a sense of collective self after the Holocaust, it was not enough to fashion a myth of destruction and rebellion; the Holocaust would yield meaning only if certain of its specifics were thoroughly censored.

Upon entering the besieged city of Vilna in 1944, the first action of the partisans led by Abba Kovner was to destroy the Gestapo files on Jewish collaborators.[72] Working in the same spirit, Sutzkever went back over the poems he had written in the ghettos and even prior to the war and deleted that which might offend the memory of the dead. This spontaneous self-censorship illuminates the hidden reaches of the Jewish collective conscience in eastern Europe and distinguishes, perhaps more than anything else, eastern from western Europe and the Holocaust from the catastrophes that came before.

What little we know about the self-censorship of Jewish writer-survivors from eastern Europe has only recently come to light, thanks in large measure to the work of Yechiel Szeintuch.[73] He has shown, for instance, how Isaiah Spiegel systematically rewrote his ghetto stories to stress the redemptive details, changing the name of the collection from *Behind the Barbed Wire* to *Light from the Abyss* and tempering each tale of horror with idealized portraits of the victims.[74]

In Sutzkever's case the evidence is somewhat more complex. We have seen that he omitted or edited his most outspoken hymns to the resistance, but the reasons could be aesthetic as well as ideological: "Take Up Arms" is simply not a good poem. There is scarcely a single ghetto poem which Sutzkever did not revise before publication. His essential motive was ideological, however, when he consigned to oblivion the anger, guilt, and despair expressed in such poems as "The Circus" and "Three Roses." The survivor-poet wished to allow only his lyrical and dramatic voices to speak for the ghetto experience.

The more the gray was eliminated, the more the Holocaust as archetype could take on its specific contours. The Jewish dead were absolutely good, the Nazis and their collaborators were absolutely evil. "And thus you shall speak to the orphan," he had written in February 1943, "when he raises his fists in exhaustion / and asks: Who am I?"[75] Originally the answer given was: "Your father bowed his head to the ground"—that is to say, you belong to a generation that allowed itself to be slaughtered. Two years later the answer was changed to "Your father lifted his head in faith"—that is to say, the victims died as martyrs. The same poet who so meticulously preserved and published the writings of others excluded from his own canon, the two-volume *Poetic Works* (Tel Aviv, 1963), all the prewar paeans to the Lithuanian peasantry[76] and the single ghetto poem that depicted Jesus in a positive, Jewish light.[77] The only exception allowed was the righteous Gentiles—those Gentiles who had who risked their lives to save the lives of others: Sutzkever's "rescuers" Yanova Bartoszewicz, and Maria Fedecka.[78] Naming only select names was an essential way of shaping the archetype.

The thrust of this self-censorship on the part of writer-survivors was the very opposite of the intellectuals' revolt against the traditions of Jewish response to catastrophe after World War I and the Bolshevik Revolution. Then, poets had turned the kaddish against itself and the pogrom into a self-sufficient archetype, novelists had chronicled the rape of the shtetl, and writers of short fiction had unmasked the weakness of the lone individual. It seemed as if all the distinctions of sacred and profane, Jew and Gentile, friend and foe had been swept aside in the great European maelstrom. But after the Holocaust, to the extent that Jews regrouped as a collective—in Lodz, Paris, displaced persons camps, Palestine—group discipline was predicated upon resurrecting these distinctions. For lined up against the few thousand survivors was the full force of the Soviet secret police; native Poles, Lithuanians, and so on; and an army of former Nazis and collaborators—all of whom had good reason to suppress the crimes perpetrated against the Jews.

Any lingering hopes about the brotherhood of Jews and Gentiles in eastern Europe were dealt a decisive blow by yet another pogrom. On July 4, 1946, the Poles demonstrated through a pogrom in Kielce that even the survivors were a few thousand Jews too many. "Only" forty-two Jews were murdered in Kielce, but they were all survivors of the Holocaust whom the Polish police had disarmed the day before.[79] Kielce was the signal for Sutzkever and thousands like him to leave Poland once and for all. As in Kishinev in 1903, the Arab riots in 1929, and the Przytyk pogrom in 1936, it was a discrete act of atrocity rather than a great catastrophe that became a catalyst for action.

Before leaving, Sutzkever delivered his parting words in the poem "To Poland," a sweeping personal and collective indictment of Polish culture, a repudiation of the Polish-Jewish symbiosis that had once seduced so many, including the poet himself.[80] Yet everything that Sutzkever stood for militated against too complete a rejection. Jewish custom required that travelers, before leaving home, should visit the graves of their nearest of kin. And so Sutzkever went to the Warsaw Jewish cemetery to stand at the Peretz monument, and concluded his poem with the ringing words of Peretz's visionary drama *The Golden Chain:* "And so we stride—our souls ablaze!"

WITH help from Golda Meir, in her capacity as head of the Political Department of the Jewish Agency, the Sutzkevers (husband, wife, and two-year-old daughter, Rayne) arrived in Palestine with forged British papers in September 1947. By now Sutzkever's life, all thirty-four years of it, was so bound up with the ebb and flow of Jewish history (to stay with his own favorite metaphors of nature) that his every subsequent endeavor took on national significance. At the very moment that statehood was being proclaimed and defended, Sutzkever came out with his two most impressive achievements: an epic poem, 241 stanzas in amphibrach tetrameter, called *Geheymshtot* (Secret City), written 1945–1947, and the plans for a new Yiddish literary journal, *Di goldene keyt* (The Golden Chain). So in fact and in effect he was once again answerable to the dead—*obliged* by the Holocaust to act as its poet.

The classical forms that Sutzkever adopted in writing *Geheymshtot* were the clearest testimony of the poet's desire to impose meaning on chaos.[81] Just as the meters and rhymes insisted on reason, so too did the content. The poem tells the story of ten survivors in the sewers of Vilna during the final year of the war. When one of the ten is killed, someone else joins; when one child dies, another is born—thus completing the requisite quorum, "*a folk zalbe tsent,* a people-contained-in-ten." In fact, reality had provided the poet with his subject. Walking through the postwar ruins of Vilna, Sutzkever had come upon a man who had emerged from the sewers. "His beard was green as if a wave had gotten stuck to him," Sutzkever later recalled in an interview.[82] This twenty-five-year-old Jew, who looked like an old man, had survived in the sewers with eighty other Jews from the day of the ghetto's liquidation, September 23, 1943, until the city's liberation on July 14, 1944.

What might have been written as a *De profundis,* the last great scream of the living dead, became in Sutzkever's hands the exemplary epic of Holocaust literature, the testimony "*fun payn vos muz farvandlen zikh in shayn,* to suffering that must be transformed into beauty," as announced in the poet's invocation to the muse. By drawing on biblical myths, on the story of Creation and the Flood, on the Akedah and the Golden Calf, Sutzkever was able to fashion the Holocaust into an archetype of miraculous survival.

The inhabitants of the underground city were the distillations of the final Diaspora and as such could become, by dint of another miracle, the first settlers of the Promised Land. The task of memorialization would not be complete until Vilna was successfully relocated in Jerusalem; until each survivor, who was a world in miniature, bequeathed his odyssey to the future; until the landscape of snow became a landscape of total renewal. These were the tasks that Sutzkever took upon himself in the first fifteen years of his life in the state of Israel. The very titles of his books published in this period reveal the continuities that he sought to uphold: *In the Chariot of Fire* (1952), *In the Sinai Desert* (1957), *Oasis* (1960), and *Spiritual Soil* (1961).

Every poet, given the chance, brings together the strands of his earlier work. But for Sutzkever, obliged by history to carry more than his individual burden, the matter of recapitulation was made doubly pressing. Though there was indeed a new home in store for the final diaspora, and though from the generation that had been destroyed another would be born, there could be no recompense for the loss of a culture and a language.

All along Sutzkever had learned to obey his inner voice. The Ariel of modern Yiddish poetry (as Itsik Manger was later to dub him) had perfected his poetic craft in opposition to the *Sturm und Drang* of Yiddish cosmopolitanism, just as in the ghetto he had paid homage to the Muse though her face was in total eclipse. As a singer of hymns and as a witness for the prosecution, he briefly commanded a loyal following within the embattled community of ghetto Jews, Soviet Marranos, and Holocaust survivors. As he set out in seach of a new homeland, he composed his epic of underground survival and miraculous transplantation. But nothing could hide the fact that his culture had been murdered, abandoned, forgotten. Much as he tried to reclaim the desert, the oasis, and the spiritual soil, the contradictions of the history he had witnessed could not be reconciled on this earth alone.

Hence his recourse to myth and metaphysics. For Sutzkever, despite everything he has seen and lost, the source of the mystery has never been the destruction itself. Instead, he keeps exploring the same places: the secret of the human soul, the howling of a wolf in the forest, the beauty of a "fiddlerose." If the Holocaust wrought any change in his work, it is that his primary allegiance shifted from the living to the dead. "But there [in the ghetto]," he wrote in 1962, "I had wanted my poems to revive the living, and now it is the dead I want to revive."[83]

In his myth for the post-Holocaust world, Sutzkever created a vision of Paradise that had never existed before— a "green aquarium," where "Greens flow into greens. Body into body . . . I look in: people swim here like fish. Countless phosphorous faces. Young. Old. Youth and age combined. All those I have seen in the course of a lifetime, and death has embalmed them with green existence; they all swim in the green aquarium in a kind of silky, aery music. Here live the dead!"[84]

From the ghetto winter of 1943, when a splinter of dusk sank into the quiet depths as a modest harbinger of spring, and from the Moscow summer of 1944, when the vision of an icy frieze adumbrated the cold resurrection to come, Sutzkever arrived at this pervasive image of green. The green was the counterpoint to the snow. The aquarium was a mythic place of eternal life, of flowing spirits in arrested time.

> My eyes splash with silver oars, chasing, swimming among the faces. They are in pursuit, searching for a single face.

There at last! There it is! The dream of my dream—

"Here I am, my dearest, here I am. The wrinkles are only a nest for my longing."

My lips, swollen with blood, reach toward hers. But alas they stay suspended on the pane of the aquarium.

Her lips also swim toward mine. I feel the breath of flaming punch. The pane is a cold slaughter-knife between us.

"I want to read you a poem about yourself . . . you must hear it!"

"I know the poem by heart, my dearest, I gave you the words myself."

"Then let me feel your body once more!"

"We can't come any closer, the pane . . ."

"No, this barrier will soon vanish, I'll smash the green pane with my head—"

At the twelfth blow the aquarium burst.
Where are the lips, the voice?
And the dead, the dead—have they died?

There is no one here. In front of me—grass. Overhead—a bough of oranges, or children playing with golden bubbles.

In the dead alone, Sutzkever had a proper audience for his poems. They were perhaps the only ones worthy of his poetic efforts, yet to enter the aquarium meant to shatter the pane, dissolving the dead. The redemption of the dead and of their memory was complete; history and nature had become one; the white had turned to green; the severed past had become eternal present. But the green aquarium existed only in the mind of the poet, and even he could never resurrect the murdered Jews of Vilna in the flesh.

IN *Green Aquarium*, an extraordinary collection of fifteen prose poems, the poet is caught in a mythic struggle between the Angel of Death and the Angel of Poetry, and Sutzkever uses this rare occasion to restate the credo that had sustained him through his years in the ghetto. "The choice lies in your own hands," warns the Angel of Poetry, visiting the narrator in his ghetto lodgings at the beginning of the second poem. "If your song inspires me, I will protect you with a flaming sword. If not—don't complain . . . my conscience will be clear." Though the narrator then tells a bizarre tale of a woman's self-sacrifice for her dead husband, the prefatory warning makes it clear that the subject matter of the Holocaust is not enough to ensure poetic immortality. Poetry obeys a timeless set of rules that transcends even the most tragic vicissitudes of history. Art has a law of life and death, and salvation is guaranteed only to the great.[85]

In anyone else this Olympian stance would be regarded as poetic and personal conceit, but Sutzkever's entire career argues for the possibility of art and form and beauty in the midst of destruction. Though *we* may not believe that the Angel of Poetry rescued him from death, Sutzkever did, and that is why he never ceased to write for a moment, and never stopped revising and perfecting what he wrote. And if, after the war, it was Sutzkever who made the necessary sutures between creation and annihilation, that too is not a matter of chance. Only someone who understands the full thrust of the classical traditions, who self-consciously shapes a new poetics out of the usable past, can make such sutures after the Holocaust.

As a neoclassicist, Sutzkever brings to the new Holocaust archetype the structure of past archetypes. But his return to themes of nature, to classical meters and pervasive rhymes, to myth and archetype, is accompanied by the self-awareness and crucial ambivalence that the word "neoclassical" implies. Sutzkever has never really made his peace with his readers' demand for high rhetoric and biblical allusions, just as his experience of the war erupts beneath the orderly surface to subvert his best efforts at poetic harmony. Inside the aquarium float the demanding and often grotesque faces of the dead. And that is as it should be, for as we are now a mere two generations from the midwifery of the Holocaust archetype, it is reasonable and predictable that the sutures should be at once so obvious and so grotesque. How fortunate, also, that they are obvious, so that my chronicle of the birth of an archetype can be so specific.

Sutzkever's poetry of and about the Holocaust offers Jews a choice: follow the route of the apocalyptists, who draw their authority from the mystique of destruction and from the unknowable terror that feeds inherent Jewish fears of personal and collective disaster; or follow the neoclassical norm, unbending and absolute, with its impossible demands of order and sublimation. Without Sutzkever's example, the choice would be a foregone conclusion. Though few are likely to follow his lead, especially now, with the death of his culture, he had this to say to all the others: the greater the loss, the greater one's need to transcend it with selective memory, emphatic rhyme, and natural beauty.

CHAPTER TEN

Jews on the Cross

Mir kumen tsu kholem di yidn vos hengen af tslomin.

I dream of the Jews hanging on crosses.
Uri Zvi Greenberg, 1923

THE neoclassicist, like God, can make wholeness where only fragments remain. Mendele, for all his erratic behavior, could participate in negotiations among the warring sides in Jewish eastern Europe in a remarkably fluent Yiddish, then reemerge speaking a new synthetic Hebrew. At least a generation after the *ḥurban beit hamidrash,* the destruction of traditional faith centered in the house of study, Bialik was still able to enter into dialogue with God, addressing him in the language of Torah and Talmud. Sholem Aleichem orchestrated the perfect linguistic polyphony at a time when most Jews were reduced to speaking plain Yiddish, plain Russian, or plain English. In the midst of the First World War, which destroyed the fabric of Jewish folk life once and for all, Ansky put the finishing touches on *The Dybbuk,* the most perfect Jewish folk play ever written. When God, nature, and man all conspired toward the murder of Jews in the Second World War, Sutzkever dedicated his formidable talents to artistic permanence and to physical regeneration. And after the war, when a motley group of dreamers decided to build themselves a state, Uri Zvi Greenberg raised the great and timeless lament for the world that had just been destroyed.

The neoclassicist is most in demand in time of crisis—when the tablets are most clearly shattered, the letters most visibly struck out, and the people most widely dispersed. Later, he may be neglected or repudiated, but never is he abandoned for long. The force of recurrent catastrophe is too great. What's more, catastrophe itself acts as a crucible in which all prior responses are refined and recombined. The Jewish dialectical response, invoked so often throughout this book, is at its core a profoundly neoclassical impulse: the greater the catastrophe, the more its victims reshape the ancient archetypes in its wake.

Because most of us do not share the neoclassical point of view, we do not see the continuities. We take as the signposts of modern Jewish culture Kafka's deathbed instructions to Max Brod to burn all his manuscripts, or Walter Benjamin's suicide on the border between Vichy France and Spain, and we arrive at a sense of total break and alienation, of standing "after the tradition," at the end of Jewish history. But we arrive at a different destination if instead we look to other signs, such as the archives of destruction set up by Tcherikower and Ringelblum in the very hearts of darkness, and the Schocken Library of Jewish Classics launched in Berlin in the 1930s to provide assimilated Jews with a sense of their glorious past—an effort that had its direct counterpart in Simon Bernfeld's ingathering of the tears (*The Book of Tears,* 1923–1926), Israel Halpern's ingathering of the valor (*The Book of Valor,* 1941–1950), and the new editions in Hebrew, Yiddish, and German of Hannover's *The Deep Mire.* We see, too, the myriad acts of penitent return, from Hershele's pathetic kaddish on the graves of Kabtsiel to the rescue of the key to the old house of study in Shibush; from Kalmanovitsh's conversion to orthodox practice to Katzenelson's reversion to the substance of faith; from Sholem Aleichem's ironic tales of communal solidarity to Sutzkever's heroic epics of survival. In each case the writer's earlier rebellion was modified and qualified in the face of national disaster. The pieces that had so readily been discarded suddenly became the sole means of reconstruction.

Yosef Hayim Yerushalmi, concluding his otherwise admirable study on Jewish history and Jewish memory, would have us believe that group memory suffered a fatal blow with the beginning of emancipation in the 1780s.[1] But the shaping and preserving of group memory is precisely what Jewish writers, artists, and intellectuals have been doing since the emancipation. Those who reviled the claims of history—Halpern, Hazaz, Markish, Shapiro, Warshawski, and Weissenberg—did as much to revive the process of group memory as those writers who affirmed their place on the continuum. That the impact of neoclassicists and apocalyptists alike can now be felt only through a colossal act of retrieval is a measure not of their failure but of the break that finally did occur—the Holocaust—a break made greater by the conscious and unconscious desire of postwar Jews to trace their roots anywhere but to the devastated landscape of eastern Europe.

At this point logic seems to falter, for to emphasize the qualitative difference of the Holocaust catastrophe works against *any* claims to a continuity in the literary use of themes and archetypes of destruction. Conversely, to argue that the writers and artists managed to deal with the Holocaust by returning to the old archetypes, either through parody or affirmation, undermines the claim that the Holocaust is unique. If the Holocaust *is* a break, then the subsequent work about it should either attempt to deny it by fanciful or reactionary motifs, or attempt to capture it by entirely new modes, or face the break in great confusion. Yet the examples cited here show the Jewish writers and artists of eastern Europe doing much the same as always. Though their styles may be slightly new, the process is the same. Why doesn't the process change if the Holocaust is such a break? The answer I suggest is that the historical break—catastrophe as it was—was anticipated by the artistic process, especially in the decade following World War I, so that despite the disappearance of a culture, its means of handling catastrophe lingers on.

The Jews of eastern Europe, wherever they regrouped, sought to understand the new Destruction, which was different in kind from the previous ones, through a response that was different in degree. After the Holocaust, group memory became more precious than ever before, so that now every *landsmanshaft,* no matter how small, marshaled its resources to put out a memorial volume (*yizker-bukh*) dedicated to the lost communities. Whereas two or three such volumes appeared in the wake of the Ukrainian civil war, over 500 have been published since 1943 and more are still to come.[2] Some 8,000 writers and as many as 1,000 editors have been involved in this grassroots phenomenon over the years, most of them ordinary men and women with no literary pretensions.[3] Meanwhile the professional writers have struck out in two parallel directions at once, fashioning the Holocaust into its own archetype and subjecting all prior archetypes to radical reinterpretation: the Akedah, the Exodus, the Covenant at Sinai, the Destruction of the Temple, the pogrom, and the Crucifixion. Because Jews experienced the Holocaust as the supreme sacrilege of all time, its demonic scope could best be mapped in archetypal fashion. Regardless of their adopted language or literary mode, postwar writers of eastern European origin returned to one or another of the ancient archetypes. French-Jewish novelist Piotr Rawicz, for example, rediscovered the covenantal meaning of the tool, the irreducible fact of his Jewishness as revealed in the circumcised penis;[4] Yiddish novelist Leyb Rochman called all the Jewish books collected by the Nazis in Offenbach-am-Main to a surrealistic trial, a grand replay of proem 24 in the Midrash on Lamentations;[5] and Canadian-Jewish poet A. M. Klein self-consciously patterned his response to the Holocaust on neoclassical models, from psalms to the satires of Alexander Pope.[6] In memorial books, surrealistic novels, and verse satires, the eastern European writers on the Holocaust disassembled the catastrophe into its constituent parts: memory, parody, archetype.

Thus, the traditional response of progressive archetyping could make room even for the Great Destruction. But while this search for continuities was in progress, something unexpected happened—the Western world accepted the catastrophe into its moral landscape and honored it with a name, calling it "the Holocaust." To complicate matters, that name was not a Jewish name at all. The French, who had already used the word to denote the vast destruction of human life in World War I, resurrected it after the Second World War: David Rousset and other (non-Jewish) French writers began to speak of *l'holocauste* as soon as the war was over.[7] Two total wars in rapid succession confirmed this haunting word as the signifier of radical evil in the modern world.

For the British and Americans, who experienced the Nazi genocide at a distance, the word "Holocaust," capitalized and bracketed in time, did not reverberate with echoes of past destructions. Such terms as Deluge, Armageddon, Great War, and Great Patriotic War carried specific historical and theological imperatives, but Holocaust, to the English ear, was an apocalyptic term for a vicarious destruction. Like so many other weighty words in the English language, "Holocaust" had its roots in Latin, and though it did establish a vague connection back to the Bible for both Jews and Gentiles ("holocaust" as burnt offering), it had none of the ready connotations of the alternative names just mentioned. So much the better, for it was precisely the nonreferential quality of "Holocaust" that made it so appealing.

Shoah fulfills exactly the same function in present-day Israel. This biblical word meaning ruin, calamity, desolation, was reintroduced into modern Hebrew by poets and politicians as early as 1940 to impress upon their audiences the enormity of the destruction in Europe; but after the war, *shoah* came to mean a unique transformational event that establishes a new relationship between God and history.[8] Once Israelis, like English-speaking Jews, were caught up in a new historical era, they had no use for a term like *ḥurban/khurbm,* which harks back to a string of past catastrophes. Living after the apocalypse was still preferable to being linked to an unbroken chain of oppression.

Nor are Jewish public relations well served by any other term. To speak of the Holocaust as the Third Destruction, *der driter khurbm,* as is done in Yiddish, would be to insulate the Jews all over again. And so the best alternative is a term that nobody recognizes, even if it means obscuring the history and hatred that gave rise to the Holocaust in the first place. In this fluid environment, Gentiles are as free to impose their own understanding on the course of Jewish events as Jews are free to borrow unabashedly from the fund of universal symbols. And this fluidity, in turn, gives rise to no small measure of confusion. As catastrophe, once the most private of Jewish concerns, becomes part of the public domain, external perceptions replace inner realities, and borrowed words and archetypes are enlisted to explain the meaning of destruction not only to Gentiles but even to Jews.

It is to one such development that we now turn: the emergence of Jesus as an emblem of Jewish catastrophe. What the uses of Jesus show is the paradoxical price of success in the age of emancipation, how the same symbol has come to have concurrent opposite meanings, and how Jewish writers and artists, groping for a new audience, have themselves become the agents of uncertainty. Before tracing the roots of this development, let us look briefly at its culmination: the emergence of the Holocaust survivor as Christ figure.

When thirty-year-old Elie Wiesel sought the endorsement of François Mauriac, a meeting of like minds clearly took place, for here was a Catholic writer concerned, as was Wiesel, with the misery of man living in the absence of God. To Mauriac, the famous tableau of the angelic boy hung between two other camp inmates—Christ between the two thieves at Calvary—was the center of Wiesel's story. From this point of departure, Mauriac reappropriated the Holocaust for a renewed understanding of Christianity:

> And I who believe that God is love, what answer could I give my young questioner, whose dark eyes still held the reflection of that angelic sadness which had appeared one day upon the face of the hanged child? What did I say to him? Did I speak of that other Israeli, his brother, who may have resembled him—the Crucified, whose Cross has conquered the world? Did I affirm that the stumbling block to his faith was the cornerstone of mine, and that the conformity between the Cross and the suffering of men was in my eyes the key to that impenetrable mystery whereon the faith of his childhood had perished?[9]

Here, possibly for the first time, the Holocaust survivor was compared to Christ. From Mauriac's perspective it made perfect sense. The dark eyes and the harrowing tale endowed the survivor with mythological powers. Defined by extreme and unknowable suffering, the survivor could be viewed as a black Christ and his tale as a New Testament of Darkness, neither of which repudiated the doctrine of love but only strengthened its mysterious force. For Mauriac, dedicated since the late twenties to rehabilitating the power of love, the survivor represented the ultimate witness. But since Judaism saw no such equation between suffering and love, the cornerstone of Mauriac's faith was the stumbling block to Wiesel's. To the Christian who had found his way back to a statement of faith, the Jewish survivor was the perfect symbol of continuity, but for a Jewish sufferer to stand alone as the purveyor of a new gospel was truly a radical departure from the Jewish perspective. One man's neoclassicism was another's apocalypse.

Yet the archetype of Jesus is not new to Jewish literature and art, just as the desire to renounce Jewish particular claims to suffering is not new. If the emancipation (the granting of equal rights to the Jews of Europe), now celebrating its bicentennial, has given rise to the fantastic irony that Jews can no longer lay exclusive claim to their own catastrophe, this development can be traced through the career of the Jewish Jesus who stands as the icon of universal suffering.

AS the Jews' view of the world changed, so too did their view of the Gentiles. Through the latter half of the nineteenth century, as Jews' hope of emancipation was on the rise in eastern Europe, portrayals of non-Jews became much more favorable in Yiddish and Hebrew fiction. For the most part, however, new stereotypes of good Goyim (enlightened Russian officers, idealistic revolutionaries) merely replaced the old.[10] Not until the first decade of the twentieth century was the ancient taboo against portraying the Man on the Cross finally lifted—a real breakthrough. According to Ansky, whose trenchant essay on this topic is the springboard for my discussion, the break should be credited to Yiddish symbolist writer Der Nister.[11] The latter ended his youthful collection *Thoughts and Motifs* (Vilna, 1907) with the prayer of Mary (Jesus' mother) for the birth of a son despite Satan's dire warnings of the tragic fate that would await him.[12] This was part of Der Nister's larger claim that the paradoxical union of suffering and love would guarantee the survival, glory, and greatness of the human species.[13]

Behind this literary syncretism was an ecumenical spirit shared by a growing number of eastern European Jews on both sides of the Atlantic, the most unencumbered of whom were the very young writers and poets like Der Nister whose major concern was the aesthetic reshaping of the world. They were children of the February Revolution of 1905 who pursued their global vision not through politics but through the privacy of carefully wrought symbolist works.[14] The heretofore neglected realm of Christianity was for them as valid a source of inspiration as hasidic folklore and haiku. In this brave and beautiful world, a Greek Orthodox procession could inspire both awe and envy in the heart of a village Jew (Joseph Rolnick's "Procession"),[15] and Jesus could become a symbol of human suffering, whether as a redemptive figure on a par with the Jewish messiah (as in the work of Leivick),[16] or as a universal tragic figure (as in the early poetry of Manger).[17]

For all their radicalism, Yiddish writers could not have broken the

Jesus taboo had it not been for prior developments in Christian Europe: the various attempts to modernize and dechristianize Jesus that had been gathering momentum since the Enlightenment, and the strict separation of the Man from the Church.[18] Equally important was the reaction to this humanistic trend in the years 1890–1910. After the out-and-out historicization of Jesus popularized throughout Europe by Ernest Renan, a mythic Jesus reemerged on the other side of rationalism. From within the ranks of Russia's liberal intelligentsia, Vladimir Solovyov celebrated the mystical power of Christianity as divorced from the nationalist doctrines of the Russian Orthodox Church.[19] In western Europe, meanwhile, Albert Schweitzer's *Quest of the Historical Jesus* (1906) launched the countermovement to rehabilitate the Jesus of the spirit by getting at the roots of Christian history.[20] As a Protestant, Schweitzer had in mind a certain kind of Christian history—Lutheran, oriented toward faith and the reestablishment of an eschatological sense of the millennium. And so, from both eastern and western intellectual circles there arose a neoclassical trend that focused on the spiritual and mythic significance of Jesus in a way that was palatable, if not profoundly inspirational, to nonbelievers.

Yiddish and later Hebrew writers (though not yet their readers) were quick to respond. The separation of the Man from the Church allowed Jewish writers to disentangle the historical and human Jesus from the horrors later perpetrated in his name (an ironic reversal of the "guilty Jews" motif in Christian literature). The hope for universal redemption could be linked to the suffering man on the cross only if he was dissociated from the Crusades, blood libels, ghettos, and auto-da-fés. Whereas the nineteenth-century rescue of the historical Jesus found its disciple in Joseph Klausner, whose *Jesus of Nazareth: His Life, Times and Teaching* appeared in 1922,[21] Jewish writers and artists were mostly interested in Jesus as a mythic archetype. Under the influence of Solovyov, Jesus and Mary became symbols of a mystical struggle for unity, and under the influence of Schweitzer, Jesus was restored as a prophet of the millennium.

In 1909 the Yiddish world suddenly took up the so-called Crucifix Question when two emblematic stories, Lamed Shapiro's "The Cross" and Sholem Asch's "In a Carnival Night," appeared in consecutive issues of the same journal.[22] The two could not have been more dissimilar. Whereas Shapiro's story located the cross at the nexus of modern violence, Asch's was the first in a long line of ecumenical fantasies that were to make him an international favorite but were ultimately to drive a wedge between him and the Yiddish reading public. Briefly, Asch's story tells of a carnival in sixteenth-century Rome that was inaugurated each year by a papal procession and by the spectacle of eight venerable

Jews being chased and beaten en route. In the story, Jesus climbs down from the cross in St. Peter's Cathedral to be one of the martyrs. Mary, mother of Jesus, then joins Mother Rachel to sew the shrouds.

Through this final act, Mary and Rachel reclaim their primitive Jewishness—a key to what Asch was up to. As in his story of the Kola Street irregulars, written a few years before, Asch was trying to project a primitivist image of the past in which the legendary exploits of *ba'al-gufs*, matriarchs, and martyrs could be celebrated without regard to religious differences or historical animosities. This facile foray into comparative mythology—a kind of Yiddish *Golden Bough*—bespoke a new stage in the politics of emancipation. Asch, alone among Yiddish writers in this period, enjoyed the support of non-Jewish Polish, Russian, and German audiences. In return, he told them what they wanted to hear—that Jewish-Gentile antagonism was a thing of the past and that enlightened Jews now recognized the essential humanity of the dominant Christian culture.[23] Though writers like Ansky and Peretz were quick to challenge Asch's program of conciliation, the pattern of subtly currying favor with the Gentiles had just begun.

For Lamed Shapiro, on the other hand, the cross was a symbol of universal violence, a sign of forgiveness that became a scar of mutilation, an emblem of zealousness that turned victim into murderer. The bloody cross on his protagonist's forehead cut through the veneer of ideas and ideals designed to rationalize the violence. Against the backdrop of World War I and the Bolshevik Revolution, Halpern, Hazaz, Markish, and Rabon painted similar cruci-fictions: a universal landscape of extremity which no amount of self-sacrifice would ever redeem.

In addition to the ecumenical idealists and apocalyptists there was a third group of writers, who upheld a traditionalist view of Jesus as symbol of the eternal enmity between Christians and Jews. They refused, in other words, to separate vehicle and message. S. Y. Agnon, to judge from his private correspondence and from his published prose (especially "The Lady and the Peddler") belonged to this camp, as did Asher Barash, who expressed this view in his martyrological story of the Gonta massacres, "At Heaven's Gate."[24]

These three groups actually formed a progression. The initial enthusiasm for the historical and mythic Jesus gave way to his role as apocalyptic omen, which led in turn to his reemergence as the divinity of the enemy of Israel. In large measure, this was the progression of eastern European Jewish culture in the hundred-year period we have been following, from the 1840s to 1948. Laid out graphically, the endorsement of the world and its historical promise described an arc that peaked after World War I and the Bolshevik Revolution, then began its rapid apocalyptic descent back to the fold, and culminated in the two Great In-gatherings of the Jewish people, one in the ghettos and factories of death, the other in the Land of Israel. In the Great Catastrophe the linear arc became a vortex, and those who passed through the whirlwind became neoclassicists despite themselves. It was a path followed by so many writers and intellectuals—whether they lived in New York, Tel Aviv, Warsaw, Vilna, Kiev, or Moscow—as to be almost commonplace. Yet the career of Uri Zvi Greenberg (born 1896), the preeminent apocalyptist of his age, stands out as a guidepost to the whole progression. What's more, he himself boasted of playing this role all along.

Like Jesus hanging alone and in visible agony at all the crossroads of eastern Europe, Greenberg, the scion of great hasidic rabbis, saw himself standing "in the middle of the world and in the middle of time." With the egocentric pathos of a true expressionist, Greenberg sought to voice the pain of human existence as directly as possible, without aesthetic veils, beautiful words, or lilting rhythms. "All the literatures have been overrun in their classical stagnation," proclaimed Greenberg in his famous expressionist manifesto:

> Idyllic daydreams and the poet's elegiac serenity have been devastated by a whirlwind: WHAM! A roar issued forth from the gaping-mouthed Colossus—Man-with-a-million-heads (according to Grosz: like a machine; technological age!). The fate of the old books—the fate of the Gothic churches and Roman towers: petrified pasthoods. Horrible to behold. Even the roads pass them by in a run. World and red century hurtling downhill. Optimists fix spectacles over their eyes trying to conjure up intuitively (for the time being) a glowing bit of new moon in some far-off horizon. Meanwhile, night is setting in and the world drags the red creaking chariot of the bleeding century to its final rest. Downhill with the rotting heaps: generational excrement.[25]

Dionysian poet and advocate of upheaval, Greenberg stood at the opposite pole of Jewish culture from someone like Sutzkever. Sutzkever's lyric exaltation of nature, his high poetic diction replete with archaic words and rhymed neologisms, his classical control and private pantheism, were all anathema to Greenberg. Sutzkever's poet wandered barefoot, playing his flute; Greenberg's poet was a madman, master of the great apocalyptic scream ("He Was Crazy").[26] Conflict for Greenberg was the essence of life—the conflict between man and woman, sex and death, the individual and the collective. The greater the felt contradiction, the greater the recourse to myths of the millennium. Thus, his route to a national poetics was certain from the start. His would be the grand prophetic words; chaos and destruction would guide his self-discovery.

Why stand in awe of Jesus and other mythic figures, if one's own life has assumed mythic proportions?[27] At the center of Greenberg's private-myth-made-public were two epiphanies of horror from the First

World War. Drafted into the Austrian army in 1915, Greenberg saw active combat on the Serbian front. "At the River Sava's waters" he beheld dead soldiers hanging upside down over the barbed wire, the nails of their boots reflecting the light of the moon.[28] Years later, in his lyric poem "Yizkor," he returned to those soldiers as a revelation of absolute extremity.[29] At poem's end, the archetypal weeping for Zion by the waters of Babylon was forever superseded in his mind by his weeping on the banks of the Sava. Here was a recollection of universal terror, of God revealed in the soldiers' boots thrust into the face of heaven. "Yizkor" was not, as the title implies, the universal made particular—that is, a Jewish liturgical response to the terrors of trench warfare—but the particular made universal, the private act of mourning and memory made into a statement about the tragedy of human existence.

Greenberg deserted from the army in 1918 and returned to his hometown of Lemberg, there to experience a bloody pogrom carried out by the Polish Legion to mark the liberation of the city from the Ukrainians. Greenberg and his parents were stood up against a wall to be shot: "Why? Just like that. Because we were Jews who carried 'dogs' blood' in their veins . . . That's what they said. So be it. It was a miracle that they chose not to shoot me. It was a miracle that I could flee to a hiding place. That's how it happened. On that day I learned to recognize the symbol of terror—in the cross."[30] November, the month in which the pogrom took place, would henceforth be associated in his mind with the slaughter of helpless Jews, and because they were helpless, the cross loomed over them as the ancient sign of terror.[31]

Greenberg's immediate response to the pogroms was an outpouring of helpless grief.[32] The importance of these early sketches can hardly be overstated, for they contain some of the central motifs of his later response to the Holocaust: the snow that will not cover the blood, the two sides of the river of sorrow, the division of the world between "Us" and "Them," the picture of himself as the lone lamenter. These were Greenberg's first attempts to raise Jewish catastrophe to a mythic plane, and by so doing to find his own place in the continuum of Jewish response. With the hubris born of youth and of a life-long sense of election, the twenty-two-year-old Greenberg already fancied himself a prophet, or, at the very least, Bialik's heir. A month before the pogrom, he took up the prophetic calling, writing of his mission in his prose poem "In the Vale of Tears."[33] At the precise point that Bialik had ended "In the City of Slaughter," with God instructing the prophet to go into exile, Greenberg began his own internal debate with the Jewish people. But he was not yet ready to carry out God's specific charge—to smash the Jewish gravestones, thus signaling that an era of renewal had begun.

By the second anniversary of the pogrom, November 1920, Greenberg's frame of reference had undergone a drastic change. The universal implications of the terror had gradually become apparent and the search for archetypes now led directly to the Crucifixion, as seen in Greenberg's "Golgotha."[34] Torn between two traditional responses, the song of lament and the cry for revenge, the narrator of the poem chooses instead to identify with the man on the cross: "Each morning I'm nailed up anew on the burning red crucifix." The world has turned into one great mount of crucifixion, with thousands of severed Jewish heads strewn below like those of so many thieves.

Trench warfare at one end and the pogrom at the other became the ultimate reference points for all of Greenberg's subsequent responses to catastrophe.[35] In both cases he looked beyond the particular experience, as every poet would; but in the first the movement was centrifugal, outward to humanity, whereas the response to the pogrom moved toward the fate of the Jews. Viewing the pogrom from the top of Golgotha raised the event to universal heights but also forged a bond between the dead Christ and the dead Jews.

In death, Jesus was of limited use to Greenberg as a Jewish symbol. So long as he remained nailed to the cross, Jesus was deaf and blind to the call of Jewish history. To make him answerable to that call, Greenberg challenged him outright in an outrageous gesture: he printed the words in the form of a cross (see Figure 5): "You've become inanimate, brother Jesus. For two thousand years you've been tranquil on the cross. All around you the world expires. Damn it, you've forgotten everything. Your petrified brain can't grasp: a Star of David at your head, over the star—hands in priestly blessing. Under them, olive groves and ethrog gardens."[36] Jesus is blind to the signs of his Jewishness and deaf to the "*ur*-cry of the Jews." Vain are the poet's reminders that "Golgotha is here—all around," in the ubiquitous relics of Jewish destruction. This passive and indifferent Jesus refuses to be moved.

If verbal prodding didn't work, Greenberg had a more drastic plan: he would denounce the Christian world to its face and leave it behind once and for all. This was not to be just a personal gesture—Greenberg's egocentric pathos would never settle for so little—but rather the Tokheḥa that the Jewish people had been stifling these two thousand years. What a traditional Jew perhaps thought but would never dare utter and what a secular Jew would not even dare think, Greenberg proclaimed for all to hear: Europe was a "kingdom of the cross" where the hatred of Jews grew not from social, political, or economic causes but directly from the church and the inescapable clamor of its bells. Only among his own in the Land of Israel could a Jew finally be free of them.

Yet typically for Greenberg, he did not want to leave without rescu-

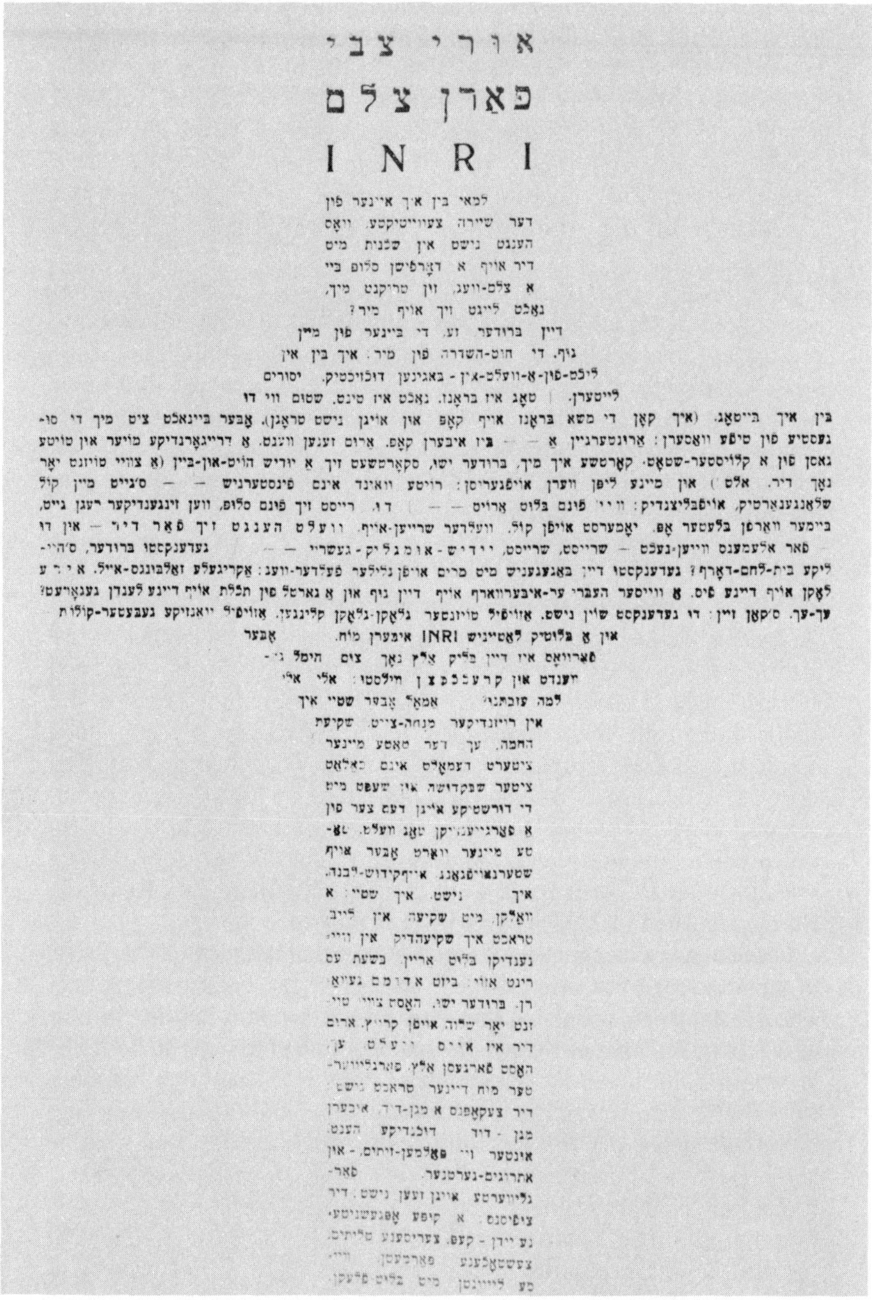

אורי צבי

פאַרן צלם

I N R I

למאי בין איך איינער פון
דער שירה צעווייטיקטע, וואָס
הענגט נישט אין שלנית מיט
דיר אויף א דזאָרפישן סלופ ביי
א צלם-וועג, זון טריקנט מיך,
נאַכט לייגט זיך אויף מיר?
דיין ברודער זע, די ביינער פון מיין
גוף. די חוט-השדרה פון מיר: איך בין אין
ליכט-פון-א-וועלט-אין - באגינען דולוויכטיק. יסורים
לייטערן. | טאָג איז בראָנז. נאַכט איז טינט. שטום ווי דו
בין איך בייטאָג. (איך קאָן די משא בראָנז אויף קאָפּ און אויגן נישט טראָגן). אָבער ביינאַכט ציט מיך די סו-
געסטיע פון טיפע וואַסערן: אַרונטערגיין אַ — — ביז איבערן קאָפּ. אַרום זענען וועגס. אַ דרייגאַרנדיקע מויער און טויטע
גאַסן פון א קלויסטער-שטאָט. קאָרטשע איך מיך, ברודער ישו, סקאָרטשעט זיך אַ יוריש הויט-און-ביין (אַ צווייטויזנט יאָר
נאָך דיר. אלס) און מיינע ליפּן ווערן אויפגעריסן: רויטע וואונד אינם פינסטערניש — — ס'ציט מיין קול
שלאַנגענאַרטיק, אויפבליצנדיק: ווי י' פונם בלוט אַרויס — — | ד ו. רייסט זיך פונם סלופּ, ווען זינגענדיקער רעגן גייט,
ביימער וואַרפן בלעטער אָפּ. יאָמערסט אויפן קול. וועלדער שרייען-אויף. וועלט הענגט זיך פאַר דיר — און דו
— פאַר אלעמענס ווייען-נעכט — שרייסט, שרייסט, יידיש-אומגליק-געשריי — — גערעדנקסטו ברודער, ס'הייליקע בית-לחם-דאָרף? געדענקסטו דיין באַגעגעניש מיט מרים אויפן גלילער פעלדער-וועג: אַקריגעלע זאַלבונגס-אייל. אירע
לאָקן אויף דיינע פיס. אַ ווייסער העברי ער-איבערוואַרף אויף דיין גוף און אַ גאַרטל פון תכלת אויף דיינע לענדן געגאַרטעט?
ער-ער. ס'קאָן זיין: דו געדענקסט שוין נישט. אזויפיל טויזנטער גלאָקן-גלאָקן קלינגען. אזויפיל יואַנזיקע געבעטער-קולות
און אַ בלוטיק לאַטייניש INRI איבערן מוח. אָבער
פאַרוואָס איז דיין בליק אַלץ נאָך צום הימל גע-
ווענדט און קרעכצן ווילסטו: אלי אלי
למה עזבתני? אמאָל אָבער שטיי איך
אין רויזנדיקער מנחה-צייט, שקיעת
החמה, ען דער טאַטע מיינער
ציטערט דעמאָלט אינם טאַלאַס
ציטער שבקדושה און שעפט מיט
די דורשטיקע אייגן דעם צער פון
א פאַרגייענדיקן טאָג וועלט. טאַ-
טע מיינער יוואַרט אָבער אויף
שטערנאויפגאַנג. אויף קידוש-לבנה.
איך נישט. איך שטיי: א
יואַלקן מיט שקיעה און לייב
טראַכט איך שקיעהדיק און ווייי-
נענדיקן בלוט אריין, בשעת עס
רינט אזוי: ביזט אדומם געוואָ-
רן, ברודער ישו. האָסט צוויי טוי-
זנט יאָר שלוה אויפן קרייץ. אַרום
דיר איז אייס ווינטער. ען
האָסט פאַרגעסן אַלץ. פאַרגליווער-
טער מוח דיינער טראַכט נישט
דיר צעקאָפּנס א מגן-דוד, איבערן
מגן - דוד דולנדיקע הענט.
אינטער ווי פאַלמען-זיתים, - און
אתרוגים-גערטנער. פאַר-
גליווערטע אויגן זעען נישט: דיר
ציפּיסנס: א קיפּע אָפּגעשניטע-
נע יידן - קעפּ, צעריסענע טליתים,
צעשטאָכענע פּאַרמעטן, ווייי-
סע לייוונטן מיט בלוט-פלעקן.

5. The original layout of Uri Zvi Greenberg's "Uri Zvi in Front of the Cross."

ing Jesus and Mary for the task of Jewish renewal. The Church had done everything possible to rob them of their true identities, even to the extent of falsifying their names—"Jesus," "Bethlehem," and "Mary" were crude Latin substitutes, he claimed—and so Greenberg shouted in defiance, "I swear by the sun, the worship of those millions is a lie! / . . . / Beit Leḥem is a *Jewish* town! / Ben-Yosef is a *Jewish* son!"[37] Since Judaism was the culture of the rising east and Christianity was the culture of the declining west, the time had come to kidnap Jesus.

Accompanying this poem, in the same issue of Greenberg's expressionist journal *Albatros*, was a virulent critique of Diaspora politics, press, and literature. As he took leave of the "woeful home on Slavic soil," Greenberg warned that Europe never had accepted and never would accept the Jews in its midst; those who were committed to staying were advised to organize for self-defense. "Place guards at your walls before the attacker comes; then you can split his head open at the Jewish thresholds."[38] The year was 1923.

GREENBERG'S prophetic powers, which no one today would deny, derived from his uncompromising view of contemporary realities. It was a prophecy born of intense self-examination coupled with an ongoing search for ancient analogies. Beginning at least in the 1920s, there were two competing voices in Greenberg's poetry—one bombastic and self-assured, the other close to existential despair. The structure of his poetry reflected the movement of his life: from indulgence of every individual passion to total identification with the collective struggle. The measure of his greatness is that this tension was never lost, not even in his massive work of national lament, *Streets of the River*, published in 1951.[39]

Greenberg's writing career likewise shows that an adequate response to the Holocaust was often shaped long before the event itself. A poet who constantly recapitulated the course of his own life, charting its flow into and against that of the people; who continued to write in both Hebrew and Yiddish; who triumphantly snatched the mantle of prophecy from Bialik; who was not content merely to explore the new meanings of ancient archetypes and messianic figures but also cultivated what he considered to be indigenous Jewish forms of expression—the Kina, Masa, and Tokheḥa (lament, oracle, and curse)—was a poet preparing to respond to the Great Destruction.

Even in works of intense self-analysis, such as *Rising Manhood* (1926), which he wrote in honor of his thirtieth birthday, Greenberg never lost sight of the larger community and its place in the world. Unlike other *engagé* poets who identified solely with those members of the tribe who would serve as vanguard of the future, Greenberg saw himself as the poet of all Jewish people, not only of the swamp-draining and road-building halutzim (pioneers) of Palestine. "From the buried treasure house of the people, from the sunken slaughterhouse of generations, the Seer is commanded to go forth into the open," he announced in the inaugural address of his "Oracle to Europe."[40] And though he now saw the history of Diaspora Jewry as a tale of unmitigated suffering (a "sunken slaughterhouse of generations"), and though his rejection of Jewish passivity was unequivocal,[41] and though he was now certain that only a return to Israel's soil and sovereignty would guarantee the revival of the nation, he also understood the spiritual power of the Diaspora and sang a song of praise to "my brothers, the Jews with earlocks." "Oh wonderful ambassadors of the Eastern kingdom," he called these orthodox and hasidic Jews of Europe as he asked their forgiveness for having ridiculed their outlandish dress and their mournful chants.[42]

In this paean, the most profound of his grandiloquent pronouncements, Greenberg recognized that the Jews with earlocks were still the backbone of eastern European Jewry despite their being a source of embarrassment to every branch of the secular movement. The Zionists and Territorialists, the Bundists and Communists, the Yiddishists and Hebraists, wrote off these millions of Jews as unreconstructed relics of the past. One could point to someone like Ansky, whose face-to-face encounters with the folk, in good times and bad, made him a spokesman for their cause; but this was the very trait for which Ansky's closest friend and associate, Chaim Zhitlovsky, never forgave him. "Ansky's indulgence for the reactionary forces in our folk life aggravated me no end," wrote Zhitlovsky, a leading Socialist and Zionist theoretician.[43] Twenty years later, Kalmanovitsh and Katzenelson would arrive at their global vision of Jewish sanctity, but it would take the Holocaust to convince them. Here, in contrast, was thirty-year-old Greenberg, fresh from his literary and sexual conquests in Warsaw and Berlin, a new convert to the pioneering cause of Palestine, who suddenly realized that the halutzim would reclaim the soil but not the spirit of Judaism. What was needed now was a vast ingathering of energy: of all the failed messiahs, from Jesus to Shabbetai Zvi, and of all the Jews, wearing khakis or *kapotes*.

Midway through his "Oracle to Europe," an impressive combination of Bialik's prophetic voice and the historiographic scope of Halpern's "A Night," Greenberg achieved his boldest appropriation of Jesus. In the poem, Jesus becomes Ahasver, not condemned to wander for rejecting the Christian savior but the sole survivor of the Bar Kokhba revolt, who is ordered to carry the message of Jewish political sovereignty throughout the generations. It is Ahasver, not Jesus, who is nailed to the cross, as he makes his way to the Temple Mount carrying a wooden beam for the sacrificial altar. The Gentiles never know it, for Ahasver is silent. And when he returns, he will announce salvation for the Jews, in the land of the Jews. Jesus, meanwhile, is killed in the electric chair of urban civilization. The poem illustrates Greenberg's wild syncretism at its peak. At the same time he began to retrieve more internal though no less controversial figures from Jewish history: Solomon Molcho, his "brother from Portugal," and Shabbetai Zvi.[44]

This attempt to rehabilitate the failed messiahs was no mere exercise in revisionist history. Greenberg's passionate identification with Jesus and then with Shabbetai Zvi were expressions of his search for the great messianic myth that would finally reconcile the contradictions of Jewish and human existence. Nor was it by chance that Greenberg first heralded the figure of Shabbetai Zvi in 1924, the year of Greenberg's "*Kfitsat-haderekh*" (Miraculous Shortcut): "There is a miraculous shortcut for the body and soul of the Holy Rabbi Israel Baal Shem Tov and there is a miraculous shortcut for the afflicted poet who fled by himself from the borders of the Slavs . . . to pitch his pauper's tent in the Judean Desert."[45] Greenberg saw his move to Palestine as the shortcut through all the landscapes of Jewish history, over "Spain-Portugal-Germany-France-Italy-Holland," but his was an itinerary with a difference: it took him on a pilgrimage to the grave of Shabbetai Zvi in Dulcingo, the Turkish Balkans (a journey that Greenberg actually made in 1918 while still in uniform).[46] In exactly the same way that Greenberg had tried, on leaving Europe, to reclaim Jesus from Christianity, he tried, on arriving in Palestine, to rescue Shabbetai Zvi from Islam. And this, in turn, was part of a comprehensive revision of Jewish archetypes. The false messiahs were true messiahs betrayed by their people's failure of nerve; the Wandering Jew was the eternal messenger of national self-determination; and Kiddush Hashem was henceforth to be understood as "Haganat Hashem," the physical defense of the people and their faith.[47] The poet of apocalypse, by merging his mythic selfhood with the fate of the collective, became an apostle of defiant affirmation.

From there the step to radical politics did not even require a shortcut. In 1929, after the Arab Riots, Greenberg joined the Revisionists. As of May 1930 he appeared regularly in the Hebrew Revisionist press and a year later was the leading candidate on the Revisionist slate for the Zionist Congress, second only to Vladimir Jabotinsky, the chief ideologue and founder of Revisionism. It was as delegate to the congress that Greenberg returned to Europe and it was then that Jabotinsky withdrew in anger from the world Zionist movement. Greenberg eventually made his way to Warsaw, where he edited the Yiddish Revisionist newspaper *Di velt* (1933–1934) and then became a regular correspondent for *Der moment* (1938–1939). With his journalist's pass and his Palestinian passport, Greenberg was able to escape from Europe and arrive home in November 1939.

There followed a period of silence—a silence far more terrible than Abramovitsh's sixty years before: between the date of Greenberg's last article for *Der moment*, September 1, 1939, and the appearance of his first lamentations on the Holocaust in July and August 1945, not only did his entire family perish but all the Jews with earlocks and their clean-shaven brothers. Again, it was Greenberg who realized the scope of the disaster. At a time when Zionist ideology required equal emphasis on the heroism of the fighters and on the Holocaust, Greenberg (the Revisionist) paid only scant attention to the resistance and then omitted these references in the final version of the poems.[48] The collective was what mattered, and that collective had perished. While other eastern European Jewish writers such as Manger and Sutzkever expunged the glowing references to Jesus and Gentiles from their earlier poetry, Greenberg did them one better by not allowing *any* of his prewar poetry to be republished (until the late 1970s). He wanted to be known exclusively as a poet of national lamentation and consolation.

Clearly, from Greenberg's perspective, there was no room for a Jewish Jesus after the great catastrophe. There was barely a place for God in a Europe devoid of Jews. And so the poet himself became the commanding presence, the supreme elegist and grand inquisitor all in one. "Go wander about Europe, God of Israel," he ordered, "and count Your sheep: how many lie in ditches, their 'Alas' grown dumb: how many in the cross's shadow, in the streets of weeping, as if in the middle of the sea."[49] In this "winter of horror," when everything was covered "by the Christain, the silent snow of the shadow of death," the Jews had become, "among the *goyim*, ashes and soap—dung for the dung heap." Since God, the Shepherd-Seer (*haro'eh-haro'eh*), had retired to heaven, leaving no convenantal rainbow behind, the few surviving Jews would continue to whore after strange gods until the poet's rebuke, steeled by centuries of sorrow, would finally rip the clouds apart, making a flood of retribution descend. Meanwhile, the murdered Jews of Europe, whose treatment at the hands of the Gentiles defied all comparisons, would remain the ultimate reference point of torture and extermination. And for the Gentiles, only one path remained: they had to renounce their pagan worship, "banish their idols from the beautiful houses of prayer," purge their own blood lust, and acknowledge "Sinai, the Tablets of the Laws, the God of Israel."[50]

Many were the blasphemers whom Jewish history returned to the fold. Many such poets of profanity were even able to argue with the God they had rejected (though they were unable to live by His rules). Greenberg's self-dramatized path of return was different from the paths followed by others. It began from inner sources of revelation in the years of the first apocalypse. With his own eyes he saw the "Great Terror and the Moon"—the revelation of God in the defiant death of the soldiers—and with his own flesh he experienced the terror of the cross. Then and there he understood that the archetypes had to be redeemed, purged, and transformed if life on earth was to continue. And so the terror and the moon, the destroyer and redeemer, the flesh and the spirit, became the two poles of his existence; and as he was torn between the one and the other, he shouted and accused, prophesied and blasphemed.

From poetry his passionate nature led him to politics, but when all further action was eclipsed by a destruction far greater than anything even he could imagine, he fell silent. Though Greenberg never said as much, his example shows more clearly than any other that the loss of faith was a much smaller price to pay for the Jews' romance with modernity than the loss of life. Faith could be regained, even the ancient land could be reclaimed, but the death of a people could not be overcome. And so Greenberg was silent—until he discovered how to mourn. Then, with the same hubris as before, he wrote a massive neoclassical Book of Lamentations that drew together all the themes, archetypes, and literary forms from his own past as from the classical tradition in order to supplant and not merely supplement the ancient laments. The catastrophe that was different in kind required a response that was different in degree.

To mourn, he showed, was to close out the world, to expiate one's own defilement privately, to express the rage, and to uphold a single truth. And that truth was tribal and exclusivist. Based on his revelations of violence, his apocalyptic reading of history, and his feeling of bereavement, he demanded a final choice between the poles of existence: there was Golgotha and there was Sinai. Those who continued to crucify on one would never receive the Tablets on the other.

THE preservation of group memory at a time of radical transition was as much the concern of eastern European Jewish artists as of their literary counterparts. Until the emancipation, the collective memory had been passed on mainly through rituals, prayers, and literary archetypes. Throughout the premodern period, not only were visual images of history lacking but also heroes of flesh and blood. No heroes emerged when the Exodus was rehearsed on Passover, when the Destruction of the Temple was lamented on the ninth of Av, when the Crusades were recalled in the weekly liturgy. In line with rabbinic practice, the ancient kings and warriors were utterly spiritualized, though in popular literature King Saul and King David were reinstated as warriors and King Solomon evinced great masculine charm over the Queen of Sheba. It was not until secular ideologies began to vie with traditional Judaism, however, that a fundamental change of attitude occurred. It was then that individual heroism and vision took on central importance, whether these were figures rediscovered from the past, such as Judah the Maccabee and Bar Kokhba, or figures who rose to fame in the present, such as Herzl and Hirsh Lekert. Jewish artists, therefore, could be doubly envious of the Gentiles, who boasted an unbroken artistic development both inside the Church and out and who took pride in the perfect icon of individual self-sacrifice: the man on the cross.

Synagogue art, though continuous, had never developed into a cumulative self-conscious tradition; and even at its finest, Jewish decorative art was anonymous. Until the late nineteenth century, no collection of Jewish religious artifacts was ever exhibited (Tcherikower cites the Paris Exhibition of 1878 as the first such instance),[51] so that the modern Jewish artist in search of a viable past would most likely turn to the classics of Christian art. Thus, whatever new forms of visual communication would develop between the Jewish artist and his audience were bound to be eclectic, and this freedom to borrow was put to good advantage. Finally, as communication through ritual and language broke down among Jews, the artist became a primary shaper of collective memory.

Catastrophe, I would argue, endowed the Jewish artist with unprecedented authority. At a time when traditional doctrines of retribution and redemption had lost their power to console, visual icons of Jewish suffering came to symbolize the staying power of the people. And these icons assumed a life of their own.

The artists' changing perception of catastrophe directly paralleled that of the professional writers. In the art as in the literature of Jewish eastern Europe, there was a progressive rebellion against the classical traditions of response to catastrophe, a rebellion expressed through various attempts to bend, shake, and reconstrue the archetypes. Although some of this reconstruing was an inevitable accompaniment of access to European modernism in all its myriad forms, most of the reconstruing was necessary in the historical milieu of a declining shtetl culture and a battle between ideologues over socialism, Zionism, nationalism, and orthodoxy. These historical pressures gave a heightened sense of mission to writers and artists, who had consequently to stretch their language, their metaphor, and their range of allusive images. The more basic the concept—exile, Kiddush Hashem, covenant, redemption—the more radical the means of reinterpretation. Only after World War I, however, and only in the build-up to World War II, did eastern European Jews realize that they could not be sustained without a new archetype. Thus, they themselves were conscious that the Holocaust could be, might well be, that new archetype. But before the new could emerge, the old archetypes had to be tried on for size. In the first years of the ghettos, the writers, artists, and ideologues ran through all the previous archetypes just to prove that a new one was necessary.

After the war, competing forces obscured what had already been achieved in the war. As the surviving Jews of eastern Europe lost the means of cultural reproduction because of new political realities and rapid linguistic assimilation, they also lost access to the art of archetyping. However significant were the neoclassical attempts of Sutzkever or Greenberg to reassemble the Holocaust archetype out of the structure of past archetypes, a sense of apocalypse was rapidly setting in that denied the validity of prior Jewish responses to catastrophe. While the Holocaust as a semantic field was being established in terms borrowed from the French, eastern European Jewish writers of influence were revising their work on the Holocaust with an eye toward a non-Jewish audience. Paradoxically, it was in the newest branch of Jewish self-expression, the graphic arts, that the modern traditions of response were carried on with less interference and that a new archetype of destruction was most clearly established.

SAMUEL Hirszenberg's epic work "Golus," or "Exile" (Figure 6) became the first icon of Jewish suffering to gain a mass audience. The scene was apparently one that he had witnessed as a youth in Cracow—Jewish victims of an expulsion trudging through the streets.[52] Now that, in the aftermath of Kishinev, the plight of the Jews had insinuated itself into the twentieth century, Hirszenberg found a way of telescoping past and present. "Exile" shows an endless throng of refugees with an old bent Jew in the lead, trudging through a barren snow-covered landscape. They are walking to the left (westward?), away from their home somewhere in eastern Europe.

The idea of exile, as David Williams has said, "requires the idea of the place from which this 'going out' takes place," of the community left behind.[53] Judging from what the refugees are carrying, theirs was a community united under God and His covenant, a true Kehillah Kedoshah, for the only objects they have salvaged for the road are a prayer shawl, a Torah scroll, and a tea kettle (see Figure 7). Perhaps the kettle is meant to be the domestic counterpart of the Torah scroll, as intimate

6. Samuel Hirszenberg, "Golus" [Exile], 1904.

7. Detail of Hirszenberg's "Golus."

a symbol of the hearth as the scroll is of the sanctuary. These objects take on added significance when one recalls that exile in the Jewish scheme is the punishment for breach of covenant. There is no evidence that this community has renounced its part of the contract. It is a patriarchal society, judging from the fact that all four figures in the foreground are male: the aged Jew in the lead with his hands in his sleeves; the middle-aged Jew with the proverbial *vander-shtekn* (wander staff) in his hand; a boy covering his ears from the cold; and, on the extreme right, a severe-looking intellectual type with steel-rimmed glasses. The composition of the group also suggests that even in exile they are one; women's shawls blend in with the tassles of the prayer shawls; the headgear is recognizably eastern European (with two bowler hats thrown in for social diversity); a father walks clutching his child.

Since exile is the supreme archetype of collective uprootedness, of separation from the sources of security and wholeness, the visual representation of exile must center its meaning on the intimation of loss. It is in the subtle mix of crowded and empty space, of old and new, of stoicism and fear, that Hirszenberg achieves the monumental quality he is after. Though in motion, the group is suspended in space, with the sky above and the snow below. The empty third of the canvas suggests an endless, inhospitable landscape. There is no sign to help define their position. Then again, how far can they go without a single wagon and with only one kettle? Though recognizably contemporary (thanks to the bowlers and the clean-shaven intellectual), this is a group suspended in time. The bearded and shawl-covered figures with their tassels, fringes, Torah scroll, and wander staff could just as well have been plucked out of the Middle Ages. Their response to their predicament is similarly ambiguous. None of them looks particularly pained, as befits a group of Jews resigned to their historic fate, but neither do they look upward, to beseech the Deity for help. The dominant figures all have their eyes fixed on the ground; only the tall woman in the middle and the doll-faced girl carrying the kettle are staring straight ahead. Thus, the internal coherence, the stoic resignation, and the signs of historic continuity make of this uprooted community more than a motley group of refugees; but the absence of recognizable landmarks, of a clear destination, and of positive expressions of faith makes this a distinctly modern archetype of exile.

Hirszenberg's painting gained instant popularity. According to Ansky, reproductions of it hung in the homes of the nationalistically minded intelligentsia;[54] and among average Jews it circulated as a postcard with Yiddish, Russian, or German captions (the YIVO archives contain samples of each). With this image of modern exile fixed in the minds of tens of thousands of Jews, all subsequent expulsions would seem like mere repetition.

For an archetype of *individual* heroism from exactly the same period, we turn to Ephraim Moses Lilien (born 1874), a Galician-born artist nine years younger than Hirszenberg. As a disciple of British "decadent" artist Aubrey Beardsley and a founder of the so-called *Jugendstil* in Germany, Lilien reveled in the juxtaposition of styles and cultural symbols.[55] Like the Zionist cause which he served with distinction, Lilien enlisted symbols from the past to glorify the present, but in so doing betrayed the European, Christian roots of the Jewish revival. To legitimate the eclecticism of his art, Lilien adopted as his motto the words of Paul, "To the pure, all things are pure" (Epistle to Titus 1:15), as if to say that because he was pure, the sources he adapted were purified in his art.[56]

As an illustrator of books and causes, Lilien catered to a mass audience that included both Jews and Gentiles. When a public campaign was launched after Kishinev to raise funds and a cry of protest, Lilien was a natural choice to do the artwork. "To the Martyrs of Kishinev" (Figure 1) was the title page he prepared for Maxim Gorky's *Sbornik* (Miscellany) on Kishinev, published in 1903 either in St. Petersburg or in Berlin (I have not been able to locate a copy). The drawing had something for everyone. For the Jewish viewer—an auto-da-fé. An old bearded Jew completely wrapped in a prayer shawl is being burned at the stake; an angel (Gabriel, perhaps), holding a Torah scroll and breastplate, is kissing the forehead of the martyred patriarch. The juxtaposition of flames and the Torah would further recall the martyrdom of Haninah ben Tardion in Hadrianic times, who in turn would recall the recent example of Moyshe-Tsvi Kigl, a synagogue attendant in Kishinev who presumably died defending the Torah. The Christian viewer would respond to a different set of images: the angel's wings spread out to suggest a crucifixion, the full moon describing a halo above the head of the martyr, and thorns decorating the upper frame. In fact, the whole motif for the drawing was nothing less than the ascension of a saint, with a male (Jewish) angel replacing the Virgin Mary of Christian iconography.

Any way you looked at it, the drawing was profoundly consolational. The perfectly upright figure of the patriarch literally and figuratively stood for the martyrs who died a meaningful death, who sacrificed their lives for the Torah. As in popular literature of the period, the one heroic death of the *shames* expiated the involuntary death of the many.

This sentimental, syncretistic approach to Jewish catastrophe went hand in glove with the idealistic appropriation of Jesus. The embedded crucifixion implied more than just a stand-in of the one for the many; it implied a vicarious sacrifice, the borderline theology between the death of Christ as the world's expiation and the medieval Jewish doctrine of Kiddush Hashem. The presence of the angel made it clear that the sacrifice had been accepted—even expected—in heaven. By covering all the symbolic bases, Lilien made the Kishinev pogrom seem so decorous, so seamlessly continuous with the past of both religious traditions, as to be almost desirable. And so, alongside Hirszenberg's epic panorama of exile, which attempted, in a neoclassical style, to portray catastrophe as the bleak fulfillment of a broken covenant, Lilien represented a second, heroic approach that sought to bridge the abyss between destruction and redemption, victim and victimizer, Jew and Gentile.

Perhaps because modern Jewish art was still in its infancy, the fund of available archetypes was severely limited. The turning point came, as in so many other areas of eastern European Jewish culture, with Ansky. It was his expedition in the years 1911–1914 to gather Jewish ethnographic materials in the towns and villages of the Ukraine that unearthed—sometimes literally—the indigenous iconography of the folk.[57] Through collecting and copying Torah covers, breastplates, ornamental silver, tombstone engravings, papercuts, woodcuts, spice boxes, marriage contracts, haggadahs, *mizrekhs*, synagogue architecture, and Ark decorations, Ansky's team of young ethnographers discovered a visual vocabulary that could become the basis of a new Jewish art form. Inspired by Ansky's example, an eighteen-year-old art student named Issachar Ber Ryback financed his own private expedition to the wooden synagogues of White Russia,[58] and a year later, in 1916, the Jewish Ethnographic Society of St. Petersburg sent him and El Lissitsky to explore the synagogues of the Ukraine.[59] Their discovery was perfectly timed to inaugurate the modernist movement in the art of revolutionary Russia. By 1919, Ryback had arrived at a new artistic credo: glorification of folk art as the source of the "people's" vision and of abstract form as the essence of art.[60] The national element, he insisted, was always expressed in its purest abstract form, though folk art in and of itself was not necessarily abstract.

Ryback lost his father in the pogroms of the civil war. The studied primitivism of his response (Figure 8) is designed to evoke both the cluttered, childlike quality of authentic Jewish folk art as well as the elemental nature of the violence. Western traditions of verisimilitude and visual depth are cast aside in favor of a two-dimensional technique. The influence of Russian icons (which he had painted for a living as a child of twelve!) is also felt in the various small scenes scattered about the central image, figures not placed in the depth but suspended over the surface.[61] Everything is happening all at once instead of in sequence.

8. Issachar Ber Ryback, "Pogrom," 1918; watercolor.

In the center is a burning wooden synagogue. A crooked ladder leads up its lopsided walls and on the top stands a Jew, one hand holding a Torah, the other raised in supplication. Flanking the synagogue are two Cossacks wearing strange hats, which look somewhat like their actual headgear as depicted in period drawings and somewhat like the dunce caps worn by Jews on Purim. A mounted Cossack on the right is guzzling from a bottle while he holds a lance in his left hand; on the tip of the lance is a pierced child surrounded by a halo in which the Hebrew word *kadosh* (holy or martyr) is inscribed. On the left is a dancing Cossack, suspended in the air; he too is drinking, and on the tip of his sabre is the severed head of a bearded Jew. The foreground is cluttered with beasts and men. At the foot of the synagogue a group of Jews huddle together, looking up to the Jew on the roof. From right to left in the very front are a pig licking the spilled blood of the victim; a stabbed Jew, the knife still in him, holding a naked Torah scroll in his arms; a (slaughtered?) bull; a huddled group of Jews; and a naked infant in a pool of blood. In the distance (the only example of perspective in the picture), one can see a shtetl in flames.

Wherever the eye settles, there is blood, fire, fear, and violence. Eventually, however, the synagogue emerges as the central image, flanked by the two savage Cossacks and framed by the outline of a mountain. The iconographic meaning of the picture is located here, on the synagogue roof, for the Jew holding the scroll is none other than Moses ascending Mount Sinai. Once this connection is drawn, Ryback's picture can be understood as a countercommentary on the revelation at Sinai. The Jews huddled below (at the foot of the mountain) look up as their leader seems to be *returning* the Torah to God. With the sanctuary in flames and the children murdered, there is nothing else to do with God's Torah but give it back.

Thus, in the short span of fifteen years, three different styles of Jewish art—the neoclassical, the neoromantic, and the primitivist—were employed in response to catastrophe. What they had in common was the reuse of ancient archetypes: the collective archetype of exile in Hirszenberg, the idealized fusion of Christian, rabbinic, and medieval martyrdom in Lilien, and the subverted Sinaitic covenant in Ryback. Each of these artistic responses, moreover, had its exact literary counterpart. The bleak revision of exile in a neoclassical mode could be found in Abramovitsh's allegorical tales of the 1890s, "Victims of the Fire" and "Shem and Japheth on the Train." Lilien's model of individual heroism was the Zionist answer to the Kishinev pogrom—the answer that Bialik hoped to achieve through his *Poems of Rage* but that poets of lesser talent attempted through legendary means. And the graphic portrayal of the rape of shtetl, with the burning synagogue at center stage, answered to the same radical agenda of those Yiddish and Hebrew writers who struggled alongside Ryback in Kiev and Berlin. It was only a matter of time before the reappropriation of Jesus in Jewish literature would also find its artistic parallel.

Though Marc Chagall (born 1887) had begun painting crucifixion scenes as early as 1912, it was not until 1938 that he used this motif as an icon of Jewish catastrophe. And here, for the first time, the Jewish artist—some say the quintessentially Jewish artist—found himself completely at odds with his literary colleagues. Unlike the writers in Yiddish and Hebrew who were constrained by their audience to respond to the trauma of history or, vice versa, were forced by history to respond to the trauma of their audience, Chagall was answerable to everyone and therefore to no one. As the world of the Jews was radically shrinking, Chagall's was ever expanding. His movement was outward whereas the whole thrust of Yiddish and Hebrew culture—in eastern Europe, America, and Palestine—was overwhelmingly inward. By 1941 everyone from Markish in Moscow and Jacob Glatstein in New York to Natan Alterman in Tel Aviv had returned to the fold, sometimes in demonstrative ways. "Good night, wide world / Big stinking world!" wrote Glatstein in April 1938.[62] "Not you but I slam shut the door." There were exceptions, to be sure, as when Sholem Asch insisted on bringing Christ into the Warsaw ghetto, but the result was mawkishly sentimental wish-fulfillment.[63] Chagall was not constrained by language and persevered in his universalism despite the pressures of history. This being so, he naturally drew upon earlier motifs and experiences in an attempt to deal with the present horror. As his career pulled him away from the fate of his people, he turned back to the figure of Jesus in order to bring the personal and collective spheres together.

A recognizably Jewish Christ with a prayer shawl for a loincloth (as described in Uri Zvi Greenberg's "In the Kingdom of the Cross") dominates the large canvas of "White Crucifixion" (1938), but all the scenes clustered around him are significantly unaffected by his presence (see Figure 9). Revolutionary mobs attack from the left, the matriarchs and patriarchs weep up above, a synagogue burns on the right, Jews flee the destruction on foot and by boat, the Torah scroll is in flames, a mother clutches her baby, an old Jew weeps. Jesus' death does not abolish the suffering around him.[64] He is holy without being divine. Surrounded by the stigmata of twentieth-century violence, the symbol of universal salvation is here transformed, in the words of Franz Meyer, into "a superpersonal symbol of pain mirroring man's diverse destiny."[65]

The Jewish viewer might ask how one could possibly call it diverse; the signs of destruction are everywhere the same—expulsion, desecration, grief, and terror—and the victims are all presumably Jews. Meyer,

9. Marc Chagall, "White Crucifixion," 1938; oil on canvas, 155 × 140 cm.

however, is quite right, for the cross propels all the visual components of the picture outward. Except for the candelabrum, which almost reaches the figure of Christ with its light, all the objects move away from the cross. The ladder does not rest on anything, so that Christ cannot be taken down, but that means that the prayer shawl cannot be taken off him either. The figure above the cross is spiritlike, so we have Christ and the Holy Ghost. What is really missing, therefore, is the Father in the Trinity, the Father who is the God of Israel. The real intimation of loss in this tableau of Jewish suffering is not the loss of life, property, or community but of God, the Old Testament Father who once protected all His sons and daughters.

Unlike the work of Yiddish and Hebrew writers of Chagall's generation, who appropriated Jesus in order to address a universalist message to a particular audience, Chagall's work shows for the first time the opposite phenomenon—an eastern European Jewish artist addressing a particularist message to a universal audience. The primary purpose of Chagall's "White Crucifixion" was to interpret the course of Jewish events in terms of an absent God and a powerless Son. The presence of red (revolutionary) banners in the upper left corner suggests that Chagall's intention was in fact to encompass *all* of recent Jewish history, not just the plight of German Jews. As we look at the next picture in the series, "The Martyr" (1940), we see his progression to a more personal, recognizably eastern European landscape (Figure 10). Vitebsk in flames, the flying animals (a partriarchal figure holding a candelabrum emerges from the leg of the goat), the fiddler with half his head missing, Chagall's father (on the lower right), and the artist himself (barely visible in the corner)—all testify to Chagall's growing desire to personalize the catastrophe, to understand its impact on the world that he knew best. Jesus is rendered as a present-day Russian Jew. He is draped in a prayer shawl and bound to the stake (not to the cross), exactly as in Lilien's drawing. But there is something strikingly feminine about the body-shape and drapery of this Jesus. The presence of Mary Magdalene, robed in magnificent colors, and his father's open book, which invokes the image of John of Revelation, add an overlay of legend to the domestic sadness. The war that was raging in Europe is depicted as the personal tragedy of a mother and son against the backdrop of their burning shtetl. The fact that Chagall chose to keep this painting may testify to its special place in his life.

By far the most affecting picture in the series is the last (Figure 11), more modest in size and executed in watercolor. Fully clothed Russian Jews hang on a series of crosses. The town is blanketed by snow. A corpse lies on the doorstep on the right, a slaughtered hen lies in the center, and a dead mother with an infant at her breast (a familiar motif)

10. Marc Chagall, "The Martyr," 1940; oil on canvas, 164 × 114 cm.

11. Marc Chagall, "The Crucified," 1944; gouache on paper, 62 × 47 cm.

lies on the left. Chagall achieves a greater sense of desecration here, because both sky and earth are barren; there is a multiplicity of crosses, and the crucified Jews at every other doorstep suggest a symbolic inversion of the Passover: no Angel of Death passes over the Israelite houses marked with blood—instead, the hands of an enemy have nailed the Jews to individual crosses in front of their houses. It is therefore a landscape abandoned by God—but not entirely by man. A benign human presence still remains in the *Judenrein* shtetl, none other than King David playing his harp, who is a symbol of the artist himself. This refusal on Chagall's part to abandon his town, his past, and his people to the forces of destruction is the sign of his faith in the redemptive powers of art.

And this is where the timing of his response came into play. For had the artist confronted the Holocaust directly, even as it was known and believed in 1944, this image of individualized murder (each Jew with a sign around his neck) as observed by the psalmist on the roof would have appeared hopelessly naïve at best and cloyingly sentimental at worst. It was not the Holocaust, however, that Chagall was painting. In the familiar dialectical response to catastrophe whereby the greater the destruction, the more it was made to recall the ancient archetypes, the Holocaust triggered in Chagall's mind the recollection of an earlier horror, the massive pogroms of the Ukrainian Civil War which he, like King David, witnessed from the safety of Vitebsk in the north. Back then, when the world was waiting to be conquered by this art, Chagall had had no occasion to mourn. Twenty years later, as he found himself cut off from both his Russian and his French homes, lost his wife, and learned, if only partially, of the ongoing slaughter, he responded with a double inversion: the Crucifixion as mass murder; the Exodus from Egypt as Crucifixion. Like Greenberg in 1923, Chagall suddenly awoke to the nightmare of martyred Jews on the cross.

DURING the Holocaust, questions as to whether this symbol or that was commensurate to the horror were rendered academic because reality itself had become archetypal. And no prior Jewish knowledge was required to make the connection. The Nazis and their willing collaborators brought the lesson home even to the uninitiated. Marcel Janco (born 1895), a founder of Dadaism, was a case in point. He made the mistake of returning to Bucharest, where the pogrom of 1940 caught him totally by surprise. In a single week, as he later explained, he was turned into a Jew and produced a series of extraordinary sketches that bore no resemblance to his earlier surrealistic style.[66] Why bother with surrealism when the world itself had gone crazy? Some of the madness depicted in these sketches is unmistakably modern: rioting crowds carry banners that read "Heraus mit die Juden"; Jewish store windows are smashed; bearded Jews are forced to do calesthenics, to wash the pavements, to dig their own graves. Other scenes, however, could have been taken from the Middle Ages: terrified Jews with packs on their backs are beaten and driven by soldiers; plundered Jewish property is heaped in the streets; and, in Figure 12, a synagogue is destroyed as soldiers burn scrolls and sacred books in an open pyre. The work is methodical: black figures scale the walls of the synagogue, smash the windows, plunder the furnishings. In the forefront a bearded Jew (the sexton, perhaps) is dragged away. Here is the Temple's destruction reenacted.

The new archetype of destruction, however, would have to incorporate greater numbers of people, for the second most common sight in the Holocaust, after murder and systematic plunder, was the mass deportation of whole communities. These deportations, which led unsuspecting millions to labor camps and death camps, were perceived at that time by the Jews themselves as the most obvious replay of the past. Had they not seen it all before—in Hirszenberg's painting and throughout World War I? And so the motif of exile is omnipresent in the graphic art and photography of the Holocaust, though stripped, of course, of its covenantal trappings. In the sketch by Charlotte Buřesova (born 1904) entitled "Deportation: The Last Road," no one carries a Torah anymore (Figure 13). But the artist has chosen nonetheless to highlight some familiar motifs: the first three figures are elderly and the one who supports himself on a cane (a version of the wander staff?) is a partriarchal symbol. Behind them are a mother and toddler, symbol of the love bond that still remains intact.

The striking similarity among most expulsion scenes is even more apparent when one notices the lack of movement in these scenes. More often than not, there are lines of bent-down or bent-over people with bent knees but no true forward motion. It seems that the reversions to archetypes reinforce a static picture of the Holocaust. Even in Chagall's "White Crucifixion," which shows a whole people in disarray, the layout of the painting is akin to that of a page in the Talmud, where a central text is surrounded by commentaries.

A version of the same scene by Bedřich Fritta (born 1909) takes us one step closer to the new archetype of destruction by allowing no room at all for consolation (Figure 14). Here is a virtually endless procession on the highway. Telegraph wires are the only accompanying presence. This mass of humanity has apparently walked all the way, despite the existence of trains, pushing and carrying its meager belongings. No single face stands out from the crowd. The only distinguishing marks are

12. Marcel Janco, sketch of the Bucharest pogrom, 1940.

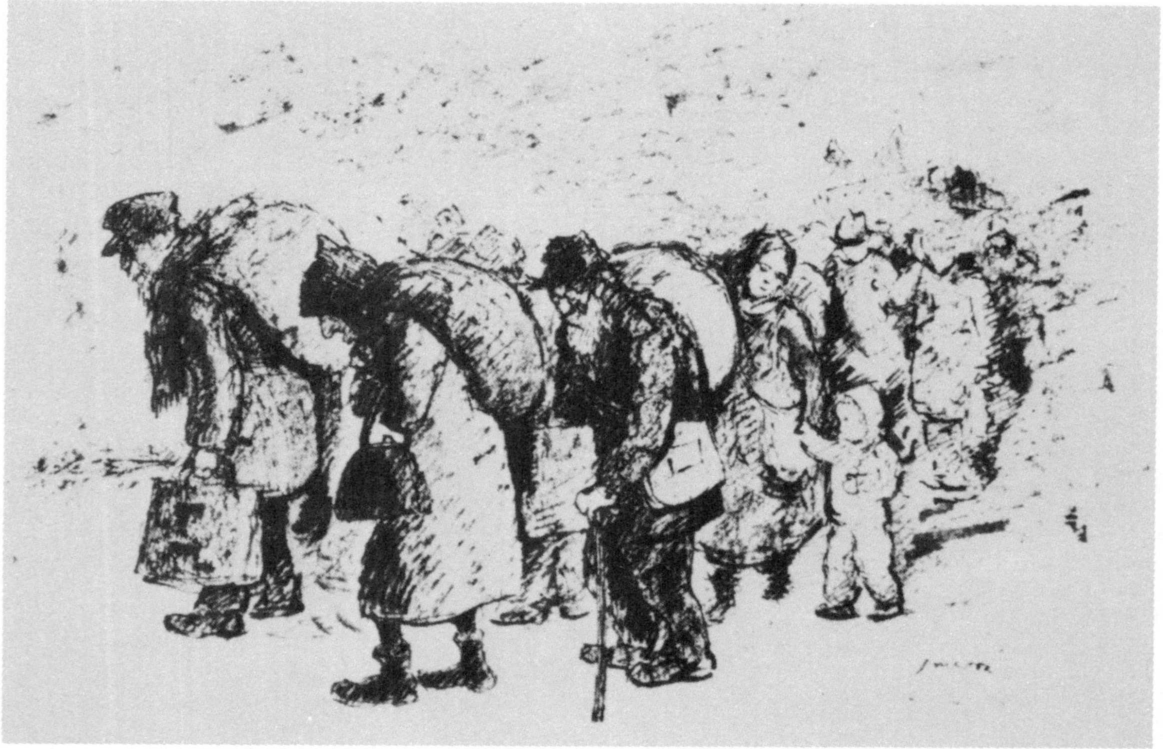

13. Charlotte Buřesova, "Deportation: The Last Road," Theresienstadt, c. 1944; pencil and ink on paper, 30 × 44 cm.

14. Bedřich Fritta [Fritz Taussig], "Incoming Transport II," Teresienstadt, undated.

the numbers on their backs, 396 on the back of one (on the extreme left), 39 on the back of another (center). They do not know their fate, but the numbers disclose the anonymous death that surely awaits them.

In this, as in other of Fritta's drawings from Theresienstadt, there are just enough recognizable features to allow Jews and other insiders an archetypal or "normal" reading of the depicted horror, while a new Holocaust metaphor is created by the unprecedented thoroughness of design. In this case, the telegraph wires and the numbers are the recognizable signs of a modern apocalypse for the remaning Jewish and non-Jewish world. Such things as a faceless dark mass of humans whose only distinguishable features are the numbers on their backs have never been seen before. At the point of unassimilable horror, the new archetype is born.

As exile gave way to genocide, so the ancient models of individual suffering and self-sacrifice were pushed to new limits during the Holocaust. Job, the Bible's archetypal loner and victim of unwarranted suffering, was a natural choice for the Jews of Warsaw in the early months of the ghetto (see Figure 4). Many artists were willing to compete for the best illustration of Job to grace the cover of Yitzhak Katzenelson's biblical drama. But hardly anyone still believed in God's desperate self-defense from out of the whirlwind.

There were some archetypes that could be wrenched free of their theological context without losing much of their power. The *ḥurban* remained a vivid image of destruction even for those, like Ansky and Levin in World War I, who did not pray for the Temple to be rebuilt. Job could be Job without his happy end. But other archetypes were wholly predicated on a presence, or at least a promise: there could be no Covenant without a God, no Exodus without a Promised Land, no Akedah without an act of faith. And so the penultimate breaking point came when all the supporting structures collapsed and nothing more than the skeleton remained: *Lekh-lekho* according to Shayevitsh; the kaddish according to Katzenelson; the Akedah according to Jürgen Stroop.

On the face of it, the photo shown in Figure 15, taken by a German army photographer in the last days of the Warsaw ghetto, admits no analogies. Everything about it is disturbing. Armed soldiers are rounding up ordinary citizens. The victims, with their hands raised awkwardly in surrender, face every which way: the soldiers, the camera, the side, but not each other. Everyone is carrying something, as if, at this late date, there were still somewhere to go. And then the eye fixes on the child, so neatly dressed, so bewildered. Whose child is he? It doesn't matter, because they will all eventually perish. Yet the child alone is surely all of us, the adult made child by the Holocaust that no one can

15. The final liquidation of the Warsaw ghetto, April–May 1943. Photograph from the report of Jürgen Stroop, S.S. officer and police general.

explain to us. And the child is alone, too, because no one seems to be coming after him—or is even concerned that he keep his hands up; he couldn't do anything with his hands down, anyway. He seems, then, to be at once imitating the adults and volunteering himself as one. So the Isaac motif is here, but now Isaac goes alone to Moriah.

The power of this photograph cannot be explained simply by the fact that it is a photograph—that is, by invoking the argument that nothing less than the documentary truth can be trusted after the Holocaust. For one thing, there is a man alive today in New Jersey who claims to have been that child, which means that to believe in this picture now requires a certain act of faith. But more than that, its meaning must be supplied by the viewer. Note again the relative absence of motion, except for the turning heads. Note also that the soldiers are not particularly malignant, that the menace is from our reading of the victims' gestures and from our knowledge of the final outcome. Because the photo leaves most of the brutality to the viewer's imagination, it has become the supreme icon of the catastrophe for such varied personalities as filmmaker Ingmar Bergman and statesman Menachem Begin and for everyone else in between. Though the photograph can be "understood" without recourse to any preexisting archetype, it is still possible, for those schooled in the exercise of archetypal thinking, to discern the skeletal remains of an Akedah. Strip away this layer, and you are left with a self-contained icon of an apocalyptic Event. Superimpose the archetype of Isaac, and the nameless boy of Warsaw takes his place on the farthest end of the line of Jewish martyrs.

Sometimes the confluence of myth and reality was so strong in the Holocaust that it is now almost impossible to separate them. Once we identify Kalmanovitsh as a prophet, and the ghetto fighters as latter-day Maccabees melting down sacred lead for bullets, or listen to Hirsh Glik's love ballad "Silence and a Starry Night," written in honor of two members of the F.P.O., it is difficult to think of these people as mere mortals. One may unravel the myth-making process to see exactly how it took shape, but one's own need of such myths is too great to leave it at that. For in the end, it is only the myth that mediates the polarities of real heroism and utter degradation. The more tragic the event, the more it cries out to be reconciled. Such was the death of Itsik Vittenberg, the first commander of the F.P.O. Thanks to the research of Yitzhak Arad, we now know what the other members of the F.P.O could not have known—that Vittenberg belonged to a Communist cell on the Aryan side of Vilna and that the Gestapo got wind of his whereabouts when someone from the cell broke under interrogation.[67] Fearing a similar fate, Vittenberg took cyanide in the Gestapo cellars and thus never betrayed the existence of the F.P.O. In contrast to this scenario, Sutzkever's memoirs of the Vilna ghetto and Kovner's testimony at the Eichmann trial[68] both recount that Vittenberg was found in the Gestapo cellars the morning after he gave himself up; his eyes had been gouged out and his arms broken and bound behind him, the implication being that he had remained silent under brutal torture.

Vittenberg was clearly a man of complex motives, but in the end what the members of the F.P.O. chose to remember was his act of voluntary sacrifice: he willingly gave himself up in order to save the ghetto from imminent destruction. And so, without changing a single detail of their version of the story, German-born artist Naftali Bezem (born 1924) drew a sketch that raised this death to mythic proportions (Figure 16). It was an Akedah in the later sense of the word: a voluntary sacrifice of one, seen as the atonement for the many. The Crucifixion had undergone a similar change of meaning: Jesus' death, which was a theological martyrdom, a divine act of bearing witness to the greater glory of God, was later claimed by the Gospels to have been a death for the sake of others. Both versions of Jesus' death were based on the notion of God-as-Father and God-as-Son. The Akedah, in contrast, was always the act of a human father and son, whether God intervened in the last instant or not. Thus, among secular eastern European Jews, with their overwhelming emphasis on collective responsibility, the Akedah as symbol had lost none of its force. It was this bond to a human community—the decision of some individuals to die for the sake of others—that made the Akedah, and not the Crucifixion, the ultimate reference point of Jewish resistance.

In the same way that the Christian doctrine of the suffering Christ has affected the traditional Jewish notions of martyrdom (as we have seen in the work of Lilien and Chagall), the secular mythology of modern political movements has made its mark on notions of herosim. Forty years after Kishinev, the movement for self-defense culminated in the last symbolic stand of the Warsaw ghetto fighters, and four years after that, plans were begun for immortalizing the battle. Whatever Mordecai Anielewicz looked like in real life, he couldn't have remotely resembled the heroic man who dominates the 1948 monument created by Nathan Rapoport (born 1911): with Molotov cocktail in hand, head high, chest bare, muscles bulging, right arm bandaged, coat thrown open, and trousers ripped, he is a latter-day "Liberty Leading the People" (see Figure 17). In fact, the young woman behind him, with one breast bare, holding a baby in her left hand, is particularly suggestive of Delacroix's Liberty, her perfect breast exposed, the Tricolore in one hand, a rifle in the other, leading the French people to victory over ruins and corpses.

But there is another side to the monument (Figure 18), dedicated not

16. Naftali Bezem, "Itsik Vittenberg," Israel, 1952; red charcoal on paper.

17. Nathan Rapoport, Warsaw Ghetto Monument, 1947–48; bronze. The inscription on the monument, in Hebrew, Yiddish, and Polish, reads: "The Jewish People—Its Fighters and Martyrs."

18. Nathan Rapoport, eastern wall of the Warsaw Ghetto Monument; stone bas-relief.

to the fighters but to the martyrs (by which is meant those who went to their deaths unprotesting). And here, unexpectedly, we come back to Hirszenberg's "Exile." Still facing the left, the composition of the group is much the same as before, except that the Jew with the wander staff is now in the lead and the Jew with the Torah has his eyes on the heavens. This would suggest a more hopeful destination than in Hirszenberg, if it were not for the more visible signs of grief: one woman tears her hair in anguish and another buries her head in her hands. A more than surface resemblance to the famous bas-relief on the Arch of Titus—Roman soldiers weighted down under booty stolen from the Temple—draws an additional link between the archetype of exile and its realization in history.

The total separation of the heroism from the martyrdom and the fact that the martyrs are relegated to the sidelines reveals what is actually going on here. Standing alone, the heroism is so blatantly derivative that it undermines its own pretense. "We too have heroes!" is what it is really saying. Meanwhile the martyrs' tableau, equally stylized, suggests that exile is a permanent and predictable feature of Jewish life which no amount of heroism can ever alter. Literally and figuratively, the tableau of exile represents the dark side of history. Something also happens to the monument once it is viewed in its context, in the middle of Warsaw. In a country whose central paradigm is the aborted uprising, such a monument becomes part of the larger mythology; or, looking ahead to the Stalinist era, it means that Mordecai Anielewicz will be seen as a Jewish Stakhanovite, a hero of Socialist labor. When mourning goes public in a public idiom, the price for accessibility can be very high indeed.

The impulse to curry favor with the non-Jewish and noncommitted world can be as strong in the literature of catastrophe as it is in bronze monuments. It is also easier to express, for all that is required is some careful editing. The original Yiddish version of Elie Wiesel's *Night* is not only four times longer and less unified than its French (and later English) version, but has a different message.[69] Themes of madness and existential despair are not as highlighted in the Yiddish narrative, which ends with the *engagé* writer's appeal to fight the Germans and anti-Semites who would consign the Holocaust to oblivion. Since no one in the literary establishment of the 1950s was ready to be preached to by a Holocaust survivor, existentialist doubt became the better part of valor. Nor would the almost-survivor fare any better. Thus, while the Yiddish readers of I. B. Singer's *The Family Moskat* were treated to a final sermon on redemption, the messianic theme was systematically excluded from the English version of the novel, which ended instead with Hertz Yanover's flip nihilism.[70] Compare the parting words of the

Yiddish edition—"Go forth and fear not. On your side is the last victory. To you will come the Messiah"—with Hertz Yanover's modernist credo delivered eleven pages earlier: "Death is the Messiah. That's the real truth." Where once the theme of catastrophe was used by modern Jewish writers to revile or to console their fellow sufferers, the same cohort of writers facing a potentially infinite audience were willing to use catastrophe for cultural rapprochement.

By expunging the "parochial" message of hope and continuity, Wiesel and Singer (who collaborated in these revisions) acknowledge a break deeper by far than existential despair, this break being the end of the dialogue between eastern European Jewish writers and their Jewish audience. Since most of that audience can no longer read what these writers have reserved for its eyes alone, it is left with the "nonparochial" message instead, and that is a message of complete despair.

In many ways this form of self-censorship is the opposite of the kind practiced by Sutzkever and Greenberg. Whereas these two writers responded to the Holocaust by excluding all glorified mention of Jesus, downplaying their earlier anger against the passivity of the Jewish people in order to project a collective image of holiness, Wiesel and Singer edited out the shared expressions of faith in order to highlight the terrifying isolation of the postwar individual. It is not coincidental that Sutzkever's metaphysics of the dead and Greenberg's defiant act of mourning have remained a closed book while the images of apocalypse—Warsaw, Dresden, Hiroshima—have attracted world attention.

THE two sides of Rapoport's Warsaw Ghetto Monument are analogous to the two sides of postwar writers like Singer and Wiesel who have allowed the tyranny of language and the politics of publishing to separate and dichotomize the knowledge of apocalypse and the statement of group survival. There are, however, signs of a possible synthesis between the two in contemporary Jewish art. Samuel Bak and Yosl Bergner, the artists with whom we conclude this discussion, have strong ties to the eastern Europe of their childhood, were profoundly affected by the Holocaust, and sought old and new artistic forms to create a new archetype of destruction. The sources of their art can be found in the work of Heironymus Bosch, famous for his terrifying representations of the powers of evil, and in surrealism—both of which gave shape to the deepest fears of the unconscious. Allegories of hell and private nightmares are the stuff that catastrophes are made of.

Both artists abandon human figures in their most direct responses to the Holocaust, and the implications of this aniconic art are worth considering. For one thing, it suggests that the Holocaust itself is without a human likeness. Though in the past, enormous evil could be dealt with figuratively, these artists seem to be arguing that the new order of atrocity—the transformation of humans into things, the utter anonymity of their death, the total denial of choice—precludes a recognizable human landscape. We are dealing, finally, with an event qualitatively different from any other, and in order to comprehend evil of such metaphysical scope, it is necessary to employ the tools of metaphysical analysis: platonic forms, spiritual geometry.

The artist, then, functions as philosopher-theologian.

Samuel Bak (born 1933) had his first exhibit at the age of nine in the Vilna ghetto. His sculpture of Moses, completed two weeks before the liquidation of the ghetto, so impressed Sutzkever that both the child prodigy and his artwork were made part of Sutzkever's epic of underground survival, *Geheymshtot.* After the war, the D.P. camps, and emigration to Israel, Bak traveled west, to Paris and Rome, where he thought he would settle. Then, in 1965–66, Bak rejected his newly acquired abstract style and returned to live in Israel. All this time he never painted his experiences of the Holocaust. But gradually, through still lifes and allegorical symbols, he began to express what it meant to be a survivor: "the absurdity of looking for any kind of moral logic in the horrific events taking place around me," and the greatest absurdity of all, "the fact of my survival."[71]

In 1975 the memories of Vilna finally began to coalesce in Bak's *Landscapes of Jewish History,* which disassembled and reassembled the actual form of the ghetto, the yellow star, and the tablets of the Decalogue. "Proposal for a Monument" (Figure 19) shows the tablets not as they were given to Moses but as they later appeared to Ansky on his mission to Galicia: with only a few words still intact. Bak, who arrived at this conception quite independently, provides his own commentary: "The desecration of the laws has created a mass grave, causing the inscriptions to be obliterated and turning the Tablets into gravestones. Throughout their long history of violation and abuse, the Tablets have maintained their eternal power to re-emerge as a guide for those who choose to accept their covenant. Their power cannot be totally annihilated: out of their fragments new Tablets are being created."[72] These tablets, Bak proposes, could also form a new kind of monument: with metal bars holding the pieces together; with the middle section chipped away, leaving the outline of a six-pointed star; with bullet holes as a sign of the most recent onslaught. Of the original inscription, all that remains is I AM THE LORD, the number 6 (for the six million Jews murdered under the sign of the violated sixth commandment), half a 9 (THOU SHALT NOT BEAR FALSE WITNESS), and 10 (THOU SHALT NOT COVET THY NEIGHBOR'S HOUSE). The spectator is thus invited to create

19. Samuel Bak, "Proposal for a Monument," 1977; oil on canvas, 80×80 cm.

his own exegesis on the meaning of these commandments after the Holocaust and on the absence of the others. Then, for a final statement, Bak would place the monument on Mount Sinai.

Thirty years after the war, the landscapes of Jewish history suddenly appear in the mind of the survivor; they are devoid of human figures but more crowded with meaning for that very reason. Jewish Vilna—that is to say, its ghetto—emerges as the quintessential "city of Jews" (Figure 20), a stone city united under God, a Kehillah Kedoshah. Wrenched together with another landscape, that of Sinai, Vilna literally stands under the sign of the covenant; it "upholds" the tablets. Yet the desecration of the landscape is unmistakable. One set of tablets is smashed and barely standing; another set is blank, with bullet holes instead of commandments, resembling nothing so much as tombstones. The city itself is barely visible and seems to be made up entirely of façades. Only the commandments are not façades. Can Jews actually live in such a precarious and claustrophobic space? The only sign of life is a smoking chimney (factory smokestack? crematorium?). Indeed, the city may very well be *sinking* under the weight of God's commandments, dying under the sign of its chosenness.

And so Bak's midrash on Jewish history reads something like this: To live as Jews means to uphold the covenant even as it is desecrated, to exist both in the shadow of eternity and on the brink of destruction. There is no return to the Decalogue except via Vilna and Ponar. The tablets have been broken—in order that they may be pieced together again. One cannot rebuild other than on ruins. The sacred symbols, though defiled, are the only ones left.

Bak's neoclassicism is exactly analogous to Sutzkever's. The memory of Vilna that weighs so heavily on both of them is first of all a mandate to explore and reexamine the full thrust of the classical traditions. As Vilna is the city of Jews, so its memorial must amalgamate earlier Jewish traditions. Yet the classical impulse can never be fully realized after the Great Destruction. It can be no more than *neo*classical, a self-conscious attempt at reimposing a semblance of order on the shattered past without an accompanying reversion to orthodox faith, to a world of internal harmony. Instead, the neoclassical statement is an exercise in arrested time, a green aquarium or set of crumbling tablets which replace the process of destruction, the movement of constant terror, the permanent apocalypse, with a single complex metaphor, a reassembled myth of origins: in the beginning was the Destruction, and now Jews proceed anew in a diminished world.

Just how diminished that world might be was left for Yosl Bergner to portray. Bergner (born 1920), the son of Yiddish poet Melech Ravitch, began as a representational artist. With memories of Warsaw still fresh

20. Samuel Bak, "City of Jews," 1978; charcoal on paper.

in his mind, the twenty-one-year-old artist painted his own version of Job crouching on the bare ground, and then a portrait entitled "Father and Sons" in which three emaciated figures are naked against a devastated urban landscape. The father wears only a fringed undergarment (a tallith katan) and covers his genitals with his hands.[73] In the early 1960s Bergner's style underwent a temporary shift to surrealism. Just as Marcel Janco had to abandon surrealism to confront the living nightmare of Bucharest 1940, Bergner had to pass through the nightmare school of painting (including illustrations of Kafka stories) to arrive at his own style, tempered by a flair for the grotesque, that would intimate the loss of life and logic brought about by the Holocaust.

"Pole Sitters" (Figure 21) is Bergner's revision of Golgotha/Calvary. Everything is in place from the original event—the loin cloth around Jesus, the nails, the threatening sky—except that vegetable graters have replaced the human figures. It is Bergner's special talent, as his admirers have often noted, that his objects bend, stretch, and move almost like human beings.[74]

Graters nailed to poles offer little hope for salvation. By the same token, an endless procession of tables, chairs, cupboards, mirrors, and samovars does not seem headed for the Promised Land. Bergner's "Destination X" (Figure 22) is the ultimate statement on the theme of exile. Objects taken from plundered Jewish homes have returned to the source of the people's beginnings—to the biblical wilderness. But with no one to lead them and no one to claim them, the journey can never end. Because of the desert, the portentous sky, the orderly, stoic quality of their march, the fate of the millions of homeless objects cannot be dismissed as merely absurd.

To recall the earlier representations of catastrophe with which Bergner was no doubt familiar is to mark the distance traveled in the intervening years. Now one looks back almost with longing to the bearded Russian Jews hanging from the individual crosses. Human figures, even as they hang and lie in Chagall's Crucifixion series, are preferable to none at all. In Chagall's burning shtetl, all the chairs are empty and overturned; King David is relegated to a rooftop. Now to see an orderly procession of the same empty chairs is somehow far more terrifying. It suggests that the killing has been anything but random and localized. Greater yet is the distance traveled from Hirszenberg's "Exile." Once there was a community of exiled Jews so united under God that it salvaged the Torah and brought only a kettle along for the road. Sixty-five years later, after the Destruction, only the kettles remain.

Through the juxtaposition of objects from disparate realms, a central technique of modern art, the Jewish artist has rediscovered the midra-

21. Yosl Bergner, "Pole Sitters," 1971; oil on canvas, 250 × 155 cm.

22. Yosl Bergner, "Destination X," 1969; oil on canvas, 100 × 100 cm.

shic procedure. One approach, that of Lilien and Chagall, has been to create a perfect blend of symbols and materials. In Bak and more fully in Bergner, the shock of disharmony is the key to the message. By denying the archetypes of crucifixion and exile to their human actors and by making the objects human, Bergner has created a new archetype of catastrophe. The salvation and redemption of the graters, kettles, and chairs, even if it were to happen, has bearing on the course of human events only if we humans have also been turned into objects.

BAK'S and Bergner's responses to catastrophe, as that of all the other eastern European Jewish writers and artists discussed in this book, could not have come about without the radical break that occurred in the modern period. The waves of violence and destruction were themselves a catalyst for many of the changes that occurred—a mad scramble for new homes, a loss of faith in the sustaining paradigm of guilt, retribution, and redemption; a need for new revelation. Impelled by ever-greater disasters to rebel more openly with tradition, the writers and artists who were still so close to the sources of that tradition arrived at a new understanding of the ancient archetypes. The reappropriation of Jesus was a part, perhaps even a necessary part, of the rebellion, but one that lost its usefulness once it became clear that the world's idea of redemption was redeeming the world of its Jews. The Holocaust, too, was only a part of this larger radical break.

Catastrophe, in fact, has always been a part of the process of rethinking the past. Like the rabbis of old who worked with any and all available materials—cultic, prophetic, apocalyptic, gnostic, mystic, platonic—so long as they could bridge the abyss left in the wake of the Great Catastrophe, the writers and artists of the nineteenth and twentieth centuries mixed symbol systems, juxtaposed sacred and profane, borrowed ferociously in order to face their ever-greater losses. Just as the Temple destructions were consciously fashioned into archetypes by the exiles in Babylonia and by the Tanaim and Amoraim, so the new destruction, the Holocaust, was lifted from the straight line of allusions back to the old archetypes and inaugurated into its own archetypal nature.

Thus, the great *imitatio Dei* of the modern period has been not the Jews' endless capacity to suffer, to be Christ figures for the world, or even their willingness to die for the sanctification of the Name. It has been their ability, in the midst and in the wake of the apocalypse, to know the apocalypse, express it, mourn it, and transcend it; for if catastrophe is the presumption of man acting as destroyer, then the fashioning of catastrophe into a new set of tablets is the primal act of creation carried out in the image of God.

Notes

Primary Sources Cited

Index

Notes

In citations from the Talmud throughout text and notes, "B." denotes the Babylonian recension and "P." the Palestinian.

1. *Ruined Cities of the Mind*

1. George Steiner, "A Kind of Survivor," in *Language and Silence: Essays, 1958–1966* (London: Faber and Faber, 1967), p. 167.

2. Hannah Arendt, *Between Past and Future* (New York: Viking, 1961), p. 28. Cited in Frank Kermode, *The Sense of an Ending: Studies in the Theory of Fiction* (New York: Oxford University Press, 1968), p. 56.

3. Nathan Wachtel, *Vision of the Vanquished: The Spanish Conquest of Peru through Indian Eyes, 1530–1570*, trans. Ben and Siân Reynolds (Hassocks, Sussex: Harvester, 1977), p. 208.

4. Paul Fussell, *The Great War and Modern Memory* (New York: Oxford University Press, 1975), p. 247.

5. Arnold J. Band, "A History of Modern Hebrew Fiction," *Prooftexts* 1, no. 1 (1981), 117.

6. Jonas Gurland, *Lekorot hagzeirot ʻal Yisrael* [To the History of Jewish Persecution], 7 vols. (1887–1892; rpt. Jerusalem: Kedem, 1972).

7. Simon Bernfeld, ed., *Sefer hadema'ot* [The Book of Tears], vol. 1 (Berlin: Eshkol, 1923), pp. 6–13.

8. Israel Halpern, ed., *Sefer hagevurah: antologia historit-sifrutit* [The Book of Valor: A literary-historical anthology], 3rd ed., 3 vols. (1941–1950; rpt. Tel Aviv: Am Oved, 1977).

9. Dror, *Payn un gvure in dem yidishn over in likht fun der kegnvart* [Suffering and Heroism in the Jewish Past in the Light of the Present], 3rd ed. (Munich: Dror, 1947).

10. Joseph Kermish, ed., *'Itonut-hamaḥteret hayehudit beVarshah* [The

Jewish Underground Press in Warsaw], vol. 1 (Jerusalem: Yad Vashem, 1979), pp. 44–45.

11. Abba Kovner, *Scrolls of Fire: A Nation Fighting for Its Life*, trans. Shirley Kaufman and Dan Laor, bilingual ed. (Jerusalem: Keter, 1981).

2. *The Liturgy of Destruction*

1. Gershon Levin, *In velt krig* [In the World War] (Warsaw, 1923), p. 76.

2. S. Ansky (Shloyme-Zanvl Rapoport), *Khurbm Galitsye* [The Destruction of Galicia: The Jewish Catastrophe of Poland, Galicia, and Bukovina] (from a diary, 1914–1917), *Gezamlte verk*, vol. 6, bk. 4 (Vilna, Warsaw, and New York, 1921), pp. 66–71.

3. Ibid., pp. 134–135.

4. Michael Fishbane, *Biblical Interpretation in Ancient Israel*, 2 vols. (Oxford: Clarendon Press, forthcoming).

5. Thomas F. Merrill, "Sacred Parody and the Grammar of Devotion," *Criticism* 23 (1981), 195–210.

6. Sidra DeKoven Ezrahi, *By Words Alone: The Holocaust in Literature* (Chicago: University of Chicago Press, 1980), p. 105.

7. Alvin H. Rosenfeld, *A Double Dying: Reflections on Holocaust Literature* (Bloomington: Indiana University Press, 1980), p. 31.

8. Mircea Eliade, *The Myth of the Eternal Return, or Cosmos and History*, trans. Willard R. Trask (Princeton: Princeton University Press, 1954), pp. 102–112.

9. Delbert R. Hillers, *Treaty-Curses and the Old Testament Prophets* (Rome: Pontifical Biblical Institute, 1964), p. 6.

10. Gerhard von Rad, *Old Testament Theology*, trans. D. M. G. Stalker (New York: Harper & Row, 1962), pp. 337–354.

11. Michael Fishbane, *Text and Texture: Close Readings of Selected Biblical Texts* (New York: Schocken, 1979), pp. 111–120.

12. Stephen P. Geller, "Introduction to Apocalyptic Literature" lecture notes, Jewish Theological Seminary of America, New York, Spring 1976.

13. Paul D. Hanson, *The Dawn of Apocalypse* (Philadelphia: Fortress, 1975), p. 21.

14. Ithamar Gruenwald, *Apocalyptic and Merkavah Mysticism* (Leiden: E. J. Brill, 1980), p. 27.

15. This was first suggested in Nahum N. Glatzer, *Untersuchungen zur Geschichtslehre der Tannaiten* (Berlin: Schocken, 1933). Quoted in Shaye J. D. Cohen, "Is History Only for Apikorsim?" *Ikka d'amrei: A Student Journal of the Jewish Theological Seminary of America* 3, no. 2 (1981), 54–55.

16. Yosef Hayim Yerushalmi, *Zakhor: Jewish History and Jewish Memory* (Seattle and Philadelphia: University of Washington Press and Jewish Publication Society of America, 1982), p. 12.

17. Brevard S. Childs, "The Canonical Shape of the Prophetic Literature," *Interpretation* 32 (1978), 46–55.

18. Ismar Elbogen, *Hatefilah beYisrael behitpatḥutah hahistorit* [Jewish Liturgy in Its Historical Development], trans. Yehoshua Amir, ed. Joseph Heinemann (Tel Aviv: Dvir, 1972), pp. 118–120.

19. Ibid., p. 132.

20. Yerushalmi, *Zakhor*, pp. 41–42.

21. Elbogen, *Hatefilah beYisrael*, p. 105.

22. Ben-Zion Lurie, ed., *Megillat Ta'anit* (Jerusalem: Mosad Bialik, 1964). Solomon Zeitlin, *Megillat Taanit as a Source for Jewish Chronology and History in the Hellenistic and Roman Periods* (Philadelphia, 1922).

23. Moses David Herr, "Persecutions and Martyrdom in Hadrian's Day," *Scripta Heirosolymitana* 23 (1972), 121. Saul Lieberman, "The Persecutions of the Jewish Religion" (in Hebrew), in *Salo Wittmayer Baron Jubilee Volume*, vol. 3: *Hebrew Section* (Jerusalem: American Academy for Jewish Research, 1974), pp. 214–215.

24. Ignatius, Bishop of Antioch, "To the Romans," in Cyril C. Richardson, ed., *Early Christian Fathers*, Library of Christian Classics, vol. 1 (Philadelphia: Westminster, 1953), pp. 102–106.

25. "The Martyrdom of Saint Polycarp," in *Early Christian Fathers*, pp. 149–158.

26. P. Sota V:7:20c, as quoted in Saul Lieberman, "The Martyrs of Caesarea," *Annuaire de l'Institut de philologie et d'histoire orientales et slaves* 7 (1939–1944), 420.

27. Lieberman, "The Martyrs of Caesarea," p. 427.

28. E[phraim] E. Urbach, *The Sages—Their Concepts and Beliefs*, trans. Israel Abrahams (Jerusalem: Magnes Press, 1975), pp. 442–448.

29. Shaye J. D. Cohen, "The Destruction: From Scripture to Midrash," *Prooftexts* 2, no. 1 (1982), 27–28. Joseph Heinemann, *Aggadot vetoldotehen* [Aggadah and Its Development: Studies in the Evolution of Traditions] (Jerusalem: Keter, 1974), pp. 131–141.

30. Herr, "Persecutions and Martyrdom," pp. 123–125.

31. Ithamar Gruenwald, "Kiddush Hashem: On the Explication of the Term" (in Hebrew), *Molad*, n.s. vol. 1, no. 4 (February–March 1968), 476–484; Herr, "Persecutions and Martyrdom," pp. 103–106; Avraham Holtz, "Kiddush and Hillul Hashem," *Judaism* 10, no. 4 (1961), 360–367; S. Safrai, "Kiddush Hashem in the Teachings of the Tannaim" (in Hebrew), *Zion* 44 (1979), 28–42.

32. *Megillath Ta'anith Bathra*, in Lurie, *Megillat Ta'anit*, pp. 200–201.

33. Gruenwald, "Kiddush Hashem."

34. Tosefta Shabbat 15:17, as quoted in Herr, "Persecutions and Martyrdom" p. 121.

35. *The Tractate "Mourning,"* trans. and ed. Dov Zlotnick (New Haven: Yale University Press, 1966).

36. Moses David Herr, "The Sages' Concept of History" (in Hebrew), in *Proceedings of the Seventh World Congress of Jewish Studies*, vol. 3 (Jerusalem: World Congress of Jewish Studies, 1981), pp. 129–138.

37. Joseph Heinemann, "The Proem in the Aggadic Midrashim: A Form-Critical Study," *Scripta Hierosolymitana* 22 (1971), 109–110.

38. Midrash Rabbah, *Lamentations,* trans. A. Cohen (London: Soncino Press, 1939).

39. Morton Cogan, *Imperialism and Religion: Assyria, Judah and Israel in the Eighth and Seventh Centuries B.C.E.* (Missoula: Society of Biblical Literature and Scholars Press, 1974), pp. 9–21. My thanks to Edward L. Greenstein for this reference.

40. Isaak Heinemann, *Darkhei ha'aggadah* [The Methods of the Aggadah], 2nd rev. ed. (Jerusalem: Magnes Press, 1954), p. 84.

41. Gerson D. Cohen, "Messianic Postures of Ashkenazim and Sephardim (prior to Sabbethai Zevi)," Leo Baeck Memorial Lecture no. 9 (New York, 1967), pp. 104–105.

42. Louis Finkelstein, "The Ten Martyrs," in *Essays and Studies in Memory of Linda R. Miller* (New York: Jewish Theological Seminary of America, 1938), pp. 29–55; Herr, "Persecutions and Martyrdom"; Lieberman, "Persecutions of the Jewish Religion"; Safrai, "Kiddush Hashem."

43. G. W. Bowersock, "A Roman Perspective on the Bar Kochba War," in William Scott Green, ed., *Approaches to Ancient Judaism,* vol. 2, Brown Judaic Studies 9 (Chico, Calif.: Scholars Press, 1980), pp. 131–141; and Peter Schäfer, "Rabbi Aqiva and Bar Kokhba," ibid., pp. 113–130.

44. Ivan G. Marcus, "From Politics to Martyrdom: Shifting Paradigms in the Hebrew Narratives of the 1096 Crusade Riots," *Prooftexts* 2, no. 1 (1982), 40–52; Leon Wieseltier, "Some Reflections on the Interpretation of Catastrophe in Medieval Jewish Culture," paper read at the eleventh annual conference of the Association for Jewish Studies, Boston, 17 December 1979.

45. Isaac Klein, *A Guide to Jewish Religious Practice* (New York: Jewish Theological Seminary of America, 1978), p. 247.

46. J. B. Soloveitchik. Attributed to a Tisha b'Av *shiur.*

47. Ernst Daniel Goldschmidt, ed., *Seder hakinot letish'ah b'Av* [The Kinot for Tisha b'Av According to the Polish Rite and the Ashkenazi Communities of Erets Yisrael] (Jerusalem: Mosad Harav Kook, 1968).

48. Judah Halevi, "Tsiyon halo' tish'ali" [O Zion, Will You Not Ask], in T. Carmi, ed. and trans., *The Penguin Book of Hebrew Verse* (New York: Viking, 1981), and in Abraham Rosenfeld, ed. and trans., *The Authorised Kinot for the Ninth of Av* (1970; rpt. New York: Judaica Press, 1979).

49. Moses Zucker, "The Responses to the Karaite Movement of the Mourners of Zion in Rabbinic Literature" (in Hebrew), in *Sefer hayovel lerabi Hanoch Albeck* (Jerusalem: Mosad Harav Kook, 1963), pp. 378–401. See also H. H. Ben-Sasson, ed., *A History of the Jewish People* (Cambridge: Harvard University Press, 1976), pp. 448–452.

50. Dov Sadan, "Shall I Weep in the Fifth Month" (in Hebrew), in *Orḥot ushvilim* [Ways and Paths], vol. 2 (Tel Aviv: Am Oved, 1978), p. 20. Written for Tisha b'Av, 1936.

51. David Flusser, "Kiddush Hashem During Second Temple Times and the Beginning of Christianity" (in Hebrew), in *Milḥemet kodesh umartirologia betoldot Yisrael uvetoldot he'amim* [Holy War and Martyrology] (Jerusalem: Historical Society of Israel, 1967), pp. 61–71.

52. "The Martyrdom of Saint Polycarp," p. 156.

53. Joseph Dan, *Hasippur ha'ivri biyemei habenayim* [The Hebrew Story in the Middle Ages] (Jerusalem: Keter, 1974), pp. 186–187. Moses David Herr, "Ten Martyrs," in *The Encyclopedia Judaica* (Jerusalem: Keter, 1971).

54. "Eileh ezkerah" [These I Shall Remember], in Adolph Jellinek, ed., *Bet ha-Midrasch,* 3rd ed., vol. 2 (Jerusalem: Wahrmann, 1967), pp. 64–72. An English translation by David Stern appears in *Fiction* 7, nos. 1–2 (1983), 75–98.

55. H. J. Zimmels, "The Historical Background of the Midrash Eleh Ezkerah," in *Semitic Studies in Memory of Immanuel Low* (Budapest, 1947), pp. 334–338. I owe this reference to Raymond Scheindlin.

56. Cohen, "Messianic Postures," pp. 35–38.

57. Gerson D. Cohen, "Hebrew Crusade Chronicles and the Ashkenazi Tradition," lecture at the Jewish Theological Seminary of America, New York, 23 October 1979.

58. Yerushalmi, *Zakhor,* pp. 41–42.

59. Solomon bar Simson, "Crusade Chronicle," in Shlomo Eidelberg, trans., *The Jews and the Crusades: The Hebrew Chronicles of the First and Second Crusades* (Madison: University of Wisconsin Press, 1977), p. 29.

60. Cohen, "Messianic Postures," pp. 104–105.

61. A. R. Malachi, "The Chronicles of the Khmelnitsky Massacres" (in Hebrew), *American Hebrew Yearbook* 10–11 (1949), 427.

62. Israel Kaplan, ed., *Dos folksmoyl in Natsi-klem* [Folk Speech under Nazi Domination: Sayings of the Ghettos and Camps], 2nd rev. ed. (Israel: Ghetto Fighters' House, 1982), p. 116.

63. James Kugel, "Two Introductions to Midrash," *Prooftexts* 3, no. 2 (1983), 131–155.

64. Marcus, "From Politics to Martyrdom."

65. Shalom Spiegel, *The Last Trial: On the Legends and Lore of the Command to Abraham to Offer Isaac as a Sacrifice: The Akedah,* trans. Judah Goldin (New York: Pantheon, 1967).

66. Eliezer bar Nathan, "Crusade Chronicle," in A. M. Haberman, ed., *Sefer gzeirot Ashkenaz veTsarfat* [The Persecutions in Germany and France, 992–1298] (1945; rpt. Jerusalem: Ophir, 1971), p. 75; and Spiegel, *The Last Trial,* pp. 19–20.

67. Ben-Sasson, *A History of the Jewish People,* pp. 504–510. SHUM is derived from the first letter of each place name in its Hebrew spelling: SHpayer, Vermayza, and Maynts.

68. Marcus, "From Politics to Martyrdom."

69. "Av haraḥamim" [May the Merciful Father], in Philip Birnbaum, ed., *Daily Prayer Book* [Ashkenaz] (New York: Hebrew Publishing Co., 1949), pp. 383–384.

70. Ernst Daniel Goldschmidt, ed., *Haggadah shel pesaḥ vetoldoteha* [The Passover Haggadah: Its Sources and History] (Jerusalem: Bialik Institute, 1969), pp. 62–64. According to Goldschmidt, the curses first appear in Maḥzor Vitry (before 1105), but the practice may have originated earlier.

71. Elbogen, *Hatefilah beYisrael,* pp. 111–112.

72. "Avinu malkenu" [Our Father Our King], in Birnbaum, *Daily Prayer Book*, pp. 99–100.

73. Meir of Rothenburg, "Sha'li serufah ve'esh" [O Law, That Has Been Consumed by Fire], in Rosenfeld, *The Authorised Kinot*, pp. 161–162.

74. Isaac bar Shalom, "Ein kamokha ba'ilmim" [There is None Like You among the Dumb], in Haberman, *Sefer gzeirot Ashkenaz*, pp. 113–114; and Jakob J. Petuchowski, *Theology and Poetry: Studies in the Medieval Piyyut* (London: Routledge & Kegan Paul, 1978), pp. 71–83.

75. Barukh ben Yehiel, "Ani hu hakkonen kinah" [I Am He Who Raises a Great Lament], in Simon Bernfeld, ed., *Sefer hadema'ot* [The Book of Tears: A History of the Decrees, Persecutions, and Destructions], vol. 2 (Berlin: Eshkol, 1924), p. 116.

76. Eleazar ben Kallir, "Zekhor Av" [Remember Abraham], in Birnbaum, *Daily Prayer Book*, pp. 697–701.

77. "Eileh ezkerah," in Ernest Daniel Goldschmidt, ed., *Maḥzor leyamim nora'im* [High Holiday Prayer Book], vol. 2 (Jerusalem: Koren, 1970), pp. 568–573.

78. Elbogen, *hatefilah beYisrael*, pp. 287–289; Spiegel, *The Last Trial*, pp. 13–16.

79. *Encyclopedia Judaica* (Jerusalem: Keter, 1971), S. V. "Purims, special"; Yerushalmi, *Zakhor*, 46–48.

80. Gerson D. Cohen, "The Story of the Four Captives," *Proceedings of the American Academy for Jewish Research* 29 (1960–61), 75.

81. "Unetaneh tokef" [Now Let Us Proclaim], in Philip Birnbaum, ed., *High Holiday Prayer Book* (New York: Hebrew Publishing Co., 1951), pp. 361–363; and Carmi, *The Penguin Book of Hebrew Verse*, pp. 207–209.

82. Gotthard Deutsch, "Amnon of Mayence," in *The Jewish Encyclopedia* (New York: Funk and Wagnalls, 1901).

83. Jacob Katz, "Martyrdom in the Middle Ages and in 1648–49" (in Hebrew), in *Sefer hayovel leYitzhak Baer* [The Yitzhak F. Baer Memorial Volume] (Jerusalem: Israel Historical Society, 1960), pp. 324–327.

84. Marcus, "From Politics to Martyrdom," p. 50.

85. Cohen, "Hebrew Crusade Chronicles."

86. Sholem Yankev Abramovitsh (Mendele Mocher Sforim), *Of Bygone Days (Shloyme reb Khayims)*, in Ruth R.Wisse, ed., and Raymond Scheindlin, trans., *A Shtetl and Other Yiddish Novellas* (New York: Behrman House, 1973), p. 334.

87. Israel Halpern, "The Jews of Eastern Europe (from ancient times until the partitions of Poland, 1772–1795)," in Louis Finkelstein, ed., *The Jews: Their History*, 4th ed. (New York: Schocken, 1970), pp. 252–255.

88. Nathan Nata Hannover, *Abyss of Despair* (*Yeven Metzulah*): *The Famous Seventeenth-Century Chronicle Depicting Jewish Life in Russia and Poland during the Chmielnicki Massacres of 1648–1649*, trans. Abraham J. Mesch (New York: Bloch, 1950).

89. Katz, "Martyrdom in the Middle Ages," pp. 330–335.

90. Shabbetai ben Meir Hacohen, "Megillat 'eifah" [The Scroll of Darkness], in Israel Halpern, ed., *Beit Yisrael beFolin* [Polish Jewry from Its Begin-

nings until the Holocaust], vol. 2 (Jerusalem: Youth Dept. of the Zionist Organization, 1953), pp. 252–255.

91. Tanhuma *Yitro* 6, as quoted in Halpern's commentary, ibid.

92. Hillel bar Jacob of Bonn, "Emunei shelumei Yisrael" [The Loyal Ones of Israel], in Haberman, *Sefer gzeirot Ashkenaz,* p. 137.

3. *Broken Tablets and Flying Letters*

1. *Rebbe* is the Yiddish designation for a hasidic leader, one who leads by virtue of charisma or descent from other *rebeim.* Some, but by no means all, were also rabbis—that is, ordained religious leaders or halachic authorities.

2. S. Ansky (Shloyme-Zanvl Rapoport), *Khurbm Galitsye* [The Destruction of Galicia], from a diary, 1914–1917, *Gezamlte verk,* vol. 6, bk. 4 (Vilna, Warsaw, and New York, 1921), pp. 58–63.

3. Dan Ben-Amos and Jerome R. Mintz, eds., *In Praise of the Baal Shem Tov* [*Shivḥei ha-Besht*] (Bloomington: Indiana University Press, 1970), tale 137.

4. Israel Halpern, "R. Levi Yitskhok of Bardichev and the Government Decrees in His Day" (in Hebrew), in *Yehudim veyahadut bemizraḥ-eiropah* [Eastern European Jewry: Historical Studies] (Jerusalem: Magnes Press, 1968), p. 340, n. 3.

5. Ibid., p. 343, n. 14.

6. Michael Stanislawski, *Tsar Nicholas I and the Jews: The Transformation of Jewish Society in Russia 1825–1855* (Philadelphia: Jewish Publication Society of America, 1983), ch. 5.

7. Ibid., ch. 1.

8. Yekhezkl Kotik, *Mayne zikhroynes* [Memoirs], 2 vols. (Berlin, 1922). Cited in Abraham Lewin, *Kantonistn* [Cantonists] (Warsaw, 1934), p. 199.

9. Yekutiel Berman, "Shnot ra'inu ra'ah" [The Years We Saw Evil], *Hamelits* 1 (1861), 251.

10. Stanislawski, *Tsar Nicholas I and the Jews,* epilogue.

11. S. M. Ginzburg and P. S. Marek, eds., *Evreiskie narodniye pesni v Rossii* [Yiddish Folksongs of Russia] (St. Petersburg, 1901), no. 44.

12. Ibid., no. 47.

13. Ibid., no. 50.

14. Ibid., no. 49.

15. Stanislawski, *Tsar Nicholas I and the Jews,* ch. 4.

16. Meir Wiener, *Tsu der geshikhte fun der yidisher literatur in 19tn yorhundert* [Toward a History of Yiddish Literature in the Nineteenth Century], vol. 1 (New York: YIKUF, 1945), pp. 150–192.

17. Isaac Baer Lebensohn, "Toldot ploni almoni hakazavi" [The Story of Evil Mr. X] (1851), in *Yalkut RIBaL* (Warsaw, 1878), pp. 6–19. Cited in Wiener, *Tsu der geshikhte,* p. 338.

18. Lewin, *Kantonistn,* pp. 185–205, 234–241.

19. Ibid., p. 185n.

20. Y. L. Katsenelson (Buki ben Yagli), "Mah shera'u einay veshame'u oznay" [What My Eyes Beheld and My Ears Heard] (Jerusalem, 1947), p. 14. Cited in Stanislawski, *Tsar Nicholas I and the Jews,* p. 33.

21. Israel Bartal, "Non-Jews and Gentile Society in East European Hebrew and Yiddish Literature, 1856–1914" (in Hebrew) (diss., Hebrew University, 1980), pp. 26–27.

22. Ibid., p. 9.

23. Ben-Ami (Chaim Mordecai Rabinowitch), "Ben-yukhid" [The Only Son: A True Story from the Time of the *Lovtshikes*] (in Russian), *Voskhod,* January 1884, pp. 151–161, and February 1884, pp. 131–156. As quoted in Lewin, *Kantonistn,* p. i.

24. Steve Jeffrey Zipperstein, "The Jewish Community of Odessa, 1794–1871: Social Characteristics and Cultural Development" (diss., University of California at Los Angeles, 1980), ch. 5.

25. Peretz Smolenskin, *Hato'eh bedarkhei haḥayim o aḥarit hato'eh* [The Wanderer in the Paths of Life, or The Wanderer's End] (Vienna, 1876), pt. 4, ch. 24. Cited in Israel Halpern, ed., *Sefer hagevurah* [The Book of Valor], 3rd ed. rev., pt. 2 (rpt. Tel Aviv: Am Oved, 1977), pp. 47–49.

26. Yekutiel Berman, *Hashodedim batsohoraim* [The Ravagers at Noon] (Vienna: Brog & Smolenskin, 1877).

27. Smolenskin, *Hato'eh bedarkhei haḥayim.*

28. Sholem Yankev Abramovitsh, *Di klyatshe oder tsar balekhaim* [The Mare, or Pity the Poor Animal: A Story of Yisrolik the Madman Published by Mendele the Bookpeddler] (Vilna: Rom, 1873), p. 100.

29. Shalom Luria, "Figurative Language in the Bilingual Works of Mendele Mocher Sefarim" (in Hebrew) (diss., Hebrew University, 1977), pp. 244–247.

30. See Arthur Hertzberg, ed., *The Zionist Idea: A Historical Analysis and Reader* (Philadelphia: Jewish Publication Society of America, 1960), pp. 143–147; Israel Zinberg, *A History of Jewish Literature,* vol. 12: *Haskalah at Its Zenith,* trans. and ed. Bernard Martin (Cincinnati and New York: Hebrew Union College Press and Ktav Publishing House, 1978), pp. 143–171.

31. Ismar Schorsch, "On the History of the Political Judgment of the Jews," Leo Baeck Memorial Lecture no. 20, (New York, 1976), pp. 12–13.

32. Bartal, "Non-Jews and Gentile Society," pp. 93–97; Luria, "Figurative Language," p. 216.

33. Luria, "Figurative Language," pp. 244–247.

34. Abramovitsh, *Di klyatshe,* p. 100.

35. Dan Miron, "Introductory Remarks on Abramovitsh's The Mare" (in Hebrew), *Hadoar* (New York), 51 (1972), 608.

36. Luria, "Figurative Language," pp. 198–203.

37. Nachman Mayzel, ed., *Dos Mendele-bukh* [The Mendele Book: Letters and Autobiographical Sketches] (New York: YIKUF, 1959), letter 68, 21 October 1882.

38. S. Y. Abramovitsh, *The Parasite* (*Dos kleyne mentshele*), trans. Gerald Stillman (New York: T. Yoseloff, 1956), p. 23. The quotation is from the preface of 1879.

39. Abramovitsh, "Biymey hara'ash" [In the Days of Tumult] (1893), in *Kol kitvei Mendele Mokher Sefarim* [The Complete Works in Hebrew] (Tel Aviv: Dvir, 1947), p. 416.

40. Abramovitsh, "Beseter ra'am" [In the Secret Place of Thunder] (1886–87), in *Kol kitvei,* p. 377.

41. Ibid., p. 384.

42. Ibid., pp. 384–388.

43. Luria, "Figurative Language," p. 216.

44. Gershon Shaked, *Bein sḥok ledema* [Between Laughter and Tears: Studies in the Work of Mendele Moykher-Sforim] (Ramat Gan: Masada, 1965).

45. Jeffrey Fleck, "Mendele in Pieces," *Prooftexts* 3, no. 2 (1983), 169–188.

46. Jury Tynianov, "On Literary Evolution" (1927), in Ladislav Matejka and Krystyna Pomorska, eds., *Readings in Russian Poetics* (Cambridge, Mass.: MIT Press, 1971), pp. 66–78.

47. Nurit Gertz, "The Place of Parody in the Change of Generations in Hebrew Literature" (in Hebrew), *Siman kri'ah* (Tel Aviv), 12–13 (February 1981), 272–277.

48. Israel Davidson, *Parody in Jewish Literature* (New York: Columbia University Press, 1907).

49. Dan Miron, *A Traveler Disguised: A Study in the Rise of Modern Yiddish Fiction in the Nineteenth Century* (New York: Schocken, 1973), ch. 5.

50. Abramovitsh, "Shem veYefet ba'agalah" [Shem and Japheth on the Train] (1890), in *Kol kitvei,* pp. 399–405. All but the opening paragraph translated by Walter Lever in Robert Alter, ed., *Modern Hebrew Literature* (New York: Behrman House, 1975), pp. 10–38.

51. Shaked, *Bein sḥok ledema.*

52. Bartal, "Non-Jews and Gentile Society," p. 114.

53. Abramovitsh, "Shem and Japheth on the Train," pp. 26–29, 33–35.

54. Abramovitsh, "Be'emek habakha" [In the Vale of Tears], preface, *Hashiloaḥ* 1 (1897), 7. I have used the later, Hebrew version, in which the allusions are more pronoucned. Cf. "Dos vintshfingerl" [The Wishing Ring], *Di yidishe folks-bibliotek* 1 (1888), 1–10, as quoted in Miron, *A Traveler Disguised,* p. 144.

55. Miron, *A Traveler Disguised,* p. 145.

56. Ibid., p. 146.

57. Jonathan Frankel, *Prophecy and Politics: Socialism, Nationalism, and the Russian Jews, 1862–1917* (Cambridge: Cambridge University Press, 1981), pt. 1.

58. Abramovitsh, "Hanisrafim" [Victims of the Fire] (1897), in *Kol kitvei,* p. 447. Translations are mine. Cf. "Victims of the Fire" in *Gems from Jewish Literature,* trans. Elsa Teitelbaum (New York: Pardes, 1953), pp. 28–41.

59. Abramovitsh, "Hanisrafim," p. 447.

60. Abramovitsh, "Seyfer habeheymes" [The Book of Beasts], 1902, preface, in *Ale verk fun Mendele Moykher-Sforim* [Complete Works in Yiddish], new ed., vol. 15 (Warsaw: Farlag "Mendele," 1928), pp. 12–14.

61. Abramovitsh, "Di antdekung fun Volin" [The Discovery of Volhynia] (1903), in *Ale verk,* vol. 16, pp. 3–11.

62. Luria, "Figurative Language," pp. 267–272.

63. Abramovitsh, "Be'emek habakha," p. 9; and idem, *Dos vintshfingerl,* in *Ale verk,* vol. 11, p. 420.

4. *The Pogrom as Poem*

1. Alan Lomax, *Folk Song Style and Culture,* American Association for the Advancement of Science, Publication no. 88 (Washington, D.C.: AAAS, 1968) p. 3.

2. Beatrice Silverman Weinreich, "Three Pogrom Songs from Russia," *YIVO-bleter* 33 (1949), 241–243; and Zosa Szajkowski, *An Illustrated Sourcebook of Russian Antisemitism, 1881–1978,* vol. 2 (New York: Ktav, 1980), p. 22.

3. Khashke di Vilnerke, "Tsu di yidishe federn" [To the Jewish Feathers], *Yudishes folks-blat* (St. Petersburg), 4 May 1882, reproduced in Szajkowski, *Illustrated Sourcebook,* vol. 2, fig. 15.

4. "Ver es hot in blat gelezn" [Oh, Have You Read in the Newspapers?], in S. Bastomski, "Yiddish Folklore Materials," in Zalmen Reisen, ed., *Pinkes far der geshikhte fun Vilne in di yorn fun milkhome un okupatsye* [Sourcebook for the History of Vilna in the Years of War and Occupation] (Vilna: Historic-Ethnographic Society, 1922), cols. 924–925; and Ruth Rubin, *Jewish Life: "The Old Country,"* Folkways record no. FS-3801.

5. "Di lid fun Byalistoker pogrom" [The Song of the Bialystok Pogrom], in a handwritten collection of Yiddish songs copied by Nathan Shaftman of Philadelphia.

6. S. Kupershmid, "Pogrom Songs" (in Yiddish), *Tsaytshrift far yidisher geshikhte, demografye un ekonomik literaturforshung, shprakhvisnshaft un etnografye* (Minsk), 2–3 (1928), 802–804.

7. Yehuda Leib Gordon, "Tsidkiyahu bevet hapekudot" [Zedekiah in Prison] (1879), in Yehuda Leib Gordon, *Shirei higayon, meshalim, shirei 'alilah* [Meditative, Parabolic, and Narrative Poems], ed. Moshe Mehler and David Nayger (Tel Aviv: Schocken, 1945), pp. 93–102.

8. Yehuda Leib Gordon, "Bein shinei arayot" [Between the Lion's Teeth], in Gordon, *Shirei higayon,* pp. 108–121.

9. Dan Miron, "Rediscovering Haskalah Poetry," *Prooftexts* 1, no. 3 (1981), 292–305.

10. A. Neubauer and M. Stern, eds., *Hebraische Berichte über die Judenverfolgungen wahrend der Kreuzzuge* (Berlin: Leonhard Simion, 1892).

11. Saul Tchernichowsky, "Barukh miMagentsa" [Baruch of Mainz], trans. Sholom J. Kahan, in Eisig Silberschlag, *Saul Tschernichowsky, Poet of Revolt* (Ithaca: Cornell University Press, 1968), pp. 114–134; and Saul Tchernichowsky, *Shirim* [Collected Poems] (Jerusalem: Schocken, 1955), pp. 181–208.

12. Paul Fussell, *The Great War and Modern Memory* (New York: Oxford University Press, 1975) p. 7.

13. Yehuda Slutsky, "Pogroms," *Encyclopedia Judaica* (Jerusalem: Keter, 1971).

14. Fussell, *The Great War and Modern Memory*, ch. 2.

15. S. Frug, "Hot rakhmones" [Have Pity], in Nachman Mayzel, ed., *Tsum hundertstn geboyrntog fun Sh. Frug* (New York: YIKUF, 1960), p. 43.

16. Szajkowski, *Illustrated Sourcebook*, vol. 2, no. 117b.

17. Ibid., no. 147.

18. Isaiah Trunk, "Letters from the Holocaust Years" (in Hebrew), *Yediot Beit Loḥamei Hageta'ot* 1–2 (April 1957), 27.

19. A. R. Malachi, "The Kishinev Pogrom as Reflected in Hebrew and Yiddish Poetry" (in Hebrew), *'Al admat Bessarabia* 3 (1963), 4–64.

20. Israel Halpern, *Sefer hagevurah* [The Book of Valor], vol. 3 (rpt. Tel Aviv: Am Oved, 1977), p. 15.

21. Ibid., p. 15n.

22. Malachi, "The Kishinev Pogrom," pp. 16–19, 42–44.

23. David Pinsky, *The Last Jew* [*Di familye Tsvi*] (1905), in *Three Plays*, trans. Isaac Goldberg (New York: B. W. Heubsch, 1918).

24. Asher Barash, "At Heaven's Gate" [Mul sha'ar hashamayim] (1925), trans. Yosef Schachter, in Robert Alter, ed., *Modern Hebrew Literature* (New York: Behrman House, 1975), pp. 165–176.

25. Ahad Ha'am (pseudonym of Asher Ginzberg), "Megillat setarim" [The Secret Proclamation] in H. Schorer et al., eds., *Hapogrom beKishinev biml'ot 60 shanah* (The Sixtieth Anniversary of the Kishinev Pogrom) (Tel Aviv: World Federation of Bessarabian Jews, 1963), pp. 113–117. The proclamation was signed "Union of Hebrew Writers" and dated 20 April 1903.

26. Halpern, *Sefer hagevurah*, vol. 2, pp. 64–88.

27. Halpern, *Sefer hagevurah*, vol. 3, pp. 20–21.

28. Chaim Nachman Bialik, "Eyewitness Accounts of the Pogrom Victims" (in Hebrew), in *'Al admat Bessarabia* 3 (1963), 167–182; and Schorer, *Hapogrom beKishinev*, pp. 29–59.

29. Bialik, "Upon the Slaughter" ['Al hashḥitah], trans. A. M. Klein, in Israel Efros, ed., *Selected Poems of Hayyim Nahman Bialik*, rev. ed. (New York: Bloch, 1965), pp. 112–113. For the Hebrew original, see Bialik, *Shirim* [The Collected Poems] (Tel Aviv: Dvir, 1966), pp. 152–153. I am indebted to Chaim Brandwein and Nili Gold for insights into the allusive layers of this poem.

30. Eleazar ben Kallir, "Melekh azur gevurah" [King Girded in Power], in Philip Birnbaum, *High Holiday Prayer Book* (New York: Hebrew Publishing Company, 1951), pp. 173–178, and E. D. Goldschmidt, ed., *Maḥzor leyamim nora'im* [High Holiday Prayer Book], vol. 1 (Jerusalem: Koren, 1970), pp. 44–46.

31. A. L. Strauss, "*'Al hashḥitah*," in Gershon Shaked, ed., *Bialik: yetsirato lesugeha bere'i habikoret* [Bialik: Critical Essays on His Work] (Jerusalem: Bialik Institute, 1974), pp. 150–155.

32. Chaim Nachman Bialik, "The City of Slaughter," trans. A. M. Klein, in Bialik, *Selected Poems*, pp. 114–128. The numeration follows the Hebrew.

33. Menakhem Perry, *Hamivneh hasemanti shel shirei Bialik* [The Semantic Structure of Bialik's Poetry: On the Theory of Semantic Change in the Text Continuum of a Poem] (Tel Aviv: Porter Institute for Poetics and Semiotics, Tel Aviv University, 1977), p. 87.

34. Halpern, *Sefer hagevurah*, vol. 3, p. ix.

35. David Aberbach, "Loss and Separation in Bialik and Wordsworth," *Prooftexts* 2, no. 2 (1982), 197–208.

36. Perry, *Hamivneh hasemanti*, pp. 152–153.

37. David Aberbach, "On Rereading Bialik: Paradoxes of a 'National Poet,'" *Encounter* 56 (June 1981), 41–48.

38. Malachi, "The Kishinev Pogrom," pp. 69–73.

39. Ba'al Makhshoves (Isidore Eliashev), "Pogrom Literature" (in Yiddish) (1906), in *Gezamlte shriftn*, vol. I (Vilna, 1910), pp. 167–174.

40. Bialik, "In shkhite-shtot" [In the City of Slaughter], in *Fun tsar un tsorn* [Of Anguish and Anger] (Odessa: Kadimah, 1906), pp. 7–22.

41. Z[almen] Khrapkovski, *Milkhome-vits* [The War Joke] (Vitebsk, 1922), p. 16.

42. Malachi, "The Kishinev Pogrom," pp. 1–98; Szajkowski, *An Illustrated Sourcebook*, vol. 2, pp. 21–41.

43. C. Abramsky, *War, Revolution and the Jewish Dilemma*, inaugural lecture delivered at University College, London, 1975; Abraham G. Duker, "Jews in the World War," *Contemporary Jewish Record* 2, no. 5 (1939), 6–29.

44. Zalmen Schneour, "The Middle Ages Draw Near!" (1913), in Ruth Finer Mintz, trans., *Modern Hebrew Poetry: A Bilingual Anthology* (Berkeley: University of California Press, 1966), pp. 90–95.

45. Maxim Gorky, "The War and the Russian Jews," *Current History* 5 (1916). As quoted in Zosa Szajkowski, *Jews, Wars, and Communism*, vol. 1: *The Attitude of American Jews to World War I, the Russian Revolution of 1917, and Communism, 1914–1945* (New York: Ktav, 1972), pp. 30–31.

46. John Reed, *The War in Eastern Europe* (New York: Scribner's, 1916), pp. 234–237.

47. Herman Bernstein, *In Sackcloth and Ashes: The Tragedy of Belgium, Poland and the Jews* (New York, 1916).

48. L. Levinson, *The Tragedy of the Jews in the European War Zone*, 12th ed. (London: Russian Jews Relief Fund, 1917).

49. Zvi Cohn, *Shvarts-bukh: di laydn fun mayn folk* [Black Book: the Suffering of My People], 2nd ed., 2 vols. (Lodz, 1917); William Poisniak, *Der shvartser bukh* [The Black Book], authorized Yiddish translation of *The Jews in the Eastern War Zone* (New York: Hebrew Publishing Company, 1916).

50. S. Dubnow, "From the Black Book of Russian Jewry" (in Russian), *Evrejskaja Starina* 10 (1918), 195–296.

51. Zvi Cohn, *Shvarts-bukh.*

52. Sholem Asch, *Gezamlte shriftn*, vol. 6: *Dos bukh fun tsar* [The Book of Anguish], 2nd ed. (New York, 1923). The second section is called "The Destruction of Poland."

53. Szajkowski, *Jews, Wars, and Communism*, vol. 1, chs. 1–2.

54. Joseph Rappaport, "The American Yiddish Press and the European Conflict in 1914," *Jewish Social Studies* 19 (1957), 121.

55. Ruth R. Wisse, "*Di Yunge:* Immigrants or Exiles?" *Prooftexts* 1, no. 1 (1981), 43–61.

56. Zishe Landau, "For All That Ever Has Been Ours" [Far undzer khorev yidish lebn] (1916), trans. Marie Syrkin, in Irving Howe and Eliezer Greenberg, eds., *A Treasury of Yiddish Poetry* (New York: Holt, Rinehart & Winston, 1969), p. 97. I have revised the last three lines to conform more closely to the original. Cf. Landau, *Lider* (New York, 1937), p. 113.

57. Moyshe-Leyb Halpern, "A Night" [A nakht] (1919), trans. with facing Yiddish text, in Kathryn Ann Hellerstein, "Moyshe Leyb Halpern's 'In New York': A Modern Yiddish Verse Narrative" (diss., Stanford University, 1980), pp. 416–536. I have made some revisions in Hellerstein's translation.

58. Hellerstein, "Halpern's 'In New York,' " pp. 672–675.

59. Ibid., pp. 674, 680–682.

60. Ibid., p. 680.

61. Nurit Govrin, "The October Revolution as Reflected in Hebrew Literature" (in Hebrew), in *Mafteḥot* [Keys: Critical Essays] (Israel: Tel Aviv University and Hakibbutz Hameuchad, 1978), pp. 99–100; Hersh Remenik, "Aleksandr Blok and Yiddish Literature" (in Yiddish), *Sovyetish heymland* 11 (November 1980), 147–151.

62. Peretz Markish, "The Aesthetics of Struggle in Modern Poetry" (in Yiddish), *Ringen* (Warsaw) 10 (1922), 35–41.

63. Peretz Markish, "Di kupe" [The Heap], excerpted in Khone Shmeruk, ed., *A shpigl oyf a shteyn* [A Mirror on a Stone: Anthology of Poetry and Prose by Twelve Murdered Soviet-Yiddish Writers], comp. Benjamin Hrushovski, Abraham Sutzkever, and Khone Shmeruk (Tel Aviv: Di Goldene Keyt & Y. L. Peretz, 1964), pp. 414–421.

64. Eliezer David Rosental, *Megillat hatevaḥ* [The Scroll of Slaughter], vol. 2 (Jerusalem–Tel Aviv, 1929), pp. 24–25. According to the sources cited by Rosental, the pogrom took place two days before Yom Kippur, 1920.

65. Benjamin Hrushovski, "Modernist Trends in Yiddish Poetry," lectures given at the Max Weinreich Center for Advanced Jewish Studies, New York, Fall 1970.

66. Peretz Markish, *Inmitn veg* [Midway] (Mayak: [Yekaterinoslav], 1919).

67. Hillel Zeitlin, "Perverted Aesthetics and the Marketing of Art" (in Yiddish), *Der Moment*, 30 (3 February 1922), 4.

68. Manes Sperber, "A Page of Memoirs" (in Yiddish), in L. Leneman, ed., *Almanakh* [Almanac] (Paris: Association of Jewish Writers and Journalists in France, 1972), pp. 16–24. This memoir originally appeared in French in 1952.

69. I. Nusinov, "From National Sorrow to Social Determination" (in Yiddish), *Di royte velt* (Kharkov) 8 (August 1929), 95–107.

70. Peretz Markish, "Ikh hob nokh blut!" [I Still Have Blood!] (1924), in Shmeruk, *A shpigl oyf a shteyn*, pp. 446–447.

71. Sholem Asch, *Kiddush Hashem* (1919), trans. Rufus Learsi (Philadelphia: Jewish Publication Society of America, 1946).

72. Asher Barash, "At Heaven's Gate."

73. H. Leivick, "On the Roads of Siberia," trans. Cynthia Ozick, in Howe and Greenberg, eds., *A Treasury of Yiddish Poetry*, p. 118.

74. H. Leivick, *The Golem*, in *The Dybbuk and Other Great Yiddish Plays*, trans. Joseph C. Landis (New York: Bantam, 1966), pp. 223–356.

75. H. Leivick, "Di shtal" [The Stable], in H. Leivick, *Ale verk* [The Complete Works], vol. 1: *Lider un poemes* (New York, 1940), pp. 189–212.

76. A. Leyeles (pseudonym of Aaron Glantz), *Di mayse fun di hundert* [The Story of the Hundred] (New York, 1921).

77. N. B. Minkov, Review of A. Leyeles, *Di mayse fun di hundert*, in *Bikher-velt* (Warsaw) 1 (1922), 279–281.

78. Isaac Lamdan, "Masada," in Leon I. Yudkin, *Isaac Lamdan: A Study of Twentieth-Century Hebrew Poetry* (Ithaca: Cornell University Press, 1971), pp. 199–234.

79. Ruth R. Wisse, "Di vokh," lecture at symposium on literature and history, Harvard University, 25 April 1982.

80. M. Lan[dau], "Przytyk," *Encyclopedia Judaica* (Jerusalem: Keter, 1971).

81. Mordkhe Gebirtig, "Undzer shtetl brent!" [Our Shtetl is in Flames], in *Ha'ayarah bo'eret* [The Town is in Flames] (Israel: Moreshet and Sifriat Poalim, 1967), unpaginated. Yiddish-Hebrew edition based on original manuscripts.

5. *The Rape of the Shtetl*

1. I. L. Peretz, "Travel Pictures," trans. Helena Frank, in Peretz, *Stories and Pictures* (Philadelphia: Jewish Publication Society of America, 1906), pp. 282–283. I have made some revisions in Frank's translation. For the Yiddish original, see "Bilder fun a provints-rayze" [Scenes from a Journey through the Provinces] (1891), in *Ale verk fun Y. L. Perets*, vol. 2 (New York: CYCO, 1947), pp. 171–172.

2. I. L. Peretz, "The Dead Town" (1895–1900), trans. Irving Howe, in Irving Howe and Eliezer Greenberg, eds., *A Treasury of Yiddish Stories* (New York: Viking, 1954), pp. 205–213.

3. Dan Miron, "Folklore and Antifolklore in the Yiddish Fiction of the *Haskala*," in Frank Talmage, ed., *Studies in Jewish Folklore* (Cambridge, Mass.: Association for Jewish Studies, 1980), pp. 219–249; and idem, "On the Classic Image of the Shtetl in Yiddish Fiction" (in Yiddish), in *Der imazh fun shtetl: dray literarishe shtudyes* [The Shtetl Image: Three Literary Studies] (Tel Aviv: I. L. Peretz, 1981), pp. 21–138.

4. Jacob Shatzky, "Studies in Peretz" (in Yiddish), *YIVO-bleter* 28 (1946), 66–77.

5. Jacob Shatzky, *Geshikhte fun yidn in Varshe* [The History of the Jews in Warsaw], vol. 3 (New York: YIVO, 1953), pp. 80–88.

6. Khone Shmeruk, "Introduction to Sholem Aleichem," in *Ktavim 'ivriim* [The Hebrew Writings] (Jerusalem: Bialik Institute, 1976), pp. 25–27.

7. Sholem Asch, "The Little Town" [*Dos shtetl*] (1904), in *Tales of My People*, trans. Meyer Levin (New York: Putnam's, 1948), pp. 3–143.

8. I. M. Weissenberg, "A Shtetl" (1906), trans. Ruth R. Wisse, in Ruth R. Wisse, ed., *A Shtetl and Other Yiddish Novellas* (New York: Behrman

House, 1973), pp. 29–78. All page references are to this translation. For the Yiddish original, see I. M. Weissenberg, *Geklibene verk,* vol. 1 (Chicago: Zelechow Society of the World, 1959), pp. 287–355.

9. Sholem Aleichem, *Der mabl* [The Deluge], *Ale verk fun Sholem-Aleykhem,* vol. 9 (Warsaw: Progress, 1912). A copy of this rare edition is in the YIVO library. Later reworked as *In shturem.*

10. Uriel Weinreich, "I. M. Weissenberg's Underrated 'Shtetl': On Liberating a Masterpiece from its Author's Biography" (in Yiddish), *Di goldene keyt* 41 (1961), 135–143.

11. Miron, "On the Classic Image," pp. 119–123.

12. Gershon Levin, *In velt krig* [In the World War] (Warsaw, 1923), p. 130.

13. S. Ansky, *Khurbm Galitsye* [The Destruction of Galicia] *Gezamlte verk,* vol. 6, bk. 4 (Vilna, Warsaw, and New York, 1921), p. 95.

14. Leyb Olitzky, *In shayn fun flamen* [In the Glow of Flames] (Vilna and Warsaw: Kletskin, 1927), p. 56. All subsequent page references are to this edition.

15. Yehuda Elzet, "Some Folklore of the World War" (in Yiddish), *Ilustrirte velt* (Warsaw), 21 August 1919.

16. Jacob Mestel, *Milkhome-notitsn fun a yidishn ofitsir* [War Notes of a Jewish Officer], vol. 1 (Warsaw: S. Jackkowski, 1924), pp. 157–160.

17. Fishl Bimko, "Brivelekh" [Letters], *Geklibene verk,* vol. 9 (New York, 1947), p. 36. Written during World War I and revised for publication.

18. William M. Glicksman, *In the Mirror of Literature: The Economic Life of the Jews in Poland as Reflected in Yiddish Literature, 1914–1939* (New York: Living Books, 1966), pp. 123–125.

19. Leyb Olitzky, *In an okupirt shtetl* [In an Occupied Shtetl] (Warsaw: Kultur-lige, 1924).

20. Olitzky, *In shayn fun flamen,* p. 51.

21. Ibid., pp. 32–50.

22. Oyzer Varshavski, *Shmuglares* [Smugglers] (1920), in *Unter okupatsye* [Under the Occupation] (Buenos Aires: Musterverk fun der yidisher literatur, 1969), pp. 22–315.

23. George J. Becker, "Modern Realism as a Literary Movement," in *Documents of Modern Realism* (Princeton: Princeton University Press, 1967), pp. 26–36.

24. Susan A. Slotnick, "Oyzer Varshavski's *Shmuglares:* A Study in Form and Meaning," in Marvin I. Herzog, Barbara Kirshenblatt-Gimblett et al., *The Field of Yiddish: Studies in Language, Folklore, and Literature—Fourth Collection* (Philadelphia: ISHI, 1980), pp. 185–236.

25. Abraham Nowersztern, "Structural Aspects of David Bergelson's Prose from Its Beginnings until *Mides-hadin*" (in Hebrew) (diss., Hebrew University, 1981), pp. 138–139.

26. David Bergelson, "Onheyb kislev TaRAT" [The Beginning of Kislev 1919], *Milgroym* (Berlin) 1 (1922), 25–26.

27. David Bergelson, "Civil War" (1922–1928), trans. Seth L. Wolitz, in Irving Howe and Eliezer Greenberg, eds., *Ashes Out of Hope: Fiction by So-*

viet-Yiddish Writers (New York: Schocken, 1977), pp. 85–123. Page references are to this translation. For the Yiddish original, see *Shturemteg* [Storm Days], vol. 5 of Bergelson's *Geklibene verk* (Vilna: Kletskin, 1928), pp. 9–64.

28. David Bergelson, "A mayse mit gvirim" [A Tale about Rich Men] (1922), in *Tsugvintn* [Storm Winds], *Geklibene verk*, vol. 8 (Vilna and Warsaw: Kletskin, 1930), pp. 51–75.

29. David Bergelson, *Mides-hadin* [The Firm Hand of Justice] (1926–1929), in *Geklibene verk*, vol. 7 (Vilna and Warsaw: Kletskin, 1929).

30. Peretz Markish, *Dor oys dor ayn* [The Generations Come and Go] (1929), vol. 1 (Warsaw: YIKUF, 1964).

31. Hayim Hazaz, "Mizeh umizeh" [From Here and There], *Hatekufah* 21 (1923), 11.

32. Hayim Hazaz, "Pirkei mahapekhah" [Chapters from the Revolution], *Hatekufah* 22 (1924), 87.

33. Hazaz, "Mizeh umizeh," pp. 1–32. On the trilogy, see Dov Sadan's seminal essay of 1934, "On Hayim Hazaz: Chapters of Turmoil" (in Hebrew), reprinted in *Bein din leḥeshbon* [Between Account and Reckoning] (Tel Aviv: Dvir, 1963), pp. 234–242.

34. Hazaz, "Pirkei mahapekhah," pp. 69–97.

35. Hayim Hazaz, "Shmuel Frankfurter," *Hatekufah* 23 (1925), 81–134. Quotation is from p. 117.

36. Israel Joshua Singer, *Steel and Iron* (1927), trans. Joseph Singer (New York: Funk & Wagnalls, 1969).

37. Isaac Bashevis Singer, *Satan in Goray* (1935), trans. Jacob Sloan (New York: Noonday Press, 1955).

38. Maximillian E. Novak, "Moral Grotesque and Decorative Grotesque in Singer's Fiction," in Marcia Allentuck, ed., *The Achievement of Isaac Bashevis Singer* (Carbondale: Southern Illinois University Press, 1969), pp. 44–63.

39. Mikhoel Burshtin, *Iber di khurves fun Ployne* [Over the Ruins of Ployne] (Buenos Aires: Tsentral-farband fun poylishe yidn in Argentine, 1949).

40. Leo Strauss, "Persecution and the Art of Writing," in *Persecution and the Art of Writing* (Glencoe: Free Press, 1952), pp. 22–37.

41. Itzik Manger, *The Book of Paradise: The Wonderful Adventures of Shmuel-Aba Abervo*, trans. Leonard Wolf (New York: Hill & Wang, 1965), p. v. The original Yiddish reads: "Baym rand funem opgrunt vert dos gelekhter nokh farshayter."

42. Mikhoel Burshtin, *Bay di taykhn fun Mazovye* [By the Rivers of Mazovia], in *Erev khurbm* [On the Eve of the Holocaust] (Buenos Aires: Musterverk fun der yidisher literatur, 1970), pp. 167–168.

43. Ismar Schorsch, "On the History of the Political Judgment of the Jews," Leo Baeck Memorial Lecture no. 20, (New York, 1976), pp. 18–19.

44. Yehuda Yaari, *K'or yahel* [Like a Dazzling Light] (1937), 2nd ed., rev. (Jerusalem: Hebrew Writers' Union in Jerusalem, 1969), p. 156. For reasons of Zionist ideology and artistic symmetry, New York, the city in which this novel—Yaari's first—was actually written, became Jerusalem in the novel itself.

45. Dan Laor, "To Begin Anew" (in Hebrew), Review of Yehuda Yaari's *K'or yahel,* in *Ha'arets,* 27 November 1981.

46. Arnold Band, *Nostalgia and Nightmare: A Study in the Fiction of S. Y. Agnon* (Berkeley: University of California Press, 1968), pp. 283–327.

47. S. Y. Agnon, *A Guest for the Night* [*Oreaḥ natah lalun*] (1938–1939), trans. Misha Louvish (New York: Schocken, 1968), p. 119. All page references are to this translation. For the Hebrew original, see vol. 4 of *Kol sipurav shel Shmuel Yosef Agnon* [The Collected Stories], 2nd ed., rev. (Jerusalem: Schocken, 1966).

48. Band, *Nostalgia and Nightmare,* pp. 46–47.

49. Ezra Mendelsohn, *Zionism in Poland: The Formative Years, 1915–1926* (New Haven: Yale University Press, 1981), pp. 26–27.

50. Nowersztern, "Structural Aspects of David Bergelson's Prose," p. 255.

6. *The Self under Siege*

1. Noyekh Prylucki, "A Historical *Tkhine*" (in Yiddish), *Historishe shriftn* (Warsaw) 1 (1929), 815–820.

2. Jacob Shatzky, Review of Leo Schwarz, *Memoirs of My People* (in Yiddish), *YIVO-bleter* 23 (1944), 389–395.

3. Jacob Shatzky, "Jewish Memoir Literature of the World War and the Russian Revolution" (in Yiddish), *Di tsukunft* 30 (August 1925), 484.

4. I. L. Peretz, Yankev Dinezon, and S. Ansky, "Appeal to Collect Materials about the World War," *Haynt* (Warsaw), 19 December 1914 (old style), rpt. *YIVO-bleter* 36 (1952), 350–351.

5. Anne Kahan, "The Diary of Anne Kahan, Siedlce, Poland, 1914–1916," *YIVO Annual of Jewish Social Science* 18 (1983), 141–371.

6. S. Ansky, *Khurbm Galitsye,* bk. 1, in *Gezamlte shriftn,* vol. 4 (Vilna, Warsaw, and New York, 1921), pp. 41–44.

7. I. Lejpuner, *Fir yor in der velt-milkhome, 1914–1918: Memuarn* [Four Years in the World War: Memoirs] (Warsaw, 1923); Gershon Levin, *In velt krig* [In the World War] (Warsaw, 1923); Joseph Tenenbaum, *Mad Heroes: Skeletons and Sketches of the Eastern Front* (1931; rpt. Freeport, N.Y.: Books for Libraries Press, 1970), originally published as *In fayer: ertseylungen fun'm shlakhtfeld fun a doktor in der alter estraykish-ungarisher armey* (New York, 1926).

8. Avigdor Hameiri, *The Great Madness* [*Hashiga'on hagadol*] (serialized 1925), trans. Jacob Freedman (New York: Vantage, 1952); Jacob Mestel, *Milkhome-notitsn fun a yidishn ofitsir* [War Notes of a Jewish Officer], 2 vols. (Warsaw, 1925).

9. S. Cohen, *Af blutike vegn: zikhroynes fun a yidishn soldat* [On Bloody Paths: Memoirs of a Jewish Soldier] (New York: Mayzl, 1923) (Cohen served in the U.S. Army); Isaac Friedman, *A yor tsvishn lebn un toyt* [A Year between Life and Death] (New York, 1932) (Friedman served in the U.S. Army); K. Ch. Heiszeryk, *In fayer un blut; memuarn fun der velt-milkhome* [In Fire and Blood: Memoirs of the World War], 2nd ed. (Warsaw: Kolektiv, 1930); Jacob Kreplak, *Fun kazarme un milkhome* [From the Barracks and from War] (New

York: Tsenter, 1927) (Tsarist army life on the eve of World War I); Avrom Zak, *Unter di fligl fun toyt* [Under the Wings of Death] (Warsaw: Di tsayt, 1921) (experiences of a tsarist soldier on the Galician front).

10. Avigdor Hameiri, *Begeihinom shel matah: reshimot katsin 'ivri bishvi Rusya* (In Hell on Earth: Notes of a Jewish Officer in Russian Captivity), 3rd ed., 2 vols. (Tel Aviv: Yosef Sreberk, 1946); Avrom Iwenicki, *Ven di vegn kreytsn zikh: togbukh fun a yidishn krigs-gefangenem* [When the Roads Intersect: Diary of a Jewish Prisoner of War] (Vilna: Union of Jewish Writers and Journalists, 1924); Jacob Wygodski, *In genem* [In the Inferno: Memoirs of German Prisons during the World War] (Vilna: Kletskin, 1927).

11. Jacob Mestel, *Soldatn- un payatsn-lider* [Songs of Soldiers and Clowns] (Warsaw, 1928), pp. 139–172. N[okhem] Oyslender, *Front* (Kiev: Kleyne bibliotek "Lirik," 1921). Avigdor Hameiri, *Bamevukha hagedolah* [In the Great Chaos], in *Sefer hashirim* [Collected Poems] (Tel Aviv: Am Hasefer, 1933), pp. 75–94. David Shimoni, "Bekeren zavit" [In a Dark Corner], in *Sefer hapo'emot* [Collected Poems], vol. 1 (Jerusalem: Masada, 1952), pp. 89–148.

12. Isaac Babel, *Diary—1920* (excerpts), in Isaac Babel, *The Forgotten Prose*, trans. Nicholas Stroud (Ann Arbor: Ardis, 1978), pp. 130–131.

13. S. Ansky, *Khurbm Galitsye*, bk. 4, pp. 81–88.

14. Jacob Shatzky, Review of S. Ansky, *Khurbm Galitsye* (in Yiddish), *Bikher-velt* (Warsaw), no. 2 (1922), 170–172.

15. S. Ansky, *Khurbm Galitsye*, bk. 3, p. 129.

16. Editorial Board to Collect and Research Materials on the Pogroms in the Ukraine, "Proclamation" (in Yiddish), reproduced in Elias Tcherikower, *Di ukrainer pogromen in yor 1919* [The Pogroms in the Ukraine in 1919] (New York: YIVO, 1965), p. 334.

17. Hirsh Dovid Nomberg, "Five Crates of Jewish Sorrows" (in Yiddish), *Der moment* (Warsaw), 28 April 1921, as quoted in Zosa Szajkowski, "The History of the Present Book" (in Yiddish), epilogue to Tcherikower, *Di ukrainer pogromen*, p. 339, n. 17.

18. Rachel Feigenberg, *A pinkes fun a toyter shtot: khurbm Dubove* [A Chronicle of a Dead Town: The Destruction of Dubove] (Warsaw, 1926).

19. Szajkowski, "The History of the Present Book."

20. "Eliezer David Rosental" [editorial note] (in Hebrew), *He'avar* 17 (1970), 83–84.

21. E[liezer] D[avid] Rosental, *Megillat hatevaḥ* [The Scroll of Slaughter], 3 vols. (Jerusalem and Tel Aviv, 1927–1930).

22. Eliezer David Rosental, "Notes from the Scroll of Slaughter" (in Hebrew), *He'avar* 17 (1970), 85–89.

23. Yehuda Elzet, "Discourses on Hebrew-Yiddish and Yiddish-Hebrew" (in Yiddish), in *Judah A. Joffe Book*, ed. Yudel Mark (New York: YIVO, 1958), pp. 252–256.

24. Hayden White, "The Forms of Wildness: Archeology of an Idea," in Edward Dudley and Maximillian E. Novak, eds., *The Wild Man Within: An Image in Western Thought from the Renaissance to Romanticism* (Pittsburgh: University of Pittsburgh Press, 1972), p. 26.

25. Sholem Asch, "Kola Street," trans. Norbert Guterman, in Irving Howe and Eliezer Greenberg, eds., *A Treasury of Yiddish Stories* (New York: Viking, 1954), pp. 260–275. Quotation is from p. 261.

26. Nathalie Babel, notes to Isaac Babel, *You Must Know Everything: Stories, 1915–1937,* trans. Max Hayward (New York: Farrar, Straus & Giroux, 1969), p. 166.

27. Fishl Bimko, "The Draft" [Biz tsum priziv], in Joachim Neugroschel, trans., *The Shtetl: A Creative Anthology of Jewish Life in Eastern Europe* (New York: Richard Marek, 1979), p. 476.

28. Fishl Bimko, *Rekrutn* (1916) (Warsaw, 1921).

29. Ruth R. Wisse, *The Schlemiel as Modern Hero* (Chicago: University of Chicago Press, 1971), p. 39.

30. Gershon Shaked, *Hasiporet ha'ivrit, 1880–1970* [Hebrew Narrative Fiction, 1880–1970], vol. 1 (Tel Aviv and Jerusalem: Hakibbutz Hameuchad & Keter, 1977), pp. 362–365.

31. Zalmen Schneour, "Revenge: Extracts from a Student's Diary," trans. Meyer Levin, in Howe and Greenberg, eds., *A Treasury,* pp. 308–316. Quotation is from p. 315. For the Yiddish original, see Schneour's *Gezamlte shriftn,* vol. 1 (Warsaw: Velt-bibliotek, 1911), pp. 80–95.

32. I. D. Berkowitz, "Bay di kranke" [Among the Sick] (1908), in *Gezamlte shriftn* (Warsaw: Hashahar, 1910), pp. 123–134. Reworked into Hebrew as "Pleitim."

33. Yosef Hayim Brenner, "The Way Out" [Hamotsa'] (1919), trans. Yosef Schachter, in Robert Alter, ed., *Modern Hebrew Literature* (New York: Behrman House, 1975), p. 145. Hebrew orig.: *Kol kitvei Y. H. Brenner,* vol. 1 (Tel Aviv: Dvir & Hakibbutz Hameuchad, 1964), pp. 450–454.

34. David Bergelson, "Among Refugees" [Tsvishn emigrantn] (1924), trans. Joachim Neugroschel, *Fiction* 2, no. 3 (1975), 20–24.

35. Israel Halpern, *Sefer hagevurah: antologia historit-sifrutit* [The Book of Valor: A Historical-Literary Anthology], vol. 3 (Tel Aviv: Am Oved, 1977), pp. 123, 215–218. Azriel Shohat, "The Pogrom in Pinsk on 5 April 1919" (in Hebrew), *Gal-Ed: On the History of the Jews in Poland* 1 (1973), 145–146.

36. S. Ansky, *Zikhroynes* [Memoirs], in *Gezamlte verk,* vol. 10 (Vilna, Warsaw, and New York, 1928), pp. 135–139.

37. Lamed Shapiro, *Der shrayber geyt in kheyder* [The Writer Goes to School] (Los Angeles, 1945), p. 31.

38. Halpern, *Sefer hagevurah,* vol. 3, p. 31.

39. Yosef Hayim Brenner, "Hu amar lah" [He Said to Her] (1905), in Halpern, *Sefer hagevurah,* vol. 3, pp. 125–129.

40. Lamed Shapiro, "Zelbstshuts" [Self-Defense] (1906), in *Ksovim* [Posthumous Writings], ed. S. Miller (Los Angeles, 1949), pp. 41–43.

41. Abraham Nowersztern, "The Pogrom Theme in the Works of Lamed Shapiro" (in Yiddish), *Di goldene keyt* 106 (1981), 126, 142–145.

42. Lamed Shapiro, "In the Dead Town" [In der toyter shtot] (1910), trans. David G. Roskies, *Mosaic* (Cambridge, Mass.) 12 (1971), 10–23.

43. Nowersztern, "The Pogrom Theme," p. 126.

44. Ruth R. Wisse, "Yiddish Writing in America, 1905–1924," lecture

notes, Max Weinreich Center for Advanced Jewish Studies, New York, Fall 1975.

45. Lamed Shapiro, "The Cross" [Der tseylem] (1909), trans. Curt Leviant, in Shapiro, *The Jewish Government and Other Stories* (New York: Twayne, 1971), pp. 114–130. Page references are to this translation.

46. Nowersztern, "The Pogrom Theme," p. 132.

47. Wisse, "Yiddish Writing in America."

48. Lamed Shapiro, "The Kiss" [Der kush] (1907), in Shapiro, *The Jewish Government,* pp. 169–172.

49. Nowersztern, "The Pogrom Theme," pp. 142–145.

50. Lamed Shapiro, "Pour Out Thy Wrath" [Shfoykh khamoskho] (1908), in Shapiro, *The Jewish Government,* pp. 144–151.

51. Lamed Shapiro, "Di yidishe melukhe" [The Jewish State] (1919), in *Di yidishe melukhe un andere zakhn* [The Jewish State and Other Things], 2nd ed. (New York: Farlag Yidish lebn, 1929), pp. 2–63. Contains the Yiddish originals of all the pogrom stories. All translations are mine, and page references are to this edition.

52. Dan Miron, "Yiddish Fiction in the Twentieth Century: Continuity and Revolt after the Classicists, 1900–1918," lecture notes, Max Weinreich Center for Advanced Jewish Studies, New York, Fall 1976.

53. S. Miller, "Biographical Notes," in Shapiro, *Ksovim,* p. 13.

54. Lamed Shapiro, "White Chalah" [Vayse khale] (1919), trans. Norbert Guterman, in Howe and Greenberg, eds., *A Treasury,* pp. 325–333. All page references are to this translation.

55. Esther Frank, "An Analysis of Four Short Stories by Lamed Shapiro," *Working Papers in Yiddish and East European Jewish Studies* 28 (November 1978), 18–27.

56. Wisse, "Yiddish Writing in America."

57. Frank, "An Analysis of Four Short Stories."

58. Nowersztern, "The Pogrom Theme," p. 138.

59. Hameiri, *The Great Madness.*

60. Nurit Govrin, "The October Revolution in the Mirror of Hebrew Literature" and "Stories on the Revolution as a Literary Genre" (in Hebrew), in *Maftehot* [Keys: Critical Essays] (Tel Aviv: Tel Aviv University and Hakibbutz Hameuchad, 1978), pp. 78–118, 140–142.

61. Eliezer Steinman, "Haḥayal hayehudi" [The Jewish Soldier], in *Sipurim* [Stories] (Warsaw, 1923), pp. 130–147. Avraham Freiman, *1919,* ed. Yehuda Slutzky (Tel Aviv: Am Oved, 1968). This is an unfinished, five-part Hebrew novel written in the Soviet Union between 1930 and 1935. Yitzhak Shenhar, "Pirkei roman" [Chapters from a Novel] (1955), in *Sipurei Yitzhak Shenhar* [Collected Stories], vol. 1 (Jerusalem: Bialik Institute, 1960), pp. 188–344.

62. Shenhar, "Basar vadam" [Flesh and Blood], in *Sipurei Yitzhak Shenhar,* pp. 50–80. Lamed Shapiro, "Rokhl mevako al boneho" [Rachel Weeps for Her Children], in *Ksovim,* pp. 320–324.

63. Israel Rabon, *Di gas* [The Street] (Warsaw: Goldfarb, 1928). Page references are to this edition.

64. Isaac Babel, "Old Shloime" (1913), in Babel, *The Forgotten Prose,* pp. 17–21.

65. Isaac Babel, "A Fine Institution" and "Premature Babies," in Babel, *You Must Know Everything,* pp. 59, 70.

66. Isaac Babel, "Observations on War" (1920), ibid., pp. 81–94.

67. Babel, "Diary—1920." Semyon Budyonny, "Open Letter to Maxim Gorky" (1928), in Babel, *The Lonely Years, 1925–1939: Unpublished Stories and Private Correspondence,* ed. Nathalie Babel, trans. Andrew R. MacAndrew (New York: Noonday, 1964), pp. 384–387.

68. Isaac Babel, "And Then There Were None" (1923), in Babel, *You Must Know Everything,* pp. 129–133.

69. Isaac Babel, "Squadron Commander Trunov" (1925), in Babel, *The Collected Stories,* trans. Walter Morison (New York: Meridian, 1960), pp. 143–152; Nathalie Babel, notes to Babel, *You Must Know Everything,* pp. 127–128.

70. Isaac Babel, *Red Cavalry* (1923–1925), in Babel, *The Collected Stories,* pp. 41–200. Page references are to this edition.

71. Arkady Lvov, "Babel the Jew," trans. Sheila Gutter, *Commentary* 75 (March 1983), 40–49.

72. Ibid.

73. Babel, "The Rabbi's Son," in *The Collected Stories,* p. 193.

7. *Laughing Off the Trauma of History*

1. Sacvan Bercovitch, "The Typology of America's Mission," *American Quarterly* 30 (1978), 135–155.

2. Murray Baumgarten, "Community and Modernity: Sholem Aleichem," in *City Scriptures: Modern Jewish Writing* (Cambridge, Mass.: Harvard University Press, 1982), pp. 72–93; Dan Miron, *Shalom Aleichem: masot meshulavot* [Sholem Aleichem: Two Related Essays], 2nd ed., rev. (Ramat Gan: Masada, c. 1980); Ruth R. Wisse, *The Schlemiel as Modern Hero* (Chicago: University of Chicago Press, 1971), pp. 3–49.

3. Nokhem Oyslender, "The Young Sholem Aleichem and His Novel *Stempenyu*" (in Yiddish), *Shriftn* (Kiev) 1 (1928), 11–12; Sholem Aleichem, "Prozdor utraklin" [The Corridor and the Palace] (1890), in Khone Shmeruk, ed., *Ktavim 'ivriim* [The Hebrew Writings] (Jerusalem: Bialik Institute, 1976), pp. 184–191 (contains Sholem Aleichem's first oblique reference to the pogroms).

4. Israel Bartal, "Non-Jews and Gentile Society in East European Hebrew and Yiddish Literature, 1856–1914" (diss., Hebrew University, 1980), p. 12.

5. Yidishe folks-tsaytung, *Hilf: a zaml-bukh fir literatur un kunst* (Warsaw: Folks-bildung, 1903).

6. David Pinsky, "From a Letter" (in Yiddish), preface to *Di familye Tsvi* [The Zvi Family] (Geneva: Bund, 1905); S. M. Dubnow, *History of the Jews in Russia and Poland from the Earliest Times until the Present,* trans. I. Freidlander, vol. 3 (Philadelphia: Jewish Publication Society of America, 1920), p. 76; Vladimir Korolenko, *Dom No. 13-ij* [House Number 13: An Episode from

the Kishinev Pogrom] (London, 1903)—a Yiddish translation was published in 1906.

7. Sholem Aleichem, "Hundert eyns" [A Hundred and One], in *Ale verk fun Sholem-Aleykhem,* vol. 17 (New York: Folksfond Edition, 1917–1925), pp. 101–115. All page references are to this version, which differs significantly from the original. Compare *Hilf,* pp. 37–47. For an English translation, see "A Hundred and One," in Sholom Aleichem, *Old Country Tales,* trans. Curt Leviant (New York: Putnam's, 1969), pp. 138–144. Daniel Gerould, "Tyranny and Comedy," in *Comedy: New Perspectives,* ed. Maurice Charney (New York: New York Literary Forum, 1978), p. 11.

8. Dubnow, *History of the Jews,* vol. 3, pp. 80–81.

9. Y. Dobrushin, "Two Basic Editions of Sholem Aleichem's *Kleyne mentshelekh mit kleyne hasoges*" (in Yiddish), *Visnshaftlekhe yorbikher* 1 (1929), 147–162; Dan Miron, "Thoughts about the Classic Image of the Shtetl in Yiddish Fiction" (in Yiddish), in *Der imazh fun shtetl: dray literarishe shtudyes* [The Shtetl Image: Three Literary Studies] (Tel Aviv: I. L. Peretz, 1981), pp. 86–101; Wisse, *The Schlemiel,* pp. 3–49.

10. Sholem Aleichem, "Di groyse behole fun di kleyne mentshelekh" [The Great Panic of the Little People] (1904), in *Ale verk,* vol. 6, pp. 155–210. Page references are to the Yiddish original. Translations are mine, based on Sholem Aleichem, "The Great Panic of the Little People," in *Old Country Tales,* pp. 81–117.

11. See, for example, [A. M. Dik], "Habehala" [The Panic], *Hamelits* 41–43 (1867). The Yiddish version appeared as *Di shtot Heres* (Vilna, 1868).

12. Sholem Aleichem, " 'Alilat-dam" [The Blood Libel] (1890) in *Ktavim 'ivriim,* pp. 140–148.

13. Volf Rabinovitsh, *Mayn bruder Sholem-Aleykhem* [My Brother Sholem Aleichem] (Kiev, 1939), p. 197.

14. Sholem Aleichem, "Pogrom-bilder" [Pogrom Scenes]: "No Hide-out for Rich or Poor" and "The Destruction of Odessa," in *Yudishes tageblat* (New York) 24 and 26 November 1905. These reports were commissioned by the paper.

15. Kh[one] Sh[meruk], "Sholem Aleichem," *Leksikon fun der nayer yidisher literatur,* vol. 8 (New York: Yidisher kultur-kongres, 1981), p. 682.

16. Sholem Aleichem, "A khasene on klezmer" [A Wedding without Musicians] (1909), in *Ale verk,* vol. 28, pp. 127–137. Page references are to the Yiddish original. Translations are mine, based on *The Tevye Stories and Others,* trans. Julius and Frances Butwin (New York: Pocket Books, 1965), pp. 56–60.

17. Yehuda Slutzky, "The Geography of the Pogroms of 1881" (in Hebrew), *He'avar* 9 (1962), 16–25.

18. Sholem Aleichem, *Motl Peyse dem khazns* [Motl the Son of Peyse the Cantor], *Ale verk,* vol. 18, pt. 1: "From Home to America." All page references are to this edition.

19. Khone Shmeruk, "The Stories of Motl the Cantor's Son, by Sholem Aleichem: The Epic Situation and the History of the Work" (in Hebrew), *Siman kri'ah* 12–13 (1981), 316–317.

20. Ruth R. Wisse, introduction to Irving Howe and Ruth R. Wisse, eds., *The Best of Sholom Aleichem* (Washington, D.C.: New Republic Books, 1979), pp. xx–xxi.

21. Khone Shmeruk, "*Tevye der milkhiker:* The Evolution of a Literary Work" (in Hebrew), *Hasifrut* 26 (1978), 35–37.

22. Sholem Aleichem, *Menakhem-Mendl* (*Nyu-york-Varshe-Vin-Yehupets*) [Menakhem-Mendl: New York-Warsaw-Vienna-Yehupets] (Tel Aviv: Beit Sholem Aleichem, 1976).

23. I. D. Berkowitz, *Undzere rishoynim* [Our Pioneers: Memoiristic Episodes about Sholem Aleichem], vol. 5 (Tel Aviv: I. L. Peretz, 1965), p. 169.

24. I. D. Berkowitz, ed., *Dos Sholem-Aleykhem-bukh* [The Sholem Aleichem Book] (New York, 1926), pp. 335–336.

25. Sholem Aleichem, "The Krushniker Delegation," trans. Sacvan Bercovitch, in Howe and Wisse, *The Best of Sholom Aleichem,* pp. 232–244; page references are to this translation except where otherwise noted. Excerpted from "Mayses fun toyznt eyn nakht" [Tales of 1001 Nights] (1915), in *Ale verk,* vol. 3, pp. 137–232.

26. Sholem Aleichem, "Mayses fun toyznt eyn nakht," p. 197.

27. Irving Howe, introduction to Howe and Wisse, *The Best of Sholom Aleichem,* p. viii; Wisse, *The Schlemiel,* p. 53.

28. Itsik Kipnis, *Khadoshim un teg un andere dertseylungen* [Months and Days and other Stories] (1926), in *Geklibene verk,* vol. 3 (Tel Aviv: I. L. Peretz, 1972).

29. Rokhl Pressman, "In Glowing Memory" (in Yiddish), *Vokhnblat* (Toronto), 25 January 1968.

30. Ruta Pups, ed., introduction to *Dos lid fun geto* [The Song of the Ghetto] (Warsaw: Yidish-bukh, 1962), p. 7.

31. Yechiel Szeintuch, "Yiddish and Hebrew Literature under the Nazi Rule in Eastern Europe: Yitzhak Katzenelson's Last Bilingual Writings and the Ghetto Writings of A. Sutzkever and I. Spiegel," vol. 1 (diss., Hebrew University, 1978), p. 33.

32. Josef Gar, *Umkum fun der yidisher Kovne* [The Destruction of Jewish Kovno] (Munich, 1948), p. 406.

33. Israel Kaplan, *Dos folksmoyl in Natsi-klem* [Jewish Folk Expression under the Nazi Yoke], 2nd ed., rev. (Israel: Ghetto Fighters' House, 1982), p. 74. Kaplan derives *ya'ales* from the *Ya'aleh veyavo* prayer recited on festivals, but also records *ya'aleh taḥanunenu* from the Kol Nidre service; see ibid., pp. 34–35.

34. Gar, *Umkum fun der yidisher Kovne,* pp. 408–409.

35. Yitzhak Arad, *Ghetto in Flames: The Struggle and Destruction of the Jews in Vilna in the Holocaust,* trans. from the Hebrew (New York: Holocaust Library, 1982), pp. 143–157.

36. S. Kaczerginski, comp., *Lider fun di getos un lagern* [Songs of the Ghettos and Camps], ed. H. Leivick (New York: CYCO, 1948), p. 205.

37. Ruth Rubin, "Hot zikh mir di zip tsezipt," in *Jewish Folk Songs in Yiddish and English* (New York: Oak Publications, 1965), pp. 42–43.

38. Emma Schaver, "The March of Death," *From the Heart of a People,*

Mercury Records MG-20052; Ruth Rubin, "Hot zikh mir di shikh tserisn," *Ruth Rubin Sings Yiddish Folk Songs,* Prestige International Records 13019.

39. Aaron Zeitlin, "Monolog in pleynem yidish" [Monologue in Plain Yiddish] (1945), in *Lider fun khurbm un lider fun gloybn* [Poems of the Holocaust and Poems of Faith], vol. 1 (New York: Bergen Belsen Memorial Press, 1967), pp. 98–104.

40. Jurek Becker, *Jacob the Liar* [Jakob der Lügner] (1969), trans. Melvin Kronfeld (New York: Harcourt Brace Jovanovich, 1975).

41. Sigmund Freud, "The Uncanny" (1919), in *The Standard Edition of the Complete Psychological Works of Sigmund Freud,* vol. 17 (London: Hogarth, 1955), p. 220.

42. Isaiah Trunk, *Lodzher geto* [Ghetto Lodz: A Historical and Sociological Study] (New York: YIVO, 1962), pp. 469–470.

43. Isaac Bashevis Singer, "The Last Demon" [Mayse Tishevits] (1959), trans. Martha Glicklich and Cecil Hemley, in *Selected Short Stories of Isaac Bashevis Singer,* ed. Irving Howe (New York: Modern Library, 1966), pp. 300–311. All page references are to this translation. For the Yiddish original, see "Mayse Tishevits," in *Der shpigl un andere dertseylungen* [The Mirror and Other Stories], ed. Khone Shmeruk (Jerusalem and Tel Aviv: Hebrew University of Jerusalem Yiddish Department and Committee for Jewish Culture in Israel, 1975), pp. 12–22.

8. *Scribes of the Ghetto*

1. Itsik Manger, "Folklore and Literature" (in Yiddish), *Afn sheydveg* 1 (April 1939), 168.

2. Elias Tcherikower, "The Tragedy of a Weak Generation" (in Yiddish), ibid., pp. 5–28.

3. Zelig Kalmanovitsh, "Under the Hammer of History" (in Yiddish), ibid., pp. 29–46.

4. S. Kaczerginski, *Ikh bin geven a partizan: di grine legende* [I Was a Partisan: The Green Legend] (Buenos Aires, 1952), pp. 41–42.

5. Lucy S. Dawidowicz, *The War against the Jews, 1933–1945* (New York: Holt, Rinehart & Winston, 1975), ch. 12.

6. John Hersey, *The Wall* (New York: Knopf, 1950).

7. Raphael Mahler, "Emmanuel Ringelblum's Letters from the Warsaw Ghetto" (in Yiddish), *Di goldene keyt* 46 (1963), 10.

8. Dawidowicz, *The War against the Jews,* p. 247. According to Yisrael Gutman, there were 2,000 building councils functioning in Warsaw by September 1940. When the ghetto was established two months later, many of these buildings were excluded from its boundaries. See *The Jews of Warsaw 1939–1943: Ghetto, Underground, Revolt* (Bloomington: Indiana University Press, 1982), p. 46.

9. Rokhl Auerbach, *Varshever tsavoes* [Warsaw Testaments: Encounters, Activities, Fates, 1933–1943] (Tel Aviv: Yisroel-bukh, 1974), p. 203.

10. Ibid., pp. 169–196; Emmanuel Ringelblum, *Ksovim fun geto* [Ghetto Writings], vol. 2 (1942–1943), ed. A. Eisenbach et al. (Warsaw: Jewish Histori-

cal Institute, 1963), pp. 76–102; Hirsh Wasser, "The Ghetto Archive: The Project of Dr. Emmanuel Ringelblum" (in Hebrew), in *Yom 'iyun lezikhro shel Dr. Emmanuel Ringelblum* [Proceedings of a One-Day Conference in Memory of Emmanuel Ringelblum] (Jerusalem: Yad Vashem, 1982), pp. 18–24; and "Code Name *Oyneg Shabes:* Emanuel Ringelblum's Underground Archives in the Warsaw Ghetto, 1940–1943" (New York: YIVO, 1983), an exhibition essay commemorating the fortieth anniversary of the Warsaw ghetto uprising.

11. Auerbach, *Varshever tsavoes,* p. 177.

12. Shalom Luria, "Zelik Hirsh Kalmanovitsh: the Man and His World" (in Hebrew), introduction to Zelig Kalmanovitsh, *Yoman begeto Vilna ukhtavim miha'izavon shenimtsa' baharisot* [A Diary of the Vilna Ghetto and Posthumous Writings Discovered in the Ruins], ed. Shalom Luria (Israel: Moreshet & Sifriat Poalim, 1977), pp. 38–44.

13. Michel Borwicz, *Ecrits des condamnés à mort sous l'occupation nazie, 1939–1945,* 2nd ed., rev. (Paris: Gallimard, 1973), p. 94.

14. Ibid., pp. 295–298.

15. Yechiel Szeintuch, "Three Footnotes to a Lecture on *The Last Writings of Yitzhak Katzenelson*" (in Yiddish), *Bay zikh* 12 (December 1978), 113–123; idem, "Yiddish and Hebrew Literature under the Nazi Rule in Eastern Europe: Yitzhak Katzenelson's Last Bilingual Writings and the Ghetto Writings of A. Sutzkever and I. Spiegel" (in Hebrew), vol. 1 (diss., Hebrew University, 1978), p. 113.

16. Szeintuch, "Yiddish and Hebrew Literature," vol. 1, pp. 21–24.

17. Ringelblum, *Ksovim fun geto,* vol. 2, pp. 82–84.

18. Borwicz, *Ecrits des condamnés à mort,* p. 227; Szeintuch, "Yiddish and Hebrew Literature," vol. 1, pp. 21–24.

19. Yechiel Szeintuch, " 'The Memoirs of a People Led to the Slaughter' by Yitzhak Katzenelson" (in Hebrew), *Mibifnim* 41, nos. 3–4 (Fall 1980), 301–315.

20. Auerbach, *Varshever tsavoes,* p. 192.

21. Szeintuch, "Yiddish and Hebrew Literature," vol. 1, pp. 7–9.

22. Hillel Zeitlin, "Answer to the Oneg Shabbat Questionnaire," in Lucy S. Dawidowicz, ed., *A Holocaust Reader* (New York: Behrman House, 1976), p. 218.

23. Israel Milejkowski, "Answer to the Oneg Shabbat Questionnaire," ibid., p. 222.

24. Auerbach, *Varshever tsavoes,* p. 248.

25. Ringelblum, *Ksovim fun geto,* vol. 2, p. 167.

26. Ber Mark, *Di umgekumene shrayber fun di getos un lagern un zeyere verk* [The Writers of the Ghettos and Camps Who Perished and Their Works] (Warsaw: Yidish-bukh, 1954).

27. Joseph Kermish and Yechiel Szeintuch, eds., *Jewish Creativity in the Holocaust* (Jerusalem: Yad Vashem, 1979), p. 26 (Catalogue of an exhibition).

28. Mark, *Di umgekumene shrayber,* pp. 147–159.

29. Wasser, "The Ghetto Archive," pp. 18–24.

30. Ringelblum, *Ksovim fun geto,* vol. 2, p. 86.

31. Yitskhok Rudashevski, *The Diary of the Vilna Ghetto, June 1941–April 1943*, trans. Percy Matenko (Israel: Ghetto Fighters' House & Hakibbutz Hameuchad, 1973), entry for 6 September 1941.

32. Joseph Kermish, ed., *'Itonut-hamaḥteret hayehudit beVarshah* [The Jewish Underground Press in Warsaw], vol. 1: May 1940–January 1941, and vol. 2: February–June 1941 (Jerusalem: Yad Vashem, 1979).

33. Dawidowicz, *The War against the Jews*, pp. 248–251.

34. Chaim A. Kaplan, *Scroll of Agony: The Warsaw Diary of Chaim A. Kaplan*, trans. Abraham I. Katsh (New York: Macmillan, 1965), entry for 21 December 1940.

35. A. Eisenbach, "Scientific Research in the Warsaw Ghetto" (in Yiddish), *Bleter far geshikhte* 1, no. 1 (1948), 55–113, and 1, no. 2 (1948), 69–84.

36. Joseph Kermish, "The Oneg Shabbat Archive" (in Hebrew), in *Yom 'iyun lezikhro shel Dr. Emmanuel Ringelblum*, pp. 25–37; Ringelblum, *Ksovim fun geto*, vol. 2, pp. 82–84.

37. Sh[imon] Huberband, "Memoranda on Rescuing Jewish Cultural Treasures in Occupied Poland" (in Yiddish), *Bleter far geshikhte* 1, no. 2 (1948), 105–110.

38. Simkhe-Bunem Shayevitsh, letter of 30 September 1941 to S. Roznshteyn, in Simkhe-Bunem Shayevitsh, *Lekh-lekho* [Go You Forth], ed. Nachman Blumental (Lodz: Central Jewish Historical Commission, 1946), pp. 21–24.

39. Mendel Grossman, *With a Camera in the Ghetto*, ed. Zvi Szner and Alexander Sened (Israel: Ghetto Fighters' House and Hakibbutz Hameuchad, 1970).

40. Yankev Herszkowicz, "Rumkovski Khayim git undz klayen," in Ruta Pups, ed., *Dos lid fun geto* [The Song of the Ghetto] (Warsaw: Yidish-bukh, 1962), no. 15.

41. Percy Matenko, notes to Rudashevski, *The Diary of the Vilna Ghetto*, n. 117.

42. Library and Reading Room of the Vilna Ghetto (6 Strashun Street), "The Ghetto Library and Ghetto Reader, 15/IX/41–15/IX/42" (in Yiddish), Sutzkever-Kaczerginski Collection no. 369–70, YIVO Archives.

43. Dror, *Payn un gvure in dem yidishn over in likht fun der kegnvart* [Suffering and Heroism in the Jewish Past in the Light of the Present], ed. Yitzhak Zuckerman and Eliyohu Gutkovsky (Warsaw, 1940; 3rd. ed. Munich, 1947).

44. Yitzhak Katzenelson, "Introduction to an Evening of the Bible" (in Yiddish), in Yitzhak Katzenelson, *Yidishe ksovim fun Varshe, 1940–1943* [Yiddish Writings from Warsaw, 1940–1943], ed. Yechiel Szeintuch (Israel: Ghetto Fighters' House and Hakibbutz Hameuchad, forthcoming), no. 8. I am indebted to Dr. Szeintuch for making the galleys available to me.

45. Szeintuch, "Yiddish and Hebrew Literature," vol. 1, p. 113.

46. Yitzhak Katzenelson, *Al naharos Bovl* [At the Waters of Babylon: A Biblical Folk Tragedy in Four Acts], in Katzenelson, *Yidishe ksovim fun Varshe*, no. 15.

47. Szeintuch, "Yiddish and Hebrew Literature," vol. 1, pp. 156–158.

48. Yitzhak Katzenelson, *Iyev* [Job: A Biblical Tragedy in Three Acts] (Warsaw Ghetto: Merkaz Dror, 1941), rpt. in Katzenelson, *Yidishe ksovim fun Varshe,* no. 24 (published in approximately 150 copies).

49. Szeintuch, "Yiddish and Hebrew Literature," vol. 1, pp. 181–204.

50. [David Yosef Bornshteyn], "On the Sources of Bialik's Poetry" (in Hebrew), *Shaviv* 1 (December 1940), 17–20; idem, "The Priests of Jewish Thought" (in Hebrew), *Shaviv* 5 (June–July 1941), 34–38; Dror, *Dror* (in Yiddish) 3 (July–August 1940) and Hano'ar Hatsioni, *Shaviv* 5 (June–July 1941), rpt. in Kermish, *'Itonut-hamaḥteret,* nos. 4, 18, 49; Mark Dworzecki, *Yerusholaim deLite in kamf un umkum* [The Jerusalem of Lithuania in Struggle and Destruction] (Paris: Jewish National Labor Alliance of America and Jewish People's Alliance of France, 1948), pp. 265, 272–273.

51. Yitzhak Katzenelson, "Yiddish Translation of Bialik's *'Al hashḥitah,*" *Dror* 3 (July–August 1940), 2–7, rpt. in Katzenelson, *Yidishe ksovim fun Varshe,* no. 3.

52. Hano'ar Hatsioni, *Shaviv* (in Hebrew) (December 1940), rpt. in Kermish, *'Itonut-hamaḥteret,* no. 18; Hashomer Hatsair, *Mima'amakim* (in Hebrew) (Kovno-Vilna, January 1940)—contains Abba Kovner's first published poem.

53. Yitzhak Katzenelson, "On This Year's Anniversary of Bialik" (in Yiddish), *Dror* 3 (July–August 1940), 1, rpt. in Katzenelson, *Yidishe ksovim fun Varshe,* no. 4.

54. Szeintuch, "Yiddish and Hebrew Literature," vol. 1, pp. 156–158.

55. Kaplan, *Scroll of Agony,* entry for 30 November 1939.

56. Mordecai Tenenbaum-Tamaroff, *Dappim min hadlekah* [Pages from the Conflagration] (Tel Aviv: Hakibbutz Hameuchad, 1947), p. 144, as quoted in Szeintuch, "Yiddish and Hebrew Literature," vol. 1, p. 122.

57. Dawidowicz, *The War against the Jews,* p. 314.

58. Ringelblum, *Ksovim fun geto,* vol. 2, pp. 59–60.

59. Hashomer Hatsair, "Mendele Moykher-Sforim," *Neged hazerem* (in Polish) 2 (February–March 1941), 33–36, rpt. and trans. in Kermish, *'Itonut-hamaḥteret,* no. 27; Poalei Zion Left, "Mendele Moykher-Sforim" (in Yiddish), *Proletarisher gedank* (March–April 1941), pp. 11–12, rpt. and trans. in Kermish, *'Itonut-hamaḥteret,* no. 32; Yugnt Bund, "Mendele Moykher-Sforim: The Grandfather of Yiddish Literature" (in Yiddish), *Yugnt-shtime* 2 (November 1940), 4–5 (literary supplement), rpt. and trans. in Kermish, *'Itonut-hamaḥteret,* no. 14.

60. Yitzhak Katzenelson, "To Mendele Moykher-Sforim's 105th Birthday" (in Yiddish), *Dror* 4 (October–November 1940), 17–22, rpt. in Katzenelson, *Yidishe ksovim fun Varshe,* no. 7.

61. Abraham Sutzkever, *Fun vilner geto* [From the Vilna Ghetto] (Moscow: Der emes, 1946), p. 105.

62. Leyb Goldin, "Khronik fun eyn mes-les" [Chronicle of a Single Day], in Ber Mark, ed., *Tsvishn lebn un toyt* [Between Life and Death] (Warsaw: Yidish-bukh, 1955), pp. 49–65 (anthology of prose works found in the Oneg Shabbat archive).

63. Simkhe-Bunem Shayevitsh, "Friling TaSHaB" [Spring 1942], in Shayevitsh, *Lekh-lekho,* ed. Blumental, pp. 51–62.

64. Shayevitsh, "Lekh-lekho," ibid., pp. 31–45. All stanza and line references are to this edition.

65. Shimon Huberband, *Kiddush Hashem: ktavim miymey hasho'ah* [Kiddush Hashem: Writings from the Holocaust, From the Ringelblum Archive in the Warsaw Ghetto], ed. Nachman Blumental and Joseph Kermish, trans. from the Yiddish (Tel Aviv: Zakhor, 1969), p. 23.

66. Szeintuch, "Yiddish and Hebrew Literature," vol. 1, p. 238.

67. Yitzhak Katzenelson, "Dos lid vegn Shloyme Zhelikhovsky" [The Song About Shloyme Zhelikhovsky], in Katzenelson, *Yidishe ksovim fun Varshe,* no. 33.

68. Szeintuch, "Yiddish and Hebrew Literature," vol. 2, pp. 220–221.

69. Yitzhak Zuckerman, "With Yitzhak Katzenelson in the Warsaw Ghetto" (in Hebrew), *Mibifnim* 13 (March 1948), 30–38, as quoted in Szeintuch, "Yiddish and Hebrew Literature," vol. 2, p. 197.

70. I. Tishby, "Kudsha-beriḵ-hu Orayta ve-Yisrael kola ḥad: The Source of the Saying in M. H. Luzzatto's Commentary to the 'Idra Rabba' " (in Hebrew), *Kiryat sefer* 50 (June 1975), 480–492.

71. Zelig Kalmanovitsh, "Pondering Jewish Fate: From Zelig Kalmanovich's Diary," in Dawidowicz, *A Holocaust Reader,* pp. 225–233.

72. Yitzhak Katzenelson, "Dos lid vegn Radziner" [The Song about the Radziner], in Katzenelson, *Yidishe ksovim fun Varshe,* no. 35. All references are to this edition.

73. Szeintuch, "Yiddish and Hebrew Literature," vol. 1, pp. 252–269.

74. Israel Rabon, "Fartseykhenungen fun yor 1939" [Notes from the Year 1939], *Untervegns* (Vilna, 1940), pp. 190–235, rpt. in *Di goldene keyt* 108 (1982), 164–197. See, also, S. Kaczerginski, *Khurbm Vilne* [The Destruction of the Jews of Vilna and Environs] (New York: CYCO, 1947), p. 213.

75. Mordkhe Gebirtig, *S'brent, 1939–1942* [Fire!] (Krakow: Regional Jewish Historical Commission, 1946).

76. Hershele [Danielewicz], "Songs from the Warsaw Ghetto" (in Yiddish), *Di goldene keyt* 15 (1953), 57–58.

77. Peretz Opoczynski, *Reshimot* [Sketches from the Warsaw Ghetto], ed. Zvi Szner, trans. Avraham Yeivin (Israel: Ghetto Fighters' House and Hakibbutz Hameuchad, 1970). The Yiddish version published in Warsaw in 1954 was subject to political censorship.

78. Yehoshue Perle, "Khurbm Varshe" [The Destruction of Warsaw], in Mark, ed., *Tsvishn lebn un toyt,* pp. 100–141.

79. Kaplan, *Scroll of Agony,* entry for 16 June 1942. I have revised this slightly to conform more closely to the Hebrew. Compare *Megilat yisurin: yoman geto Varshah,* ed. Abraham I. Katsh, annotated by Nachman Blumental (Tel Aviv and Jerusalem: Am Oved and Yad Vashem, 1966). On the phrase "like lambs to slaughter," see H. J. Zimmels, "Glossary," in *The Echo of the Nazi Holocaust in Rabbinic Literature* (Ireland: Privately printed, 1975), pp. 356–365.

80. Ringelblum, *Ksovim fun geto,* vol. 2, pp. 42–44.

81. "The Ghetto Burns" (in Yiddish) (April 1942), *Di goldene keyt* 15 (1953), 10–11.

82. Kalmanovitsh, "Pondering Jewish Fate."

83. Dworzecki, *Yerusholaim deLite*, p. 264.

84. Yitzhak Katzenelson, *Dos lid funem oysgehargetn yidishn folk* [The Song of the Murdered Jewish People] (Israel: Ghetto Fighters' House and Hakibbutz Hameuchad, 1964); idem, *The Song of the Murdered Jewish People*, trans. Noah H. Rosenbloom, rev. Y. Tobin (Israel: Ghetto Fighters' House and Hakibbutz Hameuchad, 1980), bilingual facsimile edition.

85. Noah H. Rosenbloom, "The Threnodist and the Threnody of the Holocaust," in Katzenelson, *The Song of the Murdered Jewish People*, pp. 119–133.

86. Szeintuch, "Three Footnotes."

87. Yitzhak Katzenelson, "To the Heavens" (Canto 9 of *The Song of the Murdered Jewish People*), trans. Jacob Sonntag, *Jewish Quarterly* 2 (Spring 1955), 35–36, stanzas 3–4. Subsequent citations are to this translation.

9. *The Burden of Memory*

1. Piotr Rawicz, *Blood from the Sky*, trans. from the French by Peter Wiles (New York: Harcourt, Brace and World, 1964).

2. Phillip Friedman, "The Destruction of the Jews of Lwow" (in Hebrew), in N. M. Gelber, ed., *The Encyclopedia of the Jewish Diaspora, Lwow Volume* (Israel, 1956), pp. 593–734.

3. Abraham Sutzkever, "A shmeykhl in ek velt" [A Smile at the End of the Earth] (1970), in *Griner akvarium: dertseylungen* [Green Aquarium: Stories] (Jerusalem: Yiddish Department of the Hebrew University of Jerusalem and Committee for Jewish Culture in Israel, 1975), pp. 105–117.

4. Zalmen Reisen, ed., *Pinkes far der geshikhte fun Vilne in di yorn fun milkhome un okupatsye* [Sourcebook for the History of Vilna in the Years of War and Occupation] (Vilna: Historic-Ethnographic Society, 1922).

5. Yitzhak Arad, *Ghetto in Flames: The Struggle and Destruction of the Jews in Vilna in the Holocaust*, trans. from the Hebrew (New York: Holocaust Library, 1982) pp. 209–117.

6. Abraham Sutzkever, *Fun vilner geto* [From the Vilna Ghetto] (Moscow: Der emes, 1946), p. 66.

7. Ibid., pp. 114–115.

8. Ibid., pp. 116.

9. Ibid., pp. 114–120.

10. See Mark Dworzecki, *Yerusholaim deLite in kamf un umkum* [Jerusalem of Lithuania in Struggle and Destruction] (Paris: Jewish National Labor Farband of America and Jewish People's Alliance of France, 1948); and Rachel Pupko-Krinsky, "Laurel Trees of Wiwulskiego," in Leo W. Schwarz, ed., *The Root and the Bough: The Epic of an Enduring People* (New York and Toronto: Rinehart, 1949), pp. 115–163.

11. Abraham Sutzkever, "On My Wander Flute" [Af mayn vander-fayfl] (1935), in Sarah Zweig Betsky, ed. and trans., *Onions and Cucumbers and Plums: Forty-Six Yiddish Poems in English* (Detroit: Wayne State University Press, 1958), no. 1, lines 15–20. Copyright © by the Wayne State University Press. Used by permission.

12. Ruth R. Wisse, "Sutzkever: An Appreciation," in B'nai B'rith Commission on Adult Jewish Education, *The B'nai B'rith International Literary Award 1979 (5739), Presented to Abraham Sutzkever* (Washington, D.C., 1979), unpaginated.

13. Abraham Sutzkever, letter to A. Glantz-Leyeles of 13 March 1939, quoted in Abraham Nowersztern, ed., *Abraham Sutzkever on His Seventieth Birthday,* catalogue of an exhibition at the Jewish National and University Library, text in Yiddish and Hebrew (Jerusalem, 1983), no. 34 [hereafter referred to as Nowersztern]. This is an indispensable source on Sutzkever's life and literary development. I am indebted to Dr. Nowersztern for making the manuscript available.

14. Abraham Sutzkever, "Der tsirk" [The Circus] (c. July 1941), in *Di ershte nakht in geto* [The First Night in the Ghetto: Poems, Variants, and Fragments Written during the Holocaust, 1941–1944], drawings by Samuel Bak (Tel Aviv: Di goldene keyt, 1979), pp. 6–9.

15. Sutzkever, *Fun vilner geto,* pp. 16–19.

16. Itzhak Yanasowicz, *Avrom Sutskever: zayn lid un zayn proze* (Abraham Sutzkever: His Poetry and Prose) (Tel Aviv: Israel Book, 1981), p. 68.

17. Sutzkever, "Fun der poeme 'Dray royzn' " [From the Long Poem "Three Roses"] (October 1942), in *Di ershte nakht in geto,* pp. 12–19.

18. Herman Kruk, *Togbukh fun vilner geto* [Diary of the Vilna Ghetto], ed. Mordecai W. Bernstein (New York: YIVO, 1961), p. 159.

19. Sutzkever, "Tsum kind" [To the Child] (18 January 1943), in *Poetishe verk* [Poetic Works], vol. 1 (Tel Aviv, 1963), pp. 278–279, lines 1–9. The translation is mine, done in collaboration with Hillel Schwartz.

20. International Military Tribunal, *Trial of the Major War Criminals* (Nuremberg, 1947), vol. 8, pp. 306–307.

21. Kruk, *Togbukh fun vilner geto.*

22. S. Kaczerginski, "A. Sutzkever" (in Yiddish), in *Shmerke Kaczergenski ondenk-bukh* [Memorial volume] (Buenos Aires, 1955), p. 300.

23. Abraham Sutzkever, *Siberia,* trans. Jacob Sonntag, drawings by Marc Chagall (London: Abelard-Schuman, 1961); Aaron Steinberg, "A Redemption of Yiddish" (in Yiddish), in Zalman Shazar, Dov Sadan, and M. Gros-Tsimerman, eds., *Yoyvl-bukh tsum fuftsikstn geboyrn-tog fun Avrom Sutskever* [Festschrift in Honor of Abraham Sutzkever's Fiftieth Birthday] (Tel Aviv, 1963), pp. 55–62.

24. See Mircea Eliade, *The Myth of the Eternal Return, or Cosmos and History,* trans. Willard R. Trask (Princeton: Princeton University Press, 1971; orig. pub. in French 1949).

25. Sutzkever, *Fun vilner geto,* p. 105.

26. Sutzkever, "Glust zikh mir tsu ton a tfile" [I Feel Like Making a Prayer] (17 January 1942), in *Poetishe verk,* vol. 1, p. 253. Trans. Hillel Schwartz.

27. Ruth R. Wisse, "Introduction: The Ghetto Poems of Abraham Sutzkever," in *Burnt Pearls: Ghetto Poems,* trans. Seymour Mayne (Oakville, Ontario: Mosaic Press–Valley Editions, 1981), pp. 10–12.

28. Ibid.

29. Sutzkever, "Yehoyesh" [Yehoash] (6 April 1943), in *Poetishe verk,* vol. 1, p. 296; trans. Lucy S. Dawidowicz in *The War against the Jews, 1933–1945* (New York: Holt, Rinehart and Winston, 1975), p. 255.

30. Yitskhok Rudashevski, *The Diary of the Vilna Ghetto: June 1941–April 1943,* trans. and ed. Percy Matenko (Israel: Ghetto Fighters' House and Hakibbutz Hameuchad, 1973), entry for 14 March 1943.

31. Ibid., entry for 28 January 1943.

32. S. Kaczerginski, "Shtiler, shtiler" [Still, Still, Let Us Be Still] (April 1943), in Kaczerginski, comp., *Lider fun di getos un lagern* [Songs of the Ghettos and Concentration Camps], ed. H. Leivick (New York: CYCO, 1948), pp. 88–89, original music by Alek Volkoviski. Leah Rudnitsky, "Dremlen feygl af di tsvaygn" [Birds Are Drowsing on the Branches], ibid., p. 87, set to a popular Soviet melody. Isaiah Spiegel, "Makh tsu di eygelekh" [Close Your Eyes], ibid., p. 92, original music by David Beigelman.

33. Nowersztern, no. 69.

34. Sutzkever, "Dos keyver-kind" [The Grave Child] (12 April 1942), in *Poetishe verk,* vol. 1, pp. 395–403. On the historicity of this episode, see Abba Kovner, "The Miracle in the Destruction" (in Hebrew) in *'Al hagesher hatsar: Masot be'al-peh* [On the Narrow Bridge: Essays] (Tel Aviv: Sifriat Poalim, 1981), p. 49.

35. Kruk, *Togbukh fun vilner geto,* pp. 471–472.

36. Sutzkever, "Kol-nidre" (6 February 1943), in *Poetishe verk,* vol. 1, pp. 404–426.

37. Leon Bernstein, "Abraham Sutzkever: The Person and the Poet" (in Yiddish), *In gang* (Rome) (June-July 1947), 21–30, quoted in Nowersztern, no. 69.

38. Hirsh Glik, "Zog nit keyn mol az du geyst dem letstn veg" [Never Say That This Is Your Last Road] (1943), in Kaczerginski, *Lider fun di getos un lagern,* p. 3, set to a popular Soviet melody; S. Kaczerginski, "Yugnt-himn" [Youth Hymn], ibid., p. 325, original music by Basye Rubin; Leyb Opeskin, "Far vos iz der himl" [Why Were the Heavens], ibid., p. 78.

39. "Dreamers": Sutzkever, "Di blayene platn fun Roms drukeray" [The Lead Plates at the Rom Press], in *Poetishe verk,* vol. 1, p. 335. "Revolt and revenge": idem, "Take Up Arms," April 13, 1943.

40. Arad, *Ghetto in Flames,* pp. 387–395.

41. Nowersztern, no. 73.

42. Sutzkever, "Di festung" [The Fortress] (14 July 1943), in *Poetishe verk,* vol. 1, pp. 321–322; idem, "Kling in di gleker fun toybn gevisn (Ring the Bells of Deaf Conscience] (14 July 1943), in *Di ershte nakht in geto,* p. 23; and idem, "A nem ton dos ayzn" [Take Up Arms] (13 April 1943), in *Poetishe verk,* vol. 1, pp. 299–300.

43. Sutzkever, *Lider fun yam-hamoves* [Poems of the Dead Sea: From the Vilna Ghetto, Forests, and Wanderings] (New York and Tel Aviv: Bergen-Belsen Memorial Press, 1968).

44. Sutzkever, "Lid tsu di letste" [Poem to the Last Ones] (16 March 1943), in *Poetishe verk,* vol. 1, pp. 293–295.

45. Sutzkever, "Vi azoy?" [How?] (14 February 1943), in *Poetishe verk,* vol. 1, p. 284, trans. Ruth R. Wisse in "Sutzkever: An Appreciation."

46. Wisse, "Sutzkever: An Appreciation."

47. Ibid.

48. Sutzkever, "Der novi" [The Prophet], ch. 4, in *Poetishe verk,* vol. 1, p. 373 (dated 16 August 1943 only in the manuscript); and "Di lererin Mire" [Mira the Teacher] (10 May 1943), ibid., pp. 307–309.

49. Sutzkever, "Der novi." Compare the last paragraph in *Green Aquarium.*

50. Sutzkever, "Farbrente perl" [Burnt Pearls] (28 July 1943), in *Poetishe verk,* vol. 1, p. 323, translated by Joshua Waletzky.

51. Sutzkever, "Itsik Vitnberg" (16 July 1944), in *Poetishe verk,* vol. 1, pp. 376–381, written in Vilna on the anniversary of Vittenberg Day; Subotsh-gas tsvantsik [20 Subocz Street] (December 1944), ibid., pp. 386–388; and "Golde" (19 January 1944), ibid., pp. 349–350.

52. Sutzkever, "Gezegenish" [Leave-taking] (1943–1944), in *Poetishe verk,* vol. 1, pp. 355–359. Quotation is from ch. 6.

53. Sutzkever, "Un oyb mayn folk vet blaybn bloyz a tsifer" [And If My People Will Remain Only as a Number] (30 January 1944), in *Poetishe verk,* vol. 1, p. 351.

54. Sutzkever, "Zing nit keyn troyeriks" [Don't Sing a Mournful Song] (5 February 1944), in *Poetishe verk,* vol. 1, p. 352.

55. Nowersztern, no. 73.

56. C. Shmeruk, "Yiddish Literature in the U.S.S.R.," in Lionel Kochan, ed., *The Jews in Soviet Russia since 1917* (London: Oxford University Press, 1970), pp. 261–264.

57. Y. A. Gilboa, "Hebrew Literature in the U.S.S.R.," ibid., p. 228; Elisha Rodin, *Laben* [To the Son] (Tel Aviv: Am Oved, 1943).

58. Sutzkever, "Meetings with Elisha Rodin" (in Yiddish), *Di goldene keyt* 45 (1962), 170–175.

59. Nowersztern, no. 76.

60. Ibid., no. 86.

61. Ibid., no. 92.

62. Sutzkever, "Farfroyrene yidn" [Frozen Jews] (10 July 1944), in *Poetishe verk,* vol. 1, pp. 362–363.

63. Nowersztern, no. 83.

64. Ilona Karmel, "Ślad na ścianie w baraku" [A Trace on the Barrack Wall], in Henryka and Ilona Karmel, *Śpiew za Drutami* (New York, 1947), p. 84, trans. into Yiddish by David Sfard as "A shpur af der vant," in Ruta Pups, ed., *Dos lid fun geto* [The Song of the Ghetto] (Warsaw: Yidish-bukh, 1962), no. 2.

65. Dan Pagis, "Written in Pencil on the Sealed Railway-Car" [Katuv be'iparon bakaron heḥatum], in *Points of Departure,* trans. from the Hebrew by Stephen Mitchell, introd. by Robert Alter, bilingual ed. (Philadelphia: Jewish Publication Society of America, 1981), p. 23. Copyright © by the Jewish Publication Society of America; used by permission.

66. Sutzkever, "Epitafn" [Epitaphs] in *Poetishe verk,* vol. 1, pp. 427–439.

67. Nowersztern, no. 84. Quotation is from Epitaph 14.

68. Simon Bernfeld, *Sefer hadema'ot* [The Book of Tears] (Berlin: Eshkol, 1924), vol. 2, p. 89.

69. Sutzkever, "Lid vegn a hering" [Poem about a Herring] (Warsaw, August 1946), trans. Hillel Schwartz, in *Poetishe verk*, vol. 1, p. 578, lines 20–26.

70. Sutzkever, "The Lead Plates at the Rom Press," (September 12, 1943), trans. Neal Kozodoy. Translation copyright © 1984 by Ruth Wisse, Khone Shmeruk, and Irving Howe; used by permission of Viking-Penguin, Inc. The stanza about the Maccabees (lines 7–12) is also missing from the second version of the poem published in *Yidishe kultur* (February 1945), p. 22. It first appears in *Di festung* (New York: YIKUF, 1945), p. 62.

71. *The Poetry of Abraham Sutzkever, the Vilno Poet, Reading in Yiddish*, Folkways Records FL-9947 (1960).

72. Abba Kovner, letter to the author, 22 August 1983.

73. Yechiel Szeintuch, "Yiddish and Hebrew Literature under the Nazi Rule in Eastern Europe: Yitzhak Katzenelson's Last Bilingual Writings and the Ghetto Writings of A. Sutzkever and I. Spiegel," (in Hebrew), vol. 1 (diss., Hebrew University, 1978), pp. 57–63.

74. Isaiah Spiegel, *Shtern laykhtn in tom* [Stars Light in the Abyss], 2 vols. (Tel Aviv: Israel Book, 1976).

75. Sutzkever, "Un azoy zolstu redn tsum yosem" [And So Shall You Speak to the Orphan] (12 February 1943), in *Poetishe verk*, vol. 1, pp. 281–283.

76. Sutzkever, "Litvishe poyerim," "Lashka Holub," and "Dos gezang fun hiltsernem lefl," in *Lider* [Poems] (Warsaw: Library of the Yiddish PEN Club, 1937). On these omissions, see Nowersztern, no. 20. Sutzkever also omitted the love poetry from this volume.

77. Sutzkever, "In kloyster af rudnitsker gas" [In the Church on Rudnicka Street] (23 November 1942), in *Di festung* [The Fortress: Lyric and Narrative Poems Written in the Vilna Ghetto and in the Forests, 1941–1944] (New York: YIKUF, 1945). These poems were sent to New York through the Jewish Anti-Fascist Committee in Moscow.

78. Sutzkever, "My Rescuer" (5 March 1943), and "On the Death of Yanova Bartoszewicz, Who Rescued Me," in *Burnt Pearls*, pp. 34–35, 43; idem, "Maria Fedecka," in *Poetishe verk*, vol. 1, pp. 522–524 (a chapter of *Geheymshtot*).

79. Stefan Krakowski, "Kielce," *Encyclopedia Judaica* (Jerusalem: Keter, 1971).

80. Sutzkever, "Tsu Poyln" [To Poland] (July-September 1946), in *Poetishe verk*, vol. 1, pp. 567–577.

81. Sutzkever, "Geheymshtot" [Secret City] (1945–1947), in *Poetishe verk*, vol. 1, pp. 443–537.

82. I. C. Biletzky, "Under Moonlight: An Informal Conversation with A. Sutzkever" (in Hebrew), *Basha'ar* (8 July 1948), quoted in Nowersztern, no. 122.

83. Sutzkever, "Diary Entries" (in Yiddish), *Di goldene keyt* 42 (1962), 166.

84. Sutzkever, "Green Aquarium" (1953–1954), trans. with an intro. by Ruth R. Wisse, *Prooftexts* 2, no. 1 (1982), 95–121 (contains all but one of the fifteen prose poems). Quotation is from p. 99.

85. Ruth R. Wisse, "The Prose of Abraham Sutzkever," intro. to *Griner akvarium: dertseylungen,* p. xviii.

10. *Jews on the Cross*

1. Yosef Hayim Yerushalmi, *Zakhor: Jewish History and Jewish Memory* (Seattle, London, and Philadelphia: University of Washington Press and Jewish Publication Society of America, 1982).

2. Jack Kugelmass and Jonathan Boyarin, eds., *From a Ruined Garden: The Memorial Books of Polish Jewry,* with geographical index and bibliography by Zachary Baker (New York: Schocken, 1983).

3. Abraham Wein, "Memorial Books as a Source for Research into the History of Jewish Communities in Europe," *Yad Vashem Studies* 9 (1973), 258.

4. Piotr Rawicz, *Blood from the Sky,* trans. from the French by Peter Wiles (New York: Harcourt, Brace & World, 1964).

5. Leyb Rochman, "Offenbach," a chapter of his novel *Mit blinde trit iber der erd* [With Blind Steps over the Earth] (Tel Aviv: Hamnoyre, 1968), pp. 268–318.

6. A. M. Klein, "The Hitleriad" (1944) and "The Psalter of Avram Haktani" (1944) in *The Collected Poems of A. M. Klein,* ed. Miriam Waddington (Toronto: McGraw-Hill Ryerson, 1974), pp. 186–234.

7. James Kugel, lecture delivered at Harvard Hillel, Cambridge, Mass., 10 February 1973.

8. Uriel Tal, "Excursus on the Term: *Shoah,*" *Shoah: A Review of Holocaust Studies and Commemorations* 1, no. 4 (1979), 10–11.

9. François Mauriac, foreword to Elie Wiesel, *Night,* trans. from the French by Stella Rodway (New York: Hill & Wang, 1960).

10. Israel Bartal, "Non-Jews and Gentile Society in East-European Hebrew and Yiddish Literature, 1856–1914" (in Hebrew) (diss., Hebrew University, 1980).

11. S. Ansky, "The Crucifix Question" (in Yiddish), *Dos naye lebn* (New York) 1 (1909), 610–617, 665–671.

12. Der Nister (Pinkhes Kahanovitsh), "Miriam: An Interpretation of 'The Maiden's Prayer,' " in *Gedanken un motivn: lider in proze* [Thoughts and Motifs: Prose Poems] (Vilna, 1907), pp. 12–23.

13. Khone Shmeruk, "Der Nister: His Life and Work" (in Hebrew), introd. to Der Nister, *Hanazir vehagdiyah* [The Hermit and the Goat] (Jerusalem: Bialik Institute, 1963), p. 19.

14. Ruth R. Wisse, "*Di Yunge* and the Problem of Jewish Aestheticism," *Jewish Social Studies* 38 (1976), 265–276.

15. Joseph Rolnick, "Kreshtshenye" [Procession], in *Lider* (from the *Shney* series, 14), 2nd ed. (New York, 1926).

16. H. Leivick, "Yezus" [Jesus] (1915), in *Ale verk fun H. Leyvik,* vol. 1 (New York, 1940), p. 32. See also Leivick, *The Golem,* ibid., vol. 2.

17. See Janet Hadda, "Christian Imagery and Dramatic Impulse in the Poetry of Itsik Manger," *Michigan Germanic Studies* 3, no. 2 (1977), 1–12.

18. Theodore Ziolkowski, *Fictional Transfigurations of Jesus* (Princeton: Princeton University Press, 1972), ch. 2.

19. D. S. Mirsky, *A History of Russian Literature from Its Beginning to 1900,* ed. Francis J. Whitfield (New York: Vintage, 1958), pp. 362–368.

20. Ziolkowski, *Transfigurations,* ch. 5.

21. Joseph Klausner, *Jesus of Nazareth: His Life, Times and Teaching,* trans. from the Hebrew by Herbert Danby (New York: Macmillan, 1925). See also Noah H. Rosenbloom, "Theological-Historical Conflicts with Christianity in Uri Zvi Greenberg's Poetry" (in Hebrew), *Perakim: Organ of the American Hebrew Academy* 4 (1966), 263–320.

22. Sholem Asch, "In a karnaval-nakht" [In a Carnival Night] (1909), in *Fun shtetl tsu der groyser velt* [From the Shtetl to the Wide World], ed. Shmuel Rozhansky (Buenos Aires: Musterverk fun der yidisher literatur, 1972), pp. 216–228.

23. Khone Shmeruk, "Contacts between Polish and Yiddish Literature: The Story of Esterka and King Casimir of Poland" (in Hebrew), *Hasifrut* 21 (1975), 78–79.

24. S. Y. Agnon, letter to A. M. Lifshits, 1920, as quoted in Bartal, "Non-Jews and Gentile Society," p. 275; Agnon, "The Lady and the Peddler" [Ha'adonit veharokhel] (1943), trans. Robert Alter, in Robert Alter, ed., *Modern Hebrew Literature* (New York: Behrman House, 1975), pp. 201–212; Asher Barash, "At Heaven's Gate" [Mul sha'ar hashamayim] (1925), trans. Yosef Schachter, in Alter, *Modern Hebrew Literature,* pp. 165–176.

25. Uri Zvi Greenberg, "Proclamation" (in Yiddish), *Albatros* (Warsaw) 1 (September 1922), 3–4.

26. Uri Zvi Greenberg, "Hu hayah meshuga" [He Was Crazy] (1925), in Uri Zvi Greenberg, *Be'emtsa ha'olam uve'emtsa hazman* [In the Middle of the World and in the Middle of Time: Poems], ed. Benjamin Hrushovski (Israel: Hakkibutz Hameuchad, 1979), p. 10. All citations from Greenberg's Hebrew poetry of the 1920s and 1930s are from this edition [hereafter referred to as Greenberg-Hrushovski].

27. D. Weinfeld, "Uri Zvi Greenberg's Poetry of the Twenties against the Backdrop of Expressionism" (in Hebrew), *Molad,* n.s. 31 (1981), 69.

28. Ḥanan Ḥever, ed., *Uri Zvi Greenberg on his Eightiest(!) Birthday* (in Hebrew), catalogue of an exhibition (Jerusalem: Jewish National and University Library, 1977), p. 14. All biographical information on Greenberg is based on this catalogue.

29. Uri Zvi Greenberg, "Yizkor" [Hazkarat neshamot] (1928), trans. S. J. Kahn, in *Ariel* 13 (1966), 39. For the Hebrew original, see Greenberg-Hrushovski, p. 76.

30. Uri Zvi Greenberg, "From the Archives of a Living Hebrew Poet" (in Hebrew), *Mizraḥ uma'arav* 4, no. 2 (1930), 136, as quoted in Ḥever, *Uri Zvi Greenberg,* p. 22.

31. Shmuel Huppert, "Exile and Its Legacy in the Poetry of Uri Zvi Greenberg, 1924–1945" (in Hebrew), *Hasifrut* 29 (1979), 101.

32. Uri Zvi Greenberg, "Der yam mit troyer" [The Sea of Sorrow] ("From the cycle: *After the Destruction,*" 23 December 1918) and idem, "Kaf-dalet kislev TaRAT" [The Twenty-third of Kislev 5679] ("The Last Chapter of My Book *Khurbm Lemberg,*" 17 December 1919), in Uri Zvi Greenberg, *Gezamlte verk* [Collected Yiddish Works], ed. Khone Shmeruk, vol. 1 (Jerusalem: Magnes Press, 1979), pp. 293–294, 301–303. "The Sea of Sorrow" was Greenberg's first direct response to the pogrom. It also appeared in Romanized script to meet the requirements of the Polish censor. All citations from Greenberg's Yiddish poetry are from this two-volume edition [hereafter referred to as *Gezamlte verk*].

33. Uri Zvi Greenberg, "In tol fun geveyn" [In the Vale of Tears] (25 October 1918), in *Gezamlte verk,* vol. 1, pp. 291–292.

34. Uri Zvi Greenberg, "Golgotha" (in Yiddish, 30 November 1920), ibid., pp. 304–307.

35. Stanley Nash, "The Development of Some Key Metaphors in Uri Zvi Greenberg's Poetry," unpublished paper; and Reuven Rabinovitsh, "*Baleilot reḥokei hamahut* by Uri Zvi Greenberg" (in Hebrew), in Yehuda Friedlander, ed., *Uri Zvi Greenberg: Mivḥar ma'amarei bikoret 'al yetsirato* [A Selection of Critical Essays on His Writing] (Tel Aviv: Am Oved, 1974), pp. 165–177.

36. Greenberg, "Uri Tsvi farn tseylem" [Uri Zvi in Front of the Cross] (1922), in *Gezamlte verk,* vol. 2, pp. 431–433.

37. Greenberg, "In malkhes fun tseylem" [In the Kingdom of the Cross] (1923), ibid., pp. 457–472. Quotation is from p. 464.

38. Greenberg, "Baym shlus—veytikn-heym af slavisher erd" [In Conclusion: Woeful Home on Slavic Soil] (1923), ibid., pp. 473–478.

39. On the two poetic voices in Greenberg's *Streets of the River,* see Robert Alter, "Uri Zvi Greenberg: A Poet of the Holocaust," in *Defenses of the Imagination: Jewish Writers and Modern Historical Crisis* (Philadelphia: Jewish Publication Society of America, 1977), pp. 103–118.

40. Greenberg, "Masa' el Eiropah" [Oracle to Europe] (1926), in Greenberg-Hrushovski, pp. 59–65.

41. Huppert, "Exile and its Legacy," p. 98.

42. Greenberg, "Aḥai, yehudei hapei'ot" [My Brothers, the Jews with Earlocks] (1926), in Greenberg-Hrushovski, p. 56.

43. Chaim Zhitlovsky, "Shloyme-Zanvl Rapoport-Ansky and Sociopolitical Folklore" (in Yiddish), introd. to S. Ansky, *Folklor un etnografye,* in *Gezamlte verk,* vol. 15 (Vilna, Warsaw, and New York, 1925), p. L.

44. Khone Shmeruk, "Uri Zvi Greenberg's Yiddish Work in Erez Yisrael and in Poland in the Late 20s and the 1930s" (in Hebrew), *Hasifrut* 29 (1972), 88–91.

45. Greenberg, "Kfitsat-haderekh" [The Miraculous Shortcut] (1924), in Greenberg-Hrushovski, pp. 35–41.

46. Huppert, "Exile and Its Legacy," p. 99; Shmeruk, "Greenberg's Yiddish Work," p. 89.

47. Huppert, "Exile and Its Legacy," pp. 98–100.

48. Dan Miron, personal communication, 10 December 1982. I am also indebted to Zvia Ginor for letting me read her notes from Prof. Miron's course on modern Hebrew poetry in the 1930s and 1940s, Columbia University Graduate School of Arts and Sciences, Fall 1982.

49. Greenberg, "To God in Europe, II," trans. Robert Friend, in S. Y. Penueli and A. Ukhmani, eds., *Anthology of Modern Hebrew Poetry,* vol. 2 (Jerusalem: Institute for the Translation of Hebrew Literature and Israel Universities Press, 1966), pp. 267–270, lines 26–32. For the Hebrew original of this sequence of poems, see "L'elohim be'eiropah," in Greenberg, *Reḥovot hanahar* [Streets of the River: The Book of Dirges and Power] (Jerusalem: Schocken, 1951), pp. 237–252.

50. Greenberg, "To God in Europe, III: No Other Instances," in Penueli and Ukhmani, *Anthology of Modern Hebrew Poetry,* vol. 2, pp. 271–273.

51. Elias Tcherikower, "Folk Art and Its Heir" (in Yiddish) in Tcherikower, ed., *Yisokher Ber Ribak: zayn lebn un shafn* [I. B. Ryback: His Life and Work] (Paris, 1937), p. 55.

52. Jozef Sandel, *Yidishe motivn in der poylisher kunst* [Jewish Motifs in Polish Art] (Warsaw: Yidish-bukh, 1954), pp. 153–163.

53. David Williams, "The Exile as Uncreator," in R. G. Collins and John Wortley, eds., *The Literature of Exile,* special issue of *Mosaic* 8, no. 3 (1975), 1.

54. S. Ansky, "Yitskhok Leybush Peretz" (in Yiddish, 1915), in *Zikhroynes* [Memoirs], vol. 1, p. 163, *Gezamlte shriftn,* vol. 6 (Vilna, Warsaw, and New York, 1928).

55. Milly Heyd, "Lilien and Beardsley: 'To the Pure All Things Are Pure'," *Journal of Jewish Art* 7 (1980), 58–69.

56. Ibid., p. 69.

57. Avraham Kampf, "In Quest of the Jewish Style in the Era of the Russian Revolution," *Journal of Jewish Art* 5 (1978), 50–51.

58. Sonia Ryback, "The Course of His Life" (in Yiddish), in *Yisokher Ber Ribak: zayn lebn un shafn,* pp. 7–28.

59. Kampf, "The Jewish Style in the Russian Revolution," p. 58.

60. Issachar Ber Ryback and Borukh Aronson, "The Paths of Jewish Art" (in Yiddish), *Oyfgang* (Kiev), 1919; reprinted in Tcherikower, *Yisokher Ber Ribak: zayn lebn un shafn,* pp. 87–94.

61. Mira Friedman, "Icon Painting and Russian Popular Art as Sources for Some Works by Chagall," *Journal of Jewish Art* 5 (1978), 96.

62. Jacob Glatstein, "Good Night, Wide World" (April 1938), trans. Marie Syrkin in Irving Howe and Eliezer Greenberg, eds., *A Treasury of Yiddish Poetry* (New York: Holt, Rinehart & Winston, 1969), pp. 333–335. For the Yiddish original, see Glatstein, *Gedenklider* [Memorial Poems] (New York, 1943), pp. 41–42.

63. Sholem Asch, "Kristus in geto" [Christ in the Ghetto] (c. 1941), in Asch, *Fun shtetl tsu der groyser velt,* pp. 229–248.

64. Franz Meyer, *Marc Chagall: Life and Work,* trans. from the German by Robert Allen (New York: Harry Abrams, n.d.), p. 416.

65. Ibid., p. 435.

66. Haim Be'er, Haim Gury, and Avraham Yeivin, eds., introd. to Marcel

Janco, *Kav hakets: rishumim* [The Edge of the End: Drawings] (Tel Aviv: Am Oved, 1981).

67. Yitzhak Arad, *Ghetto in Flames: The Struggle and Destruction of the Jews in Vilna in the Holocaust,* trans. from the Hebrew (New York: Holocaust Library, 1982), p. 393.

68. A. Sutzkever, *Fun vilner geto* [From the Vilna Ghetto] (Moscow: Emes, 1946), p. 194; Abba Kovner, "On the Witness Stand" (in Hebrew), in *'Al hagesher hatsar* [On the Narrow Bridge: Essays] (Tel Aviv: Sifriat Poalim, 1981), p. 103. In a Yiddish letter to me of 22 August 1983, Kovner writes: "Arad's version is close to the truth (the F.P.O. sent Itsik cyanide, but it's doubtful whether it arrived on time. Probably what happened is that the poison that [Salek] Dessler [in charge of the Jewish Police] or [Jacob] Gens [the "Ghetto Representative"] placed in his last drink took effect very quickly, in which case one can't very well speak of . . . suicide!). According to all the evidence we were able to collect at that time, the Gestapo agents never got to torture Vittenberg."

69. Elie Wiesel . . . *Un di velt hot geshvign* [And the World Was Silent] (Buenos Aires: Tsentral-farband fun poylishe yidn in Argentine, 1956).

70. Isaac Bashevis Singer, *The Family Moskat,* trans A. H. Gross (New York: Farrar, Straus & Giroux, 1950). See I. Saposnik, "Translating *The Family Moskat:* The Metamorphosis of a Novel," *Yiddish* 1, no. 3 (1973), 26–37.

71. A. Kaufman, "Conversation with the Artist," in *Bak: Paintings of the Last Decade* (New York: Aberbach Fine Art, 1974), pp. 37–39.

72. Samuel Bak, *Landscapes of Jewish History* (New York: Aberbach Fine Art, 1978), unpaginated.

73. Yosl Bergner, "Job" (1941), oil on canvas, 73 × 54 cm., and "Father and Sons" (1941), oil on canvas, 48 × 39 cm., in *Paintings, 1938–1980,* with commentary by Nissim Aloni and Rodi Bineth-Perry, text in Hebrew and English (Jerusalem: Keter, 1981), pp. 30–31.

74. Nissim Aloni, "The Longing and the Grotesque," trans. Valerie Arnon, in Bergner, *Paintings, 1938–1980,* pp. 214–185; Avraham Kampf, "The Cycle of Expulsion and Return: A Mural by Yossel Bergner," *Journal of Jewish Art* 2 (1975), 82–91. An important essay on "The Jewish Jesus" by Ziva Amishai-Maisels reached New York too late for me to incorporate its findings. According to the author, Chagall's Crucifixion series draws on a significant body of nineteenth-century Jewish art by Mark Antokolsky, Maurycy Gottlieb, and Max Lieberman and should also be understood against the backdrop of specific events in the Holocaust. See *Journal of Jewish Art* 9 (1982), 84–104.

Primary Sources Cited

The Premodern Period

Bernfeld, Simon, ed. *'Al naharot Sefarad* [By the Waters of Spain: Laments According to the Sephardi Rite on the Destruction of Jerusalem and on the Persecutions until the Decrees of 1391]. Tel Aviv: Maḥbarot lesifrut, 1956.

———, ed. *Sefer hadema'ot* [The Book of Tears: A History of the Decrees, Persecutions, and Destructions]. 3 vols. Berlin: Eshkol, 1923–1926.

Birnbaum, Philip, ed. *Daily Prayer Book* (Ashkenazi rite). New York: Hebrew Publishing Co., 1949.

———, ed. *High Holiday Prayer Book.* New York: Hebrew Publishing Co., 1951.

Danby, Herbert, ed. *the Mishnah.* London: Oxford University Press, 1933.

Dubnow, Simon. "The Second Destruction of the Ukraine (1768): Three Texts of the Folk Chronicle 'Mayse gdoyle min Uman umin Ukrayne' " (in Yiddish). *Historishe shriftn* (Berlin) 1 (1929), 27–54.

Eidelberg, Shlomo, ed. *The Jews and the Crusaders: The Hebrew Chronicles of the First and Second Crusades.* Madison: University of Wisconsin Press, 1977.

Ephraim bar Jacob of Bonn. *Sefer zekhirah* [The Book of Remembrance: Penitential Prayers and Lamentations]. Ed. A. M. Haberman. Jerusalem: Mosad Bialik, 1970.

Epstein, I., ed. *The Babylonian Talmud.* 35 vols. London: Soncino, 1935–1952.

Even-Shmuel, Yehuda, ed. *Midreshei ge'ulah* [Messianic Texts: Chapters in Jewish Apocalyptic from the Closing of the Babylonian Talmud until the Beginning of the Thirteenth Century]. 2nd rev. ed. Jerusalem and Tel Aviv: Mosad Bialik and Masada, 1968.

Gaster, Theodor H., trans. *The Dead Sea Scriptures in English Translation.* 2nd rev. ed. Garden City, N.Y.: Anchor, 1964.

Ginsberg, H. L., trans. *Lamentations.* In *The Five Megilloth and Jonah: A New Translation.* Philadelphia: Jewish Publication Society of America, 1969.

Glatzer, Nahum N., ed. *Language of Faith: A Selection from the Most Expressive Jewish Prayers.* New York: Schocken, 1967.

Goldschmidt, Ernst David, ed. *Maḥzor leyamim nora'im* [High Holiday Prayer Book]. 2 vols. Jerusalem: Koren, 1970.

———, ed. *Seder hakinot letish'ah b'Av* [The Kinot for the Ninth of Av According to the Polish Rite and the Ashkenazi Communities of Erets Yisrael]. Jerusalem: Mosad Harav Kook, 1968.

Gurland, Jonas, ed. *Lekorot hagzeirot 'al Yisrael* [To the History of Jewish Persecution]. 7 vols. Jerusalem: Kedem, 1972; orig. pub. 1887–1892.

Haberman, A. M., ed. *Sefer gzeirot Ashkenaz veTsarfat* [The Persecutions in Germany and France, 992–1298]. Jerusalem: Ophir, 1971; rpt. of 1945 ed.

Halpern, Israel, ed. *Sefer hagevurah: antologia historit-sifrutit* [The Book of Valor: A Literary-Historical Anthology]. Vol. 1: Resistance and Martyrdom from the Time of Masada until the Beginning of the Emancipation. Tel Aviv: Am Oved, 1977; rpt. of 3rd rev. ed.

Hannover, Nathan Nata. *Abyss of Despair (Yeven Metzulah): The Famous Seventeenth-Century Chronicle Depicting Jewish Life in Russia and Poland during the Chmielnicki Massacres of 1648–1649.* Trans. Abraham J. Mesch. New York: Bloch Publishing Co., 1950.

Hillers, Delbert R., trans. *Lamentations.* In *The Anchor Bible.* Garden City, N.Y.: Anchor, 1972.

Jellinek, Adolph, ed. "Eileh ezkerah" [These I Shall Remember] (midrash). In *Bet ha-Midrasch: Sammlung,* 3rd ed., vol. 2, pp. 64–72. Jerusalem: Wahrmann, 1967.

Jewish Publication Society. *The Torah: The Five Books of Moses—A New Translation of the Holy Scriptures According to the Traditional Hebrew Text.* Philadelphia: Jewish Publication Society of America, 1962.

——— *The Prophets Nevi'im: A New Translation of the Holy Scriptures According to the Masoretic Text.* Philadelphia: Jewish Publication Society of America, 1978.

Joseph ben Eliezer Lipman Ashkenazi. *Kine al gzeyres hakehiles deKaK Okrayne.* (Prague?), c. 1648. In Max Weinreich, *Bilder fun der yidisher literaturgeshikhte fun di onheybn biz Mendele Moykher-Sforim,* pp. 198–214. Vilna: Tomor, 1928.

Krauss, S. "The Decree of Expulsion of the Jews from Austria" (in Yiddish). *Historishe shriftn* (Vilna) 2 (1937), 18–25.

Lurie, Ben-Zion, ed. *Megillat Ta'anit.* Jerusalem: Mosad Bialik, 1964.

Maimonides, Moses. "Epistle to Yemen." Trans. Boaz Cohen. In Isadore Twersky, ed., *A Maimonides Reader,* pp. 437–462. New York: Behrman House, 1972.

Nissim ben Jacob ben Nissim ibn Shahin. *An Elegant Composition Concerning Relief after Adversity.* Trans. William M. Brinner. New Haven: Yale University Press, 1977.

Richardson, Cyril C., ed. *Early Church Fathers.* In *Library of Christian Classics,* vol. 1. New York: Macmillan, 1970.

Rosenfeld, Abraham, ed. *The Authorised Kinot for the Ninth of Av.* New York: Judaica Press, 1979; rpt. Israel, 1970.

Salfeld, S., ed. *Martyrologium des Nurnberger Memorbuches.* Berlin, 1898.

Shabbetai ben Meir Hacohen. *Megillat 'eifah* [The Scroll of Darkness]. In Israel Halpern, ed., *Beit Yisrael beFolin* [Polish Jewry from Its Beginnings until the Holocaust], vol. 2, pp. 252–255. Jerusalem: Youth Dept. of the Zionist Organization, 1953.

Shatzky, Jacob. "The Lamentation on the Destruction of Worms." *Filologishe shriftn* (Vilna) 2 (1929), 43–56.

Spiegel, Shalom. *The Last Trial: On the Legends and Lore of the Command to Abraham to Offer Isaac as a Sacrifice—The Akedah.* Trans. Judah Goldin. New York: Pantheon, 1967.

Stern, David, trans. "Eileh ezkerah." *Fiction* 7, nos. 1–2 (1983), 75–98.

Usque, Samuel. *Consolation for the Tribulations of Israel.* Trans. Martin A. Cohen. Philadelphia: Jewish Publication Society of America, 1964.

Weinreich, Max. *Shturemvint* [Hurricane: Scenes from Jewish History in the Seventeenth Century]. Vilna: Tomor, 1927.

Zlotnick, Dov, ed. *The Tractate "Mourning" (Śĕmaḥot̲).* Vocalized by Edward Y. Kutscher. New Haven: Yale University Press, 1966.

The Modern Period

Abramovitsh, Sholem Yankev. *Ale verk fun Mendele Moykher-Sforim* [The Complete Works in Yiddish]. 22 vols. Warsaw: Farlag Mendele, 1928.

——— *Di klyatshe oder tsar balekhaim* [The Mare, or Pity the Poor Animal]. Vilna: Rom, 1873.

——— *Kol kitvei Mendele Mokher Sefarim* [The Complete Works in Hebrew]. Tel Aviv: Dvir, 1947.

Agnon, S. Y. *A Guest for the Night.* Trans. Misha Louvish. New York: Schocken, 1968.

——— *Kol sipurav shel Shmuel Yosef Agnon* [The Complete Works]. 8 vols. Tel Aviv: Schocken, 1966.

Alter, Robert, ed. *Modern Hebrew Literature.* New York: Behrman House, 1975.

Ansky, S. *Khurbm Galitsye* [The Destruction of Galicia: The Jewish Catastrophe in Poland, Galicia, and Bukovina, from a Diary, 1914–1917]. *Gezamlte shriftn,* vols. 4–6. Vilna, Warsaw, and New York, 1921.

——— *Zikhroynes* [Memoirs]. *Gezamlte shriftn,* vols. 10–11. Vilna, Warsaw, and New York, 1922.

Asch, Sholem. *Dos bukh fun tsar* [The Book of Anguish]. *Gezamlte shriftn,* vol. 6. 2nd ed. New York, 1923.

——— *Fun shtetl tsu der groyser velt* [From the Shtetl to the Wide World]. Ed. Shmuel Rozhansky. Buenos Aires: Musterverk fun der yidisher literatur, 1972.

——— *Kiddush Hashem.* Trans. Rufus Learsi. Philadelphia: Jewish Publication Society of America, 1946.

Auerbach, Rokhl. *Varshever tsavoes* [Warsaw Testaments: Encounters, Activities, Fates, 1933–1943]. Tel Aviv: Israel Book, 1974.
——— "*Yizker* 1943" (in Yiddish). *Di goldene keyt* 46 (1963), 29–35.
Babel, Isaac. *The Collected Stories.* Trans. Walter Morison, with an introd. by Lionel Trilling. New York: Meridian, 1960.
——— *The Forgotten Prose.* Trans. Nicholas Stroud. Ann Arbor: Ardis, 1978.
——— *The Lonely Years, 1925–1939: Unpublished Stories and Private Correspondence.* Ed. Nathalie Babel, trans. Andrew R. MacAndrew. New York: Noonday, 1964.
——— *You Must Know Everything: Stories, 1915–1937.* Trans. Max Hayward. New York: Farrar, Straus & Giroux, 1969.
Bak, Samuel. *Landscapes of Jewish History.* New York: Aberbach Fine Art, 1978.
Barbusse, Henri. *Dos fayer* [The Fire] (1916). Trans. from the French by Binem Varshavski. Warsaw, 1924.
Barkahan, Khayim. *In shvere teg* [In Difficult Days]. Warsaw: Goldfarb, 1933.
Becker, Jurek. *Jacob the Liar.* Trans. Melvin Kornfeld. New York: Harcourt Brace Jovanovich, 1975.
Ben-Amos, Dan, and Jerome R. Mintz, eds. *In Praise of the Baal Shem Tov* [*Shivḥei ha-Besht*]. Bloomington: Indiana University Press, 1970.
Berdichewsky, Micah Yosef. *Fun shvere tsaytn* [From Hard Times]. *Yidishe ksovim fun a vaytn korev,* vol. 4. Berlin: Shtibl, 1924.
Bergelson, David. "Onheyb kislev TaRAT" [The Beginning of Kislev 1919]. *Milgroym* (Berlin) 1 (1922), 25–26.
——— *Mides hadin* [The Firm Hand of Justice]. *Gezamlte verk,* vol. 7. Vilna: Kletskin, 1929.
——— *Shturemteg: dertseylungen* [Storm Days: Stories]. *Gezamlte verk,* vol. 5. Vilna: Kletskin, 1928.
——— *Tsugvintn* [Storm Winds]. *Gezamlte verk,* vol. 8. Vilna: Kletskin, 1930.
Bergner, Yosl. *Paintings, 1938–1980.* With commentary by Nissim Aloni and Rodi Bineth-Perry. Text in Hebrew and English. Jerusalem: Keter, 1981.
Berkowitz, I. D. *Gezamlte shriftn* [Collected Writings]. Warsaw: Hashaḥar, 1910.
Berman, Yekutiel. *Hashodedim batsohoraim* [The Ravagers at Noon]. Vienna: Georg Brog and P. Smolenskin, 1877.
——— "Shnot ra'inu ra'ah" [The Years We Saw Evil]. *Hamelits* 1 (1861), 249–251, 269–272, 314–316, 331–333.
Bialik, Chaim Nachman. *Fun tsar un tsorn* [Of Anguish and Anger]. Odessa: Kadimah, 1906.
——— *Selected Poems of Hayyim Nahman Bialik.* Ed. Israel Efros. Rev. ed. New York: Bloch, 1965.
——— *Shirim* [The Collected Poems]. Tel Aviv: Dvir, 1966.
Bimko, Fishl. *Kelts* [Kielce]. *Geklibene verk,* vols. 9–10. New York, 1947.
——— *Rekrutn* [Recruits]. 2nd ed. Warsaw, 1921.
Blumental, Nachman, ed. *Verter un vertlekh fun der khurbm-tkufe* [Words and Sayings from the Holocaust]. Tel Aviv: I. L. Peretz, 1981.

Brenner, Yosef Hayim. *Kol kitvei Y. H. Brenner* [Collected Works]. Vol. 1. Tel Aviv: Dvir and Hakibbutz Hameuchad, 1964.
Burshtin, Mikhoel. *Bay di taykhn fun Mazovye* [By the Waters of Mazovia]. 2nd ed. Buenos Aires: Musterverk fun der yidisher literatur, 1970.
——— *Iber di khurves fun Ployne* [Over the Ruins of Ployne]. 2nd ed. Buenos Aires: Tsentral-farband fun poylishe yidn in Argentine, 1949.
Cohen, S. *Af blutike vegn* [On Bloody Paths: Memoirs of a Jewish Soldier]. New York, 1923.
Cohn, Zvi, ed. *Shvarts-bukh: di laydn fun mayn folk* [Black Book: The Sufferings of My People]. 2 vols. Lodz, 1917.
Dawidowicz, Lucy S, ed. *A Holocaust Reader*. New York: Behrman House, 1976.
Dror. *Payn un gvure in dem yidishn over in likht fun der kegnvart* [Suffering and Heroism in the Jewish Past in the Light of the Present]. Ed. Yitzhak Zuckerman and Eliyohu Gutkovsky. 3rd ed. Munich: Merkaz Dror, 1948.
Dubnow, S. "From the Black Book of Russian Jewry" (in Russian). *Evrejskaja Starina* (Petrograd) 10 (1918), 195–296.
Einhorn, David. *Rekvium* [Requiem]. Berlin, 1922.
Feigenberg, Rachel. *Megilot yehudei Rusyah* [Chronicles of Russian Jewry, 1905–1964]. Jerusalem: Kiriat Sefer, 1965.
——— *A pinkes fun a toyter shtot* (*khurbm Dubove*) [A Chronicle of a Dead Town: The Destruction of Dubove]. Warsaw, 1926.
Feld, Yehudo. *In di tsaytn fun Homen dem tsveytn* [In the Times of Haman the Second]. A collection of short stories from the Ringelblum Archive. Warsaw: Yidish-bukh, 1954.
Freiman, Avraham. *1919*. Ed. Yehuda Slutsky. 2nd ed. Tel Aviv: Am Oved, 1968.
Friedman, Isaac. *A yor tsvishn lebn un toyt* [A Year between Life and Death]. New York, 1932.
Frug, S. *Tsum hundertstn geboyrntog fun Sh. Frug* [On S. Frug's Hundredth Anniversary]. Ed. Nachman Mayzel. New York: YIKUF, 1960.
Gebirtig, M. *S'brent, 1939–1942* [Fire]. Cracow: Regional Jewish Historical Commission, 1946.
"The Ghetto Burns" (in Yiddish). *Di goldene keyt* 15 (1953), 10–15.
Gillon, Adam. "Here as in Jerusalem: Selected Poems of the Ghetto." *The Polish Review* 10, no. 3 (1965), 22–45.
Glatstein, Jacob. *Gedenklider* [Memorial Poems]. New York, 1943.
Glik, Hirsh. *Lider un poemes* [Lyric and Narrative Poems]. Ed. Nachman Mayzel. New York: YIKUF, 1953.
Gordon, Y. L. *Shirei higayon, meshalim, shirei 'alilah* [Mediative, Parabolic, and Narrative Poems]. Ed. Moshe Mehler and David Nayger. Tel Aviv: Schocken, 1945.
Gradowski, Zalmen. *In harts fun genem* [In the Heart of the Inferno: A Document from the Auschwitz Sonderkommando] (1944). Jerusalem, n.d.
Green, Gerald. *The Artists of Terezin*. New York: Hawthorn, Inc., 1969.
Greenberg, Uri Zvi. *Be'emtsa ha'olam uve'emtsa hazmanim* [In the Middle of the World and in the Middle of Time: Poems]. Ed. Benjamin Hrushovski. Tel Aviv: Hakibbutz Hameuchad, 1979.

——— *Gezamlte verk* [Collected Yiddish Works]. 2 vols. Ed. Khone Shmeruk. Jerusalem: Magnes Press, 1979.

——— *Reḥovot hanahar: sefer ha'iliyot vehakoaḥ* [Streets of the River: The Book of Dirges and Power]. 2nd ed. Jerusalem and Tel Aviv: Schocken, 1954.

Gros, Natan; Itamar Yaoz-Kest; and Rina Klinov, eds. *Hasho'ah bashirah ha'ivrit* [The Holocaust in Hebrew Poetry: An Anthology]. Israel: Yad Vashem and Hakibbutz Hameuchad, 1974.

Grossman, Mendel. *With a Camera in the Ghetto.* Ed. Zvi Szner and Alexander Sened. Israel: Ghetto Fighters' House and Hakibbutz Hameuchad, 1970.

Halpern, Israel, ed. *Sefer hagevurah* [The Book of Valor: A Historical-Literary Anthology]. Vol. 2: Resistance and Martyrdom from the Beginning of the Emancipation until the Beginnings of Zionism and Jewish Socialism. Vol. 3: The Self-Defense Movement from the First Years of Zionism and Jewish Socialism until World War I. Tel Aviv: Am Oved, 1977; rpt. of 3rd ed.

Halpern, Moyshe-Leyb. *In Nyu-york* [In New York]. New York: Vinkl, 1919.

Hameiri, Avigdor. *Begeihinom shel matah: reshimot katsin 'ivri bishvi Rusyah* [In Hell on Earth: Notes of a Jewish Officer in Russian Captivity]. 2 vols. 3rd ed. Tel Aviv: Yosef Sreberk, 1946.

——— *The Great Madness.* Trans. Jacob Freedman. New York: Vantage, 1952.

——— *Sefer hashirim* [Collected Poems]. Pp. 75–94. Tel Aviv: Am Hasefer, 1933.

Hašek, Jaroslav. *Der braver soldat Shvayk in der velt-milkhome* [The Good Soldier Svejk]. Trans. Zelig Kalmanovitsh. 2 vols. Riga: Bikher far alemen, 1928.

Hazaz, Hayim. "*Mizeh umizeh*" [From Here and There]. *Hatekufah* 21 (1923), 1–32.

——— "*Pirkei mahapeikhah*" [Chapters of the Revolution]. *Hatekufah* 22 (1924), 69–97.

——— "*Shmuel Frankfurter.*" *Hatekufah* 23 (1925), 81–134.

Heiszeryk, Kalmen Khayim. *In fayer un blut* [In Fire and Blood: Memoirs of the World War]. 2nd ed. Warsaw: Kolektiv, 1930.

Hershele [Hershele Danielewicz]. "Poems from the Warsaw Ghetto" (in Yiddish). *Di goldene keyt* 15 (1953), 57–58.

Hofstein, David. *Troyer* [Sorrow] (1920–1922). Kiev: Kultur-lige, 1922. With illustrations by Marc Chagall.

Howe, Irving, and Eliezer Greenberg, eds. *Ashes Out of Hope: Fiction by Soviet-Yiddish Writers.* New York: Schocken, 1977.

———, eds. *A Treasury of Yiddish Poetry.* New York: Holt, Rinehart & Winston, 1969.

———, eds. *A Treasury of Yiddish Stories.* New York: Viking, 1954.

Huberband, Shimon. *Kiddush Hashem: ktavim miymey hasho'ah* [Kiddush Hashem: Writings from the Holocaust]. Ed. Nachman Blumental and Joseph Kermish, trans. from the Yiddish. A collection from the Ringelblum Archive. Tel Aviv: Zakhor, 1969.

Iwenicki, Avrom. *Ven di vegn kreytsn zikh* [When the Roads Intersect: Diary of a Jewish Prisoner of War]. Vilna: Union of Jewish Writers and Journalists, 1924.

Janco, Marcel. *Kav hakets: rishumim* [The Edge of the End: Drawings]. Ed. Haim Be'er, Haim Gury, and Avraham Yeivin. Tel Aviv: Am Oved, 1981.

Kaczerginski, Shmerke, comp. *Lider fun di getos un lagern* [Songs of the Ghettos and Concentration Camps.] Ed. H. Leivick. New York: CYCO, 1948.

Kahan, Anne. "The Diary of Anne Kahan, Siedlce, Poland, 1914–1916." *YIVO Annual of Jewish Social Science* 18 (1983), 141–371.

Kalmanovitsh, Zelig. *Yoman begeto Vilna ukhtavim miha'izavon shenimtsa' baharisot* [A Diary of the Vilna Ghetto and Posthumous Writings Discovered in the Ruins]. Ed. Shalom Luria. Israel: Moreshet and Sifriat Poalim, 1977.

Kaplan, Chaim. *Megilat yishurin: yoman geto Varshah* [Scroll of Agony: A Diary of the Warsaw Ghetto]. Ed. Abraham I. Katsh. Tel Aviv and Jerusalem: Am Oved and Yad Vashem, 1966.

Kaplan, Israel. *Dos folksmoyl in Natsi-klem* [Folk Speech under Nazi Domination: Sayings of the Ghettos and Camps]. 2nd rev. ed. Israel: Ghetto Fighters' House, 1982.

Katzenelson, Yitzhak. *Yidishe ksovim fun Varshe, 1940–1943* [Yiddish Writings from Warsaw, 1940–1943]. Ed. Yechiel Szeintuch. Israel: Ghetto Fighters' House and Hakibbutz Hameuchad, in press.

——— *Ktavim aḥaronim* [Posthumous Writings, 1940–1944]. Ed. Yitzhak Zuckerman and Shlomo Even-Shoshan. 2nd rev. ed. Israel: Hakibbutz Hameuchad, 1956.

——— *The Song of the Murdered Jewish People.* Trans. Noah H. Rosenbloom, rev. Y. Tobin. Bilingual facsimile ed. Israel: Ghetto Fighters' House and Hakibbutz Hameuchad, 1980.

Kermish, Joseph, and Yisrael Bialostocki, eds. *'Itonut-hamaḥteret hayehudit beVarshah* [The Jewish Underground Press in Warsaw]. 2 vols. to date. Jerusalem: Yad Vashem, 1979.

Kermish, Joseph, and Yechiel Szeintuch, eds. *Jewish Creativity in the Holocaust.* Catalogue of an exhibition. Jerusalem: Yad Vashem, 1979.

Khrapkovski, Z[almen], ed. *Milkhome-vits* [The War Joke]. Vitebsk, 1922.

Kipnis, Itsik. *Khadoshim un teg un andere dertseylungen* [Months and Days and Other Stories]. *Geklibene verk,* vol. 3. Tel Aviv: I. L. Peretz, 1973.

Kissin, I., ed. *Lider fun der milkhome: antologye* [Poetry of This War: Anthology]. New York, 1943.

Klein, A. M. *The Collected Poems of A. M. Klein.* Ed. Miriam Waddington. Toronto: McGraw-Hill Ryerson, 1974.

Kovner, Abba. *'Al hagesher hatsar: masot be'al-peh* [On the Narrow Bridge: Essays]. Tel Aviv: Sifriat Poalim, 1981.

———, ed. *Scrolls of Fire: A Nation Fighting for Its Life.* Trans. Shirley

Kaufman, with Dan Laor. Paintings by Dan Reisinger. Bilingual ed. Jerusalem: Keter, 1981.
Kreplak, Jacob. *Fun kazarme un milkhome* [From the Barracks and War]. New York, 1927.
Kruk, Herman. *Togbukh fun vilner geto* [Diary of the Vilna Ghetto]. Ed. Mordecai W. Bernstein. New York: YIVO, 1961.
Kugelmass, Jack, and Jonathan Boyarin, eds. *From a Ruined Garden: The Memorial Books of Polish Jewry.* With geographical index and bibliography by Zachary Baker. New York: Schocken, 1983.
Kvitko, Leyb. *1919* (Poems). Berlin, 1923.
Lamdan, Isaac. "Masada." Trans. Leon I. Yudkin. In *Isaac Lamdan: A Study in Twentieth-Century Hebrew Poetry,* pp. 199–234. Ithaca: Cornell University Press, 1971.
Latzko, Andreas. *In di negl fun krig* [In the Fangs of War]. Trans. from the German by D. Kaplan. New York: Forverts, 1919.
Lehman, Shmuel. "The European War" (in Yiddish). In *Fun di milkhome-yorn.* Ed. Moyshe Shalit. Special no. of *Lebn* (Vilna) 1 (1920).
Leivick, H. *Ale verk fun H. Leyvik.* 2 vols. New York, 1940.
——— "The Golem." Trans. Joseph C. Landis. In *The Dybbuk and Other Great Yiddish Plays,* pp. 223–356. New York: Bantam, 1966.
Lejpuner, I. *Fir yor in der velt-milkhome, 1914–1918* [Four Years in the World War: Memoirs]. Warsaw, 1923.
Levin, Gershon. *In velt krig* [In the World War]. Warsaw, 1923.
Lewin, Abraham. *Kantonistn* [Cantonists: On the Drafting of Jews in Russia in the Times of Tsar Nicholas I, 1827–1856]. Warsaw, 1934.
——— *Mipinkaso shel hamoreh miyehudia* [From the Notebook of the Teacher from Yehudia: Warsaw Ghetto, April 1942–January 1943]. Ed. Zvi Szner. Israel: Ghetto Fighters' House and Hakibbutz Hameuchad, 1969.
Leyeles, A. [Glantz]. *Di mayse fun di hundert* [The Story of the Hundred]. New York, 1921.
Lunski, Khaykl. *Fun vilner geto: geshtaltn un bilder* [From the Vilna Ghetto: Characters and Scenes]. Vilna, 1920.
Mark, Ber, ed. *Megiles Oyshvits* [The Scroll of Auschwitz]. Tel Aviv: Israel Book, 1977).
———, ed. *Tsvishn lebn un toyt* [Between Life and Death]. An anthology of prose works from the Ringelblum Archive. Warsaw: Yidish-bukh, 1955.
Markish, Peretz. *Dor oys dor ayn* [The Generations Come and Go]. 2 vols. 2nd ed. Warsaw: YIKUF, 1964.
——— *Inmitn veg* [Midway]. Yekaterinoslav, 1919.
——— *Di kupe* [The Heap]. Kiev: Kultur-lige, 1922.
Mestel, Jacob. *Milkhome-notitsn fun a yidishn ofitsir* [War Notes of a Jewish Officer]. 2 vols. Warsaw: S. Jackkowski, 1924.
——— *Soldatn- un payatsn-lider* [Songs of Soldiers and Clowns]. Warsaw, 1928.
Meyer, Franz. *Marc Chagall: Life and Work.* Trans. Robert Allen. New York: Harry Abrams, n.d.

Miller, L. "Aba" (A novel). *Shriftn* (New York) Winter-Spring 1920, separate pagination.
Molodowski, Kadia, ed. *Lider fun khurbm* [Poems of the Holocaust, 1940–1945]. Tel Aviv: I. L. Peretz, 1962.
Olitzky, Leyb. *In an okupirt shtetl* [In an Occupied Shtetl]. Warsaw: Kultur-lige, 1924.
——— *In shayn fun flamen* [In the Glow of Flames]. Vilna and Warsaw: Kletskin, 1927.
Opatoshu, Joseph. *Arum di khurves* [Amid the Ruins]. *Gezamlte verk*, vol. 8. Vilna: Kletskin, 1925.
Opoczynski, Peretz. *Reshimot* [Sketches from the Warsaw Ghetto]. Trans. from the Yiddish by Avraham Yeivin, ed. Zvi Szner. Israel: Hakibbutz Hameuchad, 1970.
Oyslender, N[okhem]. *Front* (Poems). Kiev, 1921.
Peretz, I. L. *Ale verk fun Y. L. Perets*. Ed. S. Niger. 11 vols. New York: CYCO, 1947–1948.
Pinsky, David. *Di mishpokhe Tsvi* [The Zvi Family]. Geneva: Jewish Labor Bund, 1905.
Poisniak, William. *Der shvartser bukh* [The Black Book]. Authorized trans. of *The Jews in the Eastern War Zone*. New York: Hebrew Publishing Co., 1916.
Prylucki, Noah. "A Historical *Tkhine*" (in Yiddish). *Historishe shriftn* (Warsaw) 1 (1929), 815–820.
Pups, Ruta, ed. *Dos lid fun geto: zamlung* [The Song of the Ghetto: Anthology]. Warsaw: Yidish-bukh, 1962.
Rabon, Israel. "Fartseykhenungen fun yor 1939" [Notes from the Year 1939]. *Untervegns* (Vilna) (1940), 190–235; rpt. in *Di goldene keyt* 108 (1982), 164–197.
——— *Di gas* [The Street]. Warsaw: Goldfarb, 1928.
Rawicz, Piotr. *Blood from the Sky*. Trans. from the French by Peter Wiles. New York: Harcourt, Brace & World, 1964.
Reisen, Zalmen, ed. *Pinkes far der geshikhte fun Vilne in di yorn fun milkhome un okupatsye* [Sourcebook for the History of Vilna in the Years of War and Occupation]. Vilna, 1922.
Remarque, Erich Maria. *Afn mayrev-front keyn nayes* [All Quiet on the Western Front]. Trans. Isaac Bashevis [Singer]. Vilna: Kletskin, 1930.
Renn, Ludwig. *Milkhome* [War]. Trans. from the German by Elim Bornshteyn. 2 vols. Warsaw, 1930–1931.
Ringelblum, Emmanuel. *Ksovim fun geto* [Notes from the Warsaw Ghetto]. Vol. 2: Notes and Treatises (1942–1943). Ed. A. Eisenbach et al. Warsaw: Jewish Historical Institute, 1963.
Rochman, Leyb. *Mit blinde trit iber der erd* [With Blind Steps over the Earth]. Tel Aviv: Hamnoyre, 1968.
Rosental, Eliezer David. *Megilat hatevaḥ*. [The Scroll of Slaughter]. 3 vols. Jerusalem and Tel Aviv, 1927–1930.
Rozhansky, Shmuel, ed. *In pogrom* [In the Pogrom: A Literary Anthology]. Buenos Aires: Musterverk fun der yidisher literatur, 1976.

Rudashevski, Yitskhok. *The Diary of the Vilna Ghetto, June 1941–April 1943.* Trans. from the Yiddish by Percy Matenko. Israel: Ghetto Fighters' House and Hakibbutz Hameuchad, 1973.
Schneour, Zalmen. *Gezamlte shriftn* [Collected Writings]. Vol. 1. Warsaw: Velt-bibliotek, 1911.
Segalowicz, A. *Mayses fun der rusisher kazarme* [Stories of Russian Army Life]. Warsaw, 1926.
Shapiro, Lamed. *The Jewish Government and Other Stories.* Trans. Curt Leviant. New York: Twayne, 1971.
——— *Ksovim* [Posthumous Writings]. Ed. Sh[aye] Miller. Los Angeles, 1949.
——— *Di yidishe melukhe un andere zakhn* [The Jewish State and Other Things]. New York, 1929.
Shayevitsh, S[imkhe] B[unem]. *Lekh-lekho* [Go You Forth]. Ed. Nachmen Blumental. Lodz: Central Jewish Historical Commission, 1946.
Shenhar, Yitzhak. *Sipurei Yitsḥak Shenhar* [Collected Stories]. Vol. 1. Jerusalem: Mosad Bialik, 1960.
Shimoni, David. *Sefer hapo'emot* [Collected Poems]. Vol. 1. Tel Aviv: Masada, 1952.
Sholem Aleichem. *Ale verk fun Sholem-Aleykhem* [The Collected Works]. 28 vols. New York: Folksfond, 1917–1925.
——— *Ktavim 'ivriim* [The Hebrew Writings]. Ed. Khone Shmeruk. Jerusalem: Mosad Bialik, 1976.
——— *Der mabl* [The Deluge]. In *Ale verk fun Sholem-Aleykhem,* vol. 9. Warsaw: Progress, 1912.
——— *Menakhem-Mendl (Nyu-york-Varshe-Vin-Yehupets).* Tel Aviv, 1976.
——— "Pogrom Scenes" (in Yiddish). *Yudishes tageblat* (New York), 23 November–27 December 1905.
Singer, Isaac Bashevis. *The Family Moskat.* Trans. A. H. Gross. New York: Farrar, Straus & Giroux, 1950.
——— *Satan in Goray.* Trans. Jacob Sloan. New York: Noonday, 1955.
——— *Der shpigl un andere dertseylungen* [The Mirror and other Stories]. Ed. Khone Shmeruk. Israel: Yiddish Dept. of the Hebrew University of Jerusalem and Committee for Jewish Culture in Israel, 1975.
Singer, Israel Joshua. *Steel and Iron.* Trans. Joseph Singer. New York: Funk & Wagnalls, 1969.
Skalov, Zalmen. *Der haknkrayts: di hak on krayts* [The Swastika: The Ax without a Cross]. A novel from the Ringelblum Archive. Warsaw: Yidishbukh, 1954.
Spiegel, Isaiah. *Shtern laykhtn in tom* [Stars Light in the Abyss: Ghetto Writings]. 2 vols. Tel Aviv: 1976.
Steinman, Eliezer. *Sipurim* [Stories]. Warsaw, 1923.
Stryjkowski, Julian. *The Inn (Austeria).* Trans. from the Polish by Celina Wieniewska. New York: Harcourt Brace Jovanovich, 1972.
Sutzkever, Abraham. *Burnt Pearls: Ghetto Poems.* Trans. Seymour Mayne, introd. by Ruth R. Wisse. Oakville, Ont.: Mosaic Press/Valley Editions, 1981.

——— *Di ershte nakht in geto* [The First Night in the Ghetto: Poems, Variants, and Fragments Written during the Holocaust, 1941–1944]. Drawings by Samuel Bak. Tel Aviv: Di goldene keyt, 1979.

——— *Fun vilner geto* [From the Vilna Ghetto]. Moscow: Emes, 1946.

——— *Griner akvarium: dersteylungen* [Green Aquarium: Stories]. Introd. by Ruth R. Wisse. Israel: Yiddish Dept. of the Hebrew University of Jerusalem and Committee for Jewish Culture in Israel, 1975.

——— *Poetishe verk* [Poetic Works]. 2 vols. Tel Aviv, 1963.

Szajkowski, Zosa, ed. *An Illustrated Sourcebook of Russian Antisemitism, 1881–1978.* 2 vols. New York: Ktav, 1980.

Tcherikower, Elias, ed. *Yisokher Ber Ribak zayn lebn un shafn* [I. B. Ryback: His Life and Work]. Paris, 1937.

Tchernichowsky, Saul. "Baruch of Mainz." Trans. Sholom J. Kahn. In Eisig Silberschlag, *Saul Tschernichowsky, Poet of Revolt,* pp. 114–134. Ithaca: Cornell University Press, 1968.

Tenenbaum, Joseph. *Mad Heroes: Skeletons and Sketches of the Eastern Front.* Freeport, N.Y.: Books for Libraries Press, 1970; reprint of 1931 ed.

Warshawski, Oyzer. *Shmuglares* [Smugglers]. In *Unter okupatsye* [Under Occupation]. Buenos Aires: Musterverk fun der yidisher literatur, 1969.

Weissenberg, I. M. "A Shtetl." Trans. Ruth R. Wisse. In Ruth R. Wisse, ed., *A Shtetl and Other Yiddish Novellas,* pp. 29–78. New York: Behrman House, 1973.

Widen, Emil, and Daniel Widen. *Groyzame yorn* [Terrible Years]. Warsaw: Kultur-lige, 1933.

Wiesel, Elie. *Night.* Trans. from the French by Stella Rodway, foreword by François Mauriac. New York: Hill & Wang, 1960.

——— . . . *Un di velt hot geshvign* [And the World Was Silent]. Buenos Aires: Tsentral-farband fun poylishe yidn in Argentine, 1956.

World Federation of Bessarabian Jews. *Hapogrom beKishinev biml'ot 60 shanah* [Sixty Years after the Kishinev Pogrom]. Ed. Haim Schorer et al. Tel Aviv, 1963.

Wygodski, Jacob. *In genem* [In Hell: Memoirs of German Prisons during the World War]. Vilna: Kletskin, 1927.

Yaari, Yehuda. *K'or yahel* [Like a Dazzling Light]. 2nd rev. ed. Jerusalem: Union of Hebrew Writers in Jerusalem, 1969.

Yidishe folks-tsaytung. *Hilf: a zaml-bukh fir literatur un kunst* [Aid: An Almanac for Literature and Art]. Ed. Sholem Aleichem and Mordecai Spektor. Warsaw, 1903.

Zak, Avrom, ed. *Khurbm: antologye* [Anthology of Holocaust Literature]. Buenos Aires: Musterverk fun der yidisher literatur, 1970.

———, ed. *Unter di fligl fun toyt* [Under the Wings of Death]. Warsaw, 1921.

Zeitlin, Aaron. *Lider fun khurbm un lider fun gloybn* [Poems of the Holocaust and Poems of Faith]. 2 vols. New York: Bergen Belsen Memorial Press, 1967.

Index

Numbers in italics refer to pages with illustrations.